Rome II Regulation

Pocket Commentary

D1995035

Rome II Regulation

Pocket Commentary

edited by
Peter Huber

sellier.
european law
publishers

Rome II Regulation is the first volume of the
s.elp Pocket Commentaries. This volume is edited by
Peter Huber and written by

Intro; Articles 5-6, 8-9, 13, 27-32: *Martin Illmer*
Articles 1-4, 12, 14-15, 17, 20: *Ivo Bach*
Articles 7, 16, 26: *Angelika Fuchs*
Articles 10-11: *Peter Huber / Ivo Bach*
Articles 18-19, 21-25: *Markus Altenkirch*

To be cited as

Huber/*Illmer*, Rome II Regulation (2011), Intro para. 1
Huber/*Bach*, Rome II Regulation (2011), Art. 1 para. 1
Huber/*Huber/Bach*, Rome II Regulation (2011), Art. 10 para. 1

ISBN (print) 978-3-86653-092-8
ISBN (eBook) 978-3-86653-902-0

The Deutsche Nationalbibliothek lists this publication in the Deutsche Nationalbibliografie; detailed bibliographic data are available on the Internet at http://dnb.d-nb.de.

© 2011 by sellier. european law publishers GmbH, Munich.

Information contained in this book has been obtained by the publisher from sources believed to be reliable. However, neither the publisher nor its authors gurantee the accuracy or completeness of any information published herein. Neither the publisher nor its authors shall be responsible for any errors, omissions or damages arising from the use of this information. Neither the publisher nor its authors are attempting to render legal or other professional services. If such services are required, the assistance of an appropriate professional should be sought.

All rights reserved. No part of this publication may be reproduced, translated, stored in a retrieval system or transmitted, in any form or by any means, electronic, mechanical, photocopying, recording or otherwise, without prior permission of the publisher.

Production: Karina Hack, Munich. Typesetting: fidus Publikations-Service GmbH, Nördlingen. Printing and binding: Friedrich Pustet KG, Regensburg. Printed on acid-free, non-ageing paper. Printed in Germany.

This book is dedicated to
Professor Dr. Dr. h.c. Dieter Henrich
on the occasion of his 80th birthday

List of Authors

Markus Altenkirch, LL.M. (London)
Research Fellow at the University of Mainz

Dr. Ivo Bach
Junior lecturer at the University of Mainz

Dr. Angelika Fuchs, LL.M. (London)
Head of Section European Private Law,
Academy of European Law, Trier

Dr. Peter Huber, LL.M. (London)
Professor at the University of Mainz

Dr. Martin Illmer, MJur (Oxford)
Senior Research Fellow at the Max Planck Institute for
Comparative and International Private Law, Hamburg

Preface

This book has a rather long history. The original idea had been to write a short article-by-article commentary on the (then) new Rome II Regulation, and to do it on my own. Due to changes in my family life, I soon realized that I would not have the time to do so. This is when I started to bring in a team of academics and lawyers who would in their own name write certain parts of the commentary: *Markus Altenkirch*, *Ivo Bach*, *Angelika Fuchs* and *Martin Illmer*. The end of the story becomes apparent when one looks to the list of contributors of this book: They have basically written the entire book themselves (except for a rather short part which I co-author with *Ivo Bach*). My role has been reduced to coordinating the process and to be available for discussion. Looking at the book today, I have to admit: it did not do it any harm at all. I would like to congratulate the four "real" authors of the book and I hope that they will get the academic credit they deserve.

The purpose of the book is to provide a first reference to the Rome II Regulation. Rather than aiming at being comprehensive, the book tries to explain the underlying concepts and to suggest solutions for problems that may arise in the application of the Regulation.

All of us are immensely grateful to a lot of people who assisted us in the process: *Jennifer Antomo*, *Nicolas Gremminger*, *Jessica Hamed*, *Lisa Möll*, *Sarah Ott*, *Simone Rechel*, *Johanna Wald*. We owe special thanks to *Daniel Felz* who did the language editing of large parts of the book.

Mainz, March 2011 *Peter Huber*

Table of Content

Books Cited in Abbreviated Form

Ahern/Binchy	*Ahern/Binchy* (eds.), The Rome II Regulation on the Law Applicable to Non-Contractual Obligations (2009)
Anwaltskommentar BGB	*Dauner-Lieb/Heidel/Ring* (eds.), Anwaltskommentar BGB, Deutscher Anwaltverlag, 2005
Bamberger/Roth	*Bamberger/Roth*, Kommentar zum Bürgerlichen Gesetzbuch, C.H. Beck, 2nd edn. 2007
Callies, Rome Regulations	*Callies* (ed.), Rome Regulations. Commentary on the European Rules of the Conflict of Laws, Kluwer Law International 2011
Cheshire, North & Fawcett	*Cheshire/North/Fawcett* and others, Private International Law, Oxford University Press, 14th edn. 2008
Dicey, Morris & Collins	Dicey, Morris & Collins on The Conflict of Laws, Sweet & Maxwell, 14th edn., main work 2006, 4th suppl. 2010
Dickinson	*Dickinson*, The Rome II Regulation: The Law Applicable to Non-Contractual Obligations, Oxford University Press, main work 2006, 1st suppl. 2010
Fezer	*Fezer* (ed.), Kommentar zum Gesetz gegen den unlauteren Wettbewerb (UWG), C.H. Beck, 2nd edn. 2010

FS 100 Jahre DVS	*DVS, Deutscher Versicherungs-Schutzverband e.V.* (ed.), Zukunft der Wirtschaft – Versicherung der Zukunft: Festschrift zum 100-jährigen Bestehen des DVS, Deutscher Versicherungs-Schutzverband e.V., DVS Wirtschafts-Gesellschaft 2001
FS Boguslavskij	*Trunk/Knieper/Svetlanov* (eds.), Russland im Kontext der internationalen Entwicklung: Internationales Privatrecht, Kulturgüterschutz, geistiges Eigentum, Rechtsvereinheitlichung: Festschrift für Mark M. Boguslavskij, Berliner Wissenschafts-Verlag 2004
FS Henrich	*Jayme/Schwab/Gottwald* (eds.), Festschrift für Dieter Henrich zum 70. Geburtstag, Gieseking 2000
FS Hopt	*Grundmann/Merkt/Haar* (eds.), Unternehmen, Markt und Verantwortung: Festschrift für Klaus J. Hopt zum 70. Geburtstag am 24. August 2010, De Gruyter 2010
FS Jayme	*Mansel/Pfeiffer/Kronke/Kohler/Hausmann* (eds.), Festschrift für Erik Jayme, Sellier. European Law Publishers 2004
FS Kropholler	*Baetge/von Hein/von Hinden* (eds.), Die richtige Ordnung: Festschrift für Jan Kropholler zum 70. Geburtstag, Mohr Siebeck 2008
FS Müller-Freienfels	*Dieckmann/Frank/Hanisch/Simitis* (eds.), Festschrift für Wolfram Müller-Freienfels, Nomos 1986
FS Tilmann	*Keller/Plassmann/von Falck* (eds.), Festschrift für Prof. Dr. Winfried Tilmann, Heymanns 2003
Harte/Henning	*Harte-Bavendamm/Henning-Bodewig*, UWG – Gesetz gegen den unlauteren Wettberwerb, Kommentar, C.H. Beck, 2nd edn. 2009

jurisPK BGB	*Herberger/Martinek/Rüßmann/Weth* (eds.), juris Praxiskommentar BGB, juris, 5th edn. 2010
Köhler/Bornkamm	*Köhler/Bornkamm*, Gesetz gegen den Unlauteren Wettbewerb, C.H. Beck, 29th edn. 2011
Liber Amicorum Peter Hay	*Rasmussen-Bonne/Freer/Lüke* (eds.), Balancing of Interests: Liber amicorum; Peter Hay zum 70. Geburtstag, Verlag Recht und Wirtschaft 2005
Liber Fausto Pocar	*Venturini/Bariatti* (eds.), Nuovi strumenti del diritto internazionale privato – New Instruments of Private International Law: Liber Fausto Pocar, Giuffrè 2009
Münchener Kommentar BGB	*Säcker/Rixecker* (eds.), Münchener Kommentar zum Bürgerlichen Gesetzbuch, C.H. Beck, Band 10 and 11, 5th edn. 2010
Münchener Kommentar Lauterkeitsrecht	*Heermann/Hirsch* (eds.), Münchener Kommentar zum Lauterkeitsrecht, C.H. Beck 2006
Palandt	Palandt Bürgerliches Gesetzbuch, C.H. Beck, 70th edn. 2011
Plender & Wilderspin	*Plender/Wilderspin*, The European Private International Law of Obligations, Sweet & Maxwell, 3rd edn. 2009
Prütting/Wegen/Weinreich	*Prütting/Wegen/Weinreich* (eds.), BGB Kommentar, Luchterhand, 5th edn. 2010
Soergel	Soergel Bürgerliches Gesetzbuch, Kohlhammer, 13th edn. 2002 et seq.
Staudinger	Staudinger Kommentar zum Bürgerlichen Gesetzbuch mit Einführungsgesetz und Nebengesetzen, Sellier – de Gruyter

Journals Cited in Abbreviated Form

All E.R.	The All England Law Reports
Am. J. Comp. L.	American Journal of Comparative Law
Ankara L. Rev.	Ankara Law Review
CJQ	Civil Justice Quaterly
Clunet	Journal du Droit International
CML Rev.	Common Market Law Review
COM	European Commission Document
ECJL	Electronic Journal of Comparative Law
ECR	Reports of Judgments of the European Court of Justice
EIPR	European Intellectual Property Review
ELF	The European Legal Forum
ERA Forum	Journal of the Academy of European Law
EuLF	European Legal Forum
EuZA	Europäische Zeitschrift für Arbeitsrecht
EuZW	Europäische Zeitschrift für Wirtschaftsrecht
EWS	Europäisches Wirtschafts- und Steuerrecht
F.L.R.	Family Law Reports
FPR	Familie Partnerschaft Recht
GPR	Zeitschrift für Gemeinschaftsprivatrecht
GRUR Int.	Gewerblicher Rechtsschutz und Urheberrecht, Internationaler Teil
ICLQ	International & Comparative Law Quaterly
IHR	Internationales Handelsrecht
IPRax	Praxis des Internationalen Privat- und Verfahrensrecht
JBl.	Juristische Blätter
J.I.B.L.R.	Journal of International Banking Law and Regulation
J.M.L.C.	Journal of Money Laundering Control

JPIL	Journal of Personal Injury Law
J. Priv. Int. L.	Journal of Private International Law
JZ	Juristenzeitung
LJKB	Law Journal Reports, King's Bench New Series
Lloyd's Rep.	Lloyd's Law Reports
LMCLQ	Lloyd's Maritime and Commercial Law Quaterly
LQR	Law Quaterly Review
MMR	Multi-Media und Recht
NIPR	Nederlands internationaal privaatrecht
NJW	Neue Juristische Wochenschrift
NJW-RR	Neue Juristische Wochenschrift Rechtsprechungs-Report
NLJ	New Law Journal
NIPR	Netherlands International Private Law Review
OJ	Official Journal of the European Communities/Union
RabelsZ	Rabels Zeitschrift für ausländisches und internationales Privatrecht
Rec. des Cours	Académie de Droit International, Recueil des Cours
Rev. crit. dr. int. priv.	Revue critique de droit international privé
Riv. dir. int. priv. proc.	Rivista di diritto internazionale privato e processuale
RIW	Recht der Internationalen Wirtschaft
Texas Intl. L. J.	Texas International Law Journal
Tul. L. Rev.	Tulane Law Review
UKHL	United Kingdom House of Lords
VersR	Versicherungsrecht
WLR	Weekly Law Reports

WM	Zeitschrift für Wirtschafts- und Bankrecht
WRP	Wettbewerb in Recht und Praxis
YbPIL	Yearbook of Private International Law
ZEuP	Zeitschrift für Europäisches Privatrecht
ZfRV	Zeitschrift für Rechtsvergleichung
ZRvgl	Zeitschrift für Rechtsvergleichung
ZVglRWiss	Zeitschrift für vergleichende Rechtswissenschaft
ZVR	Zeitschrift für Verkehrsrecht

Regulation (EC) No 864/2007 of the European Parliament and of the Council of 11 July 2007 on the law applicable to non-contractual obligations (Rome II)

THE EUROPEAN PARLIAMENT AND THE COUNCIL OF THE EUROPEAN UNION,

Having regard to the Treaty establishing the European Community, and in particular Articles 61(c) and 67 thereof,
Having regard to the proposal from the Commission,
Having regard to the opinion of the European Economic and Social Committee[(1)],
Acting in accordance with the procedure laid down in Article 251 of the Treaty in the light of the joint text approved by the Conciliation Committee on 25 June 2007[(2)],

Whereas:

(1) The Community has set itself the objective of maintaining and developing an area of freedom, security and justice. For the progressive establishment of such an area, the Community is to adopt measures relating to judicial cooperation in civil matters with a cross-border impact to the extent necessary for the proper functioning of the internal market.

---

(1) OJ C 241, 28.9.2004, p. 1.

(2) Opinion of the European Parliament of 6 July 2005 (OJ C 157 E, 6.7.2006, p. 371), Council Common Position of 25 September 2006 (OJ C 289 E, 28.11.2006, p. 68) and Position of the European Parliament of 18 January 2007 (not yet published in the Official Journal). European Parliament Legislative Resolution of 10 July 2007 and Council Decision of 28 June 2007.

(2) According to Article 65(b) of the Treaty, these measures are to include those promoting the compatibility of the rules applicable in the Member States concerning the conflict of laws and of jurisdiction.
(3) The European Council meeting in Tampere on 15 and 16 October 1999 endorsed the principle of mutual recognition of judgments and other decisions of judicial authorities as the cornerstone of judicial cooperation in civil matters and invited the Council and the Commission to adopt a programme of measures to implement the principle of mutual recognition.
(4) On 30 November 2000, the Council adopted a joint Commission and Council programme of measures for implementation of the principle of mutual recognition of decisions in civil and commercial matters[(3)]. The programme identifies measures relating to the harmonisation of conflict-of-law rules as those facilitating the mutual recognition of judgments.
(5) The Hague Programme[(4)], adopted by the European Council on 5 November 2004, called for work to be pursued actively on the rules of conflict of laws regarding non-contractual obligations (Rome II).
(6) The proper functioning of the internal market creates a need, in order to improve the predictability of the outcome of litigation, certainty as to the law applicable and the free movement of judgments, for the conflict-of-law rules in the Member States to designate the same national law irrespective of the country of the court in which an action is brought.
(7) The substantive scope and the provisions of this Regulation should be consistent with Council Regulation (EC) No 44/2001 of 22 December 2000 on jurisdiction and the recognition and enforcement of judgments in civil and commercial matters[(5)] (Brussels I) and the instruments dealing with the law applicable to contractual obligations.
(8) This Regulation should apply irrespective of the nature of the court or tribunal seised.

---

(3) OJ C 12, 15.1.2001, p. 1.

(4) OJ C 53, 3.3.2005, p. 1.

(5) OJ L 12, 16.1.2001, p. 1. Regulation as last amended by Regulation (EC) No 1791/2006 (OJ L 363, 20.12.2006, p. 1).

(9) Claims arising out of *acta iure imperii* should include claims against officials who act on behalf of the State and liability for acts of public authorities, including liability of publicly appointed office-holders. Therefore, these matters should be excluded from the scope of this Regulation.

(10) Family relationships should cover parentage, marriage, affinity and collateral relatives. The reference in Article 1(2) to relationships having comparable effects to marriage and other family relationships should be interpreted in accordance with the law of the Member State in which the court is seised.

(11) The concept of a non-contractual obligation varies from one Member State to another. Therefore for the purposes of this Regulation non-contractual obligation should be understood as an autonomous concept. The conflict-of-law rules set out in this Regulation should also cover non-contractual obligations arising out of strict liability.

(12) The law applicable should also govern the question of the capacity to incur liability in tort/delict.

(13) Uniform rules applied irrespective of the law they designate may avert the risk of distortions of competition between Community litigants.

(14) The requirement of legal certainty and the need to do justice in individual cases are essential elements of an area of justice. This Regulation provides for the connecting factors which are the most appropriate to achieve these objectives. Therefore, this Regulation provides for a general rule but also for specific rules and, in certain provisions, for an "escape clause" which allows a departure from these rules where it is clear from all the circumstances of the case that the tort/delict is manifestly more closely connected with another country. This set of rules thus creates a flexible framework of conflict-of-law rules. Equally, it enables the court seised to treat individual cases in an appropriate manner.

(15) The principle of the *lex loci delicti commissi* is the basic solution for non-contractual obligations in virtually all the Member States, but the practical application of the principle where the component factors of the case are spread over several countries varies. This situation engenders uncertainty as to the law applicable.

(16) Uniform rules should enhance the foreseeability of court decisions and ensure a reasonable balance between the interests of the person claimed to be liable and the person who has sustained damage. A connection with the country where the direct damage occurred *(lex loci damni)* strikes a fair balance between the interests of the person claimed to be liable and the person sustaining the damage, and also reflects the modern approach to civil liability and the development of systems of strict liability.

(17) The law applicable should be determined on the basis of where the damage occurs, regardless of the country or countries in which the indirect consequences could occur. Accordingly, in cases of personal injury or damage to property, the country in which the damage occurs should be the country where the injury was sustained or the property was damaged respectively.

(18) The general rule in this Regulation should be the *lex loci damni* provided for in Article 4(1). Article 4(2) should be seen as an exception to this general principle, creating a special connection where the parties have their habitual residence in the same country. Article 4(3) should be understood as an 'escape clause' from Article 4(1) and (2), where it is clear from all the circumstances of the case that the tort/delict is manifestly more closely connected with another country.

(19) Specific rules should be laid down for special torts/delicts where the general rule does not allow a reasonable balance to be struck between the interests at stake.

(20) The conflict-of-law rule in matters of product liability should meet the objectives of fairly spreading the risks inherent in a modern high-technology society, protecting consumers' health, stimulating innovation, securing undistorted competition and facilitating trade. Creation of a cascade system of connecting factors, together with a foreseeability clause, is a balanced solution in regard to these objectives. The first element to be taken into account is the law of the country in which the person sustaining the damage had his or her habitual residence when the damage occurred, if the product was marketed in that country. The other elements of the cascade are triggered if the product was not marketed in that country, without prejudice to Article 4(2) and to the possibility of a manifestly closer connection to another country.

(21) The special rule in Article 6 is not an exception to the general rule in Article 4(1) but rather a clarification of it. In matters of unfair competition, the conflict-of-law rule should protect competitors, consumers and the general public and ensure that the market economy functions properly. The connection to the law of the country where competitive relations or the collective interests of consumers are, or are likely to be, affected generally satisfies these objectives.

(22) The non-contractual obligations arising out of restrictions of competition in Article 6(3) should cover infringements of both national and Community competition law. The law applicable to such non-contractual obligations should be the law of the country where the market is, or is likely to be, affected. In cases where the market is, or is likely to be, affected in more than one country, the claimant should be able in certain circumstances to choose to base his or her claim on the law of the court seised.

(23) For the purposes of this Regulation, the concept of restriction of competition should cover prohibitions on agreements between undertakings, decisions by associations of undertakings and concerted practices which have as their object or effect the prevention, restriction or distortion of competition within a Member State or within the internal market, as well as prohibitions on the abuse of a dominant position within a Member State or within the internal market, where such agreements, decisions, concerted practices or abuses are prohibited by Articles 81 and 82 of the Treaty or by the law of a Member State.

(24) "Environmental damage" should be understood as meaning adverse change in a natural resource, such as water, land or air, impairment of a function performed by that resource for the benefit of another natural resource or the public, or impairment of the variability among living organisms.

(25) Regarding environmental damage, Article 174 of the Treaty, which provides that there should be a high level of protection based on the precautionary principle and the principle that preventive action should be taken, the principle of priority for corrective action at source and the principle that the polluter pays, fully justifies the use of the principle of discriminating in favour of the person sustaining the damage. The question of when the person seeking compensation can make the

choice of the law applicable should be determined in accordance with the law of the Member State in which the court is seised.

(26) Regarding infringements of intellectual property rights, the universally acknowledged principle of the *lex loci protectionis* should be preserved. For the purposes of this Regulation, the term 'intellectual property rights' should be interpreted as meaning, for instance, copyright, related rights, the *sui generis* right for the protection of databases and industrial property rights.

(27) The exact concept of industrial action, such as strike action or lock-out, varies from one Member State to another and is governed by each Member State's internal rules. Therefore, this Regulation assumes as a general principle that the law of the country where the industrial action was taken should apply, with the aim of protecting the rights and obligations of workers and employers.

(28) The special rule on industrial action in Article 9 is without prejudice to the conditions relating to the exercise of such action in accordance with national law and without prejudice to the legal status of trade unions or of the representative organisations of workers as provided for in the law of the Member States.

(29) Provision should be made for special rules where damage is caused by an act other than a tort/delict, such as unjust enrichment, *negotiorum gestio* and *culpa in contrahendo*.

(30) *Culpa in contrahendo* for the purposes of this Regulation is an autonomous concept and should not necessarily be interpreted within the meaning of national law. It should include the violation of the duty of disclosure and the breakdown of contractual negotiations. Article 12 covers only non-contractual obligations presenting a direct link with the dealings prior to the conclusion of a contract. This means that if, while a contract is being negotiated, a person suffers personal injury, Article 4 or other relevant provisions of this Regulation should apply.

(31) To respect the principle of party autonomy and to enhance legal certainty, the parties should be allowed to make a choice as to the law applicable to a non-contractual obligation. This choice should be expressed or demonstrated with reasonable certainty by the circumstances of the case. Where establishing the existence of the agreement, the court has to respect the intentions of the parties. Protection should be given to weaker parties by imposing certain conditions on the choice.

(32) Considerations of public interest justify giving the courts of the Member States the possibility, in exceptional circumstances, of applying exceptions based on public policy and overriding mandatory provisions. In particular, the application of a provision of the law designated by this Regulation which would have the effect of causing non-compensatory exemplary or punitive damages of an excessive nature to be awarded may, depending on the circumstances of the case and the legal order of the Member State of the court seised, be regarded as being contrary to the public policy *(ordre public)* of the forum.

(33) According to the current national rules on compensation awarded to victims of road traffic accidents, when quantifying damages for personal injury in cases in which the accident takes place in a State other than that of the habitual residence of the victim, the court seised should take into account all the relevant actual circumstances of the specific victim, including in particular the actual losses and costs of after-care and medical attention.

(34) In order to strike a reasonable balance between the parties, account must be taken, in so far as appropriate, of the rules of safety and conduct in operation in the country in which the harmful act was committed, even where the non-contractual obligation is governed by the law of another country. The term 'rules of safety and conduct' should be interpreted as referring to all regulations having any relation to safety and conduct, including, for example, road safety rules in the case of an accident.

(35) A situation where conflict-of-law rules are dispersed among several instruments and where there are differences between those rules should be avoided. This Regulation, however, does not exclude the possibility of inclusion of conflict-of-law rules relating to non-contractual obligations in provisions of Community law with regard to particular matters.

This Regulation should not prejudice the application of other instruments laying down provisions designed to contribute to the proper functioning of the internal market in so far as they cannot be applied in conjunction with the law designated by the rules of this Regulation. The application of provisions of the applicable law designated by the rules of this Regulation should not restrict the free movement of goods and services as regulated by Community instruments, such as Directive

2000/31/EC of the European Parliament and of the Council of 8 June 2000 on certain legal aspects of information society services, in particular electronic commerce, in the Internal Market (Directive on electronic commerce)[6].

(36) Respect for international commitments entered into by the Member States means that this Regulation should not affect international conventions to which one or more Member States are parties at the time this Regulation is adopted. To make the rules more accessible, the Commission should publish the list of the relevant conventions in the *Official Journal of the European Union* on the basis of information supplied by the Member States.

(37) The Commission will make a proposal to the European Parliament and the Council concerning the procedures and conditions according to which Member States would be entitled to negotiate and conclude on their own behalf agreements with third countries in individual and exceptional cases, concerning sectoral matters, containing provisions on the law applicable to non-contractual obligations.

(38) Since the objective of this Regulation cannot be sufficiently achieved by the Member States, and can therefore, by reason of the scale and effects of this Regulation, be better achieved at Community level, the Community may adopt measures, in accordance with the principle of subsidiarity set out in Article 5 of the Treaty. In accordance with the principle of proportionality set out in that Article, this Regulation does not go beyond what is necessary to attain that objective.

(39) In accordance with Article 3 of the Protocol on the position of the United Kingdom and Ireland annexed to the Treaty on European Union and to the Treaty establishing the European Community, the United Kingdom and Ireland are taking part in the adoption and application of this Regulation.

(40) In accordance with Articles 1 and 2 of the Protocol on the position of Denmark, annexed to the Treaty on European Union and to the Treaty establishing the European Community, Denmark does not take part in the adoption of this Regulation, and is not bound by it or subject to its application,

---

(6) OJ L 178, 17.7.2000, p. 1.

HAVE ADOPTED THIS REGULATION:

Chapter I
Scope

Article 1
Scope

1. This Regulation shall apply, in situations involving a conflict of laws, to non-contractual obligations in civil and commercial matters. It shall not apply, in particular, to revenue, customs or administrative matters or to the liability of the State for acts and omissions in the exercise of State authority *(acta iure imperii)*.
2. The following shall be excluded from the scope of this Regulation:
   (a) non-contractual obligations arising out of family relationships and relationships deemed by the law applicable to such relationships to have comparable effects including maintenance obligations;
   (b) non-contractual obligations arising out of matrimonial property regimes, property regimes of relationships deemed by the law applicable to such relationships to have comparable effects to marriage, and wills and succession;
   (c) non-contractual obligations arising under bills of exchange, cheques and promissory notes and other negotiable instruments to the extent that the obligations under such other negotiable instruments arise out of their negotiable character;
   (d) non-contractual obligations arising out of the law of companies and other bodies corporate or unincorporated regarding matters such as the creation, by registration or otherwise, legal capacity, internal organisation or winding-up of companies and other bodies corporate or unincorporated, the personal liability of officers and members as such for the obligations of the company or body and the personal liability of auditors to a company or to its members in the statutory audits of accounting documents;

(e) non-contractual obligations arising out of the relations between the settlors, trustees and beneficiaries of a trust created voluntarily;
(f) non-contractual obligations arising out of nuclear damage;
(g) non-contractual obligations arising out of violations of privacy and rights relating to personality, including defamation.

3. This Regulation shall not apply to evidence and procedure, without prejudice to Articles 21 and 22.
4. For the purposes of this Regulation, "Member State" shall mean any Member State other than Denmark.

Article 2
Non-contractual obligations

1. For the purposes of this Regulation, damage shall cover any consequence arising out of tort/delict, unjust enrichment, *negotiorum gestio* or *culpa in contrahendo*.
2. This Regulation shall apply also to non-contractual obligations that are likely to arise.
3. Any reference in this Regulation to:
   (a) an event giving rise to damage shall include events giving rise to damage that are likely to occur; and
   (b) damage shall include damage that is likely to occur.

Article 3
Universal application

Any law specified by this Regulation shall be applied whether or not it is the law of a Member State.

Chapter II
Torts/Delicts

Article 4
General rule

1. Unless otherwise provided for in this Regulation, the law applicable to a non-contractual obligation arising out of a tort/delict shall be the law of the country in which the damage occurs irrespective of the country in which the event giving rise to the damage occurred and irrespective of the country or countries in which the indirect consequences of that event occur.
2. However, where the person claimed to be liable and the person sustaining damage both have their habitual residence in the same country at the time when the damage occurs, the law of that country shall apply.
3. Where it is clear from all the circumstances of the case that the tort/delict is manifestly more closely connected with a country other than that indicated in paragraphs 1 or 2, the law of that other country shall apply. A manifestly closer connection with another country might be based in particular on a pre-existing relationship between the parties, such as a contract, that is closely connected with the tort/delict in question.

Article 5
Product liability

1. Without prejudice to Article 4(2), the law applicable to a non-contractual obligation arising out of damage caused by a product shall be:
   (a) the law of the country in which the person sustaining the damage had his or her habitual residence when the damage occurred, if the product was marketed in that country; or, failing that,
   (b) the law of the country in which the product was acquired, if the product was marketed in that country; or, failing that,
   (c) the law of the country in which the damage occurred, if the product was marketed in that country.

   However, the law applicable shall be the law of the country in which the person claimed to be liable is habitually resident if he or she could not reasonably foresee the marketing of the product, or a product of the same type, in the country the law of which is applicable under (a), (b) or (c).

2. Where it is clear from all the circumstances of the case that the tort/delict is manifestly more closely connected with a country other than that indicated in paragraph 1, the law of that other country shall apply. A manifestly closer connection with another country might be based in particular on a pre-existing relationship between the parties, such as a contract, that is closely connected with the tort/delict in question.

Article 6
Unfair competition and acts restricting free competition

1. The law applicable to a non-contractual obligation arising out of an act of unfair competition shall be the law of the country where competitive relations or the collective interests of consumers are, or are likely to be, affected.
2. Where an act of unfair competition affects exclusively the interests of a specific competitor, Article 4 shall apply.
3. (a) The law applicable to a non-contractual obligation arising out of a restriction of competition shall be the law of the country where the market is, or is likely to be, affected.
   (b) When the market is, or is likely to be, affected in more than one country, the person seeking compensation for damage who sues in the court of the domicile of the defendant, may instead choose to base his or her claim on the law of the court seised, provided that the market in that Member State is amongst those directly and substantially affected by the restriction of competition out of which the non-contractual obligation on which the claim is based arises; where the claimant sues, in accordance with the applicable rules on jurisdiction, more than one defendant in that court, he or she can only choose to base his or her claim on the law of that court if the restriction of competition on which the claim against each of these defendants relies directly and substantially affects also the market in the Member State of that court.
4. The law applicable under this Article may not be derogated from by an agreement pursuant to Article 14.

Article 7
Environmental damage

The law applicable to a non-contractual obligation arising out of environmental damage or damage sustained by persons or property as a result of such damage shall be the law determined pursuant to Article 4(1), unless the person seeking compensation for damage chooses to base his or her claim on the law of the country in which the event giving rise to the damage occurred.

Article 8
Infringement of intellectual property rights

1. The law applicable to a non-contractual obligation arising from an infringement of an intellectual property right shall be the law of the country for which protection is claimed.
2. In the case of a non-contractual obligation arising from an infringement of a unitary Community intellectual property right, the law applicable shall, for any question that is not governed by the relevant Community instrument, be the law of the country in which the act of infringement was committed.
3. The law applicable under this Article may not be derogated from by an agreement pursuant to Article 14.

Article 9
Industrial action

Without prejudice to Article 4(2), the law applicable to a non-contractual obligation in respect of the liability of a person in the capacity of a worker or an employer or the organisations representing their professional interests for damages caused by an industrial action, pending or carried out, shall be the law of the country where the action is to be, or has been, taken.

Chapter III
Unjust Enrichment, Negotiorum Gestio and Culpa In Contrahendo

Article 10
Unjust enrichment

1. If a non-contractual obligation arising out of unjust enrichment, including payment of amounts wrongly received, concerns a relationship existing between the parties, such as one arising out of a contract or a tort/delict, that is closely connected with that unjust enrichment, it shall be governed by the law that governs that relationship.
2. Where the law applicable cannot be determined on the basis of paragraph 1 and the parties have their habitual residence in the same country when the event giving rise to unjust enrichment occurs, the law of that country shall apply.
3. Where the law applicable cannot be determined on the basis of paragraphs 1 or 2, it shall be the law of the country in which the unjust enrichment took place.
4. Where it is clear from all the circumstances of the case that the non-contractual obligation arising out of unjust enrichment is manifestly more closely connected with a country other than that indicated in paragraphs 1, 2 and 3, the law of that other country shall apply.

Article 11
Negotiorum gestio

1. If a non-contractual obligation arising out of an act performed without due authority in connection with the affairs of another person concerns a relationship existing between the parties, such as one arising out of a contract or a tort/delict, that is closely connected with that non-contractual obligation, it shall be governed by the law that governs that relationship.
2. Where the law applicable cannot be determined on the basis of paragraph 1, and the parties have their habitual residence in the same country when the event giving rise to the damage occurs, the law of that country shall apply.

3. Where the law applicable cannot be determined on the basis of paragraphs 1 or 2, it shall be the law of the country in which the act was performed.
4. Where it is clear from all the circumstances of the case that the non-contractual obligation arising out of an act performed without due authority in connection with the affairs of another person is manifestly more closely connected with a country other than that indicated in paragraphs 1, 2 and 3, the law of that other country shall apply.

Article 12
Culpa in contrahendo

1. The law applicable to a non-contractual obligation arising out of dealings prior to the conclusion of a contract, regardless of whether the contract was actually concluded or not, shall be the law that applies to the contract or that would have been applicable to it had it been entered into.
2. Where the law applicable cannot be determined on the basis of paragraph 1, it shall be:
   (a) the law of the country in which the damage occurs, irrespective of the country in which the event giving rise to the damage occurred and irrespective of the country or countries in which the indirect consequences of that event occurred; or
   (b) where the parties have their habitual residence in the same country at the time when the event giving rise to the damage occurs, the law of that country; or
   (c) where it is clear from all the circumstances of the case that the non-contractual obligation arising out of dealings prior to the conclusion of a contract is manifestly more closely connected with a country other than that indicated in points (a) and (b), the law of that other country.

Article 13
Applicability of Article 8

For the purposes of this Chapter, Article 8 shall apply to non-contractual obligations arising from an infringement of an intellectual property right.

Chapter IV
Freedom of Choice

Article 14
Freedom of choice

1. The parties may agree to submit non-contractual obligations to the law of their choice:
   (a) by an agreement entered into after the event giving rise to the damage occurred;
   or
   (b) where all the parties are pursuing a commercial activity, also by an agreement freely negotiated before the event giving rise to the damage occurred.
   The choice shall be expressed or demonstrated with reasonable certainty by the circumstances of the case and shall not prejudice the rights of third parties.
2. Where all the elements relevant to the situation at the time when the event giving rise to the damage occurs are located in a country other than the country whose law has been chosen, the choice of the parties shall not prejudice the application of provisions of the law of that other country which cannot be derogated from by agreement.
3. Where all the elements relevant to the situation at the time when the event giving rise to the damage occurs are located in one or more of the Member States, the parties' choice of the law applicable other than that of a Member State shall not prejudice the application of provisions of Community law, where appropriate as implemented in the Member State of the forum, which cannot be derogated from by agreement.

Chapter V
Common Rules

Article 15
Scope of the law applicable

The law applicable to non-contractual obligations under this Regulation shall govern in particular:

(a) the basis and extent of liability, including the determination of persons who may be held liable for acts performed by them;
(b) the grounds for exemption from liability, any limitation of liability and any division of liability;
(c) the existence, the nature and the assessment of damage or the remedy claimed;
(d) within the limits of powers conferred on the court by its procedural law, the measures which a court may take to prevent or terminate injury or damage or to ensure the provision of compensation;
(e) the question whether a right to claim damages or a remedy may be transferred, including by inheritance;
(f) persons entitled to compensation for damage sustained personally;
(g) liability for the acts of another person;
(h) the manner in which an obligation may be extinguished and rules of prescription and limitation, including rules relating to the commencement, interruption and suspension of a period of prescription or limitation.

Article 16
Overriding mandatory provisions

Nothing in this Regulation shall restrict the application of the provisions of the law of the forum in a situation where they are mandatory irrespective of the law otherwise applicable to the non-contractual obligation.

Article 17
Rules of safety and conduct

In assessing the conduct of the person claimed to be liable, account shall be taken, as a matter of fact and in so far as is appropriate, of the rules of safety and conduct which were in force at the place and time of the event giving rise to the liability.

Article 18
Direct action against the insurer of the person liable

The person having suffered damage may bring his or her claim directly against the insurer of the person liable to provide compensation if the law applicable to the non-contractual obligation or the law applicable to the insurance contract so provides.

Article 19
Subrogation

Where a person (the creditor) has a non-contractual claim upon another (the debtor), and a third person has a duty to satisfy the creditor, or has in fact satisfied the creditor in discharge of that duty, the law which governs the third person's duty to satisfy the creditor shall determine whether, and the extent to which, the third person is entitled to exercise against the debtor the rights which the creditor had against the debtor under the law governing their relationship.

Article 20
Multiple liability

If a creditor has a claim against several debtors who are liable for the same claim, and one of the debtors has already satisfied the claim in whole or in part, the question of that debtor's right to demand compensation from the other debtors shall be governed by the law applicable to that debtor's non-contractual obligation towards the creditor.

Article 21
Formal validity

A unilateral act intended to have legal effect and relating to a non-contractual obligation shall be formally valid if it satisfies the formal requirements of the law governing the non-contractual obligation in question or the law of the country in which the act is performed.

Article 22
Burden of proof

1. The law governing a non-contractual obligation under this Regulation shall apply to the extent that, in matters of non-contractual obligations, it contains rules which raise presumptions of law or determine the burden of proof.
2. Acts intended to have legal effect may be proved by any mode of proof recognised by the law of the forum or by any of the laws referred to in Article 21 under which that act is formally valid, provided that such mode of proof can be administered by the forum.

Chapter VI
Other Provisions

Article 23
Habitual residence

1. For the purposes of this Regulation, the habitual residence of companies and other bodies, corporate or unincorporated, shall be the place of central administration.
   Where the event giving rise to the damage occurs, or the damage arises, in the course of operation of a branch, agency or any other establishment, the place where the branch, agency or any other establishment is located shall be treated as the place of habitual residence.
2. For the purposes of this Regulation, the habitual residence of a natural person acting in the course of his or her business activity shall be his or her principal place of business.

Article 24
Exclusion of renvoi

The application of the law of any country specified by this Regulation means the application of the rules of law in force in that country other than its rules of private international law.

Article 25
States with more than one legal system

1. Where a State comprises several territorial units, each of which has its own rules of law in respect of non-contractual obligations, each territorial unit shall be considered as a country for the purposes of identifying the law applicable under this Regulation.
2. A Member State within which different territorial units have their own rules of law in respect of non-contractual obligations shall not be required to apply this Regulation to conflicts solely between the laws of such units.

Article 26
Public policy of the forum

The application of a provision of the law of any country specified by this Regulation may be refused only if such application is manifestly incompatible with the public policy (ordre public) of the forum.

Article 27
Relationship with other provisions of Community law

This Regulation shall not prejudice the application of provisions of Community law which, in relation to particular matters, lay down conflict-of-law rules relating to non-contractual obligations.

Article 28
Relationship with existing international conventions

1. This Regulation shall not prejudice the application of international conventions to which one or more Member States are parties at the time when this Regulation is adopted and which lay down conflict-of-law rules relating to non-contractual obligations.
2. However, this Regulation shall, as between Member States, take precedence over conventions concluded exclusively between two or more of them in so far as such conventions concern matters governed by this Regulation.

Chapter VII
Final Provisions

Article 29
List of conventions

1. By 11 July 2008, Member States shall notify the Commission of the conventions referred to in Article 28(1). After that date, Member States shall notify the Commission of all denunciations of such conventions.
2. The Commission shall publish in the *Official Journal of the European Union* within six months of receipt:
   (i) a list of the conventions referred to in paragraph 1;
   (ii) the denunciations referred to in paragraph 1.

Article 30
Review clause

1. Not later than 20 August 2011, the Commission shall submit to the European Parliament, the Council and the European Economic and Social Committee a report on the application of this Regulation. If necessary, the report shall be accompanied by proposals to adapt this Regulation. The report shall include:
   (i) a study on the effects of the way in which foreign law is treated in the different jurisdictions and on the extent to which courts in the

Member States apply foreign law in practice pursuant to this Regulation;

(ii) a study on the effects of Article 28 of this Regulation with respect to the Hague Convention of 4 May 1971 on the law applicable to traffic accidents.

2. Not later than 31 December 2008, the Commission shall submit to the European Parliament, the Council and the European Economic and Social Committee a study on the situation in the field of the law applicable to non-contractual obligations arising out of violations of privacy and rights relating to personality, taking into account rules relating to freedom of the press and freedom of expression in the media, and conflict-of-law issues related to Directive 95/46/EC of the European Parliament and of the Council of 24 October 1995 on the protection of individuals with regard to the processing of personal data and on the free movement of such data[(7)].

Article 31
Application in time

This Regulation shall apply to events giving rise to damage which occur after its entry into force.

Article 32
Date of application

This Regulation shall apply from 11 January 2009, except for Article 29, which shall apply from 11 July 2008.

This Regulation shall be binding in its entirety and directly applicable in the Member States in accordance with the Treaty establishing the European Community.

(7) OJ L 281, 23.11.1995, p. 31.

Done at Strasbourg, 11 July 2007.

For the European Parliament
The President
H.-G. Pöttering

For the Council
The President
M. Lobo Antunes

Commission Statement on the review clause (Article 30)

The Commission, following the invitation by the European Parliament and the Council in the frame of Article 30 of the 'Rome II' Regulation, will submit, not later than December 2008, a study on the situation in the field of the law applicable to non-contractual obligations arising out of violations of privacy and rights relating to personality. The Commission will take into consideration all aspects of the situation and take appropriate measures if necessary.

Commission Statement on road accidents

The Commission, being aware of the different practices followed in the Member States as regards the level of compensation awarded to victims of road traffic accidents, is prepared to examine the specific problems resulting for EU residents involved in road traffic accidents in a Member State other than the Member State of their habitual residence. To that end the Commission will make available to the European Parliament and to the Council, before the end of 2008, a study on all options, including insurance aspects, for improving the position of cross-border victims, which would pave the way for a Green Paper.

Commission Statement on the treatment of foreign law

The Commission, being aware of the different practices followed in the Member States as regards the treatment of foreign law, will publish at the latest four years after the entry into force of the 'Rome II' Regulation and in any event as soon as it is available a horizontal study on the application of foreign law in civil and commercial matters by the courts of the Member States, having regard to the aims of the Hague Programme. It is also prepared to take appropriate measures if necessary.

Introduction

I. Part of an Integrated System

1 Regulation (EC) No 864/2007 of the European Parliament and of the Council of 11 July 2007 on the law applicable to non-contractual obligations (Rome II)[1] marks a cornerstone in the ongoing process of harmonising the private international law within the European Union.[2] In application as of 11 January 2009, Rome II is joined by Regulation (EC) No 593/2008 of the European Parliament and of the Council of 17 June 2008 on the law applicable to contractual obligations (Rome I),[3] applying as of 17 December 2009, which replaces the Rome Convention of 1980. Both Rome I and Rome II are part of an integrated system of uniform private international law rules in civil and commercial matters throughout the member states of the European Union. Their most important co-player is Regulation (EC) No 44/2001 of 22 December 2000 on jurisdiction and the recognition and

1 OJ 2007 L 199/40.

2 The Regulation does not apply in Denmark which is not taking part in Title IV of the EC Treaty according to Protocol (No. 5) on the position of Denmark (1997), OJ 2006 C 321E/201.

3 OJ 2008 L 177/6 (Denmark equally not taking part).

enforcement of judgements in civil and commercial matters (Brussels I)[4], which is currently in its first review process.

2 As both other Regulations, Rome II is generally to be interpreted autonomously, subject to very limited exceptions that are explicitly indicated in the Regulation. In addition to the clarification and interpretation of each Regulation for itself, interplay and consistency between Rome I, Rome II and Brussels I are a new and increasingly important challenge. If the three Regulations shall form an integrated, coherent system, their interplay and consistency will have to be explored and further developed.[5] The ECJ will play a crucial role in that regard. For the first time, it is put in a position to interpret all three Regulations exclusively. This exclusive interpretative authority is fortified by the fact that due to the amendments of the Lisbon Treaty even lower national courts are allowed to refer questions for interpretation to the ECJ for a preliminary ruling.[6] Matters that prove unclear will therefore hopefully reach the ECJ for a final say much faster and far more frequently than it was the case under the old system.[7]

II. Genesis

3 After the Hague Conference on Private International Law had entered the field of conflict rules in respect of tort and delict in the early 1960's (resulting in the Convention of 4 May 1971 on the law applicable to traffic accidents and the Convention of 2 October 1973 on the law applicable to products liability), the

---

4 OJ 2001 L 12/1.

5 For further details in that regard see recently *Lein*, 10 YbPIL (2008) 177; *Haftel*, 137 Clunet (2010) 761.

6 See Art. 267 TFEU.

7 This hope is nurtured by the fact that the English High Court already made the first reference on the temporal scope of Rome II (see *Homawoo v GMF Assurance* [2010] EWHC 1941 at paras. 50 et seq.; the case is listed in the ECJ register under C-412/10).

European Economic Community's first attempt to unify the conflict rules on delict and tort dates back to 1968. Upon an initiative by the Benelux Member States, the European Commission set up a Working Group to consider possibilities of unifying the private international law of the then six Member States. The Group completed a draft EEC Convention on the law applicable to contractual and non-contractual obligations in June 1972.[8] In 1978, however, the Group decided to focus exclusively on the law applicable to contractual obligations. Their efforts resulted in the Rome Convention on the law applicable to contractual obligations of 1980.[9]

4 Anticipating the forthcoming change by the Treaty of Amsterdam (empowering the European Community pursuant to Art. 65 lit. b EC to legislate in the field of private international law by way of Regulation to promote uniformity of the rules throughout the Member States), the unification of the law applicable to non-contractual obligations was back on the agenda of the European Community in 1996. A first draft Convention was prepared in late 1998. After the Treaty of Amsterdam had entered into force on 1 May 1999, the Commission took the initiative by presenting its first draft of a Regulation on the law applicable to non-contractual obligations in May 2002.[10] Following a public consultation,[11] the Commission presented an initial proposal on 22 July 2003 supplemented by an Explanatory Memorandum.[12]

---

8 For the draft text see 21 Am. J. Comp. L. (1973) 587.

9 Convention on the law applicable to contractual obligations, opened for signature in Rome on 19 June 1980 (80/934/EEC), OJ 1980 L 266/1.

10 The first draft is accessible at http://ec.europa.eu/justice_home/news/consulting_public/rome_ii/news_hearing_rome2_en.htm.

11 Most of the submissions are accessible at http://ec.europa.eu/justice_home/news/consulting_public/rome_ii/news_summary_rome2_en.htm.

12 COM(2003) 427 final, accessible at http://europa.eu.int/eur-lex/lex/LexUriServ/site/en/com/2003/com2003_0427en01.pdf; the documents of the legislative process following this initial proposal are accessible at

Since Rome II had to be adopted under the codecision procedure according to Artt. 61 lit. c, 65, 67 and 251 EC, the European Parliament took over. Its position of 6 June 2005[13] after the first reading was based on the Report by the Committee on Legal Affairs.[14] This Report suggested deleting several special rules on tort and delict, arguing that most cases could be resolved by applying the general rule on tort and delict. For this purpose, the general rule's escape clause was supplemented by several rather vague criteria such as certainty, predictability, uniformity of results, protection of legitimate interests, and the policies underlying the law applicable but for the escape clause. The European Parliament's proposal represented a completely different approach to conflict of laws, following the US-American model. Whereas the European tradition of conflict rules is characterised by specific hard-and-fast rules with escape clauses reserved for exceptional cases, the American approach after the Second Restatement of the Conflict of Laws of 1971[15] is characterised by guiding factors striving for a more flexible solution of the individual case.[16] The European Parliament's proposal was strongly criticised as an attempt to alter the traditional systematic approach to conflict rules in tort law by importing the US conflicts revolution into European private international law despite the legal uncertainty and manifold problems it had produced. 5

In its amended proposal of 21 February 2006[17], the Commission rejected the Parliament's shift towards the US model and restated 6

http://ec.europa.eu/prelex/detail_dossier_real.cfm?CL=en&DosId=184392.

13 P6_TA(2005)0284.

14 COM(2003)0427 – C5-0038/2003 – 2003/0168(COD) (rapporteur: Diana Wallis).

15 American Law Institute, Restatement of the Law Second – Conflict of Laws, 1971.

16 See for an overview *Mathias Reimann*, Conflict of Laws in Western Europe – A Guide through the jungle (1995) 12 et seq. and 102 et seq.

17 COM(2006) 83 final.

its general approach providing for a system of *lex generalis* and *leges speciales*. Amendments to the Commission's initial proposal were limited to specific issues that had been critizised. In its common position of 25 September 2006, the Council also rejected the European Parliament's move away from the traditional European approach.[18] Instead, it approved the Commission's general approach as a matter of principle while at the same time amending several aspects of the Commission's amended proposal taking up, *inter alia*, concerns expressed by the European Parliament. Following a conciliation process focussing on the controversial aspects of Rome II, the Regulation was finally adopted by the Parliament and the Council on 11 July 2007.

Chapter I
Scope

Article 1
Scope

1. This Regulation shall apply, in situations involving a conflict of laws, to non-contractual obligations in civil and commercial matters. It shall not apply, in particular, to revenue, customs or administrative matters or to the liability of the State for acts and omissions in the exercise of State authority (acta iure imperii).
2. The following shall be excluded from the scope of this Regulation:
   (a) non-contractual obligations arising out of family relationships and relationships deemed by the law applicable to such relationships to have comparable effects including maintenance obligations;
   (b) non-contractual obligations arising out of matrimonial property regimes, property regimes of relationships deemed by the law applicable to such relationships to have comparable effects to marriage, and wills and succession;

[18] Common Position (EC) No 22/2006, OJ 2006 C 289E/68.

(c) non-contractual obligations arising under bills of exchange, cheques and promissory notes and other negotiable instruments to the extent that the obligations under such other negotiable instruments arise out of their negotiable character;
(d) non-contractual obligations arising out of the law of companies and other bodies corporate or unincorporated regarding matters such as the creation, by registration or otherwise, legal capacity, internal organisation or winding-up of companies and other bodies corporate or unincorporated, the personal liability of officers and members as such for the obligations of the company or body and the personal liability of auditors to a company or to its members in the statutory audits of accounting documents;
(e) non-contractual obligations arising out of the relations between the settlors, trustees and beneficiaries of a trust created voluntarily;
(f) non-contractual obligations arising out of nuclear damage;
(g) non-contractual obligations arising out of violations of privacy and rights relating to personality, including defamation.

3. This Regulation shall not apply to evidence and procedure, without prejudice to Articles 21 and 22.
4. For the purposes of this Regulation, 'Member State' shall mean any Member State other than Denmark.

A. General Outline

1 Article 1 delineates the Regulation's scope of application. In Art. 1(1), the Regulation sets forth the **requirements for its application**: there must exist (a) a situation involving conflicts of law, (b) a non-contractual obligation, and (c) a civil or commercial matter. In interpretating the term "civil and commercial matters" under the Regulation, case law and legal writing developed in interpreting Art. 1 Rome I and Art. 1 Brussels I are instructive, since all three provisions are similar in structure as well as in substance. Jurisprudence governing interpretation of the terms "contractual" and "non-contractual" has been developed under Art. 5(1) and (3) Brussels I; this jurisprudence should be taken into account when interpreting Art. 1(1).[1] Art. 1(2) and 1(3) exclude certain fields of law from the Regulation's scope. The exclusions in Art. 1(2) are very similar to those in Art. 1(2) of the 1980 Rome Convention on the law applicable to contractual obligations. The Guiliano/Lagarde report on the Rome Convention and ECJ interpretations of the Convention are therefore relevant in determining the scope of Art. 1(2)'s exclusions.[2]

---

[1] See Recital 7; cf. *Mankowski*, in: Magnus/Mankowski (eds.), Brussels I Regulation, Art. 5 para. 32; *Bach*, IHR 2010, 17, 24; *Bitter*, IPRax 2008, 95, 98 f.; *Thorn*, in: Palandt, Art. 1 para. 4; – differentiating: *Schmidt-Kessel*, ZEuP 2004, 1021, 1032; *Junker*, in: Münchener Kommentar BGB, Art. 1 para. 23.

[2] See *infra* paras. 33 et seq.

The Regulation's **temporal scope** of application is set forth in Art. 31. Rome II is not limited by a personal scope of application; rather, it is universally applicable throughout EU member states (as a *loi uniforme*, see Art. 3). 2

If a matter falls within the Regulation's scope, the Regulation **preempts national conflict of laws rules**. Thus, only limited application remains for domestic conflicts regimes: in civil and commercial disputes, national conflict rules govern only those claims that arise out of the fields of law Art. 1(2) excludes from the Regulation's scope. 3

B. Requirements for Application: Art. 1(1)

I. Civil and Commercial Matters

Rome II applies exclusively to "civil and commercial matters". 4
The phrase "civil and commercial" attempts to distinguish cases within the Regulation's scope from "public" matters – a distinction that often results in courts and commentators substituting the phrase "private law" in place of "civil and commercial matters." EU legislators decided to incorporate the latter into the Regulation because the phrase "private law" had been defined differently throughout EU member states.[3] The neutral term "civil and commercial matters" minimized the risk that national courts would interpret the Regulation according to established domestic understandings.[4] According to the ECJ, the term "civil

3 See Schlosser Report, OJ 1979 C 59, paras. 23 et seq.; in England and Ireland the distinction between private and public law does not exist, cf. *Rogerson*, in: Magnus/Mankowski (eds.), Brussels I Regulation, Art. 1 para. 12.

4 *Rogerson*, in: Magnus/Mankowski (eds.), Brussels I Regulation, Art. 1 para. 12.

and commercial matters" must be **interpreted autonomously**, *i.e.* without regard to national jurisprudence.[5]

5 However, Art. 1(1) does not define the term "civil and commercial matters". Instead, it merely contains examples of disputes that do *not* constitute civil or commercial matters: revenue, customs, administrative matters, and *acta iure imperii.* These examples basically serve as clarifications for countries that do not differentiate between civil and public matters (*i.e.* England and Ireland).[6] They offer little assistance to an autonomous interpretation of the term "civil and commercial matters."

6 ECJ cases that define what constitutes a "civil and commercial matter" under Art. 1(1) Brussels I offer general guidance in determining what constitutes a Rome II "civil and commercial matter".[7] In these cases, the **ECJ has defined the term negatively**: a matter is *not* "civil or commercial" if (a) a public authority is involved in creating the disputed obligations *and* (b) this public authority acts "in the exercise of its powers".[8]

---

[5] ECJ, Case C-29/76 – *LTU v Eurocontrol*, [1976] ECR 1541, para. 3; cf. Intro para. 2.

[6] *Rogerson*, in: Magnus/Mankowski (eds.), Brussels I Regulation, Art. 1 para. 12.

[7] *E.g.* ECJ, Case C-172/91 – *Sonntag v Waidmann*, [1993] ECR I-1963; ECJ, Case C-29/76 – *LTU v Eurocontrol*, [1976] ECR I-1541; ECJ, Case 814/79 – *Netherlands v Reinhard Rüffer*, [1980] ECR I-3807; ECJ, Case C-271/00 – *Gemeente Steenbergen v Luc Baten*, [2002] ECR I-10489; ECJ, Case C-7/98 – *Krombach*, [2000] ECR I-1956; ECJ, Case C-266/01 – *Préservative foncière TIARD*, [2003] ECR I-4867; cf. *Rogerson*, in: Magnus/Mankowski (eds.), Brussels I Regulation, Art. 1 paras. 12 et seq.; *Cheshire, North & Fawcett*, p. 780; *Mankowski*, in: Rauscher, Europäisches Zivilprozessrecht, Art. 1 EuGVO, paras. 1 et seq.

[8] ECJ, Case C- 29/76 – *LTU v Eurocontrol*, [1976] ECR I-1541 para. 4; ECJ, Case C-172/91 – *Sonntag v Waidmann*, [1993] ECR I-1963, para. 20; ECJ, Case C-814/79 – *Netherlands v Reinhard Rüffer*, [1980] ECR I-3807 para. 9.

From this definition it follows first that – as emphasized by Recital 8 – the nature of the court in which a proceeding is brought is irrelevant in determining whether a matter is "civil and commercial".[9] Second, as stated in Recital 9, it is also irrelevant whether a claim is brought against a state or against an official who acts on behalf of the state.[10] Third, if no public authority is involved in a case, the case may be presumed to constitute a "civil or commercial" matter. Lastly, *even if* a public authority is involved in a dispute, its involvement does not, without more, convert a case into a "public" matter. Instead, the public nature of a case depends on whether a public authority "acts in the exercise of its powers".[11] 7

Determining whether a public authority acted **"in the exercise of its powers"** is often difficult: does a policeman who causes a traffic accident act in the exercise of his powers? Does it depend on whether the accident occurred on his way to work or while patrolling or pursuing a suspect? 8

In the case of *Sonntag v. Waidmann*, the ECJ held that a teacher's personal liability for a fatal accident that killed one of his pupils on a school trip constituted a civil or commercial matter, and not a public matter. The ECJ ruled that teachers, while acting in their capacity as "supervisor" of the schoolchildren on a school trip, do not act "in the exercise of" their powers as representatives of the state. The court reasoned as follows: even if a civil servant acts on behalf of the State, he does not necessarily exercise "public powers". Instead, "public powers" are exercised only when a civil servant's conduct contains **some action *beyond* the conduct that is available under the rules that govern relations between pri-** 9

---

9 See in particular ECJ, Case C-172/91 – *Sonntag v Waidmann*, [1993] ECR I-1963, para. 19: the case was brought before a criminal court that decided on civil aspects in an adhesive procedure.

10 *Junker*, in: Münchener Kommentar BGB, Art. 1 para. 12; *Wurmnest*, in: jurisPK BGB, Art. 1 para. 38.

11 ECJ, Case C-29/76 – *LTU v Eurocontrol*, [1976] ECR I-1541, para. 4; ECJ, Case C-266/01 – *Préservative foncière TIARD*, [2003] ECR I-4867.

vate individuals. Since the teacher was merely supervising his students – an activity readily available to private childcare providers – his conduct evinced no actions that were generally unavailable to private persons. Further, the ECJ clarified in dicta that a public school teacher does not even act "in the exercise of [his] powers" when he assigns grades to students or decides that students should advance to a higher grade, since teachers at a private schools engage in identical activities.[12]

10 As a result, even if a civil servant causes injury while acting in his official capacity, the ensuing case must be assumed to constitute a "civil or commercial matter" if a private individual could have engaged in the same conduct under the same circumstances.

11 To apply the ECJ's holding to the example of the policeman stated above: a policeman that causes a traffic accident on his way to work will never do so "in the exercise of [his] powers" as a policeman. Neither will a policeman who causes an accident while patrolling so long as he does so while participating in traffic as a normal motorist. A "public matter" will arise only when the policeman causes an accident while driving under siren and rotating lights.[13]

12 Furthermore, under the ECJ's holding in Sonntag v. Wardmann, damages claims that arise from a state authority's conduct in **public procurement procedures** may well qualify as "civil or commercial" matters. Such damages are often of a non-contractual nature: they generally arise where an offeror was unsuccessful in awarding procedures and therefore claims damages representing the costs of preparing a bid or participating in the bidding process.[14] Such a claim qualifies as *culpa in contrahendo* under Art. 12 Rome II.[15]

---

12 ECJ, Case C-172/91 – *Sonntag v Waidmann*, [1993] ECR I-1963 para. 24 with reference to ECJ, Case 66/85 – *Lawrie v Blum*, [1986] ECR I-2121 para. 28.

13 Cf. *Leible/Engel*, EuZW 2004, 7, 9.

Worth noting, however, is that the ECJ has held the Brussels Convention inapplicable to **war crimes** on grounds that war crimes do not constitute a "civil or commercial matter".[16] Obviously, warfare as such relates to a "core area of state sovereignty".[17] However, the ECJ's decision is more expansive than a mere warfare exception: any wrongful acts committed by soldiers or contractors beyond the proper conduct of warfare are also excluded from the Rome regime. Thus, at least in the abstract, the EJC has held that a civil servant who acts *ultra vires* has not precluded his acts from being classified as an exercise of "public powers". 13

Under the Brussels Regime, it remains disputed whether **preliminary or incidental issues** of a public nature can preclude a matter for being considered "civil and commercial".[18] A similar problem does not arise under the Rome II Regulation. While the Brussels regulation requires the question of jurisdiction to be answered for a claim in its entirety, the Rome regime provides for applicable law to be determined for each issue separately so that the main issue (which is "civil and commercial") may be dealt with under the Rome II Regulation irrespective of whether or not the incidental issues are "civil and commercial". 14

---

14 See *e.g.* Art. 2 VII of the Council Directive 92/13/EEC of 25 February 1992 coordinating the laws, regulations and administrative provisions relating to the application of Community rules on the procurement procedures of entities operating in the water, energy, transport and telecommunications sectors.

15 See in detail Art. 12 para. 6.

16 ECJ, Case C-292/05 – *Lechouritou*, [2007] ECR I-1519 paras. 37 et seq.

17 *Plender & Wilderspin*, para. 17-030.

18 The ECJ, in one case has held that a preliminary issue may not alter the claims nature (ECJ, Case C-266/01 – *Préservative foncière TIARD v Staat der Nederlanden* [2003] ECR I-4867; critical: *Rogerson*, in: Magnus/Mankowski (eds.), Brussels I Regulation, Art. 1 para. 18.

II. Non-contractual Obligations

1. General Definition

15 The Rome regulatory regime divides the law of obligations into contractual and non-contractual obligations. The former are governed by the Rome I Regulation, the latter by Rome II. To determine which Rome Regulation applies, it is therefore necessary to distinguish between contractual and non-contractual obligations. Here again, ECJ interpretations of comparable provisions within the Brussels I regime may serve as guidance.[19]

16 Under Art. 5 Brussels I, courts must distinguish between contractual and non-contractual obligations to determine which state's courts have jurisdiction over a case: those of the place of performance (for contractual obligations) or those at the place of injury (for non-contractual obligations). In making this distinction, the **ECJ defined** the term "non-contractual" as "an independent concept covering all actions which seek to establish the liability of a defendant and which are not related to a 'contract' within the meaning of Article 5(1)".[20] Thus, the ECJ has defined the term "non-contractual" *negatively*: it encompasses every damages claim that cannot be classified as "contractual".

17 The starting point for the definition of "non-contractual" is therefore the definition of the term "contractual". The ECJ defines a "contractual" obligation as follows:[21] "[the] phrase 'matters relating to a contract' […] is not to be understood as covering a situation in which there is no obligation freely assumed by one party towards another".[22] The corollary of this negative defini-

[19] But see *supra* para. 1.

[20] ECJ, Case C-189/87 – *Kalfelis*, [1988] ECR I-5565 para. 18.

[21] See in detail *Bach*, IHR 2010, 17, 22 et seq.

[22] ECJ, Case C-26/91 – *Handte*, [1992] ECR I-3967 para. 15; ECJ, Case C-51/97 – *Réunion européenne*, [1998] ECR I-6511 para. 17; ECJ, Case C-265/02 – *Frahuil*, [2004] ECR I-1543 para. 24; cf. *Schlosser*, IPRax 1984, 65, 66 f.

tion of "contractual" is a positive definition of a "non-contractual obligaton": **any obligation that the obligor has not freely assumed** must be considered "non-contractual" and therefore within the scope of the Rome II Regulation.

2. Concurrent Liability

In certain scenarios, a tortfeasor's conduct may simultaneously give rise to contractual and tort claims. Domestic legal systems within the member states deal with such a situation in various ways. While Germany allows the victim to pursue the contractual and the tort claim concurrently, in France he is restricted to the contractual claim under the so-called *non-cumul* rule.[23] The **Regulation does not decide** in favor of either solution, but rather mitigates the difficulties that would occur if different laws governed contractual and non-contractual obligations: Art. 4(3)(2) provides a mechanism that allows[24] courts to apply the same law to contractual and tort claims.[25] 18

3. *Culpa in Contrahendo*

Applying the definition of "non-contractual" outlined above to Brussels I, the ECJ held that claims of *culpa in contrahendo* are of a non-contractual nature.[26] This holding is largely superfluous un- 19

---

23 See in detail *Schlechtriem*, Vertragsordnung und außervertragliche Haftung.

24 Admittedly, such parallelism is not guaranteed. Article 4(3) merely *allows* the court to apply the law governing the contract to tort claims, but does not *demand* that it do so, see *infra*, Art. 4 para. 79.

25 Note that the mere existence of Art. 4(3)(2) proves that the regulation does not follow the *non-cumul* rule: the opportunity for parallelism provided by Art. 4(3)(2) would be superfluous if the regulation was not to be applied to otherwise *non-cumul* cases. Cf. the commission's explanation of its proposal, COM(2003) 427, pp. 12 et seq, on Art. 3(3).

26 ECJ, Case C-334/00 – *Tacconi*, [2002] ECR I-7357 paras. 24 et seq.

der Rome II, whose Art. 12 clearly treats *culpa in contrahendo* as creating non-contractual obligations.[27]

20 It is worth noting, however, that both Art. 12 as well as ECJ decisions rely on an **autonomous understanding** of *culpa in contrahendo* that is independent of the legal traditions of any member state. Under this autonomous conception, *culpa in contrahendo* covers only violations of the duty of disclosure, breakdowns in contractual negotiations, and other "non-contractual obligations presenting a direct link with the dealings prior to the conclusion of a contract".[28]

21 Where domestic legal rules categorize other claims as *culpa in contrahendo* – such as personal injuries that occur while a contract is negotiated – the resulting obligations are not covered by Art. 12. Nevertheless, they must be considered non-contractual. This follows *a fortiori* from Recital 30 since such claims even lack a "direct link" to the contract. Recital 30 further provides that in cases of personal injury during negotiations, "Article 4 or other relevant provisions *of this Regulation* should apply" (emphasis added). For further details on the destinction between *culpa in contrahendo* and contractual obligations, see Art. 12 paras 7 et seq.

4. Questions of Agency: *Falsus Procurator* and Apparent Authority

22 The language of neither Rome I nor Rome II conclusively designates which domestic law should govern questions of agency. In fact, Art. 1(2)(g) Rome I offers the only provision of either Regulation on agency, in which it excludes "the question whether an agent is able to bind a principal" from Rome I's scope. Other questions of agency, such as the principal-agent relationship and the agent-third party relationship are not covered by this exclusion. According to the Guliano Lagarde report, these ques-

---

27 *Von Hein*, GPR 2007, 54 et seq.

28 Recital 30; cf. Art. 12 paras. 1 et seq.

tions "are included within the scope of [the Rome Convention, *i.e.* the Rome I regulation] in so far as they are of a contractual nature".[29]

23 While the relationship between principal and agent is likely contractual in nature, the relationship between agent and third party (and thus the liability of a ***falsus procurator***) appears to satisfy the ECJ's definition of a "non-contractual"[30] relationship: the *falsus procurator* intended to bind his *principal*, not himself, and thus never freely entered into obligations towards the third party. Under Rome II, the liability of a *falsus procurator* should be considered a case of *culpa in contrahendo* under Art. 12(1), since the liability of the *falsus procurator* arises out of pre-contractual dealings.[31]

24 Where the principal is bound to third parties by an agent's **apparent authority**, his liability does not normally satisfy the ECJ's requirements for a contractual obligation. At least in cases where the principal did not have actual knowledge of the "agent's" conduct, he did not enter freely into his obligations towards the third party;[32] instead, liability was imposed on the principal as a matter of law. Thus, Rome II applies and, again, under Rome II, such obligations – which arise out of pre-contractual dealings between an agent and a third party – will likely be classified as *culpa in contrahendo*.

5. Property Law, or *Rei Vindicatio*

25 The ECJ's definition of "non-contractual" raises the question of whether Rome II applies to claims which (*inter alia*) relate to the law of property such as *rei vindicatio*. The Regulation's silence on

29 OJ 1980 C-282/1/15; – contra: *Spellenberg*, in: Münchener Kommentar BGB, Art. 12 para. 23.

30 See *supra* paras. 16 et seq.

31 See in detail Art. 12 paras. 9 et seq.

32 See *Bach*, IPRax 2011, 116, 118.

this issue speaks neither for nor against excluding property law questions from its scope. In favor of exclusion is the fact that Rome II expressly enumerates the types of non-contractual obligations within its purview – tort or delict, unjust enrichment, *negotiorum gestio* or *culpa in contrahendo* – among which *rei vindicatio* does not appear. On the other hand, Art. 1(2) also enumerates the fields of law excluded from Rome II's scope, and again, *rei vindicatio* is not mentioned.

26 In the Author's opinion, Rome II's relationship to property questions should be governed as follows.[33] Where the *existence* of a property right is in question (*e.g.* **questions of title**), the Regulation should not apply. This accords with the plain fact that the Regulation provides no conflict rule to determine which state's law governs title disputes. In contrast, where an **extrinsic interference** with an existing property right is at issue, the Regulation may apply.[34] For example, violations to property rights are governed by Arts. 4 et seq. (tort/delict), while Art. 10 (unjust enrichment) regulates expenses incurred during an exercise of control over foreign property[35]. Proprietary restitution claims are governed either by Art. 4 (if the defendant gained possession through a wrongful act), Art. 11 (if the defendant gained possession as a result of a benevolent intervention with the plaintiff's affairs) or Art. 10 (in all other cases).[36]

27 Applying the regulation to extrinsic interferences with property rights finds support in the ECJ's holdings on the Brussels I regime.[37] Brussels I allocates jurisdiction over contractual and non-contractual claims (Art. 5) differently than it allocates juris-

---

33 Similarly: *Dickinson*, paras. 3.88 et seq.; *Mankowski*, in: Magnus/Mankowski (eds.), Brussels I Regulation, Art. 5 para. 195.

34 *Wurmnest*, in: jurisPK BGB, Art. 1 para. 30.

35 However, when the exercise of control is the result of a benevolent intervention with another's affairs claims for reimbursement of expenses are governed by Art. 11 *(negotiorum gestio)*.

36 Contra: *Chong*, 57 ICLQ (2008) 863, 893 et seq.

diction over claims arising from "property law" (Art. 22). In deciding whether a nuisance claim fit properly under Art. 22(1)[38] or Art. 5(3) Brussel I, the ECJ held that classification as property law is restricted to those cases where the type of violated right has "a decisive influence on the issues to be determined in the dispute". Such a "decisive influence" exists only where the plaintiff would have brought its claims "in substantially different terms if the right whose protection is sought against the alleged nuisance were of a different type, such as, for example, the right to physical integrity or a personal right".[39] Since the plaintiff would not have brought its nuisance claims in substantially different terms had its infringed rights been of a different type, the court classified the nuisance claim as a non-contractual obligation.

6. *Actio Pauliana*

In *Reichert v Dresdner Bank*, the ECJ denied an application of Art. 5(3) Brussels I to an *actio pauliana*.[40] Under the *actio pauliana*, a creditor may set aside the debtor's transfer of property to a third person under certain circumstances. Since the defendant of an *actio pauliana* is not the debtor but the third person, and since the action may succeed irrespective of whether the third person acted in bad faith, the ECJ reasoned that such action did not "seek to establish the liability of a defendant" as required under the general definition of "non-contractual"[41]. As stated above, ECJ interpretations of Art. 5 Brussels I may be considered when distinguishing between the obligations that fall under Rome I 28

37 ECJ, Case C-343/04 – *Land Oberösterreich v ČEZ*, [2006] ECR I-4557, para. 34; cf. ECJ, Case 294/92 – *Webb v Webb* [1994] I-ECR 1717, paras. 14 et seq.

38 The ECJ ruled on Art. 16(1) Brussels Convention, the predecessor of the present Art. 22(1) Brussels I Regulation.

39 ECJ, Case C-343/04 – *Land Oberösterreich v ČEZ*, [2006] ECR I-4557 para. 34.

40 ECJ, Case C-261/90 – *Reichert*, [1992] ECR I-2149.

41 For the general definition see *supra* para. 16.

and Rome II. Thus, an *actio pauliana* is **not within the scope of Rome II.**[42] Where the *actio pauliana* is connected with insolvency proceedings, the applicable law is determined under Arts. 4(2)(m), 13 of the European Insolvency Regulation.[43]

7. Collective Claims, or Suits Brought by Consumer Protection Associations

29 Under certain circumstances, contractual matters may provide the subject matter of a non-contractual obligation. Where a professional provides for unfair terms that disadvantage consumers in its General Terms and Conditions, a consumers' association may file for an injunction against the professional. While within the professional-consumer relationship the issue of unfair terms is clearly of a contractual nature, it should be classified a non-contractual matter where a consumers' association sues the professional.[44] The consumers' association does not assert the consumers' contractual rights. A consumer has no contractual rights that preclude his contractual partner from using unfair terms: EC Directive 93/13/EEC does *not* entitle the consumer to demand removal of unfair terms from the professional's General Terms and Conditions, but rather *ipso iure* invalidates the unfair terms. However, since the mere existence of unfair contractual clauses could cause consumers to comply with them, the consumers' association's claim primarily serves the purpose of preventing unfair competition and should therefore be regarded as a **non-contractual matter**.

---

42 *Junker*, in: Münchener Kommentar BGB, Art. 1 paras. 19 et seq.; – contra: *Dickinson*, paras. 3.249 et seq.

43 Council Regulation No 1346/2000 of 29 May 2000 on insolvency proceedings, OJ 2000 L 160/1.

44 Bundesgerichtshof (Germany) 9 July 2009, BGHZ 182, 24, para. 18.

8. Prize Notifications

In a series of cases,[45] the ECJ has ruled that the German and Austrian law of *Gewinnmitteilungen*, or prize notifications, may constitute contractual obligations. A prize notification occurs under the following circumstances: a professional sends a communication to a consumer, in which he informs the consumer that the latter has won or will win a prize if he performs one or more specified actions. Under contractual principles, the consumer's mere performance of the specified actions does *not* form a contract. However, German and Austrian courts imply a legal obligation to the professionel to fulfill its "promise" to the consumer despite the lack of a valid contract. The ECJ notwithstanding the lack of a valid contract, has held that the professional's implied obligation evinces the elements of a "contractual" obligation. Since the professional's communication was "sent to addressees and by the means chosen by the sender solely on its own initiative", its conduct resulted in an obligation it "freely assumed", *i.e.* a **contractual obligation**. 30

9. Restitution as a Consequence of a Void Contract

While unjust enrichment is generally within Rome II's scope, Rome I applies to claims for restitution following a finding that a contract is void (Art. 12(1)(e) Rome I).[46] In this case, therefore, Art. 12(1)(e) Rome I must be condidered **lex specialis** in relation to Art. 10 Rome II.[47] 31

---

45 ECJ, Case C-96/00 – *Gabriel*, [2002] ECR I-6367; ECJ, Case C-27/02 – *Engler*, [2005] ECR I-481; ECJ, Case C-180/06 – *Ilsinger*, [2009] ECR I-3961, para. 57; cf. *Bach*, IHR 2010, 17.

46 See Art. 12(1)(e) Rome I.

47 See in detail Art. 10 para. 9.

III. Situations Involving a Conflict of Laws

32 As mentioned above, Rome II applies only in "situations involving a conflict of laws". This restriction is misleading and dispensable at the same time. First, it is misleading in common law jurisdictions, where the term "conflict of laws" comprises not only questions of choice of law but also questions of jurisdiction and questions of enforcement of foreign judgments.[48] Rome II, however, governs only choice-of-law questions.[49] Second, the "conflict of laws" requirement is entirely dispensable: no one would consult Rome II if the the facts of a dispute displayed a connection to a single country only.[50] Even if one did, the provisions of Rome II would simply lead to an application of the state's law with which the dispute has its sole connection.

C. Specified Exclusions: Art. 1(2)

I. Family Relationships: Art. 1(2)(a)

33 Under Art. 1(2)(a), non-contractal obligations arising out of family relationships are excluded from the scope of Rome II (such obligations will be the subject of separate regulations in the near future[51]). Recital 10 sets forth that the term family relationship

---

48 *Cheshire, North & Fawcett*, p. 775.

49 *Cheshire, North & Fawcett*, p. 775; *Dicey, Morris & Collins*, para. S 3 5-175 which refer to the clearer wording of Art. 1(1) Rome Convention: "any situation involving a choice between the laws of different countries".

50 *Thorn*, in: Palandt, Art. 1 para. 8; *Junker*, in: Münchener Kommentar BGB, Art. 1 para. 9.

51 *E.g.* Regulation (EC) No 4/2009 of 18 December 2008 on jurisdiction, applicable law, recognition and enforcement of decisions and cooperation in matters relating to maintenance obligations which will enter into force in 2011; – reform of the Brussels IIa Regulation on applicable law and jurisdiction in divorce matters which has not yet been passed, see the Commission's Proposal COM(2006) 399; cf. *Pabst*, FPR 2008, 230.

"should cover parentage, marriage, affinity and collateral relatives". Three aspects of this description warrant closer notice:

First, Rome II excludes not only obligations arising out of family relationships, but also obligations arising out of relationships that have **"comparable effects"**. Under Recital 10, the "comparability" of relationships to family relationships should be judged under the *lex fori* – a (regrettable) exception to the general principle of autonomous interpretation.[52] 34

Second, obligations are excluded from Rome II's application only if they "arise out of" the family relationship. Thus, Rome II excludes only those obligations that have their **legal ground** in specific rules that govern the familial relationship. The distinction between family and non-family matters parallels that between civil and public matters: just as the exercise of public authority does not exist if any private individual could be engaged in the same conduct, an obligation does not "arise out of" a family relationship if it could exist between persons that do not share a family relationship. Therefore, *e.g.*, it is submitted that restitution of overpaid alimony is not excluded from Rome II; neither is a claim for damages resulting from a tort committed by one family member against another.[53] It should be noted, however, that the Commission's initial Rome II proposal explicitly stated that "an action for compensation for damage caused by late payment of a maintenance obligation" should fall under the exception and thereby outside the Regulation's scope.[54] 35

---

52 Critical: *Plender & Wilderspin*, para. 17-040.

53 *Dickinson*, para. 3.152; *Thorn*, in: Palandt, Anh. 74 Arts. 38-42 EGBGB, Art. 1 para. 10; *Hohloch*, 9 YbPIL (2007) 1, 16, with reference to the fact that in some legal systems maintenance claims under some circumstances are regarded as tort claims. However, such a classification obviously need not be followed under the Regulation.

54 COM(2003) 427.

36 Third, the family relationship must provide the basis for the obligation in dispute. **Preliminary questions** such as interspousal immunity or the liability of parents for acts of their children do not influence the classification of the main liability obligation.[55] By contrast, where the main liability obligation does not have its basis in the family relationship, the named preliminary issues are governed by the law designated by Rome II, see Art. 15(b) and (g).

II. Matrimonial Property Regimes, Wills, Succession: Art. 1(2)(b)

37 Under Art. 1(2)(b), Rome II excludes from its application non-contractual obligations that arise out of matrimonial property regimes, wills and successions.[56] As under Art. 1(2)(a), Art. 1(2)(b) also excludes any property regimes that are "comparable" to those enumerated in its text. Whether a property regime is comparable to matrimonal property, wills, or successorship is determined under the *lex fori*, which constitutes another (regrettable) exception from the principle of autonomous interpretation.

38 Most likely, Art. 1(2)(b) will be of minor relevance in practice because concrete situations encompassed by its wording are barely imaginable.[57] For example, a damages claim against a lawyer for negligent drafting of a will[58] is not excluded by Art. 1(2)(b) since the obligation does not arise "out of" the will.[59] In the author's

---

55 *Dicey, Morris & Collins*, para. S 35-179; *Dickinson*, para. 3.152.

56 European legislators intend to promulgate uniform conflicts rules applicable to these excluded matters in seperate regulations: for instance a Regulation on succession and wills (see the Commission's Greenbook, COM(2005) 65), a Regulation on conflict of laws in matters concerning matrimonial property regimes, including the question of jurisdiction and mutual recognition (see the Commission's Greenbook, COM(2006) 400).

57 *Dicey, Morris & Collins*, para. S 35-180.

58 Example taken from *Dicey, Morris & Collins*, para. S 35-180, fn. 67.

59 Regarding the according problem under lit. a, see *supra* para. 35.

opinion, the same reasoning applies for an unjust enrichment claim by one beneficiary to recover excess sums paid to another beneficiary,[60] as well as for a damages claim against a fraudulent "successor" for forgery of a will.[61]

III. Negotiable Financial Instruments: Art. 1(2)(c)

Under Art. 1(2)(c), Rome II excludes from its application non-contractual obligations arising under negotiable financial instruments. As **examples** of "negotiable financial instruments", Art. 1(2)(c) specifically enumerates bills of exchange, cheques and promissory notes. However, the Regulation excludes non-contractual obligations arising from all other negotiable instruments as well. Thus, "bills of lading, similar documents issued in connection with transport contracts, and bonds, debentures, guarantees, letters of indemnity, certificates of deposit, warrants and warehouse receipts are […] excluded by subparagraph (c) if they can be regarded as negotiable instruments".[62] **39**

This exclusion was "taken over from […] the Rome Convention",[63] which declined to regulate the law applicable to financial instruments to avoid excessive complexity. The Rome Convention's drafters feared that expanding the regulation's scope to such obligations would necessarily "involv[e] complicated special rules" because existing general rules were "not suited to the regulation of obligations of this kind".[64] **40**

Obligations arising out of negotiable instruments are – at least partially – governed by the **Geneva Convention** providing a uni- **41**

---

60 Contra: *Dickinson*, para. 3.155.

61 *Junker*, in: Münchener Kommentar BGB, Art. 1 para. 32.

62 Giuliano & Lagarde Report, OJ 1980 C 282/11.

63 Commission's initial proposal, COM(2003) 427, p. 9.

64 Giuliano & Lagarde Report, OJ 1980 C 282/11; the Commission explicitely justified Art. 1(2)(c) on this reasoning in its original proposal, COM(2003) 427, p. 9.

form law for bills of exchange and promissory notes (of 7 June 1930) and the Geneva Convention providing a uniform law for cheques (of 19 March 1931). Both conventions are in force in several member states.[65]

42 Note that this exclusion is limited to those obligations that arise out of the negotiable character of the financial instrument.[66] Therefore, *e.g.*, **prospectus liability** is not excluded by Art. 1(2)(c) because prospectus liability (a) does not arise out of the financial instrument and (b) may also arise in connection with non-negotiable financial instruments.[67]

IV. Company Law: Art. 1(2)(d)

43 Under Art. 1(2)(d), non-contractual obligations arising out of the law of companies or other bodies corporate or unincorporated fall ouside the scope of the Regulation. As in the previous exclusions, it must be emphasized that Art. 1(2)(d) excludes only those non-contractual obligations that *arise out of* company law. Any "regular" tort committed by a company that could equally have been committed by natural persons thus remains within the Regulation's scope.[68]

44 The question of whether a legal person has **capacity to incur liability** is also not excluded under Art. 1(2)(d).[69]

45 The exclusion of company law from Rome II's scope is likely of little practical relevance because, in the vast majority of company law cases, the obligation in question will be of a contractual nature.

---

65 A list of contracting states is available under http://untreaty.un.org.

66 *Weber*, WM 2008, 1581, 1584.

67 *Weber*, WM 2008, 1581, 1584; *von Hein*, FS Hopt, 371, 379 et seq.; *Tschäpe/Kramer/Glück*, RIW 2008, 657, 661.

68 Cf *supra* para. 35.

69 *Dickinson*, paras. 14.11 et seq.; *Dicey, Morris & Collins*, para. 35-040; cf. Art. 15 para. 5.

There is, however, one exception to this assumption: Art. 1(2)(d)'s specific exclusion of "the personal liability of officers and members as such for the obligations of the company or body", an exclusion which has not been contained in Art. 1(2)(e) of the Rome Convention. **Director liability** can be of particular relevance in non-contractual issues: where a company is liable to a third person for a tort,[70] Art. 1(2)(d) leads to the result that the conflict of law rules of the *lex fori* – not Rome II – will determine what law governs the personal liability of the company's officers and directors.

In legal literature, it is often disputed whether the exclusion of **46** "the personal liability of officers and members as such for the obligations of the company or body" from Rome II also excludes the **personal liablity of officers** for breaches of their obligations **towards the company**. Again, in most cases these obligations will be contractual and therefore not within the scope of the Regulation anyway. However, several legal systems impose non-contractual obligations on directors with regard to the companies they oversee.[71] In determining whether these obligations come within Art. 1(2)(d)'s exclusion, it should *not* be decisive whether the obligations are similar to a director's personal tort liability to third parties. Instead, the standard for exclusion under Art. 1(2)(d) should consist in one question: do the directors' duties belong to what is commonly considered "company law"? The better reasons speak for answering this question in the affirmative.[72] The duties arise from a special relationship between the officer and

70 The damages claim against the company most likely will fall within the scope of the Rome II Regulation. The exclusion of Art. 1(2)(d) does not apply since the tort does not "arise out of company law" – the mere fact that the tortfeasor is a company does not suffice for the exclusion.

71 For example the English equitable duties (see *Base Metal Trading v Shamurin* [2005] 1 WLR 1157; cf. *Dickinson*, para. 3.162) or the German claims against legal representatives or officers in § 93 Aktiengesetz or § 43 GmbH-Gesetz (cf. G. *Wagner*, IPRax 2008, 1, 2).

72 *Dickinson*, paras. 3.162 et seq.; *Plender & Wilderspin*, para. 17-045; contra: G. *Wagner*, IPRax 2008, 1, 2.

the company and do not exist between any other natural or legal persons.[73] To find that such creates an obligation of "company law" (which falls under the Art. 1(2)(d) exception) is analogous to the ECJ's approach in determining when a public authority acts "in the exercise of its powers".[74] Just as a public authority exercises its power whenever it accesses "any powers going beyond those existing under the rules applicable to relations between private individuals", so a director's obligation belongs to "company law" when it goes beyond the obligations that general civil and commercial law impose on other natural and legal persons.

47 Note that Art. 1(2)(d) also excludes from the regulation's scope "the personal liability of **auditors** to a company or to its members in the statutory audits of accounting documents".[75] Therefore an action for negligence brought against the auditor does not fall within the regulation's scope.[76]

48 The exclusion of company law does not comprise **prospectus liability**, as prospectus regulation arises from the law of capital markets rather than from company law.[77] This becomes evident considering that the liablilty does not depend on the type of company.[78]

V. Trusts: Art. 1(2)(e)

49 Under Art. 1(2)(e), "non-contractual obligations arising out of the relations between the settlors, trustees and beneficiaries of a trust created voluntarily" are excluded from the Regulation's scope. Trusts created by operation of law or by judicial decision

---

73 *Dickinson*, para. 3.167.

74 See *supra* paras. 8 et seq.

75 The Rome Convention did not contain such an exclusion in its Art. 1(2)(e).

76 *Cheshire, North & Fawcett*, p. 775.

77 *Von Hein*, FS Hopt, 371, 382; *Weber*, WM 2008, 1581, 1584; *Wurmnest*, in: jurisPK BGB, Art. 1 para. 46.

78 *Wurmnest*, in: jurisPK BGB, Art. 1 para. 46.

are *not* within the scope of the exception and are therefore governed by the Rome Regulations.[79] Article 1(2)(e)'s restriction to trusts "created voluntarily" was not contained in the Commission's initial proposal,[80] but was added by the European Parliament.[81] The Parliament supported this restriction in order "to ensure greater consistency with the **1985 Hague Convention** on recognition of trusts[[82]] and to avoid difficulty or confusion arising from the employment of the trust in common-law jurisdictions as a device for dealing with situations such as unjust enrichment".[83] This reasoning suggests that the definition of a trust provided in Art. 2 of the Hague Trust Convention may serve as a guideline for interpreting Art. 1(2)(e).[84]

Further, official reports, jurisprudence, and legal literature developed in connection with Art. 1(2)(g) Rome Convention and Art. 5(6) Brussels I[85] may be properly consulted in interpreting Art. 1(2)(e).[86] 50

---

79 *Von Overbeck*, Explanatory report on the Hague Convention on the Law applicable to trusts and on their recognition, para. 49.

80 COM(2003) 427.

81 European Parliament legislative resolution on the proposal for a regulation of the European Parliament and of the Council on the law applicable to non-contractual obligations ("Rome II"), P6_TA(2005)0284, p. 7.

82 Convention on the Law applicable to trusts and on their recognition of 1 July 1985.

83 Committee on Legal Affairs, Report on the proposal for a regulation of the European Parliament and of the Council on the law applicable to non-contractual obligations ("Rome II") (Wallis-Report), A6-0211/2005, p. 15.

84 Cf. *Mankowski*, in: Magnus/Mankowski (eds.), Brussels I Regulation, Art. 5 para. 303; – for critical views towards this definition see: *Dickinson*, paras. 3.178 et seq.

85 An exclusion of trusts from Rome II is remarkable against the background of the Brussels I Regulation, which expressly regulates trusts in Art. 5(6).

86 Of particular assistance may again be the Giuliano & Lagarde report on the Rome Convention, OJ 1980 C 282.

51 The exclusion of trusts from Rome II will likely be of minor practical relevance, as most obligations arising out of a trust that has been "created voluntarily" will be of a contractual nature and fall outside the scope of Rome II by virtue of this fact alone.[87]

VI. Nuclear Damage: Art. 1(2)(f)

52 European legislators justify excluding non-contractual obligations arising out of nuclear damage from the Regulation's scope on two grounds:[88] the importance of the economic and State interests at stake and the existence of international conventions already in place that regulate nuclear damage.[89] In interpreting the term "nuclear damage", scholars have argued that these conventions may properly provide guidance.[90] Therefore, the definition of "nuclear damage" contained in Art. I of **the 1963 Vienna Convention** is relevant in defining the scope of Art. 1(2)(f)'s exclusion.[91] For further details regarding scope and conflict rules of the Conventions see Art. 7 paras. 55 et seq.

---

87 *Dickinson*, para. 3.174.

88 COM (2003) 427, p. 9.

89 Paris Convention on Third Party Liability in the Field of Nuclear Energy of 29 July 1960; Brussels Supplementary Convention of 31 January 1963; Vienna Convention on Civil Liability for Nuclear Damage of 21 May 1963, Convention on Supplementary Compensation for Nuclear Damage of 12 September 1997 and the Joint Protocol Relating to the Application of the Vienna Convention and the Paris Convention of 21 September 1988. Note that Austria, Ireland and Luxemburg are not parties to either of the conventions.

90 *Dickinson*, para. 3.216.

91 Vienna Convention on Civil Liability for Nuclear Damage of 21 May 1963. The definition has been modified by the Protocol to Amend the 1963 Vienna Convention on Civil Liability for Nuclear Damage of 12 September 1997. The Protocol has thus far been ratified by few member states. Therefore it is arguable whether an "autonomous European definition" of "nuclear damage" can be derived from the Protocol; cf. *Dickinson*, para. 3.216.

VII. Privacy and Rights Relating to Personality: Art. 1(2)(g)

The exclusion of "non-contractual obligations arising out of violations of privacy and rights relating to personality, including defamation" in Art. 1(2)(g) is the result of a long-lasting quarrel between the Commission and (segments of) the Parliament. The Commission's initial proposal included a special rule for rights of privacy and personality that essentially established a *lex loci damni* regime.[92] This rule was heavily criticised by the (English) media lobby and – following the lobbyists' arguments – by Parliament headed by its rapporteur Diana Wallis.[93] The British press feared facing liability claims under alien legal systems that – contrary to English practice – might grant rights of personality priority over the freedom of press. The Parliament's counterproposal, therefore, called for application of the *lex loci delicti commissi* (*i.e.* the law in force at the place of action).[94] The Commission, however, objected to this counterproposal. In order to avoid disrupting legislative proceedings, the Commission, Council and Parliament eventually agreed on simply excluding the object of quarrel from the Regulation.[95] **53**

However, in their attempts to exclude the object of quarrel from Rome II, European legislators overshot the mark. Instead of excluding every tort committed by the media – *i.e.* differentiating according to the tortfeasor – legislators agreed to exclude a particular *type* **54**

---

92 COM(2003) 427, p. 38 (on Art. 6).

93 See in detail *Dickinson*, paras. 3.217 et seq.

94 *De iure* the counterproposal did not deviate from the *lex loci damni* rule; however, the place of damage was defined as "the country to which the publication or broadcasting service is principally directed"; P6_TA (2005)0284, pp. 11 et seq. (Art. 5); cf. the report of the committee on legal affairs ("Wallis-report") A6-0211/2005, pp. 21 et seq.

95 Commission's amended proposal, COM(2006) 83, p. 6 (amendment 57); Communication from the Commission to the European Parliament, COM(2006) 566, p. 3; Common Position (EC) No 22/2006, OJ 2006 C 289 E, pp. 76 et seq.

of tort (due to a failure to agree on a definition of the term "media")[96]. As a result, violations of privacy and rights relating to personality are now excluded from the Regulation's scope. This last-minute compromise leads to certain tensions and uncertainties.

55 First, the **disclosure of confidential data** (which obviously is related to violations of privacy and personality rights) plays an important role in unfair competition law and even more so in the context of intellectual property. Both fields of law are explicitly governed by Rome II in Arts. 6 and 8, respectively. Excluding claims for disclosure of data from the Regulation's application would encourage their fragmentation and also significantly weaken the Regulation, thus resulting in an increase in legal uncertainty in the fields of unfair competition and intellectual property.[97] For this reason, several scholars advocate excepting those cases from the Art. 1(2)(g) exclusion (*i.e.* subjecting them to the Rome II regime) where liability primarily arises from the law of unfair competition rather than the rights of privacy or personality of the victim.[98]

56 Second, Art. 1(2)(g)'s exclusion leads to arbitrary results in cases of **data theft**. Should the claims of a person *whose* data have been stolen fall under Art. 1(2)(g)'s "privacy and personality" exception? Should claims of the person *from whom* the data are stolen (*e.g.* a bank or telecommunication enterprise)? If the 'person' whose data are stolen is an enterprise and the competitor exploits these data, should the competitor's claim fall under the proposed[99] exception from Art. 1(2)(g) in favour of Arts. 6 and 8? If the data are stolen by a third person and sold to the competitor, should different conflicts principles govern the law applicable to the claim against the thief and the claim against the competitor?

---

96 See Communication from the Commission to the European Parliament, COM(2006) 566, p. 3.

97 *Dickinson*, para. 3.227.

98 *Dickinson*, para. 3.227; *Cheshire, North & Fawcett*, p. 785; *Plender & Wilderspin*, para. 17-055 fn. 136 and 17-059.

99 See *supra* para. 55.

Third, certain actions may constitute both defamation and another tort. For example, a public slap in the face potentially constitutes defamation and battery. Strictly applying Art. 1(2)(g) would require that two independent bodies of law determine the law which is applicable to the separate tort claims.[100] **57**

Fourth, it is not entirely clear whether **non-natural persons** enjoy rights of "privacy" and "personality". The Commission in its initial proposal repeatedly referred to the guarantee of the privacy under the ECHR and the Charter of Fundamental Rights of the European Union.[101] Under both Art. 8 ECHR and Arts. 7 and 8 of the Charter of Fundamental Rights it is at most unclear, whether the rights appertain to non-natural persons.[102] The EC data directive,[103] which Rome II explicitly references in Art. 30(2), is restricted to natural persons. **58**

In the Author's opinion, the lack of clarity in Art. 1(2)(g)'s relationship to unfair competition and intellectual property calls for a **restrictive interpretation** of the exclusion. The Regulation should, at the least, govern any case that falls under Arts. 6 or 8. This comports with the general principle, established by the ECJ and particularly emphasized by the Commission regarding all Art. 1(2) exclusions,[104] that exclusions should be interpreted restrictively.[105] **59**

---

100 Cf. *Heiss/Loacker*, JBl. 2007, p. 613 (621).

101 See *e.g.* COM(2003) 427, p. 17 (on Art. 6).

102 *Dickinson*, para. 3.227 with reference to *Lester/Pannick*, Human rights in law and practice, para. 4.8.42.

103 EC Directive 95/41 on the protection of individuals with regard to the processing of personel data and the free movement of such data, OJ 1995 L 281/31.

104 COM(2003) 427, p. 9.

105 Cf. *e.g.* ECJ, Case C-26/91 – *Handte*, [1992] ECR I-3967 para. 14; ECJ, Case C-51/97 – *Réunion européenne*, [1998] ECR I-6511 para. 16; ECJ, Case C-189/87 – *Kalfelis*, [1988] ECR I-5565, para. 19; ECJ, Case C-32/88 – *Six* Constructions, [1989] ECR I-341, para. 18.

D. Evidence and Procedure: Art. 1(3)

I. Distinction between Procedural and Substantive Matters

60 The Regulation does not apply to questions of evidence and procedure, which remain subject to the *lex fori*. The exclusion of evidentiary and procedural matters as such is primarily declaratory, as the law applicable to non-contractual obligations is purely substantive law.[106] The more complex inquiry involves delineating procedural from substantive matters.

61 Article 1(3) provides no standard for determining when a matter is "procedural". **Guidance**, however, is provided in Arts. 15 and 22. Article 15 defines the scope of national substantive law applicable under Rome II's conflicts principles: questions such as the limitation of liability (lit. b), the assessment of damages (lit. c) and prescription and limitation periods (lit. h) are governed by the designated law – and are thus considered substantive law under the Regulation.[107] Also, Art. 22(1) provides that the law designated by Rome II's rules governs questions of burden of proof and presumptions, thus also rendering these issues substantive. Under Art. 22(2), "acts intended to have legal effect" may be proved by any mode of proof recognized either by the *lex fori* or by the law(s) designated by Art. 21. This does not mean, of course, that the question of modes of proof is a substantive question for purposes of Rome II; rather Art. 22(2) provides a small exception from the general principle that procedural questions may be resolved solely under the *lex fori*.

---

106 *Cheshire, North & Fawcett*, p. 786.

107 Art. 15 para. 1. Considering these domains substantive is in line with continental traditions but represents "a radical change" for English lawyers; *Illmer*, CJQ 2009, 237, 242; *Cheshire, North & Fawcett*, p. 787. For classification as a procedural matter in English law, see *e.g. Harding v Wealands* [2006] UKHL 32.

II. Application of Foreign Law

62 One important question not addressed by the Regulation is how the court seised of jurisdiction over a Rome II-amenable action determines the *content* of applicable law. The determination of foreign law is clearly a procedural matter, but it may nevertheless exercise considerable influence over the success of Rome II. If the content of the applicable law cannot be determined, most member states allow their courts to apply another law – usually the *lex fori*.[108] Circumventing the Regulation is even easier where domestic courts are not obligated to determine the content of the foreign law on their own,[109] but may regard the content of foreign law as a matter of fact which must be pleaded and proved by the parties.[110] In such cases, the application of Rome II is subject to the parties' ability to plead and prove the foreign law. The European Parliament has proposed rules governing how courts ascertain the content of foreign law[111] which, however, have not been adopted. Pursuant to Art. 30, the Commission is merely required to submit a report on the application of the Regulation that includes "a study on the effects of the way foreign law is treated in the different jurisdictions and on the extent to which courts of the Member States apply foreign law in practice pursuant to this Regulation". Harmonising the rules on the ascertainment of foreign law has thus been shifted to a separate legislative project.[112] Whether national rules may be freely applied until such regula-

108 Cf. *Gruber/Bach*, 11 YbPIL (2009) 157, 161 et seq.; for a comparative report of the law in all member states cf. *Palao Moreno/Iglesias Buhigues/Esplugues Mota* (eds.), Application of Foreign Law (2011).

109 As *e.g.* in German law, see § 293 German ZPO.

110 As *e.g.* in English law; cf. *Cheshire, North & Fawcett*, p. 776.

111 European Parliament legislative resolution on the proposal for a regulation of the European Parliament and of the Council on the law applicable to non-contractual obligations ("Rome II"), P6_TA(2005)0284, p. 16 (Arts. 12 and 13).

112 A project initiated by the University of Valencia, the University of Genova and the Colegio de Registradores de la Propriedad y Mercantiles

tion arrives seems questionable – in particular against the background of repeated ECJ rulings emphasizing that applications of national procedural rules must not impair the effectiveness of uniform law.[113]

E. Exclusion of Denmark: Art. 1(4)

63 Article 1(4) makes explicit that, for purposes of Rome II, Denmark is not an EU member state. The provision granting the EC authority to pass Rome II was Art. 65 EC – a provision that does not bind Denmark (neither does it bind the UK and Ireland – these countries have exercised their right to opt in to Rome II).[114] Therefore, whenever the term "Member States" is used in Rome II, it refers only to the 26 remaining countries.[115]

64 However, since the Regulation is a *loi uniforme* under Art. 3[116], courts of the remaining member states must apply Danish law to a dispute if the rules of Rome II designate Danish law as applicable.[117]

de España endeavours to furnish the Commission with further regulatory proposals; cf. *Gruber/Bach*, 11 YbPIL (2009) 157, 160.

113 See *e.g.* ECJ, Case C-159/02 – *Turner v Grovit*, [2004] ECR I-3565 para. 29; ECJ, Case C-365/88 – *Kongress Agentur Hagen v Zeehaghe BV*, [1990] ECR I-1845 para. 20.

114 It is expected, however, that Denmark will adopt Rome II's provisons by way of agreement with the EU. An accordant agreement in regard to Brussels I has already been concluded, see OJ 2005 L 299/62.

115 In the Author's opinion however, the use of the term "member state" in Art. 14(3) is mistaken; see Art. 14 para. 38.

116 See Art. 3 para. 1.

117 *Spickhoff*, in: Bamberger/Roth, Anh. zu Art. 42 EGBGB para. 25.

Article 2
Non-contractual obligations

1. For the purposes of this Regulation, damage shall cover any consequence arising out of tort/delict, unjust enrichment, negotiorum gestio or culpa in contrahendo.
2. This Regulation shall apply also to non-contractual obligations that are likely to arise.
3. Any reference in this Regulation to:
   (a) an event giving rise to damage shall include events giving rise to damage that are likely to occur; and
   (b) damage shall include damage that is likely to occur.

A. Overview

The ostensible purpose of Art. 2 is to facilitate clear language throughout the Regulation. It defines several terms used continuously throughout the Regulation, thus allowing the Regulation simply to refer to, *e.g.*, "damages" instead of "damages or damage that is likely to occur". To express the Regulation's application to future non-contractual obligations, the Commission's initial proposal had repeatedly (or, as some said, indiscriminately) referred to obligations as "being likely to arise" or damage as "being likely to occur".[1] Article 2 renders such repetitive and convoluted phrasing unnecessary. 1

1 COM(2003) 427; for a detailed overview on the legislation procedure see *Dickinson*, para. 3.45 (on Art. 2) and paras. 1.44 et seq.

2 However, the definitions contained in Art. 2 also display the Article's underlying substantive purpose: to **expand the material scope** of the Regulation to encompass *future* torts, unjust enrichment, *negotiorum gestio*, and *culpa in contrahendo*.[2]

B. Material Scope: Future Obligations and Declaratory Actions

3 Article 2(2) makes clear that the Regulation not only governs the law applicable to obligations that arise from a tort, but rather also determines which law will define the principal obligation not to commit a tort in the first place. Thus, the prevention of liability falls within the Regualtion's material scope.[3] In terms of redress, the Regulation applies to **compensatory claims** as well as to **actions for injunctions**: Thus, if the potential victim of a tort claims that the tortfeasor will perform a wrongful act in the future, the Regulation supplies the law applicable to the question of whether the tortfeasor must refrain from acting.[4]

4 While declaratory judgments are of particular relevance in the context of torts (especially in the fields of intellectual property, unfair competition, environmental damages and defamation or publicity claims[5]), they are unlikely to provide any meaningful redress for other non-contractual obligations.

5 In expanding its scope to future torts, Rome II again mirrors the Brussels I Regulation – Art. 5(3) of Brussels I expressly includes torts that "may occur" within its scope.

---

2 *Thorn*, in: Palandt, Art. 2 para. 3.

3 *Hohloch*, 9 YbPIL (2007) 1, 13; *Junker*, in Münchener Kommentar BGB, Art. 2 para. 7.

4 G. *Wagner*, IPRax 2008, 1; *Thorn*, in: Palandt, Art. 2 para. 3.

5 Note however, that according to Art. 1(2)(g) violations of privacy and rights relating to personality are generally excluded from the Regulation's scope of application; but see Art. 1 para. 59.

C. Definitions

I. Art. 2(1): "Damage" Refers to "Any Consequence"

Under Art. 2(1), the term "damages" as used by the Regulation goes beyond its etymological meaning: it refers not only to loss suffered as a consequence of a tort or *culpa in contrahendo*, but also covers the consequences of the other legal institutions – unjust enrichment and *negotiorium gestio*. Using the term "damages" as shorthand for all possible consequences simplified the drafting of the Regulation's individual provisions.[6] It freed Rome II's drafters from the burden of explicitly reciting every possible consequence of a tort, an unjust enrichments, a *negotiorium gestio* and a *culpa in contrahendo* within the the Regulation's substantive provisions governing remedies.[7] For example, in addition to damages, Art. 11(2) comprehends *negotiorium gestio* as giving rise to claims reimbursement of expenses (which do not qualify as damages in their strict sense) and the restitution of enrichment. If not for Art. 2(1), Art. 11(2) would have had to individually list damages, reimbursement and restitution in order to bring all three remedies within the Regulation's scope. The same is true for Art. 14, which differentiates between a choice of law before and after an event giving rise to a "damage": again, the term "damages" encompasses all other consequences, as well, *i.e.* the event giving rise to the enrichment or expense. Other examples are Art. 18 and 23(2). 6

6 Communication from the Commission to the European Parliament, COM(2006) 566, p. 5.

7 *Thorn*, in: Palandt, Art. 2 para. 2.

II. Art. 2(3): "Damage" and "Event Giving Rise to Damage" Include Damages and Events That Are Likely to Occur

7 Article 2(3) exists for the same purposes as Art. 2(1). As mentioned above, the Commission's initial proposal was critised for its indiscriminate use of the term "likely to arise".[8] In order to satisfy its critics, simplify the Regulation's language, and ensure that declaratory actions were included in the Regulation's scope, the Council decided to eliminate the phrase "likely to arise" and instead to define the term "damage" as including "damage that is likely to occur". It followed a similar strategy in defining an "event giving rise to the damage": under the Regulation, such an "event" includes not merely past events that have caused damage, but also "events … likely to occur" that "giv[e] rise to damage".

Article 3
Universal application

Any law specified by this Regulation shall be applied whether or not it is the law of a Member State.

1 The Regulation constitutes a *loi uniforme*: it applies irrespective of whether its rules call for the application of the law of a member state. Thus, to give an exaggerated example, if a Mexican injures a Canadian in a traffic accident on the roads of New York, the question of applicable law must be answered according to the Regulation – provided, of course, that the courts of a member state preside over the case.[1]

---

8 Council Doc 16240/04, pp. 2 et seq.; cf. *Dickinson*, para. 3.45.

1 … which in the given example is only possible if the parties agree on the jurisdiction of a member state and that member state accepts such agreement (according to Art. 23(1) Brussels I such an agreement is not valid; however, the Regulation in this case is not applicable as neither party has its habitual residence in a member state).

This universal application has led to heavy debate in the legislative process[2] and continues to be criticized as exceeding the EC's legislative competence.[3] Article 65 EC, on whose authority Rome II was promulgated, requires legal measures to be "necessary for the proper functioning of the internal market". Some argue that only those regulations that govern cross-border activity within the European Union are "necessary for the proper functioning of the internal market".[4] In response, the Regulation argues its "necessity" for the proper functioning of the internal market in Recital 13 by stating that uniform rules "may avert the risk of distortions of competition between litigants". The example given by the Commission is as follows: "If there continue to be more than fifteen different systems of conflict rules, two firms in distinct Member States, A and B, bringing the same dispute between them and a third firm in country C before their respective courts, would have different conflict rules applied to them, which could provoke a distortion of competition as in purely intra-Community situations".[5] 2

---

2 See *e.g.* the Response of the Government of the UK to the Commissions initial proposal, http://ec.europa.eu/justice_home/news/consulting_public/rome_ii/govern_uk_en.pdf para. 4.

3 *Dickinson*, para. 2.110; *Remien*, 38 CML Rev. (2001) 53, 75 et seq.; *Nourissat/Treppoz*, 130 Clunet (2003) 7, 12.

4 Cf. *Dickinson*, para. 2.110 and paras. 2.34 et seq.

5 COM(2003) 427, p. 10.

Chapter II
Torts/Delicts

Article 4
General Rule

1. Unless otherwise provided for in this Regulation, the law applicable to a non-contractual obligation arising out of a tort/delict shall be the law of the country in which the damage occurs irrespective of the country in which the event giving rise to the damage occurred and irrespective of the country or countries in which the indirect consequences of that event occur.
2. However, where the person claimed to be liable and the person sustaining damage both have their habitual residence in the same country at the time when the damage occurs, the law of that country shall apply.
3. Where it is clear from all the circumstances of the case that the tort/delict is manifestly more closely connected with a country other than that indicated in paragraphs 1 or 2, the law of that other country shall apply. A manifestly closer connection with another country might be based in particular on a preexisting relationship between the parties, such as a contract, that is closely connected with the tort/delict in question.

A. Scope and Structure

I. Torts/Delicts

1. General Definition

The term "torts/delicts", as it is used throughout the Regulation, is defined autonomously, *i.e.* without reference to the legal tradition of any member state. In general, it covers **all claims that are** 1

based on a wrongdoing by the defendant. More specifically, claims for tort/delict are not solely claims for damages. According to Art. 2(2), "negatory claims" – *i.e.* claims that demand the omission of a future wrongdoing – may come under the rubric of torts/delicts as well.

2. Distruction between Torst and Unjust Enrichment

2 Whether claims that are **based solely on the gain of the other party**, do constitute claims for "torts/delicts" or rather a claim for unjust enrichment, is subject to some debate. See in more detail Art. 10 paras 2 et seq. Scholars have proposed two possible starting points for a distinction: the prerequisites and the legal consequences of a claim.

3 The latter approach would ask whether the plaintiff claims reimbursement for his damages or disgorgement of the defendant's profit. Loss based claims would be regarded as tortious, whereas gain-based claims would fall under the concept of unjust enrichment. Such a distinction, however, would lead to difficulties in practice: often the plaintiff's loss will equal the defendants profit and thus it may be hard to determine whether a claim aims at reimbursement for a loss or at disgorgement. What is more, both aspects may be melted together, each aspect being one item of a "damages calculation".

4 Therefore, the other approach seems preferable.[1] It ties in with the claim's prerequisites – concretely with the requirements to the defendant's behaviour: when claims require a wrongdoing by the defendant[2] they should as a rule be classified as tort claims rather than unjust enrichment claims. Accordingly, a claim may

---

1 *Dickinson*, paras. 4.11 et seq.; *Plender & Wilderspin*, para. 24-085 – contra: *Junker*, in: Münchener Kommentar BGB, Art. 4 para. 15.

2 *Dickinson*, para. 4.13 defines: "an act or omission of or attributable to the defendant or other event for the consequences of which the defendant is responsible to the claimant".

be regarded a claim for unjust enrichment only when it aims at disgorgement of the defendant's gain *and* the imposition of liability does not require wrongdoing by the defendant.[3]

3. Distruction between Tort Property Law

As outlined in regard to Art. 1, the Regulation applies to claims based on an **extrinsic interference with an existing property right.**[4] Violations to property rights are governed by Arts. 4 et seq. (tort/delict), while Art. 10 (unjust enrichment) or Art. 11 *(negotiorum gestio)* regulate expenses incurred during an exercise of control over foreign property. Proprietary restitution claims are governed by Art. 4 when the defendant gained possession through a wrongful act.[5] 5

4. Concurrent Liability

Where the behavior of one party may lead to tort liability as well as to other non-contractual claims, the same principles should apply that are used to determine the applicable law for concurrent contractual and non-contractual claims.[6] The law designated by Arts. 4 et seq. will determine whether tort claims arise while the law designated by Arts. 10, 11 or 12 will decide whether claims for unjust enrichment, *negotiorum gestio* or *culpa in contrahendo* exist. 6

II. Structure of the Rules on Torts/Delicts

The rules for determining the law applicable to tort claims are mainly contained in Chapter II of the Regulation (Arts. 4 through 9). These rules, however, are subject to the parties' 7

---

3 See Art. 10 paras. 2 et seq.

4 See Art. 1 para. 26.

5 If the defendant gained possession as a result of a benevolent intervention with the plaintiff's affairs, they are governed by Art. 11; in all other cases they are governed by Art. 10.

6 See Art. 1 para. 18.

choice of law, since the freedom to choose the applicable law granted by Art. 14 generally prevails over the rules of Chapter II.[7]

8 For reasons of efficiency, all issues that arise from tort claims as well as from other types of non-contractual obligations are addressed under the general provisions of Chapters V ("Common Rules") and VI ("Other Provisions"), such as, *e.g.*, which aspects of a tort claim are governed by the applicable law (Art. 15), the question of *renvoi* (Art. 24), the effect of "overriding mandatory provisons" of the *lex fori* (Art. 16), the public policy of the forum (Art. 26), and the possibility of a direct action against the insurer of the person liable (Art. 18). A very important rule concerning torts/delicts is hidden in the end of Chapter V: under Art. 17, the conduct of a person must be judged with regard to the rules of safety and conduct at the place and time of the tortfeasor's action. Thus, no matter which law is to be applied in general, the question whether or not the tortfeasor was at fault must be decided by considering the law at the place where he acted (see in detail Art. 17 para. 3).

9 A similar deviation from the law designated applicable by Arts. 4 through 9 is buried even deeper in the Regulation. According to Recital 33, "when *quantifying damages* for personal injury in cases in which [a road accident] takes place in a State other than that of the habitual residence of the victim, the court seised should take into account all the relevant actual circumstances of the specific victim, including in particular the actual losses and costs of after-care and medical attention".

III. Structure of Chapter II

10 Within Chapter II, Art. 4 provides general rules for determining the law applicable to tort claims, while Arts. 5 through 9 provide special rules for particular types of torts such as product liability

[7] A choice of law is, however, excluded for the torts of unfair competition (Art. 6(4)) and violations of intellectual property rights (Art. 8(3)), cf. Art. 14 para. 3.

(Art. 5), unfair competition (Art. 6), environmental damage (Art. 7), infringement of intellectual property rights (Art. 8) and industrial action (Art. 9). For most of these types of torts, the Regulation provides special connecting factors; however, in several cases reference is made to the general rules of Art. 4.[8] For details regarding the relationship between Art. 4 and the special rules in Arts. 5 through 9 see the comment on the relevant special rule.

The large number of exceptions and the fact that many topics are excluded from the regulation's scope by virtue of Art. 1(2) leaves the so-called "main rule" of Art. 4 with little practical impact. The priority of the parties' choice of law (Art. 14) further decreases its importance. Basically, traffic accidents constitute the only major type of torts that usually remain for an application of Art. 4:[9] The regulation neither provides for an exception in regard to traffic accidents, nor are the parties likely to agree on the applicable law. However, the field of traffic accidents may be subject to the 1971 Hague Convention on the Law Applicable to Traffic Accidents, which has been ratified by several member states[10] and which takes priority over the Rome II Regulation pursuant to Art. 28.[11] 11

IV. Structure of Art. 4

Within Art. 4 the "basic rule" is contained in subsection (1). It provides that the law applicable to a tort claim is the law of the country in which the damage occurs (*"lex loci damni"*). The basic rule of paragraph (1) is subject to the rules contained in para- 12

8 *E.g.* Art. 7 (Environmental damages) generally refers to Art. 4(1); Art. 5 (Product liability) grants priority to Art. 4(2); Art. 6 (Unfair competition) declares Art. 4 to be applicable in cases where an act of unfair competition affects the interests of one single competitor exclusively.

9 Cf. *Garcimartín Alférez*, EuLF 2007 I 77, 84.

10 Austria, Belgium, Czech Republic, France, Latvia, Lithuania, Luxembourg, Netherlands, Poland, Portugal, Slovakia, Slovenia, Spain; see http://www.hcch.net/index_en.php?act=conventions.status&cid=81.

11 See Art. 28 para. 10 – critical *von Hein*, 102 ZVglRWiss (2003) 528, 548.

graphs (2) and (3). Under paragraph (2), if the tortfeasor and the victim are habitually resident in the same country, the law of this country will be applicable rather than the *lex loci damni*. Second, if the court finds the case to be "manifestly more closely connected" with a third country, the law of this country will be applicable pursuant to paragraph (3).[12]

13 In other words, the basic rule of Art. 4(1) only applies if a) the parties have not entered a choice of law agreement, b) the claim is not for any of the types of torts governed by Arts. 5 through 9, c) the parties do not have their habitual residence in the same country and d) the courts do not find the case to be more closely connected to another country.

B. Art. 4(1): General Rule: *Lex Loci Damni*

I. General

14 Article 4(1) calls for courts to apply the *lex loci damni* to tort claims, *i.e.* the law of the country in which damage occurs.[13] The provision explicitly makes clear that, in determining *lex loci damni*, the court may consider neither the situs of the tortfeasor's actions nor the place where consequential damages occur.

15 Thus, the Regulation takes a narrower approach than the Brussels I regime. Article 5(3) Brussels I vests jurisdiction with the courts of the place "where the harmful event occurred," which

---

[12] According to the European Commission, "experience with the Rome Convention […] has shown that the courts in some member states tend to begin in fact with the exception clause and seek the law that best meets the proximity criterion", *i.e.* without first paying regard to the general rules; COM(2003) 427, p. 12.

[13] This rule corresponds with many national approaches, cf. *Kadner Graziano*, Gemeineuropäisches Internationales Privatrecht, pp. 199 et seq.; *von Hein*, 102 ZVglRWiss (2003) 528, 533 et seq.

has been held by the ECJ to comprise the situs of action as well as the place of (direct) harm.[14] This divergence may prohibit the forum granted jurisdiction under Brussels I from applying its own law under Rome II – an undesirable circumstance, since every court is most familiar with its own law.

The rationale behind the narrow approach of Art. 4(1) Rome II is expressed in Recital 16. First, equal consideration of the interests of both tortfeasors and victims requires applying neither the law of the situs of wrongful action nor the law of countries in which consequential damages occurred.[15] The place of action is often unforeseeable for and of no importance to the victim[16] and can easily be manipulated by the tortfeasor, while the place of consequential damages is unforeseeable to the tortfeasor[17] and can be easily manipulated by the victim. Second, relying on both **16**

---

14 See constitutive ECJ, Case 21/76 – *Mines de Potasse d'Alsace*, [1976] ECR I-1735 para. 25; cf. *Mankowski*, in: Magnus/Mankowski (eds.), Brussels I Regulation, Art. 5 paras. 203 et seq.

15 COM(2003) 427, pp. 11 et seq.; cf. *Stone*, 4 Ankara L. Rev. (2007) 95, 112; *de Lima Pinheiro*, Riv. dir. int. priv. proc. 2008, 5, 16; *Sonnentag*, 105 ZVglRWiss (2006) 256, 266 et seq.; *Kadner Graziano*, 73 RabelsZ (2009) 1, 13 – critical: *Benecke*, RIW 2003, 830, 834.

16 Why should the victim be entitled to choose another law merely because the tortfeasor acted in another country? This would result in undue inequality in comparison to a victim that suffers the same damage caused by a tortfeasor's identical action in the same country; cf. *Leible/Engel*, EuZW 2004, 7, 10; G. *Wagner*, IPRax 2006, 372, 377.

17 For a discussion on foreseeability of applicable law to the tortfeasor, see in detail *von Hein*, Das Günstigkeitsprinzip im Internationalen Deliktsrecht, pp. 206 et seq. *Symeonides*, 56 Am. J. Comp.L. (2008) 173, 191 points out that even the *lex loci damni* rule may lead to the application of a law that is completely unforeseeable to the tortfeasor; Symeonides therefore *de lege feranda* demands the inclusion of a foreseeability defence. However, it is submitted that the risk of applying a law unforeseeable to the tortfeasor is sufficiently balanced by Art. 17, which requires courts to take account of the rules of safety and conduct at the place of the tortfeasor's action (cf.

the place of action and the place of damage would leave a choice between two possibly applicable laws to the court (or even to a party[18]) which would render applicable law unforeseeable and thus create legal uncertainty.[19]

II. Direct and Consequential Damage

1. General

17 Courts must determine the *lex loci damni* "irrespective of the country or countries in which the indirect consequences of that event occur". Thus, only *direct* (or primary) harm is relevant to the provisions of Art. 4(1). Recital 17 expounds on the meaning of "direct" damages: the "country in which the damage occurs should be the country where the injury was sustained or the property was damaged" **(first impact rule)**. Obviously therefore, neither the place of repair of the damaged property nor the place of medical treatment may be considered. *A fortiori*, the location of the bank account where the damage leaves its eventual financial mark (because the hospital's bill must be paid from its funds) must remain unconsidered.[20]

18 In some cases, however, the line between direct and consequential loss may be hard to draw, particularly in cases in which the tort does not cause physical damage but merely economic losses. This difficulty is not new: it also arises under Art. 5(3) Brussles I and was thus the subject of several decisions of the ECJ. These

---

Wandt, in: FS 100 Jahre DVS, 127, 131). Additionally, in exceptional cases, the escape clause of paragraph (3) may be employed.

18 *E.g.* German law leaves it to the aggrieved party to choose whether the law of the place of action or the one of the place of damage shall apply (Art. 40(1) German EGBGB).

19 COM(2003) 427, p. 1.

20 *Mankowski*, in: Magnus/Mankowski (eds.), Brussels I Regulation, Art. 5 para. 234: "No 'money pocket rule' (along the line 'the damage was suffered in my pocket') applies".

decisions on Art. 5(3) Brussels I may and must guide current efforts to distinguish between direct and consequential damages under Art. 4(1) Rome II.[21] Admittedly, differences exist between the provisions of Brussels I and Rome II. Article 5(3) Brussels was an *exceptional* principle that deviated from the rule of *actor sequitor forum rei* laid down in Art. 2(1) Brussels I,[22] and its exceptional nature led to its restrictive interpretation. Since Art. 4(1) Rome II constitutes not an exception but the main principle, it might be questionable whether the restrictive interpretation of Art. 5(3) Brussels II should be extended to Art. 4(1) Rome II.[23] However, the rationale behind Art. 4(1) Rome II itself – that the place of damages must be foreseeable to the tortfeasor[24] – calls for an equivalently restrictive interpretation.[25] What is more, establishing identical standards for the interpretation of Art. 4(1) Rome II and Art. 5(3) Brussels I leads to the desirable result of parallelism of jurisdiction and applicable law (at least if the victim sues at the place of damage). The forum that is granted jurisdiction by Art. 5(3) Brussels I may then apply its hometown set of rules – which it certainly can handle best.

2. Personal Injury and Damage to Property

While the place of damage can easily be determined in most **personal injury cases**, several types of cases pose particular difficulties. 19

The German Bundesgerichtshof (Federal Supreme Court) had to decide whether, under Art. 5(3) Lugano Convention, the place of 20

21 *Dicey, Morris & Collins*, para. S 35-195; *Plender & Wilderspin*, para. 18-016; *Stone*, 4 Ankara L. Rev. (2007) 95, 111; *Kadner Graziano*, 73 RabelsZ (2009) 1, 37.

22 Cf. ECJ, Case C-168/02 – *Kronhofer*, [2004] ECR I-6009 paras. 13 et seq.; ECJ, Case C-364/93 – *Marinari* [1995] ECR I-2719 para. 13.

23 *Plender & Wilderspin*, para. 18-016; *Rushworth/Scott*, LMCLQ 2008, 274, 278.

24 See *supra* para. 16.

25 Similarly *Rushworth/Scott*, LMCLQ 2008, 274, 278.

damage for **negligent misstatement** by a doctor is the country where the doctor advised his patient to take a certain medication or the country in which the patient took the medication. The court held that since the mere misstatement by itself would not have led to a damages claim, the relevant place should be the place where the patient followed the advice and took the medication.[26]

21 The English Court of Appeal[27] faced the following question: if a victim is transported to a hospital in another country after being injured and his condition deteriorates during his stay at the hospital, does this constitute "new" direct damage under Art. 5(3) Brussels I? The court denied the question in regard to Art. 5(3) Brussels I, although under the applicable French law, "aggravation" constituted a "fresh cause of action". The court – rightfully – argued that the term "harmful event" had to be interpreted autonomously and with regard to the purpose of the Art. 5(3).[28] Since Art. 5(3) constituted an exception to the general rule of Art. 2 Brussel I Convention, it had to be interpreted restrictively. Therefore, the court decided not to regard the **deterioration in health** as a "fresh harmful event" but to consider it as "a most unfortunate consequence which flows directly from the original tort". This latter phrase, however, rather argues for the opposite result: if the deterioration indeed flows directly (!) from the original tort, it must not be regarded as a mere consequential damage. In fact, scholars had been arguing for years that *any* deterioration should be regarded as "a further detriment to the protected value [... which is ...] immediately linked with the initial wrongdoing [and] not in any way derived from some intermediate step".[29]

---

26 Bundesgerichtshof (Germany), 27 May 2008, BGHZ 176, 342 et seq.

27 Court of Appeal (England), 1 February 2002 *(Henderson v. Jaouen et. al)* [2002] 1 WLR 2971; cf. *Cheshire, North & Fawcett*, p. 798.

28 To emphasize its reasoning, the Court heavily relied on the jurisprudence of the ECJ, in particular on ECJ, Case C-220/88 – *Dumez France v Hessische Landesbank*, [1990] ECR I-49; ECJ, Case C-364/93 – *Marinari*, [1995] ECR I-2719.

However, even if the court's reasoning is capable of being misunderstood, the result reached by the court is not – and in the Author's opinion, the court's decision should be followed not only under Art. 5(3) Brussels I, but under Art. 4(1) Rome II as well.[30] While the place of injury is foreseeable to the tortfeasor, the place of medical treatment is not. What is more, if a later deterioration in the victim's health condition were considered, the victim would be given the opportunity of manipulation ("law shopping"). Therefore, the term "place of damage" should refer exclusively to the place where and the time at which the conduct of the tortfeasor first affects the victim's physical integrity.[31] 22

Accordingly, if the tortfeasor empoisons the victim in country A but the **poisonous effect** does not occur until the victim has moved to country B, only the place where the poison first comes in contact with the victim's organism may be taken into account. If *e.g.* the victim receives food poisoning from spoiled oysters in the tortfeasor's restaurant[32] at London Heathrow Airport just before his flight back to France, the place of damage must be located in London even though the sickness may not occur before the plane has reached French territory. The sickness must thus be regarded as a deterioration in health (and hence as a consequen- 23

29 *Mankowski*, in: Magnus/Mankowski (eds.), Brussels I Regulation, Art. 5 para. 235.

30 For the propriety of applying decisions on Art. 5(3) Brussels I to Art. 4(1) Rome II, see above para. 18.

31 *Dickinson*, para. 4.38; *Kadner Graziano*, 73 RabelsZ (2009) 1, 37; *Schlosser*, Art. 5 para. 19; *Junker*, in: Münchener Kommentar BGB, Art. 4 para. 30. It is further submitted that the same rule applies even when the victim later dies as a result of poisoning; cf. *von Hein*, 102 ZVglRWiss (2003) 528, 543; *Leible*, in: Rauscher, Europäisches Zivilprozessrecht, Art. 5 para. 86 fn. 324 (in regard to the Brussels I Regulation); – contra *Junker*, in: Münchener Kommentar BGB, Art. 4 para. 30.

32 Note that this might be a case of product liability, in which case Art. 5 rather than Art. 4 applies.

tial damage) that is based on the poisoning, the latter constituting the only direct damage.[33]

24 However, if the victim buys the oysters in a London store but does not consume them before he has reached France, Art. 4(1) calls for the application of French law. Such a case constitutes the typical "Distanzdelikt": the tortfeasor acts in England by selling spoiled oysters to the victim, but the damage does not occur until the victim consumes the oysters. Because the wording of Art. 4(1) explicitely denies any relevance of the place of the tortfeasor's action, no grounds exist for applying English law under Art. 4(1). However, the "escape clause" of Art. 4(3)(2) will lead to the application of as English law since it governs the contractual relationship between the parties (see in detail below § 4).

25 In case of **damage to property**, difficulties may arise when a thief has stolen from the victim in country A and sells the stolen goods in country B. In the Author's opinion, the sale should be considered as a mere consequential damage which is not relevant under Art. 4(1). Therefore, the law of country A will apply to all tort claims against the thief.[34] Obviously, however, when the victim claims damages from the buyer, this claim will be governed by the law of country B.[35]

3. Purely Economic Loss

a) The "First Impact Rule"

26 As outlined above, the location at which tortious conduct leaves its financial mark will not be considered in determining the "place of damages".[36] However, this rule does not apply when the loss is of a purely financial nature, *e.g.* in cases of fraud, en-

---

33 Similarly *Dickinson*, para. 4.57; *Plender & Wilderspin*, paras. 18-021 and 18-069.

34 *Plender & Wilderspin*, para. 18-065.

35 *Plender & Wilderspin*, para. 18-065.

36 See above II. 1.

dangering another's creditworthiness, malicious falsehood, conspiracy, prospectus liability etc.[37]

27 Since in these cases the tort is directed against another's wealth as such, it would stand to reason that the place of damage is determinded by the **situs of this person's wealth**. Unfortunately, a person's wealth rarely "exists", let alone can be located in a single country. Wealth consists of various assets and – primarily in the case of legal persons – also often of reputation and goodwill. Difficulties in determining the situs of a person's wealth may arise as soon as a single asset (*e.g.* a bank account) is located in another country.

28 A possible solution would be to locate the **"center" of the victim's wealth**. In the Author's opinion, however, this solution is not convincing for three reasons.

29 First, relying on the "center of wealth" fails to consider adequately the circumstances of the concrete case.[38] It also ignores Art. 4(1)'s express terms, which grant relevance exclusively to the place where the tort first comes into contact with the victim's legally protected interests. For example, assume that a German national lives and works in Belgium and has a bank account (and therefore the primary portion of his assets) in Luxembourg. If he travels to Cyprus, where he is led to buy a painting that he is fraudulently told is original, it seems rather arbitrary to rely on the "center of his wealth" and apply the Luxembourgian law.

---

37 *Dicey, Morris & Collins*, para. S 35-195.

38 Finding that it provided no "connection at all with the subject-matter of the dispute", the ECJ refused to rely on the location of assets in regard to Art. 5(3) Brussels I (ECJ, Case C-364/93 – *Marinari*, [1995] ECR I-2719, para. 20); similarly ECJ, Case C-18/02 – *DFDS Torline*, [2004] ECR I-1417, para. 44.

30 Second, in many cases the "center" of the victim's assets will correspond to the victim's habitual residence.[39] However, EU legislators rejected attempts to rely on a victim's habitual residence in determining the situs of damages with good reason[40] (just as the ECJ did for Art. 5(3) Brussels I[41]): doing so would unilaterally privilege the victim, while for the tortfeasor the victim's habitual residence might not be foreseeable at all. Contrary to such a clear legislative decision, the habitual residence approach should not be introduced through the back door by equating the "center of assets" with the victim's habitual residence. The argument that the victim actually perceives the damage at its habitual residence must be rejected since same holds true for personal injuries and damage of property where one does not look to the center of the injured party's injuries either. If the victim was hurt during a holiday trip in country A, he nevertheless will suffer pain and financial consequences of the injury after the return at his habitual residence in country B.

31 Third, determining the center of the victim's wealth generates difficulties in practice. The approach obviously fails if the victim is an enterprise that operates globally with assets spread throughout the world. In such a case, determining the center of the company's assets essentially requires a subjective weighing of different kinds of assets – should the factory in country A be the decisive "centering" asset, or should the seat of administration in country B or the primary bank account in country C result in the "center" of assets?

---

39 See *e.g.* Oberster Gerichtshof (Austria), 18 August 2004, ÖJZ 2005, 271. Cf. *de Lima Pinheiro*, Riv. dir. int. priv. proc. 2008, 5, 17 who proposes to set the victim's habitual residence as the place of damages in the first place; – contra *Mankowski*, in: Magnus/Mankowski (eds.), Brussels I Regulation, Art. 5 para. 240.

40 Cf. Common Position 22/2006, OJ 2006 C 289 E/68, 78.

41 ECJ, Case C-168/02 – *Kronhofer*, [2004] ECR I-6009 para. 20.

In the Author's opinion, what has been said regarding physical injuries must also be true for primary economic losses: The place of direct damage is to be located **where the tort first affects a single asset, *i.e.* a discrete component oft the victims' wealth** or – more generally speaking – one of his legally protected interests (**first impact rule**).[42] Therefore, if the tourist in the given example of the Cyprus painting pays the purchase price out of his wallet, better reasons speak for locating the place of damage where his wallet is at that moment, *i.e.* at the place of payment. Admittedly, this approach does not solve the problem but rather shifts it: what qualifies as an actual violation of the victim's legally protected interests and what does not? Comprehensive review reveals that a general rule cannot be established. Instead, different types of torts call for different rules, as is sketched in the following paragraphs:[43] 32

b) Fraud and Misrepresentation

Determining the situs of damages in cases of fraud is particularly difficult. As a rule, the **place where the victim's wealth is diminished** – as opposed to the location at which the victim receives a false statement – constitutes the place of damage. From an economic as well as a legal point of view, the misapprehension caused by the tortfeasor's falsehoods does not amount to damage, but rather to a mere preparation to cause damage.[44] Still, the place where the victim's wealth diminishes will often be difficult to localize under the first impact rule. A multitude of possible scenarios makes further differentiation necessary. 33

Scenario 1: the victim is **fraudulently induced to effect a payment** when he is under no obligation to do so. In such a case, the first financial impact (*i.e.* the damage) should be located at the 34

42 *Junker*, in: Münchener Kommentar BGB, Art. 4 para. 21; *Wurmnest*, in: jurisPK BGB, Art. 4 para. 9.

43 For examples regarding torts governed by Arts. 5 et seq., see the commentary on the relevant provision.

44 *von Hein*, Günstigkeitsprinzip im Internationalen Deliktsrecht, p. 356.

place of performance. As a rule, the place of performance is also the place of the victim's bank account or – if he pays cash – the place of actual payment.[45] If, however, the tortfeasor induces the victim to effect payment in a certain country (*e.g.* from a foreign bank account) in order to secure the application of that country's law, the inducement, and not merely the victim's payment, constitutes a detrimental part of the fraud.[46] Therefore, the damages must be located at the place where the victim would have conducted the payment if not for the fraud. It seems appropriate to presume that, in most cases, the defrauded person would have effected payment at his habitual residence.

35 Scenario 2: The victim is **induced to offer a non-monetary performance** when he is under no obligation to do so. Again, the place of performance should constitute the place of damages under the first impact rule. If the non-monetary performance consists of the provision of services, the place where the victim provides services is the situs of damages. In cases involving the delivery of goods, the place of performance is more difficult to locate. Three places deserve consideration: the place where the goods had been stored, the place where the victim loses possession over the goods, or the place where the tortfeasor gains possession. Strictly speaking, the damage does not occur until the victim loses control over the goods: even if the goods are in the custody of a carrier, the victim cannot suffer actual loss if the carrier is bound by the victim's instructions. Such a control-based solution, however, disregards that it was fraud that led the victim to ship the goods in the first place. As a result, the carriage itself constitutes a part of the damage. Thus, in the Author's opinion, the place where the carriage originates, *i.e.* **the place of storage**, must be regarded as the place of damage.[47] Such a solution corre-

45 *Dickinson*, para. 4.67.

46 *Mankowski*, in: Magnus/Mankowski (eds.), Brussels I Regulation, Art. 5 para. 239.

47 *Dickinson*, para. 4.67.

sponds to locating damages in the country of a victim's bank account in cases of monetary performance.[48]

Scenario 3: The victim is **induced to conclude a detrimental contract.** Here, two places of damage come into consideration. First, one could localize the damage at the place where the contract is concluded, since being bound by the contract may itself qualify as initial damage for the victim. Second, the location at which the victim performs his detrimental contractual obligations, *i.e.* the place that is relevant under scenario 1 or 2, may constitute the place for damage. Both alternatives contain certain difficulties. 36

Locating damages at the place of performance creates, to a certain extent, conflict with the "first impact rule" since the initial – and thus direct – damage already occurs with the conclusion of the contract: contract *formation* is the point in time when the fraud first comes into contact with the protected interests of the victim. Later performance therefore only constitutes a consolidation of the loss – in other words, a consequential damage comparable to the example of poison, which causes damage when it is swallowed instead of when the symptoms of sickness occur.[49] Nevertheless, it may be appropriate to locate damages at the place of performance, since performance irrevocably realises the damages that contract formation caused: until the victim performs his obligations, a misrepresentation defense allows him to void his obligations under the contract (presuming that the defrauder is his contractual partner), whereas performance transfers value to the defrauder.[50] 37

---

48 On the assumption that the victim does not lose control over the goods as long the carrier is bound by the victim's instructions, another solution, which will generally result in the victim's habitual residence as the place of damages, seems dogmatically feasible: in international sales, control over the goods *de facto* and *de iure* depends on the possession of lading documents. The victim thus loses control when and where he dispatches these documents.

49 See *supra* para. 23.

50 *Dickinson*, para. 4.67.

38 Locating damages at the place of contracting entails the risk of manipulation by the tortfeasor, who can induce the victim to contract in a certain country. This problem should be solved as already proposed in Scenario 1: acts of the tortfeasor that induce the victim to influence the law applicable, themselves constitute a detrimental part of the fraud.[51] Therefore, the damage occurs in the country in which the contract would have been formed but for the fraud. As a rule, it may be assumed that this "but-for country" is where the victim maintains his habitual residence.

39 Locating damages at the place of contracting can also lead to arbitrary results. For example, if two people conclude their contract in the business lounge of an international airport before flying back to their habitual residences, the place of contract formation has no connection to the contract or its parties. Such results, however, lie within the risks inherent in the *lex loci damni* rule and thus must be accepted. In individual cases, results may be adjusted under the escape clause of Art. 4(3).

40 Locating damages at the place of contracting also provides no guidance in cases where the parties do not physically meet to conclude the contract, but rather communicate via telephone or email. In these cases, the location at which the victim becomes bound by its manifestations should constitute the place of damages.[52] In determining the place where obligations arise, it matters whether the victim communicated the offer or the acceptance that led to the contract. If the victim accepted an offer, the contract is concluded (and the victim therefore bound by it) at the moment the acceptance becomes effective. In most legal systems, this occurs when notice of acceptance reaches the offeror (cf. Art. 18(2) CISG, Art. 2.1.4 PICC, Art. II. – 4:202 DCFR). The place of damage must therefore be located at the place where the offeror receives the victim's acceptance. If, on

---

51 *Mankowski*, in: Magnus/Mankowski (eds.), Brussels I Regulation, Art. 5 para. 239.

52 Similarly *Plender & Wilderspin*, para. 18-077.

the contrary, the victim was the offeror, no contract forms until the victim receives the other party's acceptance. Thus, the place of damage is presumptively the place where the victim receives the acceptance. However, when the law governing the formation of contract does not allow the offeror to withdraw or revoke its offer,[53] the offeror is *de facto* already bound by its offer. Therefore, the place where this offer becomes effective must be considered the place of damage.

At least in cases in which it was the contractual partner who fraudulently induced contract formation, it may serve as a (third) alternative to locate damages in the country whose law governs the contract. As a rule, the fraudulent behavior can be qualified as *culpa in contrahendo* – thus, locating damages in the country whose law governs the contract would result in parallel treatment of the tort and *culpa in contrahendo* aspects of the case (for applicable law to *culpa in contrahendo*, see Art. 12). However, an application of the law governing the contract cannot be based on the rule of *lex loci damni*; again the escape clause of Art. 4(3) provides a feasible solution. 41

Scenario 4 (**fraud in court proceedings**): a court renders judgment in favor of the tortfeasor because the tortfeasor submits fraudulent evidence, or the tortfeasor convinces the victim to refrain from disputing the tortfeasor's evidence.[54] In this scenario, the judgment itself qualifies as direct damage, thus rendering the forum of proceedings the place of damages under Art. 4(1). The place of enforcement or payment by the victim can only be considered the place of indirect or consequential damages. 42

53 According to Art. 16 CISG, apart from some exceptions an offer may be recoked until it is effectively accepted. By contrast, under § 145 German BGB, the offeror is bound by its offer once it has become effective (by reaching the offeree).

54 For example Bundesgerichtshof (Germany), 10 July 1986, IPRax 1987, 236.

c) Prospectus Liability

43 Localizing the place of damage for prospectus liability[55] involves problems similar to those that arose in fraudulent contract formation (above scenario 3, paras. 36 et seq.): the direct damage (*i.e.* the first impact) consists in the purchase of securities described in the prospectus, rather than in the loss of value of those securities. Therefore, **the place of purchase** (*i.e.* the place of contracting), rather than the place where the victim's funds are deposited, constitutes the place of damage.[56]

44 Generally, the place of contracting should be located at the market – *i.e.* the stock (or other) exchange – where the victim bought the fraudulent securities, even though this might not be the same place where the victim becomes bound by the contract. Balancing the interests of the parties and the purposes behind requiring a prospectus argue in favour of such a rule. First, the victim deliberately chooses the market on which it purchases securities, and the location of the market is foreseeable to the issuer. The same may not obtain in any other contractual situation, since issuers are often *not* the contractual partners of securities purchasers.[57] Second, the obligation to publish a prospectus arises

55 Under predominant opinion, the liability of an issuer of securities for information contained in its prospectuses qualifies as a tort claim rather than *culpa in contrahendo* (*von Hein*, FS Hopt, 371, 374 et seq. and 378; *Mankowski*, in: Reithmann/Martiny, Internationales Vertragsrecht (2010), para. 2530; *Wurmnest*, in: jurisPK BGB, Art. 1 para. 46 – contra *Groß*, Kapitalmarktrecht, §§ 44, 45 BörsG para. 9). Since the Regulation does not provide an special rule governing liability for information contained in prospectuses, these cases fall within the scope of Art. 4.

56 *Mankowski*, in: Reithmann/Martiny, Internationales Vertragsrecht (2010), para. 2530; *Weber*, WM 2008, 1581, 1586, the same result reaches Freitag, in: Reithmann/Martiny, Internationales Vertragsrecht, para. 1276.

57 If they were, the place of damages remains of minor importance since an accessory connection to the contract between purchaser and issuer will be opportune under the escape clause of paragraph (3)(2).

from concerns of investor protection as well as antitrust policies. For the latter, Art. 6(3)(a) requires application of the law of the affected market, and Recital 21 provides that this rule is not an exception from, but a concretisation of, the general rule of Art. 4(1). Against this background, the location of a market or stock exchange may constitute a special place of damage if the violated law aims at the protection of competition and/or the general public.[58]

d) Embezzlement

In cases of embezzlement, the location of the assets that are the object of embezzlement constitutes the place of damage. If the embezzlement results in nothing more than withdrawing a sum of money in a local bank account, the location of this bank account constitutes the place of damages. For example, assume that an English aid organization transfers a certain amount of money to the bank account of its local branch in India. The local partner does not forward the money to the designated projects but instead sees himself as worthy of development aid. In this case, the place of damage must be India. Again, however, if the local partner intended to use the money for personal purposes at the time he requested a funds transfer, the transfer itself may qualify as part of the tort (or as an independent fraud), in which case England is the place of damage.[59] **45**

It should be noted, however, that in embezzlement cases, the place of damages will rarely be relevant because the underlying contractual relationship will result in an application of the **escape clause of** subsection (3).[60] **46**

---

58 See in detail *Weber*, WM 2008, 1581, 1586.

59 Cf. Bundesgerichtshof (Germany), 6 November 2007, RIW 2008, 399 in regard to Art. 5(3) Lugano Convention.

60 See *infra* paras. 79 et seq.

e) Procuring Breach of Contract

47 If the tort consists of inducing the victim's contractual partners to breach their contractual obligations towards the victim,[61] the damage occurs **where the breached obligation should have been performed** (in cases of non-performance) or where the obligation was defectively performed (in cases of defective performance).[62] Since only the breach of contract by the other party – not the contract itself – constitutes the damage, the place of contract formation is irrelevant in determining the location of damages. The place where the tortfeasor contacts the victim's contractual partner, as the place of tortious conduct rather than the place of damages, must also not be taken into account.

48 Since, however, multiple potential locations for performance often come into question, relying on the place of performance to determine the place of damages creates a quantum of legal uncertainty. In cases of defective performance, the actual and the agreed place of action might differ. It is submitted that the actual place of performance should prevail so long as the deviation from the agreed place of performance is not due to the tort. Second, if the prevented performance consists in the delivery of goods, the place of performance can be localized at several different places: at the legally defined place of delivery (*e.g.* according to Art. 31 CISG), at the place of passing of risk (*e.g.* according to Art. 66 et seq. CISG), at the place of actual handover, or even at the place where the victim was to use the goods. From the victim's perspective, the damage most clearly occurs at the latter place. Relying on the place of use, however, would be in violation with the principle of first impact: the frustrated *use* of the goods constitutes only a consequential rather than a direct damage. Thus, setting the **legally defined place of delivery** as the place of damage offers the only fair and equitable solution and provides both parties with the necessary foreseeability and legal certainty.

---

[61] Most (but not all) inducements to breach a contract will be subject to Art. 6 rather than Art. 4.

[62] *Plender & Wilderspin*, para. 18-091.

f) Wrongful Proceedings and Fraudulent Forum Shopping

If the tort consists in an **abusive court proceeding** against the victim, the damage will regularly not be physical but exclusively economic in nature. In these cases, the proceeding itself must be regarded as the direct damage. Costs that are incurred due to the proceeding (attorneys' fees, court costs, etc.) need not be taken into account as they represent consequential damages only – analogized to physical harm, the court procedure is the injury while attorneys' fees correspond to medical costs. Therefore, the place of damages must be localized at the forum where the law suit is pending.[63] 49

If the place of forum is the result of **fraudulent forum shopping** by the tortfeasor, a different rule should apply. In such cases, the forum shopping must be regarded as being part of the tort. Thus, in determining the place of damages, jurisdictional questions are relevant: as a rule, a party can only be sued in front of his hometown courts *(actor sequitor forum rei)*. Therefore, the place of damages may be located in the country of defendant's residence. 50

g) Data Theft

In cases of data theft[64] a differentiation seems appropriate between claims of the persons whose data were stolen and claims of the person from whom the data were stolen. 51

As regards **claims of the person from whom the data were stolen**, the place of damages should be localized at the place where the 52

---

63 In regard to Art. 5(3) Brussles I, this result is disfavoured since it often grants jurisdiction to the courts of the defendant's residence. The victim of a wrongful proceeding is usually sued at its own habitual residence (Art. 2(1) Brussels I). If one designates this forum as the place of damage, the victim may file proceedings in his home forum against the tortfeasor under Art. 5(3). Such a result, however, would undermine the principle of *actor sequitor forum rei*.

64 For the question whether the tort of data theft falls within the Regulation's scope of application see Art. 1 para. 56.

data were stored, *i.e.* usually the place of the server. Locating damages at the place of stolen data protects the interests of the victim and is foreseeable to the tortfeasor.

53 As regards **claims of the person whose data were stolen**, a parallel may be drawn to violations of rights relating to personality: according to the ECJ's *Shevill* decision[65], the habitual residence of the victim should not constitute the place of damages, rather the place where the data were stored should be dispositive. If the data are later sold by the thief, each sale constitutes an independent fresh tort. Again, a parallel to the *Shevill* should be maintained: the place of damages should be located at the residence of each buyer of the data. If the person whose data were stolen is a business person (or a company), and either the thief or the buyer is a competitor, Art. 6 or 8 may displace Art. 4.

III. Damage in Different Countries

54 Relying on the place of damage rather than the place of action leads to further difficulties if one tort results in damage in several different countries (so-called "*Streudelikt*," or "scattered tort").[66] Such cases can be handled in two different ways. Option 1: each distinct incident of damage is subject to the law of the place where the damage occurred. If the damage scatters, the applicable law scatters as well (the so-called **mosaic principle**). Option 2: the totality of damage is subject to the law of one country only. This law can be determined by either localizing the "center of gravity" of the harm (**centralization principle**) or leaving the applicable law to the choice of the victim (**ubiquity principle**).

---

65 ECJ, case 68/93-Shevill, [1995] ECR I-415.

66 "Scattered torts" most likely occur when the tort affects a person's privacy or rights relating to personality. As these torts, however, are excluded from the Regulation's scope by Art. 1(2)(g), the relevance of scattered torts under the Regulation is diminished; *Hohloch*, 9 YbPIL (2007) 1, 10 et seq.

The Commission, in its first proposal for a Rome II Regulation, suggested adopting the **mosaic principle**.[67] Indeed, this principle best serves the purpose of maintaining the "closest connection" between tort and applicable law, which is one of the primary aims of Private International Law. However, scattering applicable law across multiple countries complicates the course of justice and thereby reduces legal certainty. In addition, it might be difficult to determine which procentual part of the overall damage is to be allocated to any particular country.[68] The mosaic principle seems especially unsuited to negatory claims. If a certain behaviour constitutes a tort in country A but does not in country B, the court, instead of simply enjoining the tortfeasor's behaviour, would be restricted to merely enjoining the defendant from causing damages in country A.[69] 55

At first glance, the **centralization principle** offers the charm of being plain and simple. However, legal uncertainty already occurs from the lack of criteria for determining the "center of gravity" of damages. What is more, if damages are spread equally among different countries, a "center" of the damages will hardly be determinable. 56

The **ubiquity principle** unduly privileges the victim by establishing a "personal most favorable law" approach. If, for example, a fraction of damages occurred in a country whose law permits substantial punitive damages, the victim would have the right to apply this law to all damages regardless of where they occurred throughout the world. 57

---

67 COM(2003) 427 final, p. 11; following that view: *Garcimartín Alférez*, EuLF 2007 I 77, 83; *Hohloch*, 9 YbPIL (2007) 1, 10; *de Lima Pinheiro*, Riv. dir. int. priv. proc. 2008, 5, 18; *Ofner*, ZfRV 2008, 13, 16; *Wurmnest*, in: jurisPK BGB, Art. 4 para. 10.

68 *Huber/Bach*, IPRax 2005, 73, 79.

69 Cf. in more detail *Dickinson*, paras. 4.70 et seq.

58 When deciding which of the alternatives should be followed, the ECJ's **Shevill-decision**[70] on Art. 5(3) Brussles I must be considered. There, the ECJ allowed the plaintiff either to concentrate its damages claims before the court at the place of action or to split its claims before different courts at the places of damages. Under the latter option, each domestic court is restricted to awarding only the amount of damage that occurred in its own country.[71] Thus, under the Brussels I regime, the ECJ follows the mosaic principle.

59 However, applying the mosaic principle in regard to the applicable law as well would weaken the victim's possibility to consolidate multiple proceedings: since the place of tortious conduct is *de lege lata* irrelevant under Rome II, the victim would face the dilemma of either concentrating his claims before a court that must apply the laws of many different countries or fracturing his claim to allow many courts to decide on the basis of their hometown law.[72]

60 By centralizing the case, the problems entailed by the mosaic principle are completely ameliorated when the center of damages lies in the country of tortious conduct – in such cases can the court adjudicate claims for the entire damage under its hometown law. In all other scenarios, the centralization principle offers at least considerable improvement over the mosaic principle – the court must apply only one body of foreign law.[73] The same is true for the ubiquity principle.

61 Instead of merely deciding between the mosaic and the centralization principle, a **solution that combines each principle's advantages** while avoiding its deficits is preferable. If a "centralized impact" of damages can easily be determined, following the cen-

70 ECJ, Case C-68/93 – *Shevill*, [1995] ECR I-415.

71 ECJ, Case C-68/93 – *Shevill*, [1995] ECR I-415, para. 30.

72 *Huber/Bach*, IPRax 2005, 73, 79.

73 *Huber/Bach*, IPRax 2005, 73, 79.

tralization principle seems worthwile.[74] If damages are spread equally across different countries or more than one centre of damages exists, the mosaic principle is favourable.

IV. A Nonexistent or Indeterminable *Lex Loci Damni*

Under certain circumstances, a *lex loci damni* may not exist. The clearest cases of a nonexistent *lex loci damni* involve damage that occurs in international waters or airspace.[75] In such cases, paragraph (1) no longer applies and courts must **resort to paragraphs (2) and (3)**. Although the plain language of Art. 4(3) requires that an applicable law can be determined under paragraphs (1) or (2), it is submitted that the provision should be applied analogously when the determination under paragraphs (1) and (2) fails. 62

The same reasoning should govern cases where the place of damage cannot be determined, *e.g.* because goods are packaged into a container in country A and no damage is discovered until the goods are unpackaged in country B *(res in transitu)*.[76] In such a case, neither country A nor country B may be considered the place of damage. Again, in such cases the applicable law must be determined under paragraphs (2) and (3). 63

---

74 Applying the escape clause of Art. 4(3) produces comparable results; for this reason, its application is favoured by *Plender & Wilderspin*, para. 18-027; *Junker*, in: Münchener Kommentar BGB, Art. 4 para. 32; *Sonnentag*, 105 ZVglRWiss (2006) 256, 269; *Leible/Engel*, EuZW 2004, 7, 10 et seq.

75 See in detail *infra* para. 101.

76 See in detail *infra* paras. 103 et seq.

C. Art. 4(2): Common Habitual Residence *Lex Domicilii Communis*

I. General

64 If the tortfeasor and the victim have their habitual residences in the same country, subsection (2) designates this country's law as applicable. According to the Commission's Explanatory Memorandum, the *lex domicilii communis* rule "reflects the legitimate expectations of the two parties".[77] If two residents of the same country travel together, this assumption is worthwile. If they do not, however, but instead "happen to collide with one another far away from home",[78] neither of the parties will legitimately expect its hometown law to apply.[79] In fact, in the case of a traffic accident, it may be within the interests of both[80] parties to apply the *lex loci damni* because (at least in cases involving rented vehicles) their automobile insurance may be calculated on the basis of this law.[81] Such a scenario, in which a tortfeasor's automobile insurance is set on the basis of the *lex loci damni* rather than its *lex domicilii*, may and should be balanced by employing the escape clause of paragraph (3).[82]

---

77 COM(2003) 427, p. 12.

78 *Weintraub*, Liber Amicorum Peter Hay, 451, 456.

79 *Weintraub*, Liber Amicorum Peter Hay, 451, 456; *Garcimartín Alférez*, EuLF 2007 I 77, 83; *Dickinson*, paras. 4.81 et seq.; cf. *Cheshire, North & Fawcett*, p. 798; *Leible/Lehmann*, RIW 2007, 721, 725; *Pitel*, in: Ahern/Binchy (eds.), The Rome II Regulation on the Law Applicable to Non-Contractual Obligations: A New International Litigation Regime (2009) pp. 245 et seq. (on Art. 10(2) Rome II).

80 As the parties' interests must be determined abstractely, *i.e.* independently from the concrete situation, both parties are potential victims and potential causers of an accident.

81 G. *Wagner*, IPRax 2006, 372, 378; *Sonnentag*, 105 ZVglRWiss (2006) 256, 272 and 293; *Staudinger*, EuLF 2005 I 61.

82 *Staudinger*, EuLF 2005 I 61; *Kadner Graziano*, 73 RabelsZ (2009) 1, 19; *Junker*, JZ 2008, 169, 174; *Sonnentag*, 105 ZVglRWiss (2006) 256, 293; –

Applying the *lex domicilii communis* offers the advantage of parallelism between jurisdiction and applicable law: most likely, the victim will sue the tortfeasor in the courts of the tortfeasor's country of residence (Art. 2 Brussels I) rather than resorting to the special jurisdiction of the place of the harmful event (Art. 5(3) Brussles I). Under paragraph (2), the tortfeasor's hometown court is then permitted to apply its *lex fori* to the merits of the case, thus eliminating the risk of a faulty application of foreign law.[83] **65**

II. Prerequisites

1. ... The Parties Both ...

Article 4(2) requires that "the person claimed to be liable and the person sustaining damages *both* have their habitual residence in the same country".[84] It therefore assumes that there is only one tortfeasor and only one victim.[85] In exceptional cases, and especially in the context of traffic accidents, there may exist a **multitude of tortfeasors** and/or victims. Paragraph (2) remains silent regarding its applicability in such a multi-person constellation.[86] **66**

---

contra: *Plender & Wilderspin*, para. 18-099; at least sceptical: *Junker*, in: Münchener Kommentar BGB, Art. 4 para. 57; *Wurmnest*, in: jurisPK BGB, Art. 4 para. 28.

83 *Chong*, 57 ICLQ (2008) 863, 882; *Junker*, in: Münchener Kommentar BGB, Art. 4 para. 37; *Leible/Engel*, EuZW 2004, 7, 11. However, this result could have been reached by allowing the court to apply the *lex domicilii communis* under the escape clause of paragraph (3) rather then establishing a strict rule.

84 Emphasis added.

85 *Plender & Wilderspin*, para. 18-098.

86 Art. 4(a) of the 1971 Hague Convention on the Law Applicable to Traffic Accidents provides "Where there are two or more victims the applicable law is determined separately for each of them" It is submitted that this provision may not serve as a guidance to courts: on the one hand, it could be argued that Art. 4a Hague Convention represents a General Principle that applies even without express incorporation into Rome II;

67 Although case law has yet to address this ambiguity, it has generated debate in legal literature. To understand the discussion, it is necessary to distinguish between two scenarios. Scenario 1: one tortfeasor, through a single act, causes damage to two or more victims. If only one of the victims shares a common habitual residence with the tortfeasor, two different laws potentially apply to the tortfeasor's liability – with the possible result that one victim has a damages claim while the other victim does not. Scenario 2: two or more tortfeasors cause damage two one victim. If only one tortfeasor shares a common residence with the victim, two different laws again apply to the victim's claims, potentially allowing the victim to hold only one tortfeasor liable. Within this scenario, it can be further distinguished between cases in which only the *lex loci damni* leads to liability (Scenario 2a) and cases in which only the *lex domicilii communis* entails liability (Scenario 2b).

68 In regard to Scenario 1, some have argued that it is "hard to accept" that, as a result of applying paragraph (2), only one of the victims receives compensation.[87] Still, refusing to apply paragraph (2) in scenario 1 also entails difficulties: if a claim for damages existed only under the *lex domicilii communis*, victim A (a resident of the same country as the tortfeasor) would find himself without a claim merely because the tort also injured victim B (a non-resident of the tortfeasor's country).

69 In Scenario 2, the same is true: strictly applying paragraph (2) may lead to different treatment of the two tortfeasors, leading to results that can be hard to accept.[88] However, not applying (2) again entails its own problems: in Scenario 2a, the tortfeasor

---

on the other hand, not including such a rule could be seen as a conscious decision of the legislature.

[87] *Stone*, 4 Ankara L. Rev. (2007) 95, 110, in regard to the U.S.-American case *Tooker v. Lopez*, 249 N.E.2d 394 (N.Y. 1969).

[88] *E.g.* in cases where the driver is not liable under the law of country A but is under the law of country B.

who shares the victim's habitual residence would be better off if he had caused the damage alone, since the *lex domicilii communis* would then exonerate him from liability (the opposite being true for Scenario 2b). Again, neither solution can fully convince.

Nevertheless, in the Author's opinion, it is preferable that **paragraph (2) *not* apply in multi-party-constellations**; it should instead be restricted to cases involving one tortfeasor and one victim.[89] The clearest disadvantage of applying paragraph (2) is evident when one considers the issue of contribution between tortfeasors. Generally, the tortfeasor that is sued by the victim may claim contribution from the other tortfeasor(s). Under Art. 20, a tortfeasor's contribution claim is governed "by the law applicable to the debtor's non-contractual obligation towards the creditor." In Scenario 2a, such a contribution claim will override the application of paragraph (2): the tortfeasor who is held liable under the *lex loci damni* may, under this law, claim contribution from the other tortfeasor – despite the fact that that tortfeasor is not directly liable to the victim under the *lex domicilii communis*. Thus, contribution claims in the end would generate the same results as joint liability to the victim.[90] 70

Furthermore, if paragraph (2) is applied in Scenario 2b, contribution claims themselves lead to results that are "hard to accept": if the tortfeasor who is liable under *the lex domicilii communis* can claim contribution from the other tortfeasor, the latter is thus 71

---

89 Cf. *Huber/Bach*, IPRax 2005, 73, *Hay*, EuLF 2007 I 137, 142; *de Lima Pinheiro*, Riv. dir. int. priv. proc. 2008, 5, 18; cf. *Plender & Wilderspin*, para. 18-098 and G. *Wagner*, IPRax 2006, 372, 378 who both reach this result by applying the escape clause of (3) in cases of multi-party torts; – contra: *Dornis*, JPIL 2008, 237, 241 seq.; *Staudinger*, EuLF 2005 I 61, 62 et seq.; *Kadner Graziano*, 73 RabelsZ (2009) 1, 19; *Hartley*, 57 ICLQ 899, 900; *Wurmnest*, in: jurisPK BGB, Art. 4 para. 29; *Dickinson*, para. 4.83 (however regretting this result against the background of diffulties at the stage of recourse).

90 Again, the tortfeasor would be better off had he caused the damage alone.

subjected to a law to which he has no relation and whose applicability he could not have foreseen. If, *e.g.*, a tortfeasor injured a foreign victim within his (the tortfeasor's) country of habitual residence, and the tortfeasor would not have been liable under the *lex loci damni*, he may yet owe contribution to a joint tortfeasor who coincidentally shared the victim's habitual residence. The first tortfeasor, who never left his country of residence, is judged under foreign law simply because the other tortfeasor and the victim – by pure coincidence – reside in the same country.

72 Barring the application of paragraph (2) to multi-party injuries does not lead to untenable results. In the previous example, if the *lex domicilii communis* frees the tortfeasor from liability, the tortfeasor who shares a common residence with the victim is merely barred from profiting from paragraph (2). However, a tortfeasor who causes injury in a country in which he does not reside must be prepared to be liable according to that country's law, *i.e.* the application of foreign law is foreseeable.[91] In the opposite case – the *lex loci domicilii* holds the tortfeasor liable while the *lex loci damni* does not – the victim is the one who can no longer profit from applying his hometown law to an accident that occurred on foreign territory. Still, the same is true as for tortfeasors: those who venture beyond the protecting boarders of their home country bear the risk that any damage they suffer will be governed by foreign law. In neither case should the provisons of paragraph (2) create an entitlement that allows victim or tortfeasor to invoke, and profit from, their hometown law.

2. … Have Their Habitual Residence …

73 Article 23(1) Rome II defines the "habitual resindence" of a legal person as "the place of central administration" or the location of the branch in whose course of operation the damage occurred.

---

91 *Kadner Graziano*, 73 RabelsZ (2009) 1, 36.

The habitual residence of a natural person doing business is "his or her **principal place of business**."

Article 23 does not define the habitual residence of a natural person who is acting privately, presumably because in most cases that person's habitual residence is self-evident. However, difficulties arise if a natural person has more than one residence. Under the reasoning behind Art. 23, that person's "principal" residence should constitute their habitual residence.[92] Still, Art. 23(1) allows the "**branch** in whose course of operation the damage occurred" to constitute a legal person's "habitual residence", and in light of this rule it appears appropriate to allow a natural person's non-principal residence to constitute his "habitual residence" if he caused damage while using that residence. **74**

3. … In the Same Country …

Under paragraph (2), the *lex domicilii communis* applies only when both tortfeasor and victim have their habitual residence in the same country. Legal literature argues further that paragraph (2) must also applied by way of analogy to cases in which the parties reside in different countries, but both parties' hometown laws reach the same result, and this result differs from the results under the *lex loci damni*.[93] The identical consequences of the different hometown laws, so the argument goes, justify the analogous application of paragraph (2). **75**

However, four arguments speak against such an anology. First, employing the institute of analogy is not necessary – and thus not permissible – because an application of the identical rules of both hometown laws may be achieved through the escape **76**

---

92 Cf. Art. 23 para. 11.

93 *De Lima Pinheiro*, Riv. dir. int. priv. proc. 2008, 5, 18; tending to this view: *Garcimartín Alférez*, EuLF 2007 I-77, 83; *de lege ferenda: Symeonides*, 56 Am. J. Comp. L. (2008), 173, 196 = *Symeonides*, in: FS Jayme, 935, 946; cf. *Weintraub*, 43 Texas Intl. L. J. (2008) 401, 408.

clause of paragraph (3).[94] Second, a proposal to adopt a rule that embodied this analogy was rejected during legislative drafting – thus, the legislature could not have intended to allow the analogy.[95] Third, in light of the fact that the reasoning behind paragraph (2) is questionable in many cases,[96] a flexible solution (such as the escape clause) seems more appropriate than simply expanding the scope of a rule.[97] Fourth, an analogous application of paragraph (2) bears difficulties in practice: if a court must determine whether a) the hometown laws of the parties reach the same result and whether b) this result differs from that of the *lex loci damni*, the court must apply three different laws (the *lex domicilii* of the victim, the *lex domicilii* of the tortfeasor and the *lex loci damni*).[98]

77 The same arguments counsel against another suggestion in legal literature: applying paragraph (2) by analogy when both parties reside in different member states and the damage occurred in a third state outside the EU.[99] It is submitted, however, that – once more – the inflexible rule of paragraph (2) should rather be restricted than expanded; appropriate results in a particular case are better reached via the escape clause in paragraph (3).

---

94 This solution is favoured by *Stone*, 4 Ankara L. Rev. (2007) 95, 109; *Stone*, EuLF 2004, 213, 220.

95 *Von Hein*, ZEuP 2009, 6, 17; *Kozyris*, 56 Am.J.Comp.L. (2008) 471, 481; *Junker*, in: Münchener Kommentar BGB, Art. 4 para. 43.

96 See *supra* para. 64.

97 It must be admitted that the proposed paragraph (3)-based solution runs into difficulty when a "closer connection" to a *single* country does not exist. For example, in the traffic example above, there are equally strong connections to the two countries in which the parties reside.

98 Employing the flexible escape clause rather than a strict (analogous) rule at least avoids *forcing* the courts into this difficult task – the court is free to apply the identical hometown laws but it is not obliged to do so.

99 *Garcimartín Alférez*, EuLF 2007 I 77, 83.

4. … At the Time the Damage Occurs …

78 Paragraph (2) applies only when the parties have a common residence at the time at which the damage occurs. It therefore does not apply if the parties first establish such a common residence in the course of proceedings. Instead, the law called for by paragraph (1) is unalterable.[100] If the parties wish the court to apply their newly established hometown law, they may agree on its application as permitted by Art. 14.

D. Art. 4(3): Escape Clause/Manifestly Closer Connection

I. General

79 Art. 4(3) provides for an "escape clause" from Article 4(1) and (2) where it is clear from all the circumstances of the case that the tort/delict is "manifestly more closely connected with another country" (Recital 18). The provision's purpose is to allow a certain degree of flexibility to counterbalance the disadvantages that can arise within the rule-based system provided for in (1) and (2): the court adjudicating the tort may "treat individual cases in an appropriate manner" (Recital 14).

80 To prevent the national courts from (mis-)using the escape clause to apply their *lex fori*, the legislature refused to establish paragraph (3) as a general rule, instead structuring it as an exception.[101] As a result, the escape clause **must be applied restrictively**.[102]

---

100 *Thorn*, in: Palandt, Art. 4 para. 5.

101 COM(2003) 427, p. 12.

102 *Dicey, Morris & Collins*, para. S 35-197 ("a high threshold of connection must be passed"); *Dickinson*, para. 4.85; *Garcimartín Alférez*, EuLF 2007 I 77, 84; *Hohloch*, 9 YbPIL (2007) 1, 12; *Cheshire, North & Fawcett*, p. 799; *Spickhoff*, in: Bamberger/Roth, Anh. zu Art. 42 EGBGB para. 37; cf. *Fentiman*, 82 Tul.L.Rev. (208) 2021, 2048.

81 Besides this rough guidance for application, courts have hardly been provided with a concrete scope of application for paragraph (3). As persuasive authority, §§ 6 and 145 of the ALI Restatement, Second, Conflicts of Law (1971) may aid courts in orienting themselves.[103] In literature, paragraph (3) has been criticised for its "extraordinary vagueness".[104] It is clearly subject to the risk of being interpreted differently by the national courts of member states. Therefore, in the Author's opinion, the courts of member states are obliged to refer the question to the ECJ for preliminary ruling under Art. 267 TFEU[105] so that the ECJ may forge uniform interpretations.[106]

82 According to its wording, the escape clause can be applied solely to apply a law "other than that indicated in paragraphs 1 or 2". This leads to problems if courts wish to use paragraph (3) to overcome the result of subection (2) in favour of subsection (1) (*e.g.* in cases of **multi-party torts**[107]). Strictly speaking, the escape clause does not encompass an application of the *lex loci damni*. In the Author's opinion, however, it must be concluded from the policy behind the rule in paragraph (3) (applying the law most closely connected to the case) that the rule must apply at least analogously when courts wish to resort to the *lex loci damni*.[108]

---

103 Cf. *Stone*, 4 Ankara L. Rev. (2007) 95, 114.

104 *Stone*, 4 Ankara L. Rev. (2007) 95, 113; similar: *Fentiman*, 82 Tul.L.Rev. (2008) 2021, 2039 ("Close connection is at best too ambiguous and at worst too blunt a tool"); *Weintraub*, 43 Texas Intl. L. J. (2008) 401, 405 ("There is no magic ruler to measure this distance").

105 Former Art. 234 EC.

106 Cf. *Weintraub*, 43 Texas Intl. L. J. (2008) 401, 405. A forecast on a potential decision is attempted by *Fentiman*, 82 Tul.L.Rev. (2008) 2021, 2048.

107 See *supra* para. 70.

108 *Dickinson*, para. 4.89; *Dicey, Morris & Collins*, para. S 35-197; *Cheshire, North & Fawcett*, p. 804; *Stone*, 4 Ankara L. Rev. (2007) 95, 104, *von*

As was shown in regard to paragraph (2), where there are two or more tortfeasors or victims, the escape clause may only be applied if the same law can be applied to all parties.[109] Otherwise, the problems listed above – *e.g.* a lack of remedy or lack of contribution – may arise.[110] **83**

II. Preexisting Relationship

1. General

Under paragraph (3)'s second sentence, a manifestly closer connection "might [*not*: must] be based in particular [*not*: exclusively] on a preexisting relationship between the parties"[111]. The provision names "a contract" as an example of such a relationship. It is submitted that other forms of legal relationship and – subject to some debate – even a mere factual relationship may suffice as a "preexisting relationship" (see in detail *infra* para. 90). **84**

For such an accessory connection to exist, the tort/delict must be closely connected with the preexisting relationship. Again, Art. 4 offers no guidance as to what cases exhibit such a "close connection". However, when interpreting paragraph (3), the **policy** giving rise to the accessory connection clause must be kept in mind: preventing frictions that may occur if contractual and non-contractual claims are governed by different laws. Therefore, there is a strong case for a close connection to exist whenever the victim has tort and at least colourable contractual claims against the tortfeasor arising from the same conduct. **85**

Hein, ZEuP 2009, 6, 19; *Junker*, in: Münchener Kommentar BGB, Art. 4 para. 58; – in tendency contra: *Rushworth/Scott*, LMCLQ 2008, 274, 281.

109 G. *Wagner*, IPRax 2006, 372, 378; – contra *Dornis*, JPIL 2008, 237, 241.

110 Cf. *supra* paras. 66 et seq.

111 Brackets added.

2. Contractual Relationship

a) Purpose of the Provision

86 If there is a contractual relationship between the parties, it usually best serves the parties' interests to apply the law governing that relationship (*i.e.* a relationship that the parties voluntarily entered into) to any non-contractual claims as well. What is more, in most cases the aggrieved party will have contractual as well as non-contractual claims arising from the same event. Applying different laws bears the risk of frictions between the two groups of claims. In a worst-case scenario, the law applicable to the non-contractual claims will regard the claims as of a purely contractual nature while the law applicable to the contractual relationship will provide the reverse.

b) CISG

87 Some have argued that paragraph (3)(2) must not be applied if the contractual relationship is governed by the CISG because this Convention as a special body of *contractual* law that does not contain rules for torts/delicts.[112] However, the CISG is not applicable, *e.g.*, to the seller's liability for death or personal injury (Art. 5 CISG), meaning that the CISG leaves certain *contractual* questions to be governed by applicable national law. The latter, thus, can and should be applied by way of paragraph (3) to the non-contractual liability as well.

c) Choice of Law Restrictions under Art. 14

88 The escape clause must not be misused to circumvent the restrictions Art. 14 sets up in regard to a choice of law. Under Art. 14, an anterior choice of law is only permissible "where all parties are pursuing a commercial activity". This restriction serves the purpose of consumer protection, which would be undermined if a contractual choice of law were transferred to the non-contractual relationship via paragraph (3).[113] Indeed, Art. 6(1) Rome I opens

---

[112] *Von Hein*, 64 RabelsZ (2000) 595, 611 on Art. 41 EGBGB, the German equivalent of Art. 4(3).

the possibility of a choice of law even in relation to consumers. However, the risk Art. 6(1) Rome I creates is counterbalanced by Art. 6(2) Rome I, which grants consumers the protection of their hometown law.[114] If one was to use the escape clause of paragraph (3) to import a contractual choice of law into non-contractual obligations, it must at least be accomplished under the restriction of Art. 6(2) Rome I: the consumer must not be deprived "of the protection afforded to him by provisions that cannot be derogated from by agreement by virtue of the law which, in the absence of choice, would have been applicable on the basis of [paragraphs (1) or (2)]".[115]

3. Non-Contractual Legal Relationship

A contract is named only exemplarily by paragraph (3)(2) as the typical form of a preexisting relationship. Thus, all other forms of legal relationship may also constitute an accessory connection:[116] torts between spouses may be governed by the law applicable to the effect of the marriage (the same is true in regard to an engagement); torts between parents and their children may be governed by the law applicable to the parent-child-relationship; and torts between the shareholders of a company may be governed by the law applicable to the corporation. Even an accessory connection to another non-contractual obligation is possible: when, *e.g.*, in the course of settling an unjust enrichment or a tort, one of the parties commits a fraud, the consequences of this fraud should be judged by the law applicable to the original unjust enrichment or tort. Of course, a close connection to the accordant relationship is necessary.[117] **89**

113 Cf. *Kadner Graziano*, 73 RabelsZ (2009) 1, 22.

114 Critical: *Cheshire, North & Fawcett*, p. 801.

115 It is submitted that this protection is broader than that granted by Art. 14(2) and (3) Rome II, since it is not restricted to cases where "*all* elements relevant" to a tort are located in another country.

116 *Staudinger*, EuLF 2005 I 61; 62; *Cheshire, North & Fawcett*, p. 801.

117 *Staudinger*, EuLF 2005 I 61, 62; *Junker*, JZ 2008, 169, 175, *Cheshire, North & Fawcett*, p. 801 seq.

4. Factual Relationship

90 Whether a mere factual relationship can constitute a "preexisting relationship" is subject to some debate.[118] It is submitted that this debate is misleading: mere factual relationships are not governed by any one law that can serve as the object of an accessory connection under paragraph (3)(2). In other words, whenever there is a law to which a "preexisting relationship" can be connected, the relationship is already a legal one and paragraph (3)(2) may apply.[119] Purely factual relationships may, however, become relevant under paragraph (3)(1).

E. Particular Cases

I. Traffic Accidents

91 Damages claims that result from traffic accidents should regularly be governed by the *lex loci damni*. If, by chance, the drivers of the two vehicles involved reside in the same country, the *lex domicilii communis* applies under paragraph (2) – even though the policy behind paragraph (2) may not be served.[120] As argued above, however, paragraph (2) should not apply whenever other parties are involved in the accident who do not share this common residence.[121] Such a situation may even arise if the car is owned by a third person residing in a different country; as a rule, it will occur in cases involving mass accidents.

---

118 Pro: *Spickhoff*, in: Bamberger/Roth, Anh. zu Art. 42 EGBGB para. 37; *Staudinger*, EuLF 2005 I 61, 62; – contra: *Thorn*, in: Palandt, Art. 4 para. 13; *Junker*, JZ 2008, 169, 175; G. *Wagner*, IPRax 2008, 1, 6.

119 Purely factual circumstances of course may be considered under paragraph (3)(1); cf. *Huber/Bach*, IPRax 2005, 73, 7; *Staudinger*, EuLF 2005 I 61, 62.

120 See *supra* para. 64.

121 See *supra* para. 70.

An application of paragraph (2) to traffic accidents may be further avoided by employing the escape clause of (3). In particular, applying paragraph (3) seems appropriate if the tortfeasor's automobile insurance is calculated on the basis of the *lex loci damni* rather than the *lex domicilii communis*, *e.g.* because the **car was rented at the place of damage**. In this case, it better protects the "legitimate interests" of the parties to apply the law of the place of damage (*i.e.* the law of the place where both parties participate in public traffic) rather than relying on the mere coincidence that the parties share a common residence far away from the place of damage.[122] **92**

If the victim was transported by the tortfeasor, the law governing the **transport agreement** (if there is one) should also be applied to the claim for tort/delict under Art. 4(3).[123] **93**

Lastly, in every case arising from a traffic accident, courts must consider Art. 28, which grants priority over Rome II to the **1971 Hague Convention** on the Law Applicable to Traffic Accidents, which is in force in 12 member states.[124] **94**

II. Internet Torts

The term "internet tort" is commonly used to describe several different constellations. In its narrower sense, an internet tort consists of **destroying PC software** with a virus, worm, or similar **95**

---

122 *Staudinger*, EuLF 2005 I 61; *Kadner Graziano*, 73 RabelsZ (2009) 1, 19; *Junker*, JZ 2008, 169, 174; *Sonnentag*, 105 ZVglRWiss (2006) 256, 293; – contra: *Plender & Wilderspin*, para. 18-099; at least sceptical: *Junker*, in: Münchener Kommentar BGB, Art. 4 para. 57; *Wurmnest*, in: jurisPK BGB, Art. 4 para. 28.

123 *Junker*, JZ 2008, 169, 175 et seq.; *Staudinger*, EuLF 2005 I 61, 62.

124 See *infra* para. 11.

program. In such cases, the place where the damaged PC is located serves as the place of damages.[125]

96 In its broader sense, the term comprises all kinds of "classic" **torts committed by using the internet**, such as fraud. In these cases, the rules that designate the applicable law for the underlying tort must be applied. However, courts must account for Recital 35, which provides that the determination of applicable law "should not restrict the free movement of goods and services as regulated by Community instruments, such as the [e-commerce directive]".[126] Note that the Recital suggests *e contrario* that the e-commerce directive does not contain its own conflict rules[127] – a question that is hotly disputed amongst scholars.[128]

III. Collision of Ships or Airplanes

97 If two ships[129] collide **in international waters**, the absence of a *lex loci damni* results in the inapplicability of paragraph (1). Instead, applicable law must be determined under paragraph (2) or (3).[130] Legal literature argues that applying paragraph (2) is appropriate whenever the two ships are registered in the same country, have their home-port in the same country or are held by owners that reside in the same country. However, only the latter constellation (if any) should be subsumed under paragraph (2), as the shipowner – and not the ship itself – is the one damaged by tortious

[125] *Spickhoff*, in: Bamberger/Roth, Anh. zu Art. 42 EGBGB para. 54; *Thorn*, in: Palandt, Art. 4 para. 29; *Wurmnest*, in: jurisPK BGB, Art. 4 para. 43.

[126] Directive 2000/31/EC of the European Parliament and of the Council of 8 June 2000 on certain legal aspects of information society services, in particular electronic commerce, in the Internal Market (Directive on electronic commerce), OJ 2000 L 178/1.

[127] *Plender & Wilderspin*, para. 18-040.

[128] See *Dickinson*, paras. 16-11 et seq.

[129] The same problems occur in regard to the collision of airplanes in international airspace and should be resolved under the same principles.

[130] See *supra* para. 62.

conduct. Still, an application of paragraph (2) requires that – first – the owner of the other ship may be regarded as the tortfeasor, and – second – that he is the *only* person who can be considered the tortfeasor, as otherwise (in the author's opinion[131]) paragraph (2) is not applicable. Applying the escape clause of (3) again seems to be the more appropriate means of determining applicable law.

If there are no common elements between shippers, legal literature argues that, since no basis for any alternative exists, the hometown law[132] of the damaged ship should apply. Since in most cases both ships will be damaged, this approach will lead to different laws being applied to the different ships – a result at odds with the purpose of conflicts rules (especially if the laws lead to different results). Nevertheless, lacking any more convincing alternative, the approach should be followed. Where one ship is wholly at fault, it seems reasonable to apply the hometown law of the innocent ship to the entire case.[133] **98**

Fortunately, in most cases, **international conventions** that prevail over the Rome II Regulation will apply to collisions in international waters (*e.g.* the 1910 Convention for the Unification of Certain Rules of Law with respect to Collisions between Vessels). **99**

IV. Torts/Delicts onboard a Ship or Airplane

If damage occurs onboard a ship or airplane while the vessel is **in territorial waters or airspace**, Art. 4(1) designates as applicable the law of the country to which the waters or airspace belong. However, courts should readily employ the escape clause of Art. **100**

---

131 See *supra* para. 70.

132 *Dickinson*, para. 4.56. There exists debate over whether the law of the ship's flag, the law of the ship's home port, or the law of the ship's owner constitutes a ship's "hometown" law; cf. *Thorn*, in: Palandt, Art. 18 para. 13.

133 *Plender & Wilderspin*, para. 18-048.

4(3) in cases when no other connection to this country exists. Such cases most likely have a closer connection to the law of the flag or to the port of departure or destination.[134]

101 If the tort is committed **in international territory**, the law of the flag should be applied in the first place:[135] for conflicts purposes, either the ship/airplane may be regarded as part of the country under whose flag it operates or – more convincing – the flag may be considered as establishing a manifest close connection under paragraph (3).[136]

102 If the **airline is party to the tort** (be it as tortfeasor be it as victim), the law governing the transportation contract may be applied under the "preexisting relationship" provision of paragraph (3). The same can be said for torts committed by the board crew against the airline: Art. 4(3)(2) opens the door for an accessory connection to the employment contract.

V. Damage to *Res in Transitu*

103 If goods are damaged while in transit, in most cases the law governing the transportation contract will be applicable by virtue of (3)(2). If not, two primary difficulties arise in determining what law governs goods damaged during shipping:

104 First and most evidently, it may be **impossible to identify the exact place of damages**. If, *e.g.*, goods are packaged into a container in country A and are discovered damaged in country B, it cannot be determined whether the damage occurred before or after the

---

134 *Plender & Wilderspin*, para. 18-050; *Wurmnest*, in: jurisPK BGB, Art. 4 para. 36.

135 ECJ, Case C-18/02 – *DFDS Torline*, [2004] ECR I-1417, para. 44 (in dicta); cf. *Plender & Wilderspin*, para. 18-047; *Junker*, in: Münchener Kommentar BGB, Art. 4 para. 35; *Wurmnest*, in: jurisPK BGB, Art. 4 para. 36.

136 Cf. *Garcimartín Alférez*, EuLF 2007 I 77, 84; *Plender & Wilderspin*, para. 18-047.

goods passed the border between the two countries. In regard to Art. 5(3) Brussels I, the ECJ ruled that the place of discovery of the damage is irrelevant in determining the applicable law. Rather, **the place of actual delivery** is dispositive.[137] Often, however, the place of delivery and the place of discovery will be identical. The decision of the ECJ first makes sense when one considers the particular facts of the case: the goods were transported by several different carriers and the damage could be allocated to one single carrier. Thus, the crucial point of the ECJ's ruling is that the place of damage is not the place of *final* delivery, but instead the place where the carrier *in whose possession the goods were damaged* was to deliver the goods. If the decision is reduced to an abstract formula, the following seems to best reflect the ECJ's holding: if damages can be allocated to a distinct segment of the transport operation, the place of delivery at the end of this segment is the place of damages. If such precise allocation is not possible, the place of *final* destination of the goods is the place of damages. However, under the Brussels I regime the ECJ was forced to "create" a more or less fictitious place of damages. Under the Rome II Regulation there is no need for such artificial "creations" – and it is therefore more convincing to employ the flexible approach embodied in the escape clause of paragraph (3). Thus, if the place of damage cannot be determined, paragraph (1) is inapplicable and courts should determine applicable law under paragraph (3).[138]

Second, while traveling from country A to country B onboard a ship or airplane, damage to goods may occur **in international** **105**

[137] ECJ, Case C-51/97 – *Réunion européenne*, [1998] ECR I-6511, para. 33. The ECJ reasoned that relying on either place "would in most cases mean attributing jurisdiction to the courts for the place of the plaintiff's domicile", para. 34; contra: *Cheshire, North & Fawcett*, p. 797: "for choice of law purposes it is hard to see any other solution than that of where the damage was discovered".

[138] Cf. *Garcimartín Alférez*, EuLF 2007 I 77, 84; *Plender & Wilderspin*, para. 18-062.

waters or airspace. In light of the ECJ decision mentioned above, the destination of the air or sea transport should constitute the place of damages. However, this approach differs from what is generally proposed in legal literature for torts in international waters/airspace, *i.e.* to rely on the ship's/airplane's flag (see above 101). In the Author's opinion, the result – whether destination-based, flag-based, or other – should be reached by way of the escape clause of paragraph (3). Such an approach allows the court the necessary flexibility to decide which approach seems to best fit the circumstances of the individual case.

106 Again, under Art. 28, many cases of damage over international waters will be governed by **international conventions** that prevail over the Rome II regime (such as the 1956 Convention on the Contract for the International Carriage of Goods by Road).

VI. Damage to Third Parties

107 Article 15(f) provides which law should apply if the tort causes damages to third parties (*e.g.* if parents of an injured minor must pay the minor's hospital bills, or if the parent company is detrimentally affected by a tort directed against its subsidiary). In such cases, the law designated applicable to the "direct" victim also governs the damages claims of third parties. Under Art. 15(f), the designated law shall govern "persons entitled to compensation for damage suffered personally", and the Commission's Explanatory Memorandum states that "such damage might be non-material, as in the pain or suffering caused by bereavement, or financial, as in the loss sustained by the children or spouse of a deceased person".[139] In the Author's opinion, Art. 15(f) also governs cases in which damage to a third party is not of purely financial but also of a physical nature (*e.g.* if the closest relatives of the deceased suffer medically ascertainable psychological injuries).[140]

---

139 COM(2003) 427, p. 24, Art. 11.

140 See Art. 15 para. 20.

The rule contained in Art. 15(f) is consistent with the "direct damages" principle of Art. 4(1). Damage to third parties constitutes a consequential loss, even if the primary and exclusive impact the tort has is on the third party. Damages are consequential not only when they flow from another, more immediate harm to the injured person, but also when they arise from harm to another person.[141] Even when damage to a third person is of a physical (as opposed to financial) nature, it does not constitute a new "direct" damage, but rather a consequential damage that flows from the harm to the person originally injured through tortious conduct.[142] The law applicable to the third person under paragraph (1) is therefore the law of the place where the direct damage occurred to the direct victim[143] – notwithstanding paragraphs (2) and (3). **108**

Article 15(f) and a consistent interpretation of Art. 4(1) is in line with the ECJ's case law on Art. 5(3) Brussels I: in *Dumez v Hessische Landesbank*, the court held that the harm that occurred to parent companies through financial losses originally suffered by their subsidiaries was "merely the indirect consequence" of the subsidiaries' losses. It therefore held the place of damage to the subsidiaries was dispositive in deciding the place of damage to the parent companies.[144] **109**

---

141 ECJ, Case C-168/02 – *Kronhofer*, [2004] ECR I-6009, para. 20; *Dickinson*, paras. 4.42 et seq.; *Kropholler*, Europäisches Zivilprozessrecht, Art. 5 para. 91; *Leible*, in: Rauscher, Europäisches Zivilprozessrecht, Art. 5 Brussels I para. 86c; – differentiating: *Mankowski*, in: Magnus/Mankowski, (eds.) Brussels I Regulation, Art. 5 para. 237, – contra: *Cheshire, North & Fawcett*, p. 798.

142 *Von Hein*, Günstigkeitsprinzip im Internationalen Deliktsrecht, pp. 310 et seq.

143 *Kropholler*, Europäisches Zivilprozessrecht, Art. 5 para. 91; – contra: *Cheshire, North & Fawcett*, p. 798.

144 ECJ, Case C-220/88 – *Dumez France v Hessische Landesbank*, [1990] ECR I-49.

110 The direct damages principle should govern even if the harm to a third person derives from a ***novus actus interveniens***: for example, as a result of his injuries in a car accident in country A, the victim suffers a personality change and attacks a third person in country B.[145] The third person claims damages from both the car driver and the attacker. Obviously, the claim against the attacker should be governed by the law of country B. However, as regards the claim against the car driver, the attack should be seen as an indirect consequence of the accident, and thus the law of country A should apply.[146]

VII. Collective Claims, or Suits Brought by Consumer Protection Associations

111 Where a professional provides for unfair terms that disadvantage consumers in its General Terms and Conditions, some legal systems allow consumers' associations to file an action for an injunction against the professional. While the issue of unfair terms is clearly of a contractual nature as between the professional and the consumer, it should be classified as non-contractual where a consumers' association sues the professional.[147] According to the (German) *Bundesgerichtshof*,[148] the law applicable to such lawsuits may be determined under Art. 4. The court left open the question of whether Art. 6 applies as a *lex specialis*: in the court's opinion, Art. 6 constitutes a mere concretisation of Art. 4, meaning that both provisions necessarily lead to the same result. The court ruled that, in determining the place of damages for cases of unfair terms in General Conditions, courts should consider where the unfair terms were used or would probably be used in the future. In the case decided by the *Bundesgerichtshof*, a Latvian airline had placed their General Conditions on a German-language website. The court concluded that the airline had used their unfair terms

145 Cf. *Plender & Wilderspin*, para. 17-012.

146 Contra: *Plender & Wilderspin*, para. 17-012.

147 See Art. 1 para. 29.

148 Bundesgerichtshof (Germany), 9 July 2009, BGHZ 182, 24.

in Germany and held German law to be applicable. Thus, the court reached the correct result under the wrong rule: rather than Art. 4, the special rule in Art. 6 now appears to govern associations' suits against a professional's unfair terms. Unfortunately, the *Bundesgerichtshof* refused to bring the matter before the ECJ under Art. 267 TFEU.

Article 5
Product liability

1. Without prejudice to Article 4(2), the law applicable to a non-contractual obligation arising out of damage caused by a product shall be:
   (a) the law of the country in which the person sustaining the damage had his or her habitual residence when the damage occurred, if the product was marketed in that country; or, failing that,
   (b) the law of the country in which the product was acquired, if the product was marketed in that country; or, failing that,
   (c) the law of the country in which the damage occurred, if the product was marketed in that country.

   However, the law applicable shall be the law of the country in which the person claimed to be liable is habitually resident if he or she could not reasonably foresee the marketing of the product, or a product of the same type, in the country the law of which is applicable under (a), (b) or (c).
2. Where it is clear from all the circumstances of the case that the tort/delict is manifestly more closely connected with a country other than that indicated in paragraph 1, the law of that other country shall apply. A manifestly closer connection with another country might be based in particular on a pre-existing relationship between the parties, such as a contract, that is closely connected with the tort/delict in question.

A. Overview

I. Legislative History

1 The legislative history of Art. 5 Rome II is a tangled one.[1] The special conflict rule on product liability in the first draft by the Commission of May 2002 provided for a combination of cumulative and alternative connecting factors,[2] which was close to the conflict regime of the Hague Convention on the law applicable to products liability of 1973. The special rule in the Commission's initial proposal of July 2003 differed substantially. It provided for a rule consisting of only two elements: the habitual residence of the injured person as the connecting factor, and lack of consent to marketing of

[1] For a detailed account of the legislative history see *Illmer*, 73 RabelsZ (2009) 269, 272 et seq.; *Plender & Wilderspin*, paras. 19-001 et seq.

[2] See Art. 5 of the first draft, accessible at http://ec.europa.eu/justice_home/news/consulting_public/rome_ii/news_hearing_rome2_en.htm.

the product in that country as a defence for the person claimed to be liable. In case of marketing without his consent in the country of the habitual residence of the injured person, the applicable law was that of the allegedly liable person's habitual residence.[3] As with regard to other special conflict rules of the initial proposal, the European Parliament in its first reading[4] suggested to delete the conflict rule on product liability. Instead, the general rule (which is now Art. 4) should apply. Its escape clause (which is now Art. 4 (3)) was enlarged extensively by adding numerous criteria for a deviation from the basic connection to the place where the event giving rise to the damage occurred (which is now Art. 4(1)). Those included rather vague aspects such as certainty, predictability, uniformity of results, protection of legitimate interests, and the policies underlying the law applicable but for the escape clause. Not surprisingly, this approach was rejected by the Commission in its amended proposal insisting on its initial rule[5] and by the Council.[6] It was a clear and intended break with the traditional European conflict of laws model, following instead the US model after the Second Restatement of the Conflict of Laws of 1971[7] although the latter had proven rather unsuccessful.[8]

In its common position,[9] the Council suggested an altogether new special rule, strongly rejecting Parliament's approach but also deviating from the Commission's proposals. The rule contained a 2

---

3 See Art. 4 of the initial proposal COM(2003) 427 final.

4 See Art. 6 of the European Parliament's legislative resolution after the first reading (P6-TA(2005)0284 of 6 July 2005).

5 See Art. 6 of the amended proposal COM(2006) 83 final.

6 Statement of the Council's Reasons, OJ 2006 C 289E/79.

7 *American Law Institute*, Restatement of the Law Second, Conflict of Laws, 1971.

8 See *von Hein*, ZEuP 2009, 6, 18; *idem*, 82 Tul.L.Rev. (2008) 1663, 1685 seq.; rather in favour of such a flexible approach *Symeonides*, 56 Am. J. Comp. L. (2008) 173.

9 Common Position (EC) No 22/2006 of 25 September 2006, OJ 2006 C 289E/68.

cascade system with three connecting factors supplemented by a foreseeability defence in Art. 5(1). The common habitual residence rule – by reference to Art. 4(2) – and the escape clause – by restating Art. 4(3) in Art. 5(2) – of the general rule were kept. The Council's proposal was accepted by both the Commission[10] and Parliament so that it could make its way through to the final version of Art. 5 of the Regulation.

II. Structure

3 Art. 5 is the first of a set of provisions (Art. 5 to 13) dealing with specific torts. In that respect it is ***lex specialis*** to the *lex generalis* in Art. 4. It has no predecessor in any of the national laws of the Member States.

4 According to Recital 20 Rome II the main object of the rule in Art. 5 is to spread the risks inherent in a modern high-technology society fairly by striking a balance between the interests of the person potentially liable and the person sustaining the damage caused by the product. The differentiated cascade structure of Art. 5(1)1 complemented by a foreseeability defence in Art. 5(1)2 is mainly motivated by this goal. Whether a less complex rule may also have achieved it, is another matter.[11]

5 The system of Art. 5 consists of **three elements**: the cascade connections as the general rule in Art. 5(1)1, a foreseeability defence

---

10 Although the Commission regretted the unnecessary increase in complexity of the rule, see COM(2006) 566 final; similarly critical towards the complexity of the rule G. *Wagner*, IPRax 2008, 1, 7; *Plender & Wilderspin*, para. 19-063; *Hartley*, 57 ICLQ (2008) 899, 906.

11 The rule proposed initially by the Commission was far less complex and the Commission doubted whether the more complex structure would result in a higher degree of justice to the parties (COM(2006) 83 final); rather critical also *von Hein*, ZEuP 2009, 6, 26; *Spickhoff*, in: FS Kropholler (2008) 671, 672; G. *Wagner*, IPRax 2008, 1, 7; *Thorn*, in: Palandt, Art. 5 para. 1; *Wurmnest*, in: jurisPK BGB, Art. 5 para. 3.

in Art. 5(1)2 and an escape clause in Art. 5(2). The law applicable to an international product liability claim is, however, not only determined by the connections in Art. 5. Rather, Art. 5 is intertwined with several other provisions of Rome II and forms only the core of a complex system of connections: First, Art. 14 takes precedence over any of the objective connections of Art. 5. Secondly, the common habitual residence connection of Art. 4(2) is incorporated into Art. 5(1)1 prevailing over the subsequent cascade connections. And thirdly, the escape clause of Art. 4(3) is restated in Art. 5(2). Due to this intertwined structure, Art. 5 is in effect only replacing Art. 4(1) while the application of the rules embodied in Art. 4(2) and (3) is preserved even in cases of product liability.

As a consequence, the law applicable to international product liability is not only determined by the three levels of the cascade of Art. 5(1)1,[12] but by a **ladder of six connections**,[13] descending in the following order: (i) choice of law (Art. 14), (ii) common habitual residence (Art. 5(1)1 in combination with Art. 4(2)), (iii) habitual residence of the person sustaining damage if the product was marketed in that country (Art. 5(1)1(a)) and if this marketing was reasonably foreseeable for the producer (Art. 5(1)2), (iv) place of acquisition of the product if the product was marketed in that country (Art. 5(1)1(b)) and if this marketing was reasonably foreseeable for the producer (Art. 5(1)2), (v) place of occurrence of damage if the product was marketed in that country (Art. 5(1)1(c)) and if this marketing was reasonably foreseeable for the producer (Art. 5(1)2), with connections 2 to 5 being subject to (vi) a manifestly closer connection to another country (Art. 5(2)). Furthermore, each connection may be modified by Art. 17 when assessing the conduct of the person claimed 6

---

12 See *infra* paras. 22 et seq. for more detail.

13 Some authors list 7 steps since they take the foreseeability defence in Art. 5(1)2 as a separate step; this is, however, inaccurate since the foreseeability defence has to be read together with each of the three levels of the cascade of Art. 5(1)1.

to be liable.[14] This relates to the rules of safety and conduct at the place and time of marketing of the product[15] since it is that marketing which gives rise to liability.[16]

III. Relationship with the 1973 Hague Convention

7 The Hague Convention of 2 October 1973 on the Law Applicable to Products Liability is amongst the Member States in force in Finland, France, Luxembourg, the Netherlands, Slovenia and Spain.[17] Since third countries are also amongst the signatory states, the relationship between the Rome II Regulation's regime on product liability and the Hague Convention is governed by Art. 28(1) Rome II: the Hague Convention takes precedence over Rome II. Attempts to align the two regimes during the legislative process failed.[18] Consequently, **two regimes** determining the law applicable to international product liability will apply within the EU: The Hague Convention applies in the said six Member States while Art. 5 Rome II applies in the remaining 21. While this fragmented state of the law is already very unsatisfactory in itself,[19] it is even aggravated by the **exclusion of ren-**

---

14 *Thorn*, in: Palandt, Art. 5 paras. 8 and 14; *Junker*, in: Münchener Kommentar BGB, Art. 5 para. 54; *Wurmnest*, in: jurisPK BGB, Art. 5 para. 5; *Huber/Illmer*, 9 YbPIL (2007) 31, 39; for a detailed account see *Plender & Wilderspin*, paras. 19-133 et seq.

15 *Thorn*, in: Palandt, Art. 5 para. 14; *Wurmnest*, in: jurisPK BGB, Art. 5 para. 38.

16 See *infra* paras. 27 et seq.

17 In total, the Convention on the law applicable to products liability is currently signed by 14, ratified and in force in 11 states (besides the 6 Member States these are Croatia, Montenegro, Norway, Macedonia and Serbia).

18 *R. Wagner*, in: FS Kropholler (2008) 715, 726; for a discussion of the options concerning the relationship between the Hague Conventions and Rome II see Art. 28 para. 3.

19 *Illmer*, 73 RabelsZ (2009) 269, 311; *Dickinson*, para. 5.53; *Spickhoff*, in: FS Kropholler (2008), 671, 673; *Garriga*, 9 YbPIL (2007) 137, 143; *Joubert*,

voi in Art. 24 Rome II preventing external harmony of decisions between "Rome II States" and "Hague Convention States".[20] Thus, the primary goal of the Rome II Regulation to establish a uniform system of private international law applicable in all Member States to avoid forum shopping[21] is not achieved in a core area of the law of non-contractual obligations.

De lege ferenda, the best solution would be a denunciation of the Hague Convention by the minority of the six signatory Member States since the Convention did not prove very successful due to its complex system of connections.[22] *De lege lata*, the parties can avoid the application of the Hague Convention before the courts of a signatory Member State either by a choice of court agreement 8

---

in: Corneloup/Joubert (eds.), Le règlement communautaire "Rome II" sur la loi applicable aux obligations non contractuelles (2007) 55, 62 et seq.; G. *Wagner*, IPRax 2008, 1, 3; *von Hein*, 102 ZVglRWiss. (2003) 528, 554 seq.; *Hamburg Group for Private International Law*, 67 RabelsZ (2003) 1, 56.

20 *Von Hein*, 73 RabelsZ (2009) 461, 474 and *idem*, in: Ahern/Binchy, p. 153, 158 (considering to achieve external harmony of decisions by applying the escape clauses of Art. 4(3) and 5(2) Rome II); *Junker*, in: Münchener Kommentar BGB, Art. 28 para. 9.

21 In that regard one should bear in mind, that there is range of available fora; under the Brussels I Regulation the plaintiff in a product liability case has a choice between the defendant's domicile (Art. 2), the place where the event giving rise to the damage occurred and the place where the damage occurred (Art. 5 Nr. 3 as interpreted by the ECJ, see Case 21/76 – *Mines de Potasse d'Alsace* [1976] ECR 1735 paras. 19 et seq.; Case C-68/93 – *Shevill* [1995] ECR I-415 para. 20; Case C-167/00 – *Verein für Konsumenteninformation* [2002] ECR I-8111 paras. 42 et seq.; Case C-168/02 – *Kronhofer* [2004] ECR I-6009 para. 16).

22 *Staudinger*, EuLF 2005, I-64 et seq.; *Kadner Graziano*, in: Basedow/Baum/Nishitani (eds.), Japanese and European Private International Law in Comparative Perspective (2008) 243, 245; *Wurmnest*, in: jurisPK BGB, Art. 5 para. 12; *Kropholler*, Internationales Privatrecht, 6th ed 2006, § 53 V. 3.; *Lorenz*, 37 RabelsZ (1973) 317, 328 et seq.

providing for the exclusive jurisdiction of a member state which is not a party to the Hague Convention or by derogating the Hague Convention's application, so that Art. 5 Rome II will apply.[23] The possibility of derogating the application of the Hague Convention has been accepted by French[24] and Austrian courts.[25]

9 The **reach of the Hague Convention's precedence** is not entirely clear. As a matter of course, the Hague Convention forecloses the application of the respective conflict rules in Art. 5, 14 Rome II that are directly concerned with the law applicable to the product liability claim. Whether the Hague Convention also forecloses the application of the more general, supplementary provisions of the Rome II Regulation, particularly those concerning direct actions (Art. 18), subrogation (Art. 19) and multiple liability (Art. 20), is, however, less clear. As a general rule, those provisions of Rome II should apply even if the law applicable to the product liability claim itself is determined by the Hague Convention.[26] They do not prejudice the application of the Hague Convention within the meaning of Art. 28(1) Rome II since the issues are not addressed by the Hague Convention. Just as they supplement Art. 5 Rome II, they may equally supplement the conflict rules on product liability of the Hague Convention.

---

23 Art. 28(1) can hardly apply in such a case since its rationale of respecting international commitments of the Member States does not apply if the respective "Hague Convention State" allows party autonomy to prevail; in the words of Art. 28(1) the application of the Hague Convention is not prejudiced since the "Hague Convention State" itself would not apply it.

24 Cour de Cassation (France), 19 April 1988 – 85-18.715; 78 Rev. crit. d. i. p. (1989) 68.

25 Oberster Gerichtshof (Austria), 30 January 2003 – 2 Ob 10/03i, 44 ZRvgl. (2003) 148; 26 January 1995 – 2 Ob 11/94, 36 ZR vgl. (1995) 212.

26 *Brière*, 135 Clunet (2008) 31, 72 et seq. ("… the gaps should be filled by applying Rome II to those aspects …").

B. Scope

I. Material Scope

1. Non-Contractual Liability for Damage Caused by a Defective Product

Art. 5 covers **strict and fault-based liability.**[27] 10

Art. 5 applies only to **non-contractual liability**. This relates in particular to direct claims by subsequent purchasers or unrelated third parties, whether under the implemented Product Liablity Directive or the national laws of tort/delict.[28] In case of concurrent contractual liability, *e.g.* claims by initial purchasers or lessees of a product, the law applicable to liability in contract is determined by Art. 3, 4 and 6 Rome I. Since the contract will regularly constitute a manifestly closer connection under Art. 5(2)2 Rome II, the same law will apply to the non-contractual claim.[29] Whether the claim is of a contractual or non-contractual nature is to be qualified autonomously. Any direct claim based on an obligation not freely assumed by the person claimed to be liable is of a non-contractual nature. Accordingly, the French *action directe* is a form of non-contractual liability for the purposes of determining the applicable law under Art. 5 Rome II.[30] The European Court of Justice took this view with regard to Art. 5 No. 1 vis-à-vis Art. 5 No. 3 Brussels I[31] and the same should apply in 11

27 See the Explanatory Report by the Commission (COM(2003) 427, p. 15); *Schwartze*, NIPR 2008, 430, 431; *Huber/Illmer*, 9 YbPIL (2007) 31, 37; *Wurmnest*, in: jurisPK BGB, Art. 5 para. 8; *Thorn*, in: Palandt, Art. 5 para. 3.

28 *Illmer*, 73 RabelsZ (2009) 269, 282; *Brière*, 135 Clunet (2008) 31, 47.

29 *Spickhoff*, in: FS Kropholler (2008) 671, 678.

30 *Illmer*, 73 RabelsZ (2009) 269, 283; *Spickhoff*, in: FS Kropholler (2008) 671, 679.

31 ECJ, Case C-26/91 – *Handte* [1992] ECR I-3967 paras. 15 et seq. (at the same time stressing that concepts under Brussels I are not necessarily the

respect of Rome I vis-à-vis Rome II. Therefore, the *action directe* is a non-contractual claim which is available if Art. 5 Rome II designates the application of French law.

12 Art. 5 requires damage caused by a **product**. In that respect, one can draw on the definition of product in Art. 2 of the Product Liability Directive.[32] Furthermore, Art. 5 covers only liability caused by a **defective product** whereas liability for damage caused by a non-defective product or by an aspect unrelated to the defect in the product is governed by the law determined by the general rule in Art. 4 Rome II.[33] For Art. 5 to apply it is, however, sufficient that the person sustaining damage claims that the product is

---

same under the Rome Convention which was at the time in force); ECJ, Case 51/97 – *Réunion européenne* [1998] ECR I-6511 paras. 15 et seq.; ECJ, Case C-334/00 – *Tacconi* [2002] ECR I-7357 paras. 22 et seq.; see *Rushworth/Scott*, LMCLQ 2008, 274, 299 seq. for further details on the concept of non-contractual versus contractual.

32 See the Explanatory Report by the Commission (COM(2003) 427 final at p. 13); *Illmer*, 73 RabelsZ (2009) 269, 283; *Dickinson*, para. 5.10; *Schwartze*, NIPR 2008, 430; *Spickhoff*, in: FS Kropholler (2008) 671, 678; *Leible/Lehmann*, RIW 2007, 721, 727; *Junker*, in: Münchener Kommentar BGB, Art. 5 para. 13; *Brière*, 135 Clunet (2008) 31, 46; critical in that respect *Plender & Wilderspin*, paras. 19-021 et seq. (Art. 2 of the Directive being too narrow in requiring a tangible and moveable product which excludes software and information stored by electronic means).

33 *Illmer*, 73 RabelsZ (2009) 269, 283; *Junker*, in: Münchener Kommentar BGB, Art. 5 para. 15; *Kozyris*, 56 Am. J. Comp. L. (2008) 471, 487; *von Hein*, ZEuP 2009, 6, 26; *Plender & Wilderspin*, para. 19-018; *Wurmnest*, in: jurisPK BGB, Art. 5 para. 8; similar *Rushworth/Scott*, LMCLQ 2008, 274, 283 (they seem to see the problem in an obligation not only *concerned* with damage caused by a product but *arising out of* damage caused by a product); a different view is taken by *Brière*, 135 Clunet (2008) 31, 47 (any product); *Dickinson*, para. 5.15 (Art. 5 should in particular also apply to inherently dangerous products such as cigarettes or firearms; in this case, however, Art. 4 should rather apply since damage is then rather caused by the use of the non-defective product than by the product itself;

defective. Whether this is actually the case, is together with the other prerequisites of the product liability claim (causation, damage etc.) a matter to be determined by the applicable law.

2. Relationship with Other Provisions of the Regulation

a) Art. 7 (Environmental Damage)

In case of an overlap of the material scope of Art. 5 and 7, *i.e.* environmental damage[34] caused by a defective product, Art. 7 prevails so that Art. 5 disapplies.[35] First, the centre of gravity in such a case is not the defective product but the damage to the environment. Whether pipes used in a cooling system of a factory are defective due to manufacturing defects or whether they are damaged by man should not make a difference when it comes to determining the law applicable to the resulting environmental damage. Secondly, the protection of the environment is given special attention in Art. 191 TFEU and Recital 25 Rome II.[36] Thirdly, in comparison, Art. 7 appears to be even more special than Art. 5 in relation to the case scenarios with which the overlap situation is concerned.[37] 13

b) Art. 12 (*Culpa in Contrahendo*)

An overlap between Art. 5 and 12 may arise particularly in relation to **pre-contractual duties of information in relation to a defective product**. One has to distinguish:[38] There is no overlap 14

---

concurring in that regard *Junker*, in: Münchener Kommentar BGB, Art. 5 para. 15).

34 Note that Art. 7 covers environmental damage and damage sustained by persons or property as a consequence of environmental damage.

35 See also Art. 7 para. 40; concurring *Dickinson*, para. 5.17; *Plender & Wilderspin*, para. 19-053; *Junker*, in: Münchener Kommentar BGB, Art. 5 para. 20; *Thorn*, in: Palandt, Art. 5 para. 3; *Wurmnest*, in: jurisPK BGB, Art. 5 para. 10.

36 *Thorn*, in: Palandt, Art. 5 para. 3.

37 *Junker*, in: Münchener Kommentar BGB, Art. 5 para. 20.

38 *Spickhoff*, in: FS Kropholler (2008) 671, 679.

where the person claimed to be liable for the defect is not identical with the person claimed to be liable for the omission to provide the required pre-contractual information: the former will be liable under the law determined by Art. 5, the latter under the law determined by Art. 12. An overlap does, however, exist where the person claimed to be liable for the defect is identical with the person claimed to be liable for the omission to provide the required pre-contractual information, *e.g.* contract negotiations with a test run of the product in the face of a direct purchase from the producer.[39] Such overlap should be solved by clearly distinguishing the bases of the respective claims. As far as the claim is based on a breach of pre-contractual duties, *e.g.* information duties, the applicable law is determined by Art. 12. As far as it is based on the defect of the product unrelated to the existing pre-contractual duties, the applicable law is determined by Art. 5. Thus, different laws will apply to the two different claims which appears to be sound in principle. If, however, the damage resulting from the breach of the pre-contractual duty and the defect in the product are the same or factually difficult to separate, there is a risk of double compensation. To avoid that, the court should strive at applying the same law to both claims in making use of the escape clauses in Art. 5 and 12, preferably, Art. 5(2).[40]

3. Relationship with the E-Commerce Directive

15 With regard to the sale and supply of **society information services** sold and delivered via electronic means[41] Art. 5 Rome II

---

39 *Spickhoff*, in: FS Kropholler (2008) 671, 679; the range of persons potentially liable under the law determined by Art. 5 is, however, broader than only the producer (see *infra* para. 18) so that an overlap may generally arise in case of identity of the person owing the pre-contractual information and the person claimed to be liable under Art. 5.

40 *Junker*, in: Münchener Kommentar BGB, Art. 5 para. 21; *Spickhoff*, in: FS Kropholler (2008) 671, 680.

41 According to Art. 2 lit a of the E-Commerce Directive in connection with Art. 1(2) of Directive 98/34/EC as amended by Directive 98/48/

must, according to Art. 27 Rome II, not prejudice the country of origin-principle of Art. 3(1) and (2) of the E-Commerce Directive.[42] Whether the latter amounts to a conflict rule or not, is contested,[43] but in the end not decisive:[44] if one regards the country of origin-principle as a conflict rule, Art. 3(1) and (2) of the E-Commerce Directive replace Art. 5 Rome II according to Art. 27 Rome II. If one does not regard the country of origin-principle as a conflict rule, Recital 35 provides that the country of origin's provisions in the respective field covered by the other Community law instrument (which will mainly be those of public economic/regulatory law[45]) take precedence on the level of substantive law in case of incompatibility with the applicable substantive law.

In any event, the application of the E-Commerce Directive is **restricted in two ways.** First, "society information services" do not cover physical goods but only products sold *and delivered* via electronic means such as software or mp3 files downloaded from a 16

EC, this is any service normally provided for remuneration, at a distance, by electronic means and at the individual request of a recipient of services; a service is provided by electronic means if it is sent initially and received at its destination by means of electronic equipment for the processing (including digital compression) and storage of data, and entirely transmitted, conveyed and received by wire, by radio, by optical means or by other electromagnetic means.

42 Directive 2000/31/EC of the European Parliament and of the Council of 8 June 2000 on certain legal aspects of information society services, in particular electronic commerce, in the Internal Market (Directive on electronic commerce), OJ 2000 L 178/1.

43 For details and references see Art. 6 paras. 25 et seq.

44 Concurring *Spickhoff*, in: FS Kropholler (2008), 671, 674; *Thorn*, in: Palandt, Art. 6 para. 15; for a detailed analysis see Art. 27 paras. 7 et seq.

45 *De Lima Pinheiro*, Riv. dir. int. priv. proc. 2008, 5, 37 with further references; in case of the E-Commerce Directive only provisions within the coordinated field pursuant to its Art. 2.

website. Consequently, the classic distance online sale of a product then physically delivered to the buyer is not covered by the E-Commerce Directive.[46] Secondly, even society information services are not governed by the E-Commerce Directive if a consumer is involved. Although Art. 3(4)(a)(ii) fourth indent of the E-Commerce Directive provides so explicitly only with regard to national laws, it should *a maiore ad minus* equally apply with regard to a uniform European regime replacing national law.[47]

II. Personal Scope

17 The **person sustaining the damage** may be any person. The application of Art. 5 is not restricted to consumers.[48]

18 The **person claimed to be liable** may equally be *any* person for the purposes of Art. 5. Reference to the range of persons addressed by Art. 3 of the Product Liability Directive (producer, quasi-producer, importer, supplier etc.) in the Explanatory Memorandum of the Commission[49] does neither restrict nor enlarge the group of potentially liable persons. Whether the person *claimed* to be liable is actually liable (in particular within the range of persons potentially liable), is a matter to be determined by the applicable law.[50]

---

46 Concurring *Lurger/Vallant*, RIW 2002, 188, 190; *Spickhoff*, in: FS Kropholler (2008) 671, 674; *Spindler*, 66 RabelsZ (2002) 633, 692 (listing several instances of services provided online).

47 *Illmer*, 73 RabelsZ (2009) 269, 310.

48 *Dickinson*, para. 5.09; *Plender & Wilderspin*, para. 19-018; *Illmer*, 73 RabelsZ (2009) 269, 284; *Wurmnest*, in: jurisPK BGB, Art. 5 para. 9.

49 COM(2003) 427 final, p. 15.

50 *Illmer*, 73 RabelsZ (2009) 269, 284; *Leible/Lehmann*, RIW 2007, 721, 727; *Junker*, in: Münchener Kommentar BGB, Art. 5 para. 19.

III. Territorial Scope

The rule in Art. 5 applies in all Member States apart from those six which have ratified the Hague Convention on products liability.[51] 19

C. Determination of the Applicable Law

I. Ladder of Connections

1. Choice of Law

A **choice of law** pursuant to Art. 14 prevails over any of the objective connections of Art. 5. 20

2. Common Habitual Residence

In case of a **common habitual residence** the law of that country applies according to Art. 5(1)1 in connection with Art. 4(2). It prevails over any of the subsequent cascade connections of Art. 5(1)1 and is not qualified by any of the considerations relevant under the cascade, in particular the marketing requirement and foreseeability of such marketing. The escape clause of Art. 5(2), however, is applicable.[52] 21

3. The Cascade of Art. 5(1)1 lit. a to c

a) Overview

The core of the special rule in Art. 5 are the **cascade connections** of Art. 5(1)1 lit. a to c, supplemented by a common foreseeability 22

---

51 See *supra* para. 7.

52 *Junker*, in: Münchener Kommentar BGB, Art. 5 para. 50; *Thorn*, in: Palandt, Art. 5 para. 7; *Plender & Wilderspin*, para. 19-129; the application of the escape clause is denied by *Rushworth/Scott*, LMCLQ 2008, 274, 283 seq.; *Dickinson*, para. 5.46.

defence in Art. 5(1)2. The cascade has three levels. Each level consists of two cumulative elements: a varying connecting factor and the common marketing element. The varying connecting factors are: habitual residence of the persons sustaining the damage (first level), place of acquisition of the product (second level) and place where the damage occurred (third level). The common marketing element requires that the product (or a product of the same type[53]) was marketed in the respective country indicated by the connecting factor. A subsequent level of the cascade may only be entered if the cumulative elements of the prior level are not met (this differentiates the cascade from alternative connections).

b) The Three Varying Factors

23 The **three varying connecting factors** are commonly used in private international law and present only few difficulties.

24 The concept of **habitual residence** in lit. a is defined with regard to companies, other bodies (corporate or unincorporated) and natural persons acting in the course of their business capacity (Art. 23 Rome II), but not as regards natural persons acting in their private capacity. This accords with the flexibility of the concept: the habitual residence of a person may depend on a wide range of criteria differing in light of the individual circumstances of the case.[54] The Brussels I and IIa Regulations[55] as well as several Hague Conventions[56] pursue the same approach. The na-

---

[53] See *infra* paras. 31 et seq. for a detailed analysis of this problem.

[54] For further details see Art. 23 para. 11.

[55] Art. 60 Brussels I is equally limited to defining the habitual residence of companies, other bodies (corporate or unincorporated) and natural persons acting in the course of a business activity.

[56] See *e.g.* the Hague Convention on the Law Applicable to Traffic Accidents (4 May 1971); the Hague Convention on the Law Applicable to Maintenance Obligations (2 October 1973); the Hague Convention on the Law Applicable to Products Liability (2 October 1973); the Hague Convention on the Law Applicable to agency (14 March 1978).

tional courts are sufficiently familiar with the concept so as to apply it autonomously, taking account of the goal to apply it uniformly throughout the Member States.[57] The habitual residence is tied to the moment when the direct damage occurred, *i.e.* damage to the legally protected interest, as opposed to an indirect, consequential loss.[58]

The **place of acquisition** in lit. b is the place where the product was acquired, not necessarily purchased,[59] by the person sustaining the damage.[60] If other persons are damaged at the place of acquisition, lit. b will not apply. Rather the applicable law will then either be determined by lit. c (rather rarely) or, in the majority of cases, by Art. 5(2) (bystander-problem).[61] In case of distance sales the place of acquisition is the place of receipt of the product.[62] **25**

---

57 *Hohloch*, 9 YbPIL (2007) 1, 11 et seq. denies the need for an autonomous interpretation (apart from the constellations dealt with by Art. 23) but at the same time presents such an autonomous interpretation by referring to habitual residence as the factual centre of life activities.

58 See the Explanatory Memorandum by the Commission, COM(2003) 427 final, p. 11; concurring *von Hein*, ZEuP 2009, 6, 16; *Illmer*, 73 RabelsZ (2009) 269, 287; *Spickhoff*, in: FS Kropholler (2008) 671, 681; *Junker*, in: Münchener Kommentar BGB, Art. 5 para. 31; G. *Wagner*, IPRax 2008, 1, 7; *Hohloch*, 9 YbPIL (2007) 1, 7 seq.; *Ofner*, 49 ZRvgl (2008) 13, 16; *Heiss/Loacker*, JBl. 2007, 613, 624; *Leible/Lehmann*, RIW 2007, 721 724; *Huber/Bach*, IPRax 2005, 73, 76.

59 See *Plender & Wilderspin*, paras. 19-075 et seq.; *Dickinson*, para. 5.39 (acquisition of physical possession and control, as opposed to title); *Junker*, in: Münchener Kommentar BGB, Art. 5 para. 35.

60 *Junker*, in: Münchener Kommentar BGB, Art. 5 para. 37 (reaching that result by way of a teleological interpretation of the wording "was acquired" which could point to anyone).

61 *Illmer*, 73 RabelsZ (2009) 269, 287; *Junker*, in: Münchener Kommentar BGB, Art. 5 para. 38; *Thorn*, in: Palandt, Art. 5 paras. 9 and 13; for further details on the bystander issue see *infra* para. 44.

62 *Dickinson*, para. 5.38; *Wurmnest*, in: jurisPK BGB, Art. 5 para. 20.

26 The **place where the damage occurred** in lit. c is taken from the general rule in Art. 4.[63]

c) The Cumulative Marketing Element

27 Whereas the three connecting factors are rather designed to protect the interests of the person sustaining the damage, the **cumulative marketing requirement** aims at striking a fair balance by serving the predictability interests of the person potentially liable. In that regard it corresponds with the foreseeability defence which builts upon a marketing of the product in the country of the respective connecting factor.

28 The marketing requirement comprises of two problematic issues: the meaning of "marketing" and, in particular, the question whether the marketing relates only to the *product* or also to *products of the same type*.

aa) Marketing

29 **Marketing** of the product takes place in every country where the product is distributed, *i.e.* offered for sale and/or supply to end users.[64] While mere advertising is not regarded as marketing, advertising with a view to sales (which may in fact amount to an offer already) does amount to marketing in the respective country.[65] Distribution may take place face to face but likewise online via the internet. In the latter case the product is marketed in

---

63 For further details see Art. 4 paras. 13 et seq.

64 *Illmer*, 73 RabelsZ (2009) 269, 288 et seq.; *Plender & Wilderspin*, paras. 19-106 et seq.; *Stone*, 4 Ankara L. Rev. (2007) 95, 122; *Wurmnest*, in: jurisPK BGB, Art. 5 para. 24; *von Hein*, ZEuP 2009, 6, 26; *Leible/Lehmann*, RIW 2007, 721, 728; *Junker*, in: Münchener Kommentar BGB, Art. 5 para. 29; *Hamburg Group for Private International Law*, 67 RabelsZ (2003) 1, 16 (country of commercialisation); *Hartley*, 57 ICLQ (2008) 899, 904 requires "organized, mass selling of a standardized product" which appears to be without any basis in the wording of Art. 5 though.

65 *Dickinson*, para. 5.20; for a detailed account see *Plender & Wilderspin*, paras. 19-110 et seq.

every country where a potential buyer would be supplied with it.[66] Restrictions on distribution imposed by the manufacturer do not affect an actual marketing but become relevant when considering the foreseeability defence.[67]

The place where the product is first put into circulation by the manufacturer, *i.e.* where the product leaves the manufacturing site, is irrelevant for the purposes of Art. 5. *Marketing of the product* is therefore different from *putting into circulation* under Art. 6(1) lit. c, (2) and 7 lit. f of the Product Liability Directive,[68] although the terms used in Art. 5 Rome II and in the Product Liability Directive concur in other language versions.[69] First, the marketing element is solely product-related, not tied to the person of the producer/manufacturer. Otherwise the foreseeability defence would have no scope of application: Unforeseeability of marketing becomes only relevant in relation to distribution by persons different from the producer/manufacturer in other countries (those of lit. a to c) than the one where the product was manufactured and first put into circulation. Secondly, whereas *putting into circulation* is directed at setting the relevant point in time for assessing the acts or omissions of the person claimed to be liable as a matter of substantive law, *marketing of the product* is directed at determining the applicable law taking account of the predictability concerns of the persons involved.[70] 30

66 *Illmer*, 73 RabelsZ (2009) 269, 291.

67 For details see *infra* paras. 39 seq.

68 Council Directive 85/374/EEC of 25 July 1985 on the approximation of the laws, regulations and administrative provisions of the Members States concerning liability for defective products, OJ L 210/29 as amended by Directive 1999/34/EC of the European Parliament and of the Council of 10 May 1999 amending Council Directive 85/374/EEC on the approximation of the laws, regulations and administrative provisions of the Member States concerning liability for defective products, OJ L 141/20.

69 Cf. the German language version "Inverkehrbringen".

70 *Illmer*, 73 RabelsZ (2009) 269, 290; concurring *Dickinson*, para. 5.23; *Wurmnest*, in: jurisPK BGB, Art. 5 para. 24; *Schwartze*, NIPR 2008, 430,

bb) *Product* or also *Product of the Same Type*?

31 By its wording the marketing element in Art. 5(1)1 requires a **marketing of the product** while the foreseeability defence in Art. 5(1)2 refers not only to the *product* but also to *products of the same type*. Nevertheless, it is submitted that the marketing requirement of Art. 5(1)1 is satisfied even if not the individual product that caused the damage but **products of the same type** were marketed in the country indicated by the respective varying connecting factor of lit. a to c.[71]

32 The structure of the cascade itself presupposes this understanding. If the marketing element was only satisfied with regard to the individual product causing the damage, the three varying connecting factors would be replaced by one single connection – the place of marketing – since the individual product is by definition marketed in only one country. Under the existing cascade the place of marketing would regularly coincide with the place of acquisition under lit. b. One would, however, not even require the additional varying connecting factor of lit. b. The place of

---

431 seq.; in contrast referring to Art. 7 lit. a Product Liability Directive *Thorn*, in: Palandt, Art. 5 para. 11.

[71] For a detailed analysis see *Illmer*, 73 RabelsZ (2009) 269, 292 et seq.; furthermore *Plender & Wilderspin*, paras. 19-091 et seq.; *Junker*, in: Münchener Kommentar BGB, Art. 5 paras. 27 et seq.; *Leible/Lehmann*, RIW 2007, 721, 728 (extending it comprehensively to products of the same type); *G. Wagner*, IPRax 2008, 1, 7 (product of the same type insofar covered as it bears the same safety features as the specific product causing the damage); *Thorn*, in: Palandt, Art. 5 para. 11 (also based on the criterion of the same safety features); *Spickhoff*, in: FS Kropholler (2008) 671, 685; *Garcimartín Alferéz*, ELF 2007 I-77, 85; *Dickinson*, para. 5.21 takes an intermediate view distinguishing between the actual product including identical products but not non-identical products (criteria are such as pure markings and packaging versus modifications in a material respect); the opposite narrow view (only the actual product that caused the damage) is taken by *von Hein*, ZEuP 2009, 6, 27 et seq. and *idem*, 82 Tul.L.Rev. (2008) 1663, 1696 seq. as well as *Hartley*, 57 ICLQ (2008) 899, 904.

marketing would do. This would **seriously undermine the cascade system** and in fact reverse the structure of Art. 5(1).[72] The three varying connecting factors are the decisive elements for determining the applicable law while the marketing requirement is only an additional element with limited functions: it structures the three connecting factors as a cascade and serves as a broad filter with regard to the potentially applicable laws. This view is strongly supported by the legislative process.[73] The proposals of the Commission provided for only one connecting factor (the injured party's habitual residence) and a foreseeability defence.[74] The Council's Common Position extended the one to three connecting factors while keeping the foreseeability defence and it laid down the marketing requirement expressly to enable the cascade structure (in the Commission's proposals it was implied since lack of consent to marketing requires actual marketing).[75]

A limitation to the individual product would, however, not only undermine the cascade structure. It would also **interfere with the foreseeability defence** as the decisive instrument for the protection of the legitimate predictability interests of the person claimed to be liable. The foreseeability defence builds upon the marketing requirement: the term "not reasonably foreseeable" refers to the object of marketing of the cascade connections. Consequently, the defence that marketing of products of the same type was not reasonably foreseeable could hardly ever be invoked 33

72 *Illmer*, 73 RabelsZ (2009) 269, 292 seq.; concurring explicitly *Plender & Wilderspin*, para. 19-095; *Wurmnest*, in: jurisPK BGB, Art. 5 para. 25; it is a completely different matter whether the place of marketing would have been the better connecting factor as several authors put forward, see *Kadner Graziano*, Europäisches Internationales Deliktsrecht, 2003, 74 et seq.; G. *Wagner*, IPRax 2008, 1, 6; *von Hein*, ZEuP 2009, 6, 28.

73 For a detailed analysis see *Illmer*, 73 RabelsZ (2009) 269, 288 et seq.

74 See Art. 4 of the initial proposal (COM(2003) 427 final) and Art. 6 of the amended proposal (COM(2006) 83 final).

75 See Art. 5 of the Common Position (EC) No 22/2006 of 25 September 2006, OJ 2006 C 289E/68.

if the marketing element of Art. 5(1)1 required marketing of the individual product causing the damage.[76] This systematic link strongly supports an alignment of the two marketing-related mechanisms of Art. 5. Furthermore, the marketing requirement of Art. 5(1)1 would establish a level of protection to the person claimed to be liable that the foreseeability defence would not provide. First, it operates only as a defence. Secondly, the person claimed to be liable may not circumvent the application of a specific law by simply arguing that marketing of the individual product was not reasonably foreseeable for him as long as marketing of products of the same type was foreseeable.[77]

34 The decisive criterion to distinguish products of the *same* type from products of a *different* type is the **identity of the safety features**.[78] These are features, such as material, construction or instruction, which are relevant for incurring liability for damage caused by a defective product as opposed to those features, such as name, style, colour or appearance, bearing no relevance for the safety of the product. However, not any difference in the safety features suffices to establish different types of products. Rather, the issue must be viewed **case-specific**: Different types of products require different safety features in relation to the specific damage to person or property.[79] To illustrate, different locations of the tank of a car do not render the cars different types of products in relation to damage caused by the identical gas pedal constructions.[80] The criterion of safety features enables product diversifi-

---

76 *Plender & Wilderspin*, para. 19-092 even argue that the forseeability defence would be redundant.

77 As regards the potential precautionary measures see *infra* paras. 38 et seq.

78 Concurring: *Huber/Illmer*, 9 YbPIL (2007) 31, 43; G. *Wagner*, IPRax 2008, 1, 7; *Wurmnest*, in: jurisPK BGB, Art. 5 para. 26; *Thorn*, in: Palandt, Art. 5 para. 11; *Junker*, in: Münchener Kommentar BGB, Art. 5 para. 28; *Dickinson*, para. 5.35 lists (although with regard to the foreseeability defence) five factors for "substantial identity" (as this is his standard for products of the same type).

79 *Wurmnest*, in: jurisPK BGB, Art. 5 para. 26.

cation between different countries within an existing product range. The person claimed to be liable has to adapt only the safety features to the respective countries of marketing while he does not have to diversify his range of product types with regard to other features. He may, *e.g.*, distribute the same kettle in different countries merely using different fuses and materials while not changing the general design of the kettle, or distribute the same baby stroller model simply using different wheels and a different brake handle.

Whether the **price-risk interrelation** calls for a shift towards the interests of the person potentially liable by limiting the object of marketing to the actual product that caused the damage, is a matter *de lege ferenda*. It relates to the idea that the person claimed to be liable may want to adopt a variable pricing policy that reflects the different liability risk in the respective countries of marketing which may rest on other aspects than the safety standards, in particular heads of damages, presumptions and the quantum of damage awards.[81] The person sustaining the damage should not be put into a position where he paid a price for the product reflecting a low standard of product liability in one country but then obtains a damage award reflecting the much higher standard of product liability of the country indicated by the varying connecting factor which he could usually only obtain by paying a significantly higher price.[82] Whether such price diversification takes place 35

80 On the level of the conflict rule this does not, however, require a detailed causation test (which is a matter of substantive law). Rather, only cases where obviously no connection between the feature in question and the damage exists are caught: The person claimed to be liable must not point at any different safety feature if it obviously bears no relevance for the damage that occurred.

81 Pursuant to Art. 15 lit. a, b, c and Art. 22 Rome II these aspects are all governed by the applicable law as determined by Art. 5 Rome II.

82 *Wandt*, Internationale Produkthaftung (1995) para. 1063; *Sonnentag*, 105 ZVglRWiss. (2006) 256, 282; *Kadner Graziano*, 54 ICLQ (2005) 475, 481; *von Hein*, VersR 2007, 440, 447 seq.; G. *Wagner*, IPRax 2006, 372, 382.

and would work, is, however, questionable. First, as far as the manufacturer or importer is concerned, it will rather be their aim to avoid liability in the first place either by adjusting the safety features of the product to the respective product liability standard instead of charging higher prices for the potential risk of product liability or by taking precautionary measures rendering marketing in specific countries *ab initio* not reasonably foreseeable so that he can invoke Art. 5(1)2.[83] Secondly, the manufacturer as the person primarily liable in tort/delict (for lack of a contractual relationship with the injured party) will regularly not be the person that markets the product. His influence on pricing policies eventually taken vis-à-vis the end users of the product is therefore limited.

cc) Lack of Marketing

36 In case of a **lack of marketing** of the product or products of the same type in one of the countries indicated by the varying connecting factors of lit. a to c, the law of the country of the habitual residence of the person claimed to be liable applies by way of an analogous application of Art. 5(1)2.[84] The law designated in case of unforeseeability of marketing, has to apply *a maiore ad minus* if the product or products of the same type were not marketed in one of the countries indicated by the connecting factors of Art. 5(1)1(a) to (c) at all. In particular, one must not revert to the general rule of Art. 4[85] as Art. 5(1)1(c) indicates that the law of

---

83 For details see *infra* paras. 38 et seq.

84 *Illmer*, 73 RabelsZ (2009) 269, 296 seq.; G. *Wagner*, IPRax 2008, 1, 7; *Schwartze*, NIPR 2008, 430, 433; *de Lima Pinheiro*, Riv. dir. int. priv. proc. 2008, 5, 23; *Wurmnest*, in: jurisPK BGB, Art. 5 para. 31; *Leible/Lehmann*, RIW 2007, 721, 728; *Junker*, in: Münchener Kommentar BGB, Art. 5 para. 48; *Thorn*, in: Palandt, Art. 5 para. 11; *von Hein*, ZEuP 2009, 6, 28; *Garcimartín Alferéz*, EuLF 2007, I-77, 85; *Plender & Wilderspin*, para. 19-052.

85 This approach is, however, favoured by *Hartley*, 57 ICLQ (2008) 899, 905 and by *Spickhoff*, in: FS Kropholler (2008) 671, 686 seq. (but he is pre-

the country where the damage occurred shall not apply if the product was not marketed there.

4. Foreseeability Defence

The interests of the person claimed to be liable are mainly served by way of a defence: if marketing of the product or products of the same type in the country indicated by one of the cascade connections of Art. 5(1)1 was not reasonably foreseeable for the person claimed to be liable, the law of the country of his habitual residence shall apply pursuant to Art. 5(1)2. As a consequence of the understanding of the cascade's marketing element,[86] the foreseeability defence plays the **central role in the attempts of the person claimed to be liable to limit the number of applicable laws**. 37

Marketing is not reasonably foreseeable worldwide simply because of globalised trade and distribution of products via the internet.[87] Otherwise, the foreseeability defence would be a farce, in effect amounting to an irrebuttable presumption of foreseeability. Rather, foreseeability depends mainly on the **precautionary measures** taken by the person claimed to be liable in order to avoid marketing of the product or products of the same type in specific countries.[88] In that regard, one should distinguish between absolute and relative precautionary measures. 38

Absolute precautionary measures are physically tied to the product (and products of the same type!), *i.e.*, restrictions of distribution are set out on the product itself. As such they last for the life of the product. Examples are: "For sale in the UK only", "Not 39

---

pared to take the rationale of Art. 5(1)2 into account via the escape clause of Art. 4(3)).

86 See *supra* paras. 27 et seq.

87 *Illmer*, 73 RabelsZ (2009) 269, 298 seq.; *Thorn*, in: Palandt, Art. 5 para. 11; but this view is staken by *Kadner Graziano*, 73 RabelsZ (2009) 1, 43.

88 One should, however, note that such restrictions of distribution may, within the EU, be incompatible with EU antitrust law.

for sale in the US and Canada" or "For use in Germany only". The use of absolute precautionary measures may be a way to establish unforeseeability *a priori*. Distributors and buyers of the product are aware of the restriction. If they act in breach of it, they do so at their own risk with regard to the applicable law.

40 **Relative precautionary measures** are only legally tied to the product, regularly by way of contractual provisions imposing territorial restrictions with regard to distribution. As such, they are only binding for the contracting parties but not for subsequent traders or users in the distribution chain unless the restrictions are passed on along the chain of distribution.[89] Nevertheless, contractual restrictions will usually satisfy the foreseeability defence, at least if they are supplemented by a duty of the other party to pass on those restrictions in case of further distribution prior to supply to the end user. Apart from exceptional circumstances or specific indications to the contrary, it is not reasonably foreseeable that distributors will market the product in breach of an explicit territorial restriction.

41 Irrespective of such precautionary measures, foreseeability is a matter of the **individual circumstances of each case**. If the product is suitable for use in specific countries only (in particular owed to industry standards or technical specifications), neither the manufacturer nor distributors usually have to anticipate distribution into other countries. If in contrast, a product is supplied into a free trade area (such as EFTA, NAFTA, Mercosur, COMESA, GAFTA or the EU), this may require additional measures to establish that distribution amongst its Member States was not reasonably foreseeable.

---

89 This will usually be done by contractual provisions imposing a duty on the buyer of the product to impose the same territorial restrictions on subsequent buyers of the product.

5. Escape Clause

The escape clause in Art. 5(2) is identical to the one in Art. 4(3) and could also have been incorporated by way of reference. It is the necessary correlative to the rigid connections of Art. 5(1) and prevails over any of them. A choice of law pursuant to Art. 14 prevails, however, even over Art. 5(2). 42

The most important field of application, a **pre-existing contractual relationship**, is explicitly mentioned. This relates in particular to the relationship between the seller or lessor as the person claimed to be liable and the purchaser or lessee as the person sustaining damage: Contractual and non-contractual claims will be governed by one single law. It is disputed whether this also applies to guarantees given by manufacturers to purchasers or lessees of the product to whom they have not themselves sold or leased the product. Since the guarantee is usually given only in relation to the proper functioning of the product as such, as opposed to damage caused to person or property, it may be argued that a guarantee does not establish a closer connection that would justify application of the escape clause of Art. 5(2).[90] 43

Another major field of application, specifically with regard to product liability, are **bystanders**. Bystanders are third parties having no pre-existing relation to the product causing the damage. They neither acquired nor used it. The damage strikes them unexpectedly. From the perspective of such a bystander the tort/delict will usually have a manifestly closer connection to the law of the country where the damage occurred than to the laws applicable under the cascade connections (lit. c also points to this country but requires marketing there).[91] 44

---

90 *Wurmnest*, in: jurisPK BGB, Art. 5 para. 34; *Thorn*, in: Palandt, Art. 5 para. 12; an application of Art. 5(2) even to guarantees is considered by *Schaub*, in: Prütting/Wegen/Weinreich, Art. 5 para. 8.

91 *Hamburg Group for Private International Law*, 67 RabelsZ (2003) 1, 18; *von Hein*, ZEuP 2009, 6, 29; *Leible/Lehmann*, RIW 2007, 721, 728 (although

D. Burden of Proof

45 As regards the **facts underlying the connections of Art. 5(1)1**, the burden of proof (and disproof if he wants to plead the application of a law on a lower step on the ladder of connections) lies with the person sustaining the damage.[92] Since he will usually be the plaintiff, this accords with the general rule on the burden of proof under most national laws. It should, however, apply even in case of a negative declaratory action by the person claimed to be liable. The burden of proof is regarded as a matter of substantive law by Rome II (cf. Art. 22) so that the burden of proof should not shift depending on the procedural scenario.

46 As regards **foreseeability under the defence of Art. 5(1)2** the burden of proof lies with the person claimed to be liable.

47 As regards the **escape clause of Art. 5(2)** the burden of proof lies with the party claiming a manifestly closer connection.

E. Jurisdiction Issues

48 The connections of Art. 5 Rome II are **not systematically coordinated** with the jurisdiction rules of the Brussels I Regulation, particularly Art. 5 No. 3 Brussels I as the practically most rele-

---

they note that this requires an extensive interpretation of the escape clause); *Huber/Bach*, IPRax 2005, 73, 77; *Spickhoff*, in: FS Kropholler (2008), 671, 689; *Thorn*, in: Palandt, Art. 5 para. 13; similar *Wurmnest*, in: jurisPK BGB, Art. 5 para. 35.

92 *Illmer*, 73 RabelsZ (2009) 269, 303; *Spickhoff*, in: FS Kropholler (2008) 671, 682; critical with regard to the aspect of disproof *Dickinson*, para. 5.28 (however, it appears to be no undue burden to disprove the application of any prior sub-rule; furthermore, otherwise, the cascade would be turned into a set of three alternative connections from which the person sustainting the damage could chose).

vant jurisdiction for claims in tort/delict. The criterion of Art. 5 No. 3 Brussels I, *i.e.* the place where the harmful event occurred, refers to the place where the damage occurred as well as to the place where the event giving rise to the damage took place,[93] so that it matches only with the criterion of Art. 5(1)1(c). The complex cascade structure aiming to strike a fair balance between the interests involved ties into other (and too many) directions compared to the straight-forward single connection as regards jurisdiction. The latter is mainly concerned with proximity of the forum to the place of the harmful event. In practice, there is nevertheless regularly congruence in the most common case of a purchase abroad with a resulting injury back home: the injured party can sue under Art. 5 No. 3 Brussels I at his habitual residence as the place where the damage occurred and Art. 5(1)1 lit. a Rome II results in the application of the *lex fori*.[94]

In ***b2b*** *relationships* the parties may of course provide for synchronisation of jurisdiction and applicable law. In case of a pre-existing contractual relationship they are free to agree on a combined jurisdiction and choice of law clause pursuant to Art. 23 Brussels I and Art. 14(1)(b) Rome II (subject to Art. 14(2), (3), 16 Rome II). If such an *ex ante* choice is missing, they are free to agree on an *ex post* choice either by jurisdiction agreement or submission to the jurisdiction according to Art. 24 Brussels I combined with a choice of law pursuant to Art. 14(1)(a) Rome II (again subject to Art. 14(2), (3), 16 Rome II). 49

In ***b2c*** *relationships* several restrictions concerning jurisdiction agreements (Art. 23(5) in connection with 13(1), 17(1) and 21 50

---

93 See in particular ECJ, Case 21/76 – *Mines de Potasse d'Alsace* [1976] ECR 1735 paras. 19 et seq.; Case C-68/93 – *Shevill* [1995] ECR I-415 para. 20; Case C-167/00 – *Verein für Konsumenteninformation* [2002] ECR I-8111 paras. 42 et seq.; Case C-168/02 – *Kronhofer* [2004] ECR I-6009 para. 16.

94 G. *Wagner*, IPRax 2008, 1, 7; *Junker*, in: Münchener Kommentar BGB, Art. 5 para. 33; *Plender & Wilderspin*, para. 19-062.

(1) Brussels I) and choice of law (not ex ante under Art. 14(1)(b) Rome II) apply, but a submission to the jurisdiction under Art. 24 Brussels I combined with a choice of law pursuant to Art. 14(1)(a) Rome II might work.

Article 6
Unfair competition and acts restricting free competition

1. The law applicable to a non-contractual obligation arising out of an act of unfair competition shall be the law of the country where competitive relations or the collective interests of consumers are, or are likely to be, affected.
2. Where an act of unfair competition affects exclusively the interests of a specific competitor, Article 4 shall apply.
3. (a) The law applicable to a non-contractual obligation arising out of a restriction of competition shall be the law of the country where the market is, or is likely to be, affected.
   (b) When the market is, or is likely to be, affected in more than one country, the person seeking compensation for damage who sues in the court of the domicile of the defendant, may instead choose to base his or her claim on the law of the court seised, provided that the market in that Member State is amongst those directly and substantially affected by the restriction of competition out of which the non-contractual obligation on which the claim is based arises; where the claimant sues, in accordance with the applicable rules on jurisdiction, more than one defendant in that court, he or she can only choose to base his or her claim on the law of that court if the restriction of competition on which the claim against each of these defendants relies directly and substantially affects also the market in the Member State of that court.
4. The law applicable under this Article may not be derogated from by an agreement pursuant to Article 14.

A. Overview

1 Art. 6 covers **two distinct areas of law** which are closely related but do not necessarily overlap: **unfair competition and acts restricting free competition**. While the Commission's initial proposal concerned only unfair competition,[1] the Council added a rule on acts restricting free competition.[2] As a result, Art. 6 provides for conflict rules on unfair competition in Art. 6(1) and (2) and on acts restricting free competition in Art. 6(3).[3] With regard to both of them, a choice of law is excluded by Art. 6(4); whether this exclusion applies to Art. 6(2) is, however, contested.[4]

---

1 See Art. 5 of the initial proposal (COM(2003) 427 final), likewise Art. 7 of the amended proposal (COM(2006) 83 final).

2 See the Common Position (EC) No 22/2006 of 25 September 2006, OJ 2006 C 289E/68; for further details on the background of Art. 6(3) see *infra* paras. 62 et seq.

3 For a comprehensive account of the legislative history of both conflict rules see *Plender & Wilderspin*, paras. 20-001 et seq.; *Dickinson*, paras. 6-01 et seq.

4 For details see *infra* para. 54.

B. Unfair Competition

I. Structure and Relationship between Art. 6(1) and 6(2)

2 The conflict rule in Art. 6 distinguishes **two different types of acts of unfair competition**: market-related and competitor-related acts.[5] If the act affects the public, *i.e.* competitors and consumers at large (market-related act), Art. 6(1) provides for the law of the country where the interests protected by the law of unfair competition (competitive relations, collective interests of consumers and the proper functioning of the market as such) are affected. In contrast, if the act affects exclusively the interests of a specific competitor (competitor-related act; such as acts of sabotage or espionage, disclosure of a competitor's business/trade secrets[6] and enticing away a competitor's staff), Art. 6(2) refers to the general rule of Art. 4. In the latter case, there is no difference compared to usual torts/delicts towards another person which would justify a deviation from the general rule.[7]

3 The **relationship between the two connections** is one of rule (Art. 6(1)) and exception (Art. 6(2)). Accordingly, Art. 6(2) must be interpreted narrowly. It applies only if the act has (objectively[8]) no direct effect on further competitors, consumers or the market public (indirect repercussions on the market are irrele-

---

5 For a detailed account of the legislative history of the conflict rule on unfair competition see *Mankowski*, in: Münchener Kommentar Lauterkeitsrecht, IntWettbR paras. 19 et seq.

6 For the relationship with Art. 8 in that regard see Art. 8 para. 10 and *Wadlow*, EIPR 2008, 309, 310.

7 *Leistner*, in: Basedow/Drexl/Kur/Metzger (eds.), Intellectual Property in the Conflict of Laws (2005) 129, 137; *Lindacher*, GRUR Int 2008, 453, 457; *Mankowski*, in: Münchener Kommentar Lauterkeitsrecht, Int WettbR para. 243.

8 A subjective approach as initially suggested by the Commission (see Explanatory Report to the initial proposal COM(2003) 427 final, p. 16: "… where an act of unfair competition targets a specific competitor") is

3

vant[9]), *i.e.* if the act is limited (again objectively) to directly damaging a specific competitor.[10] As soon as there is a direct effect on the market, even only a slight one, which goes beyond indirect repercussions, Art. 6(1) applies. Consequently, Art. 6(2) does not apply to acts that are targeted at a specific competitor but operate via consumers or other competitors, *e.g.* requests for boycotts, unjustified requests towards customers to refrain from purchasing or distributing goods or services of a specific competitor and other forms of denigration of specific competitors on the market.[11] The **distinguishing criterion** is not the (subjective) target but the (objective) effect. In that respect the rule is *in dubio pro* Art. 6(1). The scope of Art. 6(2) is thus limited. In the case of uncertainty even under the (objective) effect-based approach one may pursue the matter from the other end, *i.e.* from the respective connections that would apply. The crucial question then is whether the application of Art. 4(2) and (3) appears to be justified; since Art. 6(1) is, according to Recital 21, only a clarification of the general rule in Art. 4(1) and since Art. 6(2) invokes Art. 4 as a whole, the real difference between Art. 6(1) and 6(2) is the applicability of Art. 4(2) and (3).

---

rightly rejected by *Dickinson*, para. 6.29; *Plender & Wilderspin*, para. 20-035.

9 *Sack*, WRP 2008, 845, 850; *Leistner*, in: Basedow/Drexl/Kur/Metzger (eds.), Intellectual Property in the Conflict of Laws (2005) 129, 149; *Hellner*, 9 YbPIL (2007) 49, 56.

10 Similar *Dickinson*, para. 6.28; *Köhler*, in: Köhler/Bornkamm, Einl. UWG, para. 5.44; *Leistner*, in: Basedow/Drexl/Kur/Metzger (eds.), Intellectual Property in the Conflict of Laws (2005) 129, 149; *Wurmnest*, in: jurisPK BGB, Art. 6 para. 24; Bundesgerichtshof (Germany), 11 February 2010, I ZR 85/08, para. 19 (not yet published); for a detailed analysis of the rationale and scope of Art. 6(2) see *Lindacher*, GRUR Int. 2008, 453, 457 et seq.; for examples under English law see *Dickinson*, para. 6.30; for examples under German law see *Sack*, WRP 2008, 845, 851.

11 *Sack*, WRP 2008, 845, 851.

II. Scope

1. Material Scope

a) Acts of Unfair Competition

The concept of "acts of unfair competition" which is not defined by Art. 6 Rome II requires an **autonomous interpretation**[12] as it defines the material scope of a uniform European conflict rule. However, since this uniform conflict rule operates against the background of and in relation to substantially different national laws of unfair competition,[13] the autonomous interpretation has to take the national laws' concepts and scope into account.[14] This 4

---

12 *Köhler*, in: Köhler/Bornkamm, Einl. UWG, para. 5.31; *Wurmnest*, in: jurisPK BGB, Art. 6 para. 5; *Glöckner*, in: Harte/Henning, Einl. C, para. 89; *Dickinson*, para. 6.17; *Handig*, GRUR Int 2008, 24, 26; *Sack*, WRP 2008, 845, 846; *Mankowski*, in: Münchener Kommentar Lauterkeitsrecht, IntWettbR para. 11; *Dicey, Morris & Collins*, para. S 35-215; *Mankowski*, GRUR Int. 2005, 634, 635; *Schaub*, in: Prütting/Wegen/Weinreich, Art. 6 Rom II para. 2; *Plender & Wilderspin*, paras. 20-011 et seq. point out rightly that despite an autonomous interpretation the ECJ will look at the national laws.

13 The national laws range from no general tort of unfair competition in England (see lately *L'Oreal SA v Bellure NV* [2007] EWCA Civ 968 at paras. 135 et seq.; instead protection by single torts such as passing off, inducing breach of contract, interference with contractual relations, breach of confidence, slander, libel, defamation; for a discussion of characterisation issues see *Fitchen*, 5 J. Priv. Int. L. (2009) 337, 348 et seq.) to an application of the general law of torts in France (case law evolving around Art. 1382, 1383 Code civil) to a specific tort of unfair competition in Germany (Gesetz gegen den unlauteren Wettbewerb [UWG], particularly Art. 3 with the very wide general tort of unfair competition and Art. 4 providing for the most common instances); for more detailed accounts of foreign substantive laws of unfair competition see *Köhler*, in: Köhler/Bornkamm, UWG, Einl. UWG, ch. 4; briefly in relation to various EU Member States also *Plender & Wilderspin*, paras. 20-011 et seq.

14 *Plender & Wilderspin*, para. 20-011.

implies a wide and flexible understanding which is supported by Recital 21 Rome II. The recital emphasises the manifold interests protected by unfair competition law and highlights their broad unifying goal to ensure "that the market economy functions properly".

aa) *Prima Facie* Acts of Unfair Competition

5 Striving for consistency in Community law, rather clear instances of unfair competition are provided by related **European secondary legislation** concerning the harmonisation of the national substantive laws of unfair competition, in particular the Unfair Commercial Practices Directive[15] and the Directive on Misleading and Comparative Advertising.[16] Although the material scope of Rome II's uniform conflict rule reaches further than the scope of the Directives, it should at least cover those acts that are regarded as unfair competitive behaviour by those Directives as European legislation pursuing the same interests as the conflict rule.[17] They are, however, only *prima facie* instances of unfair competition providing a starting point which is neither exhaustive nor restrictive for the purposes of Art. 6 Rome II.[18]

6 Bearing this in mind, unfair practices as defined by Art. 5(2) to 5 (5) in connection with Art. 6 to 9 and Annex 1 of the Unfair Commercial Practices Directive as well as unlawful advertising under the Directive on Misleading and Comparative Advertising are *prima facie* acts of unfair competition under Art. 6 Rome II.[19]

15 Directive (EC) No 2005/29, OJ 2005 L 149/22.

16 Directive (EC) No 2006/114, OJ 2006 L 376/21.

17 *Honorati*, in: Malatesta (ed), The Unification of Choice of Law Rules on Torts and Other Non-Contractual Obligations in Europe (2006) 127, 142 concurs and even suggests that "[t]he … Directive [Dir. 2005/29] helps to overcome such a situation by providing first of all a European and binding definition of what it is intended to be covered by 'unfair competition'".

18 Concurring: *Plender & Wilderspin*, para. 20-027.

19 Concurring: *Dickinson*, para. 6.23; *Köhler*, in: Köhler/Bornkamm, Einl. UWG, para. 5.31.

As already explained, even though the Directives' terms and definitions have to be interpreted autonomously for the purposes of the Directives, national implementations and their application by the national courts should be taken into account for the purposes of Art. 6 Rome II.

The fact that the term "unfair commercial practices" was considered[20] but rejected[21] during the legislative process of Rome II does not prejudice a reference to the Unfair Commercial Practices Directive.[22] The term was likely rejected against the background that Art. 2(d) of the Unfair Commercial Practices Directive defines it specifically with regard to *b2c* relationships (reflecting the personal scope of the Directive) while Art. 6 Rome II contains no such restriction. 7

bb) Definition and Criteria

A clear-cut, abstract definition of the term "unfair competition" appears to be unrealistic as many attempts in the past have shown.[23] However, one may define a frame by establishing a set of criteria for acts of unfair competition to characterise potential instances under the national laws of unfair competition for the purposes of Art. 6 Rome II. 8

Inspiration may be sought in the Commission's Explanatory Memorandum,[24] Art. 10bis of the 1883 Paris Convention for the Protection of Intellectual Property[25] to which all Member States are parties, Art. 1 of the Conflict-of-Laws Rules on Unfair Competition by the Institut de Droit International (Cambridge Ses- 9

20 See Art. 7 of the amended proposal (COM(2006) 83).

21 See Art. 6 of Common Position (EC) No 22/2006 of the Council.

22 More hesitant *Plender & Wilderspin*, para. 20-025.

23 Concurring *Plender & Wilderspin*, para. 20-031; *Mankowski*, GRUR Int. 2005, 634, 635; *Glöckner*, in: Harte/Henning, Einl. C, para. 87.

24 See COM(2003) 427 final, p. 17.

25 Art. 10bis itself does not constitute a conflict rule which would prevail over Art. 6 Rome II according to Art. 28(1) Rome II.

sion 1983)[26] and Art. 1 to 6 of the WIPO Model Provisions on Protection against Unfair Competition.[27] The Explanatory Memorandum refers to "acts calculated to influence demand (misleading advertising, forced sales, etc.), acts that impede competing supplies (disruption of deliveries by competitors, enticing away a competitor's staff, boycotts), and acts that exploit a competitor's value (passing off and the like)" as well as industrial espionage, disclosure of business/trade secrets and inducing breach of contract. This encompasses market-related as well as competitor-related acts. According to Art. 10bis(2) of the Paris Convention "[a]ny act of competition contrary to honest practices in industrial or commercial matters constitutes an act of unfair competition." This abstract definition is illustrated by examples in Art. 10bis(3) such as acts creating confusion and acts containing false, discrediting allegations as to the establishment, the goods, or the industrial or commercial activities, of a competitor as well as indications or allegations misleading the public as to the nature, the manufacturing process, the characteristics, the suitability for their purpose, or the quantity, of the goods offered. Art. 1 of the WIPO Model Provisions contains a definition very similar to the one laid down in Art. 10bis(2) of the Paris Convention and Art. 2 to 6 of the WIPO Model Provisions classify acts of unfair competition in a similar fashion as Art. 10bis(3). Art. 1 of the Conflict-of-Laws Rules on Unfair Competition by the Institut de Droit International (Cambridge Session 1983) refers explicitly to the definition in Art. 10bis(2) of the Paris Convention but it adds further examples such as unfair price competition (in this area there may be overlap with antitrust[28]) and defamation or disparagement of a competitor in relation to his products or business.

---

26 Concurring *Hellner*, 9 YbPIL (2007) 49, 68; *Dicey, Morris & Collins*, para. S 35-215.

27 WIPO Publication No. 832(E) of 1996.

28 For a solution regarding such overlap constellations see *infra* paras. 22 et seq.

Drawing from these international sources and the national concepts one may define an act of unfair competition in a rather abstract fashion as *an act in the competitive context contrary to honest and fair business practice*. With regard to market-related acts one may add: *interfering with the competitive interests of competitors or the collective interests of consumers*. In relation to competitor-related acts one may add: *interfering exclusively with the competitive interests of a specific competitor*. Far more telling than this abstract definition are the illustrations and the key elements indicated by the illustrations: the competitive context of the act, its dishonest and/or misrepresenting nature, the direction of the act vis-à-vis competitors, consumers or the public at large and its detrimental effect on a competition on the merits. 10

b) Defamation

Defamation and related acts in the business context are covered by Art. 6 even though Art. 1(2)(g) Rome II excludes "violations of privacy and rights relating to personality, including defamation" from the Regulation's material scope.[29] Taking account of the legislative history, the exclusion mainly concerns violations of privacy and personality rights in the media context, the yellow press in particular.[30] This *ratio legis* as well as the wording of lit. g indicate that defamation is not excluded as such from the material scope of Rome II but only to the extent that it serves as a cause of action in relation to violations of privacy and personality rights. In the business context, defamation does not vindicate those rights. Rather, it protects rights in relation to a business, *i.e.* products, trademarks, services or the reputation of an enterprise. Since such business rights are *rationae materiae* not covered by the exclusion in lit. g, this exclusion likewise does not cover 11

---

29 Cf. Art. 1 paras. 53 et seq.; concurring: *Cheshire, North & Fawcett*, p. 785 and 809; *Dicey, Morris & Collins*, para. S 35-215 and 219; *Glöckner*, in: Harte/Henning, Einl. C, para. 83 seq.; *Wurmnest*, in: jurisPK BGB, Art. 6 para. 6.

30 See the Explanatory Report by the Commission to its initial proposal COM(2003) 427 final, p. 17 seq.

defamation in relation to those rights. Thus, Art. 6 covers actions such as defamation and malicious falsehood in the business context under English law, *Verleumdung* or *Anschwärzung* according to §§ 4 No. 7, 8, 10 of the German *Gesetz gegen den unlauteren Wettbewerb* (UWG) and the like acts under other national laws.

c) Criminal Law Provisions

12 Under several national unfair competition laws issues such as disclosure of business/trade secrets and breach of confidence are not only acts of unfair competititon sanctioned by private law remedies. In addition, they are criminal offences; the respective provisions are part of the national **criminal law**. Despite an autonomous interpretation of the material scope of Art. 6 Rome II the criminal law provisions are not covered by it.[31] Whether they apply, is a matter of the national conflict rules of criminal law. By its very nature and the empowering provisions of the EC Treaty (Art. 61, 65 in particular which is now Art. 81 TFEU), the Rome II Regulation concerns only private law.

d) Relationship with Other Provisions of the Regulation

aa) Relationship between Art. 6(1) and Art. 4

13 Since Art. 6(2) refers to Art. 4, a conflict may only arise as between Art. 6(1) and Art. 4. If the act in question is only interfering with the protected interests of Art. 6(1), it is exclusively governed by the law determined by Art. 6(1); if the act is lawful under this law, it may not be rendered unlawful by the law that would be applicable under Art. 4. Art. 6(1) prevails as a *lex specialis*.[32] If the act interferes with the protected interests under Art. 6(1) but at the same time violates interests not protected by Art. 6 but by Art. 4, such as real property or the right to the name, Art. 6 and Art. 4 will apply respectively; most of these

---

31 *Köhler*, in: Köhler/Bornkamm, Einl. UWG, para. 5.30; *Handig*, GRUR Int 2008, 24, 25; *Hausmann/Obergfell*, in: Fezer, Einleitung I, para. 42.

32 *Drexl*, in: Münchener Kommentar BGB, IntUnlWettbR para. 119.

cases will, however, be competitor-related acts under Art. 6(2), so that qualification is less relevant.

bb) Relationship between Art. 6(1) and Art. 8

Although the law of unfair competition and that of intellectual property are despite their common roots by now distinct areas of law, there are links and borderline cases which present difficulties in allocating the claim in question to the respective conflict rule of Rome II. 14

(1) General

If an act of unfair competition amounts to the infringement of an intellectual property right, *e.g.* the infringement of a trademark by comparative advertising, none of the two conflict rules in Art. 6(1) and 8 prevails in that it would govern all aspects of the case.[33] Which conflict rule applies, will rather depend on the **basis of the claim** chosen by the plaintiff.[34] If he bases his claim on the infringement of the intellectual property right, the law determined by Art. 8 will govern the claim. If, however, he bases his claim on the unfair comparative advertising or other act of unfair competition, the law determined by Art. 6(1) will govern the claim (including the issue whether the existence of an IP right bars a claim based on unfair competition). The law determined by Art. 6 or 8 is limited to the respective claim. 15

Despite this guidance for distinguishing the scope of the two conflict rules, the distinction is in practice regularly irrelevant since 16

---

33 Concurring *Drexl*, in: Münchener Kommentar BGB, IntUnlWettbR para. 128; *Sack*, WRP 2008, 845, 859; but see in contrast: *Thorn*, in: Palandt, Art. 6 para. 4; *Grünberger*, 108 ZVglRWiss (2009) 134, 142; *Dickinson*, para. 6.34.; *Wurmnest*, in: jurisPK BGB, Art. 6 para. 9 who regards Art. 8 as *lex specialis* if the act of unfair competition infringes an intellectual property right.

34 *Sack*, WRP 2008, 845, 859.

in the majority of cases Art. 6 and 8 will determine the same law to govern both unfair competition and intellectual property rights.[35]

(2) Supplementary Protection under Unfair Competition Law

17 If a technical innovation, idea or other achievement by the plaintiff lacks protection under an intellectual property right but appears to be worthy of protection against exploitation and blatant acts of copying by the defendant, these **gaps in the system of intellectual property rights** are in many national laws filled by the law of unfair competition.[36] The claim then does not attach to the infringement of an intellectual property right but to the unfair act by the defendant. It is therefore to be qualified as an action arising out of an act of unfair competition. The applicable law is not determined by Art. 8 but by Art. 6(1).[37] As a plaintiff, a party has two options. If he believes in the existence of the intellectual property right, he may first plead its infringement and only failing that rely on unfair competition law. In that case, Art. 8 will determine the law applicable to the existence and infringement of the intellectual property right, while Art. 6(1) would determine the law applicable to the action based on unfair competition law.[38] Alternatively, if the plaintiff acknowledges the lack of protection by an intellectual property right, he may rather base his claim on unfair competition only. In that case, Art. 6(1) will determine the law applicable to the main action,

---

35 Concurring *Plender & Wilderspin*, para. 22-021.

36 For instance, under German law, this is referred to as "ergänzender wettbewerbsrechtlicher Leistungsschutz", codified under § 4 No. 9 UWG.

37 *Sack*, WRP 2008, 845, 859; *Rosenkranz/Rohde*, NIPR 2008, 435, 437; *Grünberger*, 108 ZVglRWiss (2009) 134, 141 seq.; *Wurmnest*, in: jurisPK BGB, Art. 6 para. 9; *Drexl*, in: Münchener Kommentar BGB, IntUnl WettbR para. 122; *Heinze*, Einstweiliger Rechtsschutz im europäischen Immaterialgüterrecht (2007) 30.

38 *Sack*, WRP 2008, 845, 859.

while Art. 8 would only govern the preliminary question of the existence of an intellectual property right.[39]

Since applicability, scope and conditions of the supplementary protection under unfair competition law are intertwined with the law of intellectual property under most national laws and since the availability of specific remedies and/or the assessment of damages is equally dependant on the intellectual property infringement proceedings (in particular to avoid double recovery), it would be best to apply the same law to both claims. In practice, this goal is regularly achieved despite the application of two different conflict rules (Art. 6(1) and Art. 8). The overlap situation presupposes that the infringement of the alleged intellectual property right occurs in the country whose market is affected by the (infringing) act of unfair competition so that both Art. 6(1) and Art. 8 will point at the law of the (national) market for which intellectual property protection is claimed. **18**

(3) Geographical Indications and Designations of Origin

On the one hand, **geographical indications and designations of origin** such as those protected by Regulation 510/2006 are regarded as intellectual property rights by Art. 1(2) in conjunction with Art. 22 et seq. TRIPS as well as Art. 2(1)(c)(iv) of the EC Product Piracy Regulation.[40] Furthermore, according to Art. 1 of the EC Enforcement Directive,[41] intellectual property rights include (although only for the purposes of the Directive) industrial property rights. This corresponds with Art. 1(2), 10 of the Paris Convention for the Protection of Intellectual Property and ECJ case law in relation to Art. 30 EC Treaty/Art. 36 TFEU,[42] **19**

39 *Rosenkranz/Rohde*, NIPR 2008, 435, 437.

40 Regulation (EC) No 1383/2003, OJ 2003 L 196/7.

41 Directive 2004/48/EC of the European Parliament and of the Council of 29 April 2004 on the enforcement of intellectual property rights, OJ 2004 L 195/16 (including the corrigendum).

42 ECJ, Case C-87/97 – *Gorgonzola* [1999] ECR I-1301 para. 20; ECJ, Case C-216/01 – *Budějovický Budvar* [2003] ECR I-13617 paras. 99 seq.; ECJ,

both regarding geographical indications as industrial property rights.

20 On the other hand, misrepresentations in relation to the geographical origin as well as the exploitation of good will attached to the geographical origin are regarded as acts of unfair competition according to Art. 6(1)(b) Unfair Commercial Practices Directive.

21 Applying the criteria laid down under (1) above, the application of Art. 8 Rome II versus Art. 6(1) Rome II depends on the basis, *i.e.* the **subject-matter of the claim**: if the subject-matter is the infringement of a geographical indication or designation of origin as an intellectual property right, *e.g.* by unauthorized use or by using imitations, Art. 8 will determine the law governing the infringement action;[43] if the subject-matter is the misrepresentation in relation to the geographical origin, *e.g.* by advertising sausages from Spain as original Vienna Sausages,[44] Art. 6 will determine the law applicable to this act of misleading advertising. Furthermore, as explained above under (2), gaps in the system of intellectual property rights in relation to geographical indica-

---

Case C-469/00 – *Ravil v Bellon and Biraghi (Grana Padano)* [2003] ECR I-5053 para. 49; ECJ, Case C-108/01 – *Prosciutto di Parma* [2003] ECR I-5121, para. 64, ECJ, Case C-478/07 – *Budějovický Budvar* [2009] ECR I-7721, paras. 75, 94, 110.

43 *Sack*, WRP 2008, 845, 860 seq.; *Heinze* in: jurisPK BGB, Art. 8 para. 11; the opposite view (applying Art. 6 generally to geographical indications and designations of origin) is taken by *Plender & Wilderspin*, para. 22-019.

44 Similar cases can be found in the English law of passing off, for the purposes of Rome II to be qualified as an act of unfair competition under Art. 6 (see *e.g. Bollinger v Costa Brava* [1960] Ch 262; *Chocosuisse Union des Fabricants Suisses de Chocolat v Cadbury Ltd* [1998] RPC 117 (Ch.) and [1999] RPC 826 (CA); *Diageo North America Inc v InterContinental Brands Ltd* [2010] EWHC 17).

tions and designations of origin may be filled by unfair competition law in which case the law for such claims is determined by Art. 6(1) Rome II.[45]

cc) Relationship between Art. 6(1) and Art. 6(3)

Areas of potential overlap between Art. 6(1) and Art. 6(3) are in particular boycotts, discrimination and the protection of distribution systems.[46] While it has been suggested that the relationship between Art. 6(1) and Art. 6(3) is generally one of mutual exclusivity[47] and that in cases of overlap Art. 6(3) should prevail,[48] it seems preferable to allow both conflict rules to apply even to the same act. If the act violates the law applicable under one of the two conflict rules, that gives de facto rise to its prohibition altogether. There is no convincing reason why either one country's law of unfair competition or another country's antitrust law should be disregarded if the protected interests on the respective market are affected. 22

Hence, in cases of overlap, both conflict rules should apply while the scope of the applicable laws would be limited to provisions in the respective field (qualified autonomously for these purposes). If a provision of national law covers aspects of both fields, the centre of gravity will determine whether it falls under Art. 6(1) or Art. 6(3).[49] In the majority of cases, though, the matter is of little practical relevance since the applicable law determined by Art. 6(1) and Art. 6(3) will concur.[50] 23

---

45 *Sack*, WRP 2008, 845, 862.

46 *Henning-Bodewig/Schricker*, EIPR 2002, 271, 272.

47 In that direction *Dickinson*, para. 6.31.

48 *Henning-Bodewig/Schricker*, EIPR 2002, 271, 272; *Wurmnest*, in: jurisPK BGB, Art. 6 para. 16 with further details.

49 *Mankowski*, in: Münchener Kommentar Lauterkeitsrecht, IntWettbR, para. 7; *Hausmann/Obergfell*, in: Fezer, Einleitung I, para. 32.

50 For the difference between the connecting factors (*Einwirkungs- versus Auswirkungsprinzip*) see *infra* paras. 37 et seq.; *Fitchen*, 5. J. Priv. Int. L. (2009) 337, 350 overlooks this when regretting that it "... is unfortunate

24 Likewise, if aspects of antitrust law arise as preliminary issues of a claim based on unfair competition, *e.g.* in case of restrictive distribution systems, both conflict rules apply with the scope of each limited to the respective field.

e) Relationship with the Country of Origin-Principle

aa) E-Commerce and Audiovisual Media Services Directives

25 Art. 3 E-Commerce Directive[51] and Art. 2, 2a Audiovisual Media Services Directive[52] are sector-specific rules bearing relevance for **marketing and advertising via internet or audiovisual media services (mainly television)** as potential acts of unfair competition. Whether the country of origin-principle pursued by both Directives constitutes a conflict rule is highly contested.[53] If so, according to Art. 27 Rome II the country of origin-principle in Art. 3 E-Commerce Directive and Art. 2, 2a of the Audiovisual Media Services Directive would replace the conflict rule of Art. 6(1) Rome II.

---

that the structure of Art. 6 cannot be relied upon to allow the domestic court to 'consolidate' the different choice of law in such a situation …"

[51] Directive 2000/31/EC of the European Parliament and of the Council of 8 June 2000 on certain legal aspects of information society services, in particular electronic commerce, in the Internal Market (Directive on electronic commerce), OJ 2000 L 178/1.

[52] Council Directive 89/552/EEC of 3 October 1989 on the coordination of certain provisions laid down by Law, Regulation or Administrative Action in Member States concerning the pursuit of television broadcasting activities, OJ 1989, L 298/23, as amended by Directive 2007/65/EC, OJ 2007 L 332/27.

[53] For an overview on the matter see generally *Deinert*, 17 EWS (2006) 445; *Michaels*, 2 J. Priv. Int. L. (2006) 195; with regard to unfair competition in particular see *Drexl*, in: Münchener Kommentar BGB, Int-UnlWettbR paras. 53 et seq.; *Mankowski*, in: Münchener Kommentar Lauterkeitsrecht, IntWettbR, paras. 48 et seq.; *Hausmann/Obergfell*, in: Fezer, Einleitung I, paras. 121 et seq.; *Glöckner*, in: Harte/Henning, Einl. C, paras. 25 et seq.

According to the prevailing view, the country of origin-principle does not constitute a conflict rule. Rather, it operates on the level of the substantive law once this has been determined by the respective conflict rules.[54] This view is strongly supported by Recital 23 and Art. 1(4) of the E-Commerce Directive. They explicitly state that the Directive does not establish additional rules of private international law.[55] Consequently, the relationship between Art. 3 E-Commerce Directive/Art. 2, 2a of the Audiovisual Media Services Directive and Art. 6(1) Rome II is not governed by Art. 27.[56] Rather, the country of origin-principle and the conflict rule in Art. 6(1) Rome II operate on different levels: once the applicable law is determined according to Art. 6(1) Rome II, the law of the country of origin prevails on the level of substantive law in case of incompatibility with the applicable law in so far as the latter imposes further restrictions than the former upon the marketing or advertising in question. The law of the country of origin does, however, not add on to lower standards of the law of the affected market.[57] As a result, any restrictions under the applicable law within the coordinated fields and scope of the E-Commerce and Audiovisual Media Servides Di- **26**

---

54 *Plender & Wilderspin*, paras. 18-031 et seq. and para. 20-075; *Drexl*, in: Münchener Kommentar BGB, IntUnlWettbR paras. 72 et seq.; *Ahrens*, in: FS Tilmann (2003) 739, 745; *Schack*, MMR 2000, 59, 61; *Halfmeier*, ZEuP 2001, 837, 864 et seq.; *Glöckner*, in: Harte/Henning, Einl. C, para. S32; *Sack*, WRP 2008, 845, 855; *Dicey, Morris & Collins*, para. S 35-173; *Leible*, in: Reichelt (ed.), Europäisches Gemeinschaftsrecht und IPR, 2007, 31, 47 seq.; *Wilderspin*, NIPR 2008, 408, 409 seq.; *de Lima Pinheiro*, Riv. dir. int. priv. proc. 2008, 5, 36; see also Art. 27 para. 9; the issue will very likely soon be clarified by the ECJ in Case C-509/09 – *eDate Advertising* (which is still pending as of January 2011) upon a reference by the Bundesgerichtshof (Germany), 10 November 2009 – VI ZR 217/08, EuZW 2010, 313 (Question 3).

55 This is particularly stressed by *Sack*, WRP 2008, 845, 855 et seq.

56 See Art. 27 para. 9.

57 *Köhler*, in: Köhler/Bornkamm, Einl. UWG, para. 3.47.

rectives will apply only up to the level of the country of origin.[58] Thus, an advertising scheme that is lawful in its country of origin must not be prohibited on the basis of the law determined by Art. 6 Rome II.

27 According to the view[59] which regards the country of origin-principle as a conflict rule,[60] the Directives would operate on the same level, *i.e.* the level of conflict rules. Their relationship would be governed by Art. 27 Rome II. Hence, the country of origin-principle of Art. 3 E-Commerce Directive and Art. 2, 2a Audiovisual Media Services Directive would replace the conflict rule of Art. 6(1) Rome II. The law of the country of origin would apply directly and exclusively, not only in case of incompatibility with the law of the affected market.

28 In any event, the scope of application of the Audiovisual Media Services and the E-Commerce Directive is **limited in relation to acts of unfair competition**.

---

58 *Glöckner*, in: Harte/Henning, Einl. C, para. 32; *Drexl*, in: Münchener Kommentar BGB, IntUnlWettbR para. 77 makes one exception: if the advertising and marketing activities in question are exclusively addressed at a foreign market (and not also the market of the country of origin), then the law of the country of origin plays no role (proposing a restrictive interpretation of Art. 3(2) E-Commerce Directive in such constellations).

59 See for that view *e.g. Höder*, Die kollisionsrechtliche Behandlung unteilbarer Multistate-Verstöße (2002) 200 et seq.; *Thünken*, 51 ICLQ (2002) 909, 940 seq.; *Grundmann*, 67 RabelsZ (2003) 246, 273; *Mankowski*, in: Münchener Kommentar Lauterkeitsrecht, IntWettbR, para. 97; *Mankowski*, 100 ZVglRWiss (2001) 137, 179; *Lurger/Vallant*, MMR 2002, 203, 207.

60 The two views presented here are only the two main lines of argument which argue either on the level of conflict rules or on the level of the substantive law; in fact, there are several variations of those two views, see *Drexl*, in: Münchener Kommentar BGB, IntUnlWettbR paras. 53 et seq.

The Audiovisual Media Services Directive contains several particularly relevant limitations: First, the country of origin-principle of the Audiovisual Media Services Directive applies only in relation to the Directive's coordinated field (Art. 10 et seq.). The coordinated field, however, mainly concerns media-specific aspects whereas it does not cover most areas of unfair competition,[61] particularly misleading and comparative advertising.[62] Most aspects of unfair competition in relation to audiovisual media services are therefore governed solely by the law determined by Art. 6 Rome II. Secondly, the personal scope of the Audiovisual Media Services Directive is limited considerably in relation to unfair competition since the Directive does not apply to the person responsible for the marketing or advertising but only to the media service provider, *e.g.* a television broadcasting company.[63] Thirdly, the territorial scope of application of Art. 2, 2a Audiovisual Media Services Directive is limited to intra-Community constellations whereas Art. 6(1) and (2) Rome II apply universally (Art. 3 Rome II). This results in a fragmented system of conflict rules in relation to the coordinated field of the Audiovisual Media Services Directive: marketing and advertising of products or services may be subject to one standard within Europe (the country of origin's standard) while the standards outside Europe may vary depending on the applicable law determined by Art. 6(1) Rome II. 29

The E-Commerce Directive contains fewer limitations: the coordinated field[64] is broader so as to effectively enabling EU-wide online marketing and advertising subject to a single standard of 30

---

61 *Sack*, WRP 2008, 845, 857; *Schricker*, GRUR Int. 1999, 771, 775.

62 See ECJ, Case C-34/95 – *de Agostini* [1997] ECR I-3843 paras. 37 seq.

63 *Sack*, WRP 2008, 845, 858; *Mankowski*, in: Münchener Kommentar Lauterkeitsrecht, IntWettbR, para. 100.

64 Whether the country of origin-principle extends even beyond the coordinated field is not clear, pro *Mankowski*, in: Münchener Kommentar Lauterkeitsrecht, IntWettbR, para. 56; contra: *Köhler*, in: Köhler/Bornkamm, Einl. UWG, para. 3.47.

unfair competition – the one of the country of origin.[65] The territorial scope of application is, however, likewise limited to intra-Community constellations.

bb) The Basic Freedoms of the TFEU

31 While the matter is contested, the prevailing opinion takes the view that the basic freedoms of the TFEU, in particular the free movement of goods (Art. 34 TFEU) and services (Art. 56 TFEU), neither constitute a conflict rule providing for the law of the country of origin themselves nor require one or the other principle (country of origin versus country of destination) to be adopted in a conflict rule established by secondary EC law like the Rome II Regulation.[66] Rather, the applicable national (substantive) law of unfair competition has to accord with the basic freedoms, in particular the free movement of goods, as it was developed by the ECJ in a line of cases starting with *Cassis de Dijon*[67] via *Oosthoek*[68] and *GB-INNO*[69] to *Keck and Mithouard*[70] and the

---

65 *Thorn*, in: Palandt, Art. 6 para. 15; *Köhler*, in: Köhler/Bornkamm, Einl. UWG, para. 3.47.

66 *Köhler*, in: Köhler/Bornkamm, Einl. UWG, paras. 5.3 and 5.21 et seq.; *Glöckner*, in: Harte/Henning, Einl. C, paras. 22 seq.; *Mankowski*, in: Münchener Kommentar Lauterkeitsrecht, IntWettbR paras. 123 et seq. and 148 et seq.; *Drexl*, in: Münchener Kommentar BGB, IntUnlWettbR paras. 44 et seq.; *Honorati*, in: Malatesta (ed), The Unification of Choice of Law Rules on Torts and Other Non-Contractual Obligations in Europe (2006) 127, 140 et seq.; *Ahrens*, in: FS Tilmann (2003) 739, 742 et seq.; *Halfmeier*, ZEuP 2001, 837, 853; *Ohly*, GRUR Int. 2001, 899, 901; *Sack*, WRP 1994, 281, 284 seq.; for the opposing view that the basic freedoms provide for the law of the country of origin to apply see in particular: *Basedow*, 59 RabelsZ (1995) 1, 12 et seq.; *Bernhard*, EuZW 1992, 437, 440; *Grandpierre*, Herkunftsprinzip contra Marktortanknüpfung (1999) 106, 118; *Hamburg Group for Private International Law*, 67 RabelsZ (2003) 1, 19 seq. (only with regard to intra-Community constellations).

67 ECJ, Case 120/78 – *Cassis de Dijon* [1979] ECR 649, see for a detailed account of the case law *Körber*, Grundfreiheiten und Privatrecht (2004) 136 et seq.

subsequent case law.[71] In case of incompatibility, the respective national provisions are rendered inapplicable by virtue of the basic freedoms. This accords with the understanding of the country of origin-principle in European secondary legislation, in particular the E-Commerce and the Audiovisual Media Services Directives.[72]

f) Relationship with EC Directives on Unfair Competition

The EC Directives directly concerned with unfair competition, 32
i.e. the Directive on misleading and comparative advertising[73] and the Directive on unfair commercial practices,[74] contain no conflict rules which would prevail according to Art. 27 Rome II. Their purpose is limited to harmonising the substantive laws of unfair competition of the Member States. Likewise, the Directive on privacy and electronic communications,[75] the Directive on injunctions for the protection of consumers' interests[76] and the Regulation on consumer protection cooperation[77] do not contain any conflict rules.

2. Personal Scope

Art. 6(1) and (2) Rome II are not restricted to *b2c* relationships 33
as is the Unfair Commercial Practices Directive. As long as the

68 ECJ, Case 286/81 – *Osthoek* [1982] ECR 4575 (concerning a provision of Dutch unfair competition law).

69 ECJ, Case C-362/88 – *GB-INNO-BM* [1990] ECR I-683.

70 ECJ, Joined Cases C-267/91 and C-268/91 – *Keck and Mithouard* [1993] ECR I-6097.

71 See in particular ECJ, Case C-405/98 – *Gourmet International Products* [2001] ECR I-1795; ECJ, Case C-322/01 – *Doc Morris* [2003] ECR I-14887.

72 See *supra* paras. 26 et seq.

73 Directive (EC) No 2006/114, OJ 2006 L 376/21.

74 Directive (EC) No 2005/29, OJ 2005 L 149/22.

75 Directive (EC) No 2002/58, OJ 2002 L 201/37.

76 Directive (EC) No. 1998/27, OJ 1998 L 166/51.

77 Regulation (EC) No 2006/2004, OJ 2004 L 364/1.

act in question occurs in a competitive context, this act may be committed by anyone towards anyone. This reflects the range of protected interests.

3. Territorial Scope

34 As the other provisions of Rome II, Art. 6 is a *loi uniforme*.[78] Suggestions to differentiate between intra-Community (principle of origin) and extra-Community constellations (market effects principle)[79] were not taken up by the legislating European institutions.

III. Determination of the Applicable Law

1. Market-Related Acts

35 According to Art. 6(1) market-related acts of unfair competition are governed by the law of the country where **competitive relations or the collective interests of consumers are, or are likely to be, affected.**

a) Structure

36 Art. 6(1) is an entirely inflexible conflict rule.[80] The common habitual residence connection of Art. 4(2) as well as the escape clause of Art. 4(3) are not applicable to market-related acts of unfair competition[81] even though Art. 6(1) is only a clarification of Art. 4(1) (see Recital 21). A choice of law pursuant to Art. 14 is excluded by Art. 6(4). This is due to the fact that Art. 6(1), as opposed to Art. 6(2), pursues a direct, microeconomic function in

---

78 See Art. 3 para. 1.

79 See *Hamburg Group for Private International Law*, 67 RabelsZ (2003) 1, 19 seq.

80 *Cheshire, North & Fawcett*, p. 810; G. *Wagner*, IPRax 2008, 1, 8; *Sack*, WRP 2008, 845, 849.

81 *Dickinson*, paras. 6.12 et seq.; *Dicey, Morris & Collins*, para. S 35-217; *Glöckner*, in: Harte/Henning, Einl. C, paras. 125 seq. and 129.

relation to competitors and consumers collectively, combined with an indirect, macroeconomic function in relation to the proper functioning of the market (see Recital 21).[82] The market protection function leaves no room for deviations in the common interests of the parties. At the same time, it justifies the exception in Art. 6(2) in relation to acts of unfair competition which are exclusively competitor-related, *i.e.* bear no relevance for the proper functioning of the market. From a systematic perspective, the non-application of Art. 4(2) and (3) equally follows from an *argumentum e contrario* in relation to Art. 5 which explicitly refers to Art. 4(2) and replicates the escape clause of Art. 4(3) in Art. 5(2).

b) The Market Effects Principle

Although Art. 6(1), in contrast to Art. 6(3), does not mention the term *market*, the reference to the law of the country where competitive relations or the collective interests of consumers are, or are likely to be, affected, is commonly regarded as the traditional effects[83] or market effects principle[84] as it is pursued by several national laws. Competitive relations and the collective interests of consumers are often equated with the market,[85] so that Art. 6 could also read "... the law of the country whose market is, or is likely to be, affected." This equasion of competitive relations and the collective interests of consumers with the market could align the connecting factors of Art. 6(1) concerning acts of unfair competition and of Art. 6(3) concerning acts restricting free competition. It is, however, **contested whether Art. 6(1) and 6(3) provide for the same connecting factor**. In- 37

82 *Honorati*, in: Malatesta (ed), The Unification of Choice of Law Rules on Torts and Other Non-Contractual Obligations in Europe (2006) 127, 135 and 145 seq.

83 *Hamburg Group for Private International Law*, 67 RabelsZ (2003) 1, 19.

84 *Honorati*, in: Malatesta (ed), The Unification of Choice of Law Rules on Torts and Other Non-Contractual Obligations in Europe (2006) 127, 148 et seq.; *Huber/Bach*, IPRax 2005, 73, 78.

85 *Hellner*, 9 YbPIL (2007) 49, 56; *Plender & Wilderspin*, para. 20-050.

consistent terminology adds to the uncertainty surrounding the so called effects or market effects principle in relation to both conflict rules.

38 The majority argues towards a differentiation: whereas the market effects principle under Art. 6(1) shall refer to the law of the country where the competitive interests collide, *i.e.* the country where the act of unfair competition takes effect vis-à-vis competitors and the market counter-part, *i.e.* consumers *(Einwirkungsprinzip)*, the market effects principle under Art. 6(3) shall refer to the law of the country where free competition is restricted as a result of the anti-competitive act *(Auswirkungsprinzip)*.[86] The different connecting factors reflect the different goals pursued by the two areas of law: while unfair competition law regulates the competitive *conduct* on a market, antitrust law concerns the *consequences* of anti-competitive behaviour on the market.[87] The rationale of unfair competition law, *par conditio concurrentium*, requires a connection to the country where the market players compete for customers, *i.e.* where the competitive interests collide, instead of the country where the consequences for (free) competition are finally felt.[88] This accords with the *Einwirkungsprinzip* since it reflects the direct microeconomic function of unfair competition law.

39 In contrast, others argue towards a uniform principle assuming that both Art. 6(1) and 6(3) provide for the law of the country where the effects of the unfair or anti-competitive acts materia-

---

[86] *Drexl*, in: Münchener Kommentar BGB, IntUnlWettbR paras. 131 and 134; *Hausmann/Obergfell*, in: Fezer, UWG, Einleitung I, paras. 224 et seq.; *Wurmnest*, in: jurisPK BGB, Art. 6 paras. 17 and 27; *Mankowski*, in: Münchener Kommentar Lauterkeitsrecht, IntWettbR, paras. 142 et seq.; *Sack*, WRP 2008, 845, 846 seq.; according to *R. Wagner*, in: FS Kropholler (2008) 715, 723, this was also the position of the Council.

[87] *Mankowski*, in: Münchener Kommentar Lauterkeitsrecht, IntWettbR, para. 142; *Dickinson*, para. 6.31.

[88] G. *Wagner*, IPRax 2008, 1, 8; see also the Commission's Explanatory Memorandum COM(2003) 427 final at p. 16.

lise.[89] The emphasis is rather on the macroeconomic function of unfair competition law which brings it closer to antitrust law.

Overall, the differentiating view is more convincing. It reflects the triple objective and is mirrored by the different wording of Art. 6(1) and Art. 6(3). By specifically referring to the competitive relations and the collective interests of consumers, the conflict rule on unfair competition goes beyond the macroeconomic market protection function. The decision for one or the other view is, however, usually not of crucial importance. In the vast majority of cases, the country where the unfair act interferes with the protected interests and the country where the consequences for competition are felt, is one and the same.[90] Rare instances where those countries differ, are advertising and sales activities abroad addressing customers on holiday with subsequent delivery in their home country (act of unfair competition takes effect abroad, but consequences materialise back home)[91] and domestic advertising activities for products to be acquired and distributed abroad.[92] 40

Hence, one may refer to the "market effects principle" in relation to the conflict rules of Art. 6(1) and in fact Art. 6(3) as long as it does not result in misleading associations of a concurrence of the connecting factors of Art. 6(1) and Art. 6(3). Just as the protected interests behind the notion of "market" differ, the countries indicated by the market effects under Art. 6(1) and Art. 6(3) may differ. 41

---

89 *Glöckner*, in: Harte/Henning, Einl. C, paras. 100 et seq.; *Honorati*, in: Malatesta (ed), The Unification of Choice of Law Rules on Torts and Other Non-Contractual Obligations in Europe (2006) 127, 149; similar also *Hellner*, 9 YbPIL (2007) 49, 56 (with reference to the legislative history).

90 Particularly when considering that the *Auswirkungsprinzip* does by no means attach to the indirect consequences of the act of unfair competition or the act restricting free competition (cf. Art. 4 and Recital 17).

91 *Drexl*, in: Münchener Kommentar BGB, IntUnlWettbR para. 135.

92 *Rosenkranz/Rohde*, NIPR 2008, 435, 437.

42 By pursuing the market effects principle, the conflict rule in Art. 6(1) rejects the country of origin-principle.[93] The major goal of the market effects principle is to provide a level playing field for competitors on a (national) market *(par conditio concurrentium)*,[94] particularly against the background of diverging standards of fair versus unfair competition in the national laws (not only of the Member States since Art. 6(1) applies universally). It bars competitors from exporting their national standard of unfair competition like an attachment to their products or services onto a foreign market. Instead, it ensures that all competitors entering a national market play the competitive game according to the same rules while also realising the concept of the closest connection since an act of unfair competition is regularly most closely connected to the country where the protected interests are affected.

c) The Country where the Protected Interests are Affected

aa) The Relevant Country

43 According to the *Einwirkungsprinzip* (see above under b), the country where the protected interests are affected is the **country where the act of unfair competition operates vis-à-vis competitors or consumers, i.e. where the person claimed to be liable interferes with one of the protected interests** (an interference with all of them is not required[95]).[96] The country where the person claimed to be liable acted (or even only took preparatory ac-

---

[93] For the relationship with the country of origin-principle of the E-Commerce and the Audiovisual Media Services Directive see *supra* paras. 25 et seq.; for a general discussion on the country of origin-principle versus the country of destination-principle (which reflects the effects principle) see *Drasch*, Das Herkunftslandprinzip im internationalen Privatrecht (1996); *Bruinier*, Der Einfluss der Grundfreiheiten auf das internationale Privatrecht (2002); *Körber*, Grundfreiheiten und Privatrecht (2004) 432 et seq.

[94] *Sack*, WRP 2008, 845, 847; G. *Wagner*, IPRax 2008, 1, 8; *Garcimartín Alferéz*, EuLF 2007, I-77, 86.

[95] *Köhler*, in: Köhler/Bornkamm, Einl. UWG, para. 5.32.

tion) and the country where indirect consequential effects of the act occur are irrelevant.[97] This follows from Recital 21 according to which Art. 6(1) is only a clarification of Art. 4(1).

Acts directed not at competitors or consumers, but at traders, distributors and other persons in the chain of distribution at large, should also be covered by Art. 6(1).[98] The rule's personal scope is not limited to *b2c* relationships. Distributors as a group may be as vulnerable as consumers as a group and the detrimental effect on a proper functioning of the market is similar. In relation to manufacturers and other persons upstream in the chain of distribution, traders and distributors are also on the demand-side just as consumers are in relation to them. This view accords with the material scope of Art. 6 which is not restricted to acts of unfair competition towards consumers but likewise covers acts of unfair competition towards traders under the Directive on Misleading and Comparative Advertising.[99] 44

Applying the market effects principle one may distinguish **several stages**: 45

96 *Drexl*, in: Münchener Kommentar BGB, IntUnlWettbR paras. 133 et seq.; *Hausmann/Obergfell*, in: Fezer, Einleitung I, paras. 224 et seq.; *Mankowski*, in: Münchener Kommentar Lauterkeitsrecht, IntWettbR paras. 142 et seq.; *Sack*, WRP 2008, 845, 846 seq.; *Thorn*, in: Palandt, Art. 6 para. 9; G. *Wagner*, IPRax 2008, 1, 8; *Rosenkranz/Rohde*, NIPR 2008, 435, 437.

97 *Sack*, WRP 2008, 845, 847.

98 *Köhler*, in: Köhler/Bornkamm, Einl. UWG, para. 5.32 assumes an analogous application of Art. 6 but it may well apply directly considering Recital 21 providing for a proper functioning of the market economy as the underlying rationale of the protected interests; *Dickinson*, para. 6.24 applies Art. 6 in this case directly as it is suggested here but requires "some (appreciable) effect either on a specific competitor or upon a class of market participants, whether competitors or consumers". Whether this aims at establishing two categories of cases or an appreciability thereshold, is not clear.

99 See *supra* para. 6.

46 As regards **acts of unfair competition in the course of advertising or other marketing activities** such as sales promotions, the country where the protected interests are affected is the country where the advertising or marketing operates vis-à-vis the customers (not necessarily consumers), *i.e.* where it is noticed by them.[100] In the rare cases in which the country of advertising or marketing and the country where the product or service is delivered/performed differ,[101] the country of delivery is irrelevant.[102] The advertising or marketing is usually intended to be recognized where it physically takes place, *e.g.* by displaying adverts on walls or other special advertising spaces (perimeter advertising in football stadiums, adverts at bus stops, airports etc.), by handing out flyers to people, whether randomly on the street, directly at the point of sale or by inserting them into magazines, or by approaching people in the course of other marketing activities. In case of advertising via television, radio or internet it is the country or countries where the advert is receptible by the addressees if the product or service is also distributed in the respective country (often indicated by disclaimers or the language used in the advert) which reduces the otherwise exorbitant number of countries.[103] This regularly raises the issue of multi state torts/delicts.[104] The problem of multiple standards under multiple laws is, however, within the EU substantially reduced by the country of origin-principle under the E-Commerce and the Audiovisual Media Services Directive.[105]

---

100 *Köhler*, in: Köhler/Bornkamm, Einl. UWG, para. 5.34.

101 For instances where those countries differ see *supra* para. 40.

102 *Glöckner*, in: Harte/Henning, Einl. C, paras. 139 et seq. and 144; *Sack*, WRP 2008, 845, 848; *Thorn*, in: Palandt, Art. 6 para. 9; *Drexl*, in: Münchener Kommentar BGB, IntUnlWettbR para. 135.

103 *Sack*, WRP 2008, 845, 852.

104 See *infra* paras. 55 et seq.

105 For the way, the country of origin-principle operates in connection with Art. 6 see *supra* para. 26.

As regards **acts of unfair competition in the course of the sale and supply of goods or services** the country where the protected interests are affected is the country where the product or service is offered for sale. Examples for such unfair acts are sales contrary to market regulatory laws, misrepresentations by selling the product (such as passing off)[106] and the sale of copies (if original creation is not protected by an IP right so that it may amount to an act of unfair competition). The country where the sold product or service is delivered or performed and the country where the product was produced are irrelevant.[107] If the act of unfair competition concerns the contract formation process, the country where the protected interests are affected will usually be the country where the relevant representation or other act in the course of the formation was brought to the attention of the other party.[108] This is the country where the unfair act takes effect vis-à-vis the contracting partner. 47

As regards **acts of unfair competition in the aftermath of a sale and supply of goods or services** the country where the protected interests are affected is again the country where such act takes effect vis-à-vis the contracting partner, *e.g.* in case of misrepresentations or statements concerning consumer rights the country where such false representations are received by the contracting partner. 48

bb) Affected or are Likely to be Affected

Affected or are likely to be affected refers to actual as well as imminent interference with the protected interests. This covers claims for damages in relation to actual or past acts as well as 49

106 If the misrepresentation takes places in the course of advertising, it will be the country of advertising which will usually but not necessarily be identical with the country of sale.

107 *Sack*, WRP 2008, 845, 850.

108 *Köhler*, in: Köhler/Bornkamm, Einl. UWG, para. 5.35 seq.

injunctive relief (*ex parte* and interim as well as final injunctions, including cease and desist orders) concerning impending acts of unfair competition.[109]

cc) Appreciability

50 Contrary to earlier drafts of the conflict rule on unfair competition,[110] the rule finally adopted in Art. 6 Rome II **does not provide for an appreciability threshold**. Against the background of this legislative history any attempts to keep an appreciability threshold in relation to the finally adopted rule alive,[111] are not convincing.

---

109 *Thorn*, in: Palandt, Art. 6 para. 8.

110 See Art. 5 of the Commission's (initial) proposal and Art. 7 of the Commission's amended proposal ("direct and substantial effect").

111 *Cheshire, North & Fawcett*, p. 810 mistakenly still refer to the Commission's Explanatory Memorandum to justify the requirement of a direct substantial effect; *Dickinson*, para. 6.55 suggests that spillover effects are indirect consequences which are irrelevant for determining the applicable law – a solution which still sits uncomfortably with the deletion of the appreciability threshold by the Council in the Common Position; *Glöckner*, in: Harte/Henning, Einl. C, para. 152 and *Rosenkranz/Rohde*, NIPR 2008, 435, 437 argue that the appreciability threshold is inherent in the requirement of effects on the respective market (drawing mainly from an alleged parallelism of the antitrust and unfair competition law connections in Art. 6); similarly still requiring an appreciable effect *Wurmnest*, in: jurisPK BGB, Art. 6 para. 22; *Leible/Lehmann*, RIW 2007, 721, 729; *Handig*, GRUR Int. 2008, 24, 28 would welcome an appreciability threshold by way of case law; *Spickhoff*, in: Bamberger/Roth, Anh. zu Art. 42 EGBGB para. 59 requires an appreciable effect by drawing a reverse conclusion from Art. 4(3); *Plender & Wilderspin*, para. 20-032 concur that appreciability is a matter for the applicable substantive law, not for the conflict of laws, but suggests on the level of conflict of laws a *de minimis*-filter which is, however, for similar reasons equally not convincing.

Consequently, in the present author's opinion, there is no spill-over protection on the level of conflict of laws. A national law may apply even though the effects occurring in the respective country are neglectable. Whether effects not appreciable and/or only interfering indirectly do in fact constitute an act of unfair competition, is a matter to be determined by the applicable law.[112] Hence, spillover protection is moved from the level of conflict rules to the level of the substantive law. 51

2. Competitor-Related Acts

According to Art. 6(2), the law applicable to a competitor-related act[113] of unfair competition is determined by the general rule of Art. 4. By providing for the application of Art. 4, competitor-related acts are regarded as simple torts inflicting harm on another person. Consequently, Art. 4 should generally be applied without modifications. In particular, the common habitual residence connection of Art. 4(2) and the escape clause of Art. 4(3) apply, both lacking under the regime of Art. 6(1) with regard to market-related acts. 52

In case of competitor-related acts of unfair competition, the country where the damage occurs within the meaning of Art. 4(1) is the country where the specific competitor is directly damaged, *i.e.* where his competitive position on the market is affected. This may be the country of his seat (*e.g.* in case of espionage at the seat),[114] but it may also be the country where an employee is enticed away.[115] 53

---

112 *Thorn*, in: Palandt, Art. 6 para. 13; *Hellner*, 9 YbPIL (2007) 49, 64; *Sack*, WRP 2008, 845, 854; *Dicey, Morris & Collins*, para. S 35-217 (although Dickinson's approach [see fn. 113] is also considered).

113 For the relationship with Art. 6(1) see *supra* paras. 2 et seq.

114 *Lindacher*, GRUR Int. 2008, 453, 457 et seq.; *Sack*, WRP 2008, 845, 850; critical in that regard *Glöckner*, in: Harte/Henning, Einl. C, paras. 118 et seq.

115 *Hellner*, 9 YbPIL (2007) 49, 57.

54 It is submitted that, although the wording of Art. 6(4) seems to point into another direction, the **exclusion of a choice of law** according to Art. 6(4) does not apply in relation to competitor-related acts under Art. 6(2).[116] First and foremost, the exclusion's rationale does not apply in case of competitor-related acts of unfair competition. The coice of law is excluded with regard to Art. 6(1) since it is irreconcilable with its macroeconomic function under the triple objective including wider interests of competitors and consumers at large.[117] Competitor-related acts do not affect such wider interests of the market. Secondly, since party autonomy is a guiding principle under the Rome II Regulation, its exclusions must be interpreted narrowly, particularly in relation to Art. 6(2) as a narrow exception to the general rule of Art. 6(1).[118] Thirdly, the non-applicability of Art. 4(2) and 4(3) under Art. 6(1) follows the same rationale as the exclusion of party autonomy. Therefore, since Art. 4(2) and 4(3) apply under Art. 6(2), Art. 14 providing for a choice of the applicable law equally applies.[119]

3. Multi-State Acts

a) The Mosaic Approach

55 In case of multi-state acts of unfair competition, *i.e.* acts affecting the protected interests in more than one country, the market effects principle of Art. 6(1) results in the application of several national laws following the **mosaic approach**.[120] Art. 6(3)(b) does not apply according to its wording (referring only to restrictions

---

[116] Concurring G. *Wagner*, IPRax 2008, 1, 8; *Leible/Lehmann*, RIW 2007, 721, 730 seq.; *Thorn*, in: Palandt, Art. 6 para. 19; *Plender & Wilderspin*, para. 20-053; *Dickinson*, para. 6.75; *Rosenkranz/Rohde*, NIPR 2008, 435, 438; *Wurmnest*, in: jurisPK BGB, Art. 6 para. 36; an exclusion of a choice of law even in relation to Art. 6(2) is, however, favoured by *von Hein*, ZEuP 2009, 6, 23; *Handig*, GRUR Int. 2008, 24, 29.

[117] G. *Wagner*, IPRax 2008, 1, 8; *Plender & Wilderspin*, para. 20-053.

[118] See *supra* para. 3.

[119] *Thorn*, in: Palandt, Art. 6 para. 19.

of competition) and systematic structure (being only lit. b of sub-paragraph 3 instead of a separate sub-paragraph as is sub-paragraph 4 which applies to both Art. 6(1) and (3)(a)).[121]

Multi-state acts of unfair competition occur regularly in case of advertising and/or sale via television, internet and print media. While the burden of the mosaic approach is reduced (on the level of the substantive law) by the country of origin-principle in relation to internet and, to a lesser extent, television advertising,[122] the mosaic approach applies without modifications in relation to print media. **56**

The effects of the mosaic approach differ with regard to **concurrent, but separable versus single acts** on the one hand, and **damages claims versus injunctive relief** on the other hand. In the present author's opinion, the following guidelines should apply. **57**

b) Concurrent Acts of Unfair Competition

In case of concurrent, but separable acts of unfair competition, *e.g.* e-mail adverts sent to a large number of potential customers or publication of the same advert in print magazines published in various countries, the determination of the applicable law is rather straight-forward: According to Art. 6(1), each act is judged separately by applying the law of the country where the **58**

---

120 *Köhler*, in: Köhler/Bornkamm, Einl. UWG, para. 5.38 seq.; *Sack*, WRP 2008, 845, 851 seq.; *Wurmnest*, in: jurisPK BGB, Art. 6 para. 20.

121 *Wurmnest*, in: jurisPK BGB, Art. 6 para. 20; *Glöckner*, in: Harte/Henning, Einl. C, para. 176; *Sack*, WRP 2008, 845, 851 seq.; *Thorn*, in: Palandt, Art. 6 para. 21; *Plender & Wilderspin*, paras. 20-068 et seq.; *Dicey, Morris & Collins*, para. S 35-217; *R. Wagner*, ibid. at 724; *G. Wagner*, IPRax 2008, 1, 8, however, argues in favour of an analoguous application of Art. 6(3)(b) to Art. 6(1); *Heiss/Loacker*, JBl 2007, 613, 630 would *de lege ferenda* generally welcome an extension of Art. 6(3)(b) to all multi-state cases in tort/delict.

122 See *supra* para. 26.

act takes effect vis-à-vis potential customers.[123] Thus, the same act may be unlawful in one country, but lawful in another. Damages and injunctive relief are likewise limited to the respective country under the respective national law: The amount of damages in relation to each act is limited to the loss incurred by this act in the respective country. Injunctive relief results only in a prohibition of the advert in the respective country.

c) Single Acts of Unfair Competition

59 In case of a single act of unfair competition taking effect vis-à-vis competitors or customers in several countries, *e.g.* online misrepresentation on a company website or misleading keyword advertising on Google, one has to distinguish between damages and injunctive relief.

60 Concerning damages, the issue is similar to concurrent but separable acts: the claim for damages is determined for each country separately by the respective national law, and the amount of damages under each claim is limited by the loss incurred in the respective country. According to ECJ case law, the plaintiff has a choice as regards jurisdiction. He may either bring the claim at the domicile or seat of the defendant under Art. 2; this court may comprehensively determine the damage claim by applying the different laws proportionally. Or he may bring the claim under Art. 5(3) in the country where the act of unfair competition takes effect; the court seized is then, however, limited to determining the damages claim in relation to the loss that occurred in the forum state.[124]

61 Concerning injunctive relief, the issue lies differently. While the mosaic approach likewise applies in theory, the result is different in practice. The plaintiff may apply for injunctive relief under the

123 *Sack*, WRP 2008, 845, 852; *Köhler*, in: Köhler/Bornkamm, Einl. UWG, para. 5.39.

124 ECJ, Case C-68/93 – *Shevill* [1995] ECR I-415 para. 33.

strictest unfair competition law (lacking an appreciability threshold, there is no spillover protection under Art. 6(1)). This will result in a prohibition of the act in that country. Since the act is inseparable, such national prohibition will effectively result in a world-wide prohibition of the single act of unfair competition.[125] This holds true even in online advertising cases covered by the E-Commerce Directive's country of origin-principle since it is tied to the inseparability of the respective act regardless of the law that applies to it.

C. Acts Restricting Free Competition

I. Legislative History and Background

While the Commission's preliminary draft proposal of 2002 contained a conflict rule on restrictions of competition, its initial and amended proposal did not contain such a rule.[126] This self-restraint was motivated by the parallel initiative of the Commission on private enforcement of competition law which led to a Green and a White Paper on Damages Actions.[127] At the time when the Commission published its amended proposal on Rome II, the consultation phase of the Green Paper was still running and the Commission did not want to interfere with the controversial de- **62**

125 *Thorn*, in: Palandt, Art. 6 para. 9; *Wurmnest*, in: jurisPK BGB, Art. 6 para. 21; *Sack*, WRP 2008, 845, 852; *Köhler*, in: Köhler/Bornkamm, Einl. UWG, para. 5.41; *Lindacher*, GRUR Int. 2008, 453, 455; *Schaub*, in: Prütting/Wegen/Weinreich, Art. 6 Rom II para. 4.

126 For a detailed account of the legislative history see *Mankowski*, RIW 2008 177, 178 seq.; *Roth*, in: FS Kropholler (2008), 623, 632 et seq.; *Dickinson*, paras. 6.01 et seq.

127 Green Paper on Damages Actions for Breach of the EC antitrust rules of 19 December 2005, COM(2005) 672 final, supplemented by a Commission Staff Working Paper of 19 December 2005, SEC(2005) 1732 as an annex to the Green Paper.

bate.[128] Any move by the Commission in relation to antitrust matters within the Rome II Regulation would have driven the discussion into one direction or the other. However, the Commission did explicitly state in its amended proposal that, depending on the replies to the Green Paper, it "may wish to support a different solution in the course of the codecision procedure."[129]

63 From early 2006 onwards, the general conflict rule on restrictions of competition, which is now Art. 6(3)(a), was discussed in the Council. Following fierce debate, the affected market-rule was adopted and became part of the Council's common position in September 2006.[130] The supplementary conflict rule in Art. 6(3)(b) was introduced by the European Parliament in the codecision procedure based on critique in relation to the general rule and proposals for a solution by the Commission (as it had indicated in its amended proposal). As a result of the late and sudden birth of Art. 6(3), legislative material providing guidance on the operation and interpretation of the rule, particularly lit. b, is nearly non-existent.

64 The conflict rule in Art. 6(3) is closely linked to the **strategy by the Commission to foster private enforcement of antitrust law within the EU**.[131] It is an instrument for the intermediate term until the Commission's White Paper[132] may pave the way to a harmonised or even uniform private enforcement regime throughout

---

128 See Amendment 29 (p. 6) of the amended proposal (COM(2006) 83 final).

129 See again Amendment 29 (p. 6) of the amended proposal (COM(2006) 83 final).

130 Common Position (EC) No 22/2006 of 25 September 2006, OJ 2006 C 289 E/68.

131 For a brief, but concise outline see *Pineau*, 5 J. Priv. Int. L. (2009) 311, 312 et seq.; for further details on the private enforcement policy of the EU see *Basedow* (ed.), Private Enforcement of Competition Law (2007).

132 White Paper on Damages Actions for Breach of the EC antitrust rules of 2 April 2008, COM(2008) 165 final, supplemented by a Commission

Europe. Although Art. 6(3) applies universally, many aspects of the rule demonstrate the serving function for the private enforcement of EU antitrust law. The most obvious witness is the optional rule of Art. 6(3)(b).

II. Scope

1. Material Scope

a) EU Antitrust Law

The **applicability of EU antitrust law** of the TFEU is not determined by the Rome II Regulation. Rather, the antitrust provisions of the TFEU, namely Art. 101 and 102, are mandatory provisions of Community law.[133] They determine their material and territorial scope themselves under the effects doctrine as laid down by the ECJ in the *Wood Pulp* case.[134] Since they do not contain provisions on private enforcement, damages claims in particular, Art. 6(3) determines the national law to fill this gap in accordance with the ECJ's judgments in *Courage*[135] and *Manfredi*.[136] 65

b) Civil and Commercial Matters

According to Art. 1(1) Rome II, the Regulation's material scope is throughout limited to non-contractual obligations in civil and commercial matters. Art. 6(3) does not constitute an exception in that regard.[137] Rather, the general limitation of the Regulation's material scope implies that the material scope of Art. 6(3) 66

Staff Working Paper of 2 April 2008, SEC(2008) 404 as an annex to the White Paper.

133 *Thorn*, in: Palandt, Art. 6 para. 6; *Roth*, in: FS Kropholler (2008), 623, 634.

134 ECJ, Joined Cases 89, 104, 114, 116, 117 and 125 to 129/85 – *Ahlström* [1988] ECR 5193.

135 ECJ, Case C-453/99 – *Courage* [2002] ECR I-6297.

136 ECJ, Joined Cases C-295/04 and C-298/04 – *Manfredi* [2006] ECR I-6619.

137 *Pineau*, 5 J. Priv. Int. L. (2009) 311, 319; *Mankowski*, RIW 2008, 177, 180.

runs along the dichotomy of legal provisions concerning public versus private enforcement. National as well as EU law provisions forming an integral part of public enforcement (including sanctions) are outside the scope of Art. 6(3).[138] Consequently, Art. 6(3) Rome II only determines the law applicable to the aspects of private enforcement while the national conflict rules still apply in relation to the public enforcement regime.[139] This corresponds with the rationale of Art. 6(3) in fostering private enforcement of antitrust law.

c) Contractual versus Non-Contractual Obligations

67 Since Art. 6(3) is limited to non-contractual obligations, the issue of invalidity or unenforceability of a **contractual claim for breach of antitrust law** is outside its scope. It is generally governed by the Rome I Regulation, more precisely by Art. 9(3) Rome I which concerns foreign mandatory provisions.[140] However, if the contract is caught by EU antitrust law, Art. 101(2) TFEU which provides for the invalidity of contracts in breach of EU antitrust law has binding effect upon all Member State courts without requiring a conflict of laws-entry door for its application.

68 The matter lies differently if a purchaser claims damages incurred by paying prices under a contract that were fixed by a cartel or concerted practice. Such claim is not based on the contract. In fact, no breach occurred; the contract was performed by both parties. Rather, the claim for damages is based on the non-contractual, namely statutory duty not to violate antitrust laws and is thus governed by Art. 6(3).[141]

---

138 *Pineau*, 5 J. Priv. Int. L. (2009) 311, 319; *Wurmnest*, in: jurisPK BGB, Art. 6 para. 12; *Thorn*, in: Palandt, Art. 6 para. 7; *Mankowski*, RIW 2008, 177, 180 seq.; *Garcimartín Alferéz*, EuLF 2007, I-77, 86; *Cheshire, North & Fawcett*, p. 812.

139 *Thorn*, in: Palandt, Art. 6 para. 7; *Mankowski*, RIW 2008, 177, 181 seq.

140 *Mankowski*, RIW 2008, 177, 182.

141 *Plender & Wilderspin*, para. 20-040.

d) Acts Restricting Free Competition

The core issue in relation to the material scope of Art. 6(3) is the scope of the term "acts restricting free competition" which has to be interpreted autonomously. **69**

The starting point for an autonomous interpretation is **Recital 23**. According to it, prohibitions on agreements between undertakings, decisions by associations of undertakings and concerted practices as well as the abuse of a dominant position are covered by the concept of restrictions of competition. The list corresponds with the activities prohibited under Art. 81, 82 EC Treaty (now Art. 101 and 102 TFEU). The additional wording "... where such agreements, decisions, concerted practices and abuses are prohibited by Articles 81 and 82 of the Treaty or by the law of a Member State" does not require the specific act in question to be unlawful as a prerequisite for the application of the conflict rule. Rather, as the unlawfulness is a matter for the applicable substantive law, the reference to acts prohibited under EU or national antitrust law is a general one: all acts generally prohibited under EU or national antitrust law are covered by Art. 6(3).[142] This implies that the jurisprudence of the ECJ defining the material scope of Art. 81, 82 EC Treaty/Art. 101, 102 TFEU will be of particular relevance when determining the scope of acts restricting free competition under Art. 6(3) Rome II.[143] Since Art. 6(3) claims universal application, the limited wording of Recital 23 does not result in an indirect restriction of the territorial scope of Art. 6(3).[144] Rather, in light of an autonomous interpretation one may, even in relation to acts affecting the market(s) of Non-Member States, refer (non-exhaustively) to the concepts of EU antitrust law in order to determine whether they constitute an act restricting free competition. **70**

---

142 *Mankowski*, RIW 2008, 177, 182.

143 Concurring *Wurmnest*, in: jurisPK BGB, Art. 6 para. 11.

144 For details see *infra* para. 77.

71 Recital 23, however, does not claim to be exhaustive.[145] The range of anti-competitive phenomena covered by Art. 6(3) is wider. It aims at comprehensively covering any act restricting free competition by distorting the competitive order of the market. This has several implications.

72 First, as **Recital 22** states explicitly, anti-competitive acts within the EU under the national laws that are not covered by the material scope of Art. 101, 102 TFEU may be covered by Art. 6(3) Rome II.[146] A particularly relevant example are unilateral acts by strong, but not dominant market players that do not fall under Art. 102 TFEU but may well be prohibited under national antitrust law.[147] In relation to Non-Member State laws the potential coverage beyond Art. 101, 102 TFEU may be even larger.

73 Secondly, beyond cartels, concerted practices and the abuse of a dominant position, non-contractual damages claims in the context of mergers, joint ventures and other concentrations are also covered by Art. 6(3) Rome II.[148] They may likewise interfere with free competition. Within the EU, cross border concentrations are governed by the Merger Regulation No. 139/2004.[149] As in relation to Art. 101, 102 TFEU, Art. 6(3) Rome II fills the gap for determining the national law applicable to the damages claim.[150]

---

145 Concurring *Mankowski*, RIW 2008, 177, 179; *Roth*, in: FS Kropholler (2008) 643 seq.; *Rosenkranz/Rohde*, NIPR 2008, 435, 436.

146 *Wurmnest*, in: jurisPK BGB, Art. 6 para. 12.

147 *Roth*, in: FS Kropholler (2008) 623, 644.

148 *Plender & Wilderspin*, para. 20-039; *Wurmnest*, in: jurisPK BGB, Art. 6 para. 11.

149 Council Regulation (EC) No 139/2004 of 20 January 2004 on the control of concentrations between undertakings (the EC Merger Regulation), OJ 2004 L 24/1.

150 It may even fill the gap of the Merger Regulation in relation to its territorial scope of application if one is prepared to read Art. 6(3) not only as referring to the law of a country or, alternatively, to accept the EC Merger

Beyond such mergers, joint ventures and other concentrations, Art. 6(3) furthermore covers actions for damages by aggrieved competitors against recipients of unlawful state aid.[151] First, both the rules on antitrust and state aid are part of the same chapter in the TFEU entitled "rules on competition" (Title VII, Chapter 1). Secondly, unlawful state aid may just as a cartel or an unlawful merger restrict free competition. In contrast to damages claims based on a violation of Art. 101, 102 TFEU, damages claims based on unlawful mergers, joint ventures and other concentrations as well as unlawful state aid depend entirely on a corresponding action under the applicable national law. The ECJ did not require that such damages claims lie as a matter of EU law as it did in relation to private enforcement claims based on a violation of Art. 101, 102 TFEU. Furthermore, one should note in relation to unlawful state aid that Art. 6(3) governs only the (private law) relationship between competitors whereas the relationship state – recipient and state – aggrieved competitor is, according to its Art. 1(1) Rome II, outside the material scope of Art. 6(3).[152] 74

2. Personal Scope

The personal scope of Art. 6(3) Rome II is unrestricted. In particular, it is not a matter for the conflict rule to determine the range of potential claimants, *i.e.* the victims of acts restricting free competition.[153] Rather, it is a matter for the applicable sub- 75

Regulation as the law of the country of each Member State for the purposes of Art. 6(3); see *Mankowski*, RIW 2008, 177, 180.

151 *Plender & Wilderspin*, para. 20-039; *Hellner*, 9 YbPIL (2007) 49, 69.

152 *Wurmnest*, in: jurisPK BGB, Art. 6 para. 11.

153 The concerns of *Fitchen*, 5 J. Priv. Int. L. (2009) 337, 340 seq. and 366 et seq. (equating effects on the market with damage to a specific victim) are therefore misplaced; the matter is problematic (cf. the Commission Staff Working Paper and the White Paper on damages actions for breach of the EC antitrust rules) but one of the substantive law (therefore dealt with in the White Paper concerning the harmonisation of the substantive laws in relation to private enforcement of EC antitrust law).

stantive law to determine whether the claimant suffered damage resulting from an act restricting free competition which would entitle him to bring a damages claim and whether the person claimed to be liable is actually liable.

3. Territorial Scope

76 Although the Regulation claims universal application according to Art. 3, one has to distinguish with regard to the territorial scope of Art. 6(3).

77 The general rule in lit. a is a *loi uniforme*. Hence, it is not restricted to designating EU or Member State laws but may designate any law worldwide.[154] The limited reference in Recital 23 to acts restricting competition within a Member State or within the internal market does not restrict the territorial scope of Art. 6(3). The recital solely concerns the interpretation of the concept of restrictions of competition but not the territorial scope. Furthermore, Art. 6(3) itself does not contain a territorial restriction. Rather, it refers to the "law of the country …". Likewise, Art. 3 provides for a universal application of the Regulation. It would require explicit language if a recital addressing the qualification of certain acts under a conflict rule superseded such provisions of the Regulation. Recitals usually explain and supplement the provisions of a legislative act but do not contradict or even supersede them.

78 In contrast, the optional rule in lit. b will always designate the law of a Member State (even in relation to damage suffered in

[154] *Mankowski*, RIW 2008, 177, 187 seq.; *Roth*, in: FS Kropholler (2008) 637 et seq.; *Wurmnest*, in: jurisPK BGB, Art. 6 para. 29; *de Lima Pinheiro*, Riv. dir. int. priv. proc. 2008, 5, 24; *Plender & Wilderspin*, para. 20-041 and 20-054; *Pineau*, 5 J. Priv. Int. L. (2009) 311, 320; *Fitchen*, 5 J. Priv. Int. L. (2009) 337, 353, G. *Wagner*, IPRax 2008, 1, 8; *Leible/Lehmann*, RIW 2007, 721, 730.

Non-Member States), which does, however, not have an impact on the territorial scope of lit. a.[155]

III. Structure

The basic, multilateral conflict rule is contained in Art. 6(3)(a). It pursues the affected market-rule as connecting factor without any appreciability or substantiality threshold. In contrast, most Member States' laws pursue a unilateral conflict rule based on the effects doctrine in relation to public and private law antitrust matters.[156] **79**

Art. 6(3)(b) provides a supplementary, optional rule allowing for the application of a single law to the entire damage even in case of several co-defendants. It aims at avoiding the mosaic approach in certain multi-state as well as multi-party private enforcement actions as advocated by the European Parliament and the Commission. At the same time, it contains safeguards to prevent forum shopping as advocated by the Council. The result is a differentiated, complex compromise between those aims. **80**

Art. 6(3) is supplemented by two extensive Recitals (22 and 23) which provide some guidance on several issues arising under the rule. **81**

A choice of law is excluded by Art. 6(4).[157] **82**

---

155 *Mankowski*, RIW 2008, 177, 187; *Pineau*, 5 J. Priv. Int. L. (2009) 311, 320.

156 *Adolphsen*, 1 J. Priv. Int. L. (2005) 151, 158; *Pineau*, 5 J. Priv. Int. L. (2009) 311, 318.

157 For a critical analysis of this absolute ban see *Pineau*, 5 J. Priv. Int. L. (2009) 311, 326 et seq. (generally endorsing it) and *Fitchen*, 5 J. Priv. Int. L. (2009) 337, 344 et seq. (rejecting an absolute ban).

IV. Operation

83 The operation of the conflict rule in Art. 6(3) differs depending on several criteria: follow-on versus stand-alone actions and EU versus national antitrust prohibitions.

1. Follow-On Actions

84 The majority of damages actions, at least in relation to EU antitrust prohibitions, will be follow-on actions. In this constellation the violation of the respective antitrust prohibition[158] has already been determined either by the Commission or by a national cartel authority (in particular under Regulation 1/2003[159]).

85 According to Art. 16 of Regulation 1/2003 (mentioning explicitly only Commission decisions), any such decision by the Commission or a Member State's national cartel authority on the violation of EU antitrust prohibitions is binding upon a Member State court seized with a damages claim. Art. 6(3) Rome II governs all remaining aspects of the claim, such as standing, limitation periods, assessment of damages, award of punitive damages[160] and the issues listed (non-exhaustively) in Art. 15 Rome II. According to Art. 1(3) Rome II, matters of evidence and procedure are governed by the *lex fori*.[161]

---

[158] For the sake of simplicity, I will only refer to antitrust prohibitions in the following sections; all statements apply accordingly to illegal mergers and state aid.

[159] Council Regulation (EC) No 1/2003 of 16 December 2002 on the implementation of the rules on competition laid down in Articles 81 and 82 of the Treaty, OJ 2003 L 1/1.

[160] Concurring *Pineau*, 5 J. Priv. Int. L. (2009) 311, 315.

[161] For a detailed analysis of the dichotomy of substance and procedure see *Illmer*, 28 CJQ (2009) 237.

86 By contrast, a decision on the violation of national antitrust prohibitions by a national cartel authority[162] is not automatically binding upon the court seized with the damages claim. Instead, recognition or any other form of taking the decision into account in the damages claim will depend on the *lex fori*.[163]

2. Stand-Alone Actions

87 In case of a stand-alone actions the court seized has to determine itself whether the respective EU or national antitrust prohibition is violated. In doing so, the court will first consider a violation of EU antitrust prohibitions. Since these prohibitory provisions, Art. 101, 102 TFEU in particular, determine their scope and application themselves, Art. 6(3) Rome II does not play a role in this first step.[164] If, however, the act in question does violate EU antitrust prohibitions, the court will then determine the law governing the other aspects of the damages claim according to Art. 6(3) Rome II. If the act in question does not violate EU antitrust prohibitions (since they are inapplicable for territorial or material scope-reasons, *e.g.* national prohibitions on abuse of a dominant position reaching further than Art. 102 TFEU), the court will determine the law governing the violation of antitrust prohibitions and all other aspects of the damages claim according to Art. 6(3) Rome II. Hence, in case of cross-border scenarios not involving EU antitrust prohibitions, the conflict rule of Art. 6(3) determines the law applicable to all aspects of the damages claim com-

162 Within the EU such cases (involving a cross-border element) will be rather rare; they may only arise in relation to national cartel law going beyond the prohibition of an abuse of a dominant position in Art. 102 TFEU. They may, however, arise more frequently in relation to decisions by Non-Member State cartel authorities.

163 Cf. in that regard § 33(4) of the German Act Against Restrictions of Competition (*Gesetz gegen Wettbewerbsbeschränkungen* – GWB) providing for a binding effect of the establishment of a violation of antitrust law in a decision by the German competition authority.

164 *Wurmnest*, in: jurisPK BGB, Art. 6 para. 13.

prehensively. This includes the law applicable to the issue of a violation of antitrust prohibitions.[165]

V. Determination of the Applicable Law

88 The applicable law is generally determined by Art. 6(3)(a) whereas Art. 6(3)(b) constitutes only an option for the plaintiff in case of multi-state and multi-party constellations involving an EU Member State.

1. General Rule

89 The general rule in Art. 6(3)(a) adopts the market effects principle previously employed by most national laws. Like Art. 6(1) it is an entirely inflexible conflict rule. Both the common habitual residence connection of Art. 4(2) and the escape clause of Art. 4(3) are not applicable. Furthermore, Art. 6(4) bars a choice of law.

a) Market Effects Principle

90 The market effects principle of Art. 6(3)(a) is close, albeit **not identical, to the connecting factor of Art. 6(1)**. One may express this by contrasting the *Einwirkungsprinzip* under Art. 6(1) with the *Auswirkungsprinzip* under Art. 6(3).[166] The differentiation corresponds with the different emphasis of unfair competition law versus antitrust law in relation to the protected interests. Whereas unfair competition law pursues a triple objective with an emphasis on microeconomic aspects (protection of competitors, consumers and the market public at large), antitrust law em-

---

165 Concurring *Wurmnest*, in: jurisPK BGB, Art. 6 paras. 14 seq.; *Immenga*, in: Baur/Sandrock/Scholtka/Shapira (eds.), Das Auswirkungsprinzip des internationalen Wettbewerbsrechts als Gegenstand einer Gemeinschaftsverordnung (2009) 725, 727 et seq; however, the application of the foreign antitrust prohibition will also depend on whether it claims to apply; see *infra* paras. 102 et seq.

166 See the detailed discussion *supra* paras. 37 et seq.

phasizes the macroeconomic objective of protecting competition on the market as such, *i.e.* in particular unrestricted access to, and free competition on the market. The protection of competitors or consumers is merely a repercussion of this predominant goal. Corresponding with this objective, the law of any country where effects on free competition triggered by an anti-competitive act are felt applies. The seat of the companies involved in the anti-competitive activities and the country where the person(s) claimed to be liable acted (or even only took preparatory action), *e.g.* the place where the cartel was agreed, are irrelevant.[167]

aa) Market

The concept of the market under Art. 6(3) is a geographic one. **91**

In a first step, one should apply the concept of the geographic market as developed by the Commission and the ECJ in relation to the substantive antitrust law of Art. 81, 82 EC Treaty.[168] In terms of simplicity, it is generally easier to refer to a concept that has been developed over the decades than to introduce a new one. What is more, in the majority of cases, which will be follow-on actions, the market will already have been determined by the competition authority or a court once the follow-on action is brought. Thus, neither the parties nor the court seized with the damages claim will have to engage in this difficult task.[169] In terms of consistency, substantive EU antitrust law and Art. 6(3) Rome II both pursue the market effects principle. Hence, the aspects relevant to establish the geographic market are therefore the same despite the different purpose for which this market is established. Furthermore, the interests protected by both substantive law and the conflict rule are congruent. **92**

167 *Roth*, in: FS Kropholler (2008) 623, 640.

168 *Hellner*, 9 YbPIL (2007) 49, 60; *Plender & Wilderspin*, para. 20-056; *Wurmnest*, in: jurisPK BGB, Art. 6 para. 27.

169 Concurring: *Dickinson*, paras. 6.62 seq. (cost and convenience).

93 In a second step, the cross-border geographic market resulting from the application of the concept of substantive EU antitrust law has to be split up into national markets for the purposes of Art. 6(3). This will regularly lead to a mosaic approach under Art. 6(3)(a), a scenario which Art. 6(3)(b) aims to avoid. The reason for this second step is that the concept of the geographic market under substantive EU antitrust law is predominantly an economic one linked to the relevant product market. It is not restricted to national territories so that the geographic market will regularly spread over several countries. By contrast, the concept of the geographic market under Art. 6(3)(a) is a territorial one, tied to national markets.[170] To determine the law of one country or several countries governing the damages claim, the national market(s) that are affected by the anti-competitive act have to be established.

bb) Effects

94 The criterion of effects, or more precisely "affected", under Art. 6(3) is neutral, objective and therefore potentially very wide. It covers *any* alteration in the competitive conditions on a market.[171] As such, it slightly differs from the concept of implementation[172] as established by the ECJ in relation to Art. 81, 82 EC Treaty:[173] While the affected market(s) will often coincide with the market(s) where the anti-competitive act is implemented, the notion of effects is potentially wider than that of implementation. Likewise, effects are not tantamount with interference, impairment or any other criterion that carries a value judgment on the alteration of the competitive conditions.[174]

---

170 *Mankowski*, RIW 2008, 177, 185.

171 *Mankowski*, RIW 2008, 177, 185.

172 *Roth*, in: FS Kropholler (2008) 640; *Mankowski*, RIW 2008, 177, 185; *Wurmnest*, in: jurisPK BGB, Art. 6 para. 29 regards both criteria as substantially nearly identical.

173 ECJ, Joined Cases 89, 104, 114, 116, 117 and 125 to 129/85 – *Ahlström* [1988] ECR 5193 para. 16 (the *Wood Pulp* case).

174 Concurring *Roth*, in: FS Kropholler (2008) 640.

cc) Indications

There are various indications for an effect on a particular market by the defendant's anti-competitive act. For instance, any market on which the defendant is generating turnover is potentially affected; even any business operations by the defendant may suffice. Likewise, a market on which both plaintiff and defendant compete for customers is potentially affected. Beyond those prima facie cases there are numerous other factual settings where market effects have to be determined by applying the neutral criterion of alterations of the competitive conditions. **95**

b) Affected or Likely to be Affected

The wording "affected or are likely to be affected" refers to actual as well as imminent acts restricting free competition. This covers foremost (non-contractual) claims for damages in relation to actual or past acts as well as injunctive relief (*ex parte* and interim as well as final injunctions) concerning impending anti-competitive acts.[175] **96**

c) Directly and Substantially Affected

While the optional rule of Art. 6(3)(b) explicitly requires a direct and substantial effect in the country whose law the plaintiff wants to choose, **neither the general rule of Art. 6(3)(a) nor a recital explicitly provide for such restrictive filters**. A recital to that extent[176] was deleted during the final conciliation process between Parliament and Council. Reasons for the deletion were not indicated. Considering the nature of Art. 6(3) as a mere clarification of the general rule in Art. 4 as well as the purpose and effect of such filters, it is submitted that Art. 6(3)(a) requires a direct, but no substantial effect.[177] Again, spillover protection is **97**

---

175 Cf. *Mankowski*, RIW 2008, 177, 182 et seq.

176 See Recital 20 of the Common Position (EC) No 22/2006 of 25 September 2006, OJ 2006 C 289E/68.

177 Concurring *Pineau*, 5 J. Priv. Int. L. (2009) 311, 322 seq.; *Dickinson*, para. 6.65; presumably also *Fitchen*, 5 J. Priv. Int. L. (2009) 337, 366 et seq.

moved from the level of private international law to the level of the substantive law.

98 The matter is, however, contested. Several authors regard a filtering threshold on the level of conflict of laws as being inherent in the potentially wide market effects principle.[178] There is, however, no unanimity amongst those authors: Some do not require a direct effect, but a substantial one,[179] others even add a requirement of foreseeability.[180]

aa) Direct Effect

99 The requirement of a **direct effect** is closely linked to Art. 4 Rome II on the one hand and to the passing on defence in substantive antitrust law on the other hand. According to Recital 21 the special rule in Art. 6 is no exception, but a clarification of Art. 4. Since it is common ground with regard to Art. 4 that indirect consequences of the damage to the protected interest are irrelevant for determining the country where the damage occurs,[181] the matter seems also settled in relation to Art. 6(3): indirect effects are no market effects for the purposes of determining the applicable law.

100 This view holds even true when considering the passing on defence, *i.e.* the question whether the defendant may succeed with the argument vis-à-vis direct purchasers that the overcharges paid by them due to a price fixing cartel were passed on to the final purchasers so that, on balance, the direct purchasers did not suffer any loss. If the respective substantive antitrust law grants

---

178 *Mankowski*, RIW 2008, 177, 186; *Rosenkranz/Rohde*, NIPR 2008, 435, 437.

179 *Leible/Lehmann*, RIW 2007, 721, 730; *Plender & Wilderspin*, para. 20-067 argue into that direction; *Roth*, in: FS Kropholler (2008) 623, 641 rejects a substantiality threshold but considers a *de minimis* threshold instead.

180 *Mankowski*, RIW 2008, 177, 185; disagreeing: *Hellner*, 9 YbPIL(2007) 49, 62.

181 See Art. 4 paras. 17 et seq.

this defence, it is regularly combined with granting final purchasers, usually consumers, a right to bring a damages claim although they suffer only indirect loss. First, the defendant should not be able to get away without paying any damages for his anti-competitive behaviour. Secondly, the final purchaser did actually suffer a loss resulting from the anti-competitive behaviour.

For this reason, it should be avoided that different laws apply to 101
the claim of the direct purchaser (country of the direct effect) and the claim of the final purchaser (country of the indirect effect).[182] If the law that denies the passing on-defence applies to the claim of the direct purchaser, and if the law that permits the passing on-defence applies to the claim of the indirect purchaser, the defendant may face two damages claims or, in the reverse case, no damages claim at all. Both scenarios would require the most difficult task of *Anpassung* (adaptation) on the level of conflict of laws and/or the substantive law – a highly undesirable result. Consequently, the law of the country whose market is directly affected by sales to direct purchasers governs claims by direct and indirect purchasers, including the passing on-defence.[183]

bb) Substantial Effect

The requirement of a **substantial effect** is repeatedly requested 102
based on the argument that substantiality or at least an appreciability threshold forms part of EU as well as most national antitrust laws.[184] Hence, if it were not to be applied in the context of Art. 6(3)(a) Rome II when determining the applicable law, a substantive antitrust law might be applied which, according to its own standards, is not applicable for lack of an appreciable or substan-

---

182 *Plender & Wilderspin*, para. 20-066.

183 It is important to note that the requirement of a direct effect is only relevant for determining the applicable law. It does not determine the existence of a damage claim by indirect purchasers which is a matter for the substantive law (of the country of direct effects).

184 *Mankowski*, RIW 2008, 177, 186; *Hellner*, 9 YbPIL (2007) 49, 61 et seq.

tial effect on the respective country's market.[185] While it is convincing that a national antitrust law should not be applied contrary to its self-determined scope, this does not mandate an appreciability or even substantiality threshold on the level of conflict of laws. To the contrary, in order to give full effect to the self-determination of the scope of foreign antitrust law, the matter must be dealt with on the level of the substantive law, *i.e.* the respective foreign antitrust law. Otherwise, one uniform European threshold under Art. 6(3)(a) Rome II would replace the national laws' self-determination. This has the further advantage that the threshold applies on the level where it is located by the national laws, *i.e.* the level of the substantive law. The consequences of such a "substantive level-approach" are straight forward: if the substantive law determined by Art. 6(3)(a) Rome II requires a substantial effect for its antitrust regime or specific prohibitions to apply, there simply lies no damage claim under the respective law in relation to the damage suffered in the respective country.[186]

103 The rationale might lead even further: Foreign antitrust law should only apply if it claims application in relation to the specific case, whether for reasons of appreciability or substantiality of the effects or any other reason. Consequently, a unilateral conflict rule in the national law determined by Art. 6(3)(a), that establishes whether domestic antitrust law is applicable, should be given full effect.[187] The exclusion of renvoi in Art. 24 Rome II does not bar such a view. It aims at avoiding reference to a further law or even laws under the conflict regime of Rome II. It does, however, not extend the applicability of foreign substantive law beyond its own self-determined scope.[188]

---

185 *Hellner*, 9 YbPIL (2007) 49, 62.

186 Concurring *Pineau*, 5 J. Priv. Int. L. (2009) 311, 322.

187 *Roth*, in: FS Kropholler (2008) 623, 641.

188 *Roth*, in: FS Kropholler (2008) 623, 641.

2. Multi-State and Multi-Party Constellations

While the general rule in Art. 6(3)(a) applies equally to multi-state (several affected markets) and multi-party (several co-defendants) constellations, the optional rule in Art. 6(3)(b) offers in such constellations a limited choice for a single law applicable to the entire damage claim even against several co-defendants. It is closely intertwined with the jurisdiction regime of the Brussels I Regulation. 104

a) Several Affected Markets

In case of several affected markets, one has to distinguish between the application of the general rule of Art. 6(3)(a) and the application of the optional rule of Art. 6(3)(b). 105

Under the **general rule of Art. 6(3)(a)**, anti-competitive acts affecting several markets are governed by the mosaic principle: the law of each country whose market is affected applies in relation to the damage that occurs in that country.[189] 106

Under the **optional rule of Art. 6(3)(b)**, the plaintiff is offered an indirect choice of one single law for the entire damage, irrespective of the country where the damage occurred. If he sues at the defendant's domicile in a Member State, he may opt for the *lex fori* if the market of the forum Member State is amongst those directly and substantially affected by the anti-competitive act (the substantiality threshold not being provided by the general rule[190]). 107

The **rationale of the optional rule** is to reduce costs and the duration of litigation as well as the risk of a wrong decision by enabling the court to determine all aspects of the case under the 108

---

189 *Dicey, Morris & Collins*, para. S 35-221; *Mankowski*, RIW 2008, 177, 188; *Dickinson*, para. 6.68; *Pineau*, 5 J. Priv. Int. L. (2009) 311; *Roth*, in: FS Kropholler (2008) 623, 644 seq.

190 See *supra* paras. 97 et seq.

lex fori.[191] It pays due credit to the fact that under the mosaic principle an action for damages is regularly so burdensome that it may discourage private enforcement *ab initio*. Although the optional rule is not limited to intra-Community cases, the violation of EU antitrust law is the model case for which the rule was designed. First, EU antitrust law applies only if the anti-competitive act may affect trade between Member States, so that it will regularly involve multi-state scenarios. Secondly, the difficulty to allocate the conglomerate damage to the respective national markets where the mosaic portions of the damage occurred arises particularly in cases of violation of EU antitrust law since its application does not require such an allocation. Even in follow-on actions, the plaintiff would have to establish the law applicable to the mosaic portions amongst the plurality of affected markets.

109 Art. 6(3)(b) does not set the terms for making use of the option (timing, form etc.) since these issues are matters of procedure. According to Art. 1(3) Rome II they are governed by the national procedural law of the court seized.[192]

110 While it is required that the **defendant's domicile is located in a Member State** and that this Member State's market is amongst those directly and substantially affected, the other affected markets may be those of Non-Member States.[193] In the latter scenario, however, the indirect choice of the plaintiff does not extend to the question of antitrust infringement. It is limited to the aspects of private enforcement, *i.e.* the private law aspects of the

---

[191] *Pineau*, 5 J. Priv. Int. L. (2009) 311, 323; *Mankowski*, RIW 2008, 177, 188; *Plender & Wilderspin*, para. 20-070; rather critical for good reasons *Wurmnest*, in: jurisPK BGB, Art. 6 para. 3.

[192] *Wurmnest*, in: jurisPK BGB, Art. 6 para. 34.

[193] *Pineau*, 5 J. Priv. Int. L. (2009) 311, 324; *Roth*, in: FS Kropholler (2008) 623, 647.

damages claim.[194] Consequently, the issue of infringement of an antitrust prohibition is not governed by the antitrust law of the *lex fori* under Art. 6(3)(b), but by the antitrust law of the affected market under Art. 6(3)(a). Otherwise, the antitrust law of the *lex fori*, regularly EU antitrust law, would be applied to effects in Non-Member State markets for which it does not claim application under the effects doctrine.[195] Conversely, foreign antitrust law would be disregarded in respect of effects for which it claims application. Limiting the operation of Art. 6(3)(b) to the private enforcement aspects does not contradict the optional rule's purpose to overcome the practical difficulties of the mosaic approach. In follow-on actions, which constitute the majority of cases, the real difficulty of multi-state constellations does not lie in establishing the infringement of antitrust law, even a foreign one, but rather in the application of different regimes of private enforcement under the mosaic approach.

The notion of domicile in Art. 6(3)(b) is identical with that un- 111
der Art. 2, 60 Brussels I.[196] It is an overarching concept of EU private international law as well as European international civil procedural law, and Art. 6(3)(b) is related to actions regularly brought under the Brussels I Regulation.

The optional rule in Art. 6(3)(b) requires that the domicile 112
Member State is **amongst those directly and substantially affected** by the anti-competitive act. The requirement of a direct effect does not add anything, since such effect is inherently also required under Art. 6(3)(a).[197] The requirement of a substantial effect, however, goes beyond Art. 6(3)(a). Its main aim is to avoid

---

194 *Roth*, in: FS Kropholler (2008) 623, 647 seq.; *Wurmnest*, in: jurisPK BGB, Art. 6 para. 33; *Plender & Wilderspin*, para. 20-072 (suggesting the application of Art. 17 Rome II in that regard); *Scholz/Rixen*, EuZW 2008, 327, 331.

195 *Roth*, in: FS Kropholler (2008) 623, 647.

196 *Mankowski*, RIW 2008, 177, 189.

197 See *supra* paras. 99 et seq.

forum shopping and to ensure a significant link between at least one of the affected markets and the applicable law. At one end of the spectrum, substantial appears to be more than appreciable.[198] At the other end of the spectrum, substantial does not require that the respective country is the centre of gravity of anti-competitive effects.[199] This is clearly demonstrated by the wording "amongst" which implies that there may be several markets that are substantially affected. Between those ends of the spectrum, turnover and market shares on the respective (national) markets will be important criteria for substantiality.[200] Eventually, such criteria will have to be determined by case law and largely depend on the circumstances of each individual case.

b) Several Co-Defendants

113 If in a multi-state case the action lies against several co-defendants (provided that they may be sued jointly under the respective rules of jurisdiction, *e.g.* Art. 6 Brussels I), the option for the *lex fori* is restricted to those cases where the claim against each of them is based on a restriction of competition directly and substantially affecting the market of the forum Member State. The rationale of this further option is largely identical with that of the first option. In addition, the concentration of claims is desirable to avoid diverging or even conflicting judgments.

c) Interplay with EU Antitrust Law

114 The two options of Art. 6(3)(b) are tailored to the two categories of anti-competitive behaviour under the TFEU. While multi-state constellations involving only one defendant may often occur in case of an abuse of a dominant position under Art. 102 TFEU, the additional multi-party scenario will usually arise in case of a cartel or concerted practice under Art. 101 TFEU which

---

198 *Roth*, in: FS Kropholler (2008), 623, 646; *Dickinson*, para. 6.71; *Wurmnest*, in: jurisPK BGB, Art. 6 para. 32.

199 *Mankowski*, RIW 2008, 177, 189; *Roth*, ibid. at 646.

200 *Roth*, in: FS Kropholler (2008) 623, 646.

will regularly involve several co-defendants, namely the members of the cartel or concerted practice.

d) Interplay with the EU Jurisdiction Regime

The optional rule in Art. 6(3)(b) is closely intertwined with and designed in light of the jurisdictional framework in multi-state and multi-party constellations under the Brussels I Regulation as developed by the ECJ. 115

In case of a **multi-state constellation**, the plaintiff has **several options** under the Brussels I Regulation where to file his claim. As a first and second option, he may sue the defendant under Art. 5 No. 3 Brussels I either at the place where the damage occurred or at the place where the event giving rise to the damage took place.[201] An action at the place where the damage occurred implies distinct claims in each country whose market is affected, with the jurisdiction of the respective court limited to the damage that occurred on the respective market (one mosaic piece per each claim).[202] An action at the place where the event giving rise to the damage took place may cover the entire damage although the mosaic principle will apply (all mosaic pieces per one claim).[203] As a third option, the plaintiff may sue the defendant under Art. 2 Brussels I at his domicile where he may also recover 116

---

201 See in particular ECJ, Case 21/76 – *Mines de Potasse d'Alsace* [1976] ECR 1735 paras. 19 et seq.; Case C-68/93 – *Shevill* [1995] ECR I-415 para. 20; Case C-167/00 – *Verein für Konsumenteninformation* [2002] ECR I-8111 paras. 42 et seq.; Case C-168/02 – *Kronhofer* [2004] ECR I-6009 para. 16.

202 ECJ, Case C-68/93 – *Shevill* [1995] ECR I-415 para. 30.

203 ECJ, Case C-68/93 – *Shevill* [1995] ECR I-415 para. 32; for further details see G. *Wagner*, 62 RabelsZ (1998) 243, 277 et seq.; *Mäsch*, IPRax 2005, 509; see also Oberster Gerichtshof (Austria), 28 May 2002 – 4 Ob 116/02s, RdW 2002, 603; Oberlandesgericht München (Germany), 20 January 2000 – 29 U 5819/99, MMR 2000, 277; Hanseatisches Oberlandesgericht Hamburg (Germany), 19 April 2007 – 1 Kart U 5/06, GRUR-RR 2008, 31; Cour de Cassation (France), 16 July 1997 – 95-17.163, 125 Clunet (1998) 136.

the entire damage (again all mosaic pieces per one claim). The conflict rule in Art. 6(3)(b) Rome II does away with the mosaic approach (with regard to the private law elements of the claim) in allowing the plaintiff to opt for the *lex fori* at the domicile of the defendant in relation to the entire damage. The place where the event giving rise to the damage took place will regularly coincide with the defendant's domicile.[204] The combined effect of Art. 2 Brussels I (or the place where the event giving rise to the damage took place under Art. 5 No. 3 Brussels I) and Art. 6(3)(b) Rome II is to allow recovery of all mosaic pieces per one claim under one single law.

117 In case of a **multi-party constellation**, the plaintiff may sue several co-defendants in one court according to Art. 6 No. 1 Brussels I. In case of a cartel or concerted practice, the requirement of a close connection between the claims against each of them is met,[205] while this may not always be the case with acts in abuse of a dominant position under different national antitrust laws (which may impose stricter standards than Art. 102 TFEU).[206] As a logical extension of the first option, the second option of Art. 6(3)(b) Rome II grants the choice for one single law even in such multi-party constellations regularly occurring in case of a violation of Art. 101 TFEU. The combined effect of Art. 2, 6 No. 1 Brussels I and Art. 6(3)(b) Rome II is to allow recovery of all mosaic pieces from the co-defendant per one claim under one single law.

---

204 G. *Wagner*, IPRax 2008, 1, 8.

205 *Mäsch*, IPRax 2005, 509, 512 seq.; *Leible/Lehmann*, RIW 2007, 721, 730; *Mankowski*, RIW 2008, 177, 191; see also *Roche Products Ltd. v Provimi Ltd* [2003] EWHC 961 paras. 41 et seq. (an action in the aftermath of the vitamins cartel); for a detailed analysis of the decision see *Bulst*, 4 EBOR (2003) 623, in relation to Art. 6 Brussels I at 631 seq. and 643.

206 *Scholz/Rixen*, EuZW 2008, 327, 332.

d) Tactical Considerations

Within the regime of Art. 6(3)(b) there is little room for tactical considerations due to the requirement of a direct and substantial effect of the anti-competitive act at the domicile of the defendant. This renders forum shopping at least under the first alternative of lit. b hardly possible. In fact, the avoidance of forum shopping was the very purpose of introducing the additional threshold which is not contained in the general rule of Art. 6(3)(a). Under the second alternative of lit. b, however, there is room for forum shopping as between the domiciles of at least some of the co-defendants since the home markets of cartel members are usually amongst those directly and substantially affected.[207] **118**

As regards the choice between Art. 6(3)(a) and Art. 6(3)(b), the optional rule in lit. b may be advantageous for the plaintiff in the majority of multi-state scenarios for the reasons given above. Nevertheless, it is worth weighing advantages versus disadvantages in the individual case, particularly in relation to the matters listed (non-exhaustively) in Art. 15 Rome II. While costs and time efficiency will generally militate in favour of the optional rule, an advantageous assessment of damages under a specific *lex causae* may outweigh those general advantages. The plaintiff may then file several actions under Art. 5(3), each in respect of the damage suffered on the respective (national) market, rather than filing one single claim at the defendant's domicile. Furthermore, the fact that according to Art. 1(3) matters of evidence and procedure are governed by the *lex fori* may outweigh cost and time advantages. **119**

207 *Mankowski*, RIW 2008, 177, 191; *Heiss/Loacker*, JBL 2007, 613, 630; *Roth*, in: FS Kropholler (2008) 623, 646.

Article 7
Environmental damage

The law applicable to a non-contractual obligation arising out of environmental damage or damage sustained by persons or property as a result of such damage shall be the law determined pursuant to Article 4(1), unless the person seeking compensation for damage chooses to base his or her claim on the law of the country in which the event giving rise to the damage occurred.

A. Introduction

1 Art. 7 establishes a special provision for environmental liability. In distinguishing the general rule of Art. 4(1) to which Art. 7 explicitly refers, the law applicable to environmental damage is the law of the country in which the damage occurs *unless* the person seeking compensation for damage chooses to base his or her claim on the law of the country in which the event giving rise to the damage occurred. It must be emphasised that Art. 7 refers only to Art. 4(1); it does not refer to the other paragraphs in

Art. 4 and is therefore not subject to either the common domicile nor the closer connection exception. This is due to the fact that the victim's right of election is motivated by **substantial policy** (see below paras. 10-12 and 25-27). Choice of law under Art. 14 is, however, possible,[1] and it has been frequently used in practice.[2]

Only in cases of environmental damage does Rome II provide for the **principle of ubiquity**, which takes into account the place of injury and the law of the place of conduct. However, it should be noted that the alternatives in Art. 7 do not have the same standing, as the *lex loci damni* will apply unless the claimant opts for the law of the country of the event giving rise to damage. As the decision on the applicable law depends on the choice of the victim, this will result in applying the law that is more favourable to the injured party: so-called **most favourable law principle** (Günstigkeitsprinzip).[3] 2

To sum up, pursuant to Art. 14, parties may choose the applicable law; if this is not done, the claimant may opt in favour of the law of the place of conduct; and if this is not the case, the law of the place of injury will apply to environmental liability. 3

During the drafting process, the principle of ubiquity and its combination with the victim's option to choose the law of the place of conduct were heavily criticised. 4

1 *von Hein*, 82 Tul.L.Rev. (2008) 1663, 1699; *Garcimartín Alférez*, EuLF 3-2007, 77, 87; *Thorn*, in: Palandt, Art. 7 para. 6; *Junker*, in: Münchener Kommentar BGB, Art. 7 para. 6; cf. Art. 14 para. 1.

2 *E.g.* in the famous case ECJ, Case 21/76 – *Mines Potasse d'Alsace*, [1976] ECR 1735; *Kadner Graziano*, 73 RabelsZ (2009) 1, 45.

3 *Junker*, in: Münchener Kommentar BGB, Art. 7 para. 1; *Wurmnest*, in: jurisPK BGB, Art. 7 para. 1.

B. Justification of the Principle of Ubiquity and the Victim's Option to Choose the Law of the Place of Conduct

I. Basic Rule

5 Following the principle of ubiquity, it is either the law of the place of injury or the law of the place of conduct that will apply. The basic connection to the law of the **place of injury** *(Erfolgsort)* does not need any further justification. As set forth above, this rule considers both the interests of tortfeasor and victim[4] and intends to guarantee full compensation for the person suffering the loss according to the law of the state of his or her habitual residence. Furthermore, the rule is in accordance with the policy of prevention, as it removes the incentive to operate in a low-protection country and to rely exclusively on its legal system with its (low) level of damages.[5]

6 It is not required that the place of injury could have been foreseen by the tortfeasor.[6] This is to say that the tortfeasor cannot exclude liability arguing that he could not reasonably have foreseen the country in which the damage occurred.

7 The inclusion of the **place of conduct** (or place where the wrongful act was committed; *Handlungsort*) is set out in Recital 25.[7] All

---

4 See Art. 4 para. 15.

5 Proposal for a Regulation of the European Parliament and the Council on the law applicable to non-contractual obligations ("Rome II"), 22 July 2003, COM(2003) 427 final, p. 19; *Cheshire, North & Fawcett*, p. 813.

6 *Thorn*, in: Palandt, Art. 7 para. 7.

7 "Regarding environmental damage, Art. 174 of the Treaty, which provides that there should be a high level of protection based on the precautionary principle and the principle that preventive action should be taken, the principle of priority for corrective action at source and the principle that the polluter pays, fully justifies the use of the principle of discriminating in favour of the person sustaining the damage."

the principles mentioned in the Recital justified alternatively applying the law of the state of emission in the eyes of the legislature. The operator should not be given any incentive to establish his facilities at the border and pollute or discharge waste almost exclusively to the neighbouring country, thus benefiting from the lower damage awards in the neighbouring country. In short, the rule should contribute to raising the general level of environmental protection.[8] Following this reasoning, an international treaty and a bilateral agreement have already embodied the most favourable law principle.[9] The solutions in domestic legal systems varied widely, and only very few national laws provided for a special conflict of law rule for environmental damage.[10] Several European countries were applying the principle of ubiquity in their national laws.[11]

II. Criticism

Diana Wallis, the rapporteur of the European Parliament's Committee on Legal Affairs argued against a special rule for violations 8

8 Proposal for a Regulation of the European Parliament and the Council on the law applicable to non-contractual obligations ("Rome II"), 22 July 2003, COM(2003) 427 final, p. 19.

9 Art. 3 para. 2 of the Nordic Environmental Protection Convention of 1974; Art. 4 para. 3 of the Bilateral Agreement of 19 December 1967 between Germany and Austria on the effects of the establishment of the Salzburg Airport.

10 See in particular: Art. 138 of the Swiss Law on Private International Law: claims resulting from harmful emissions emanating from an immovable property are governed, at the choice of the injured party, by the law of the State in which the real property is located or by the law of the State in which the harmful event occurred.

11 Czech Republic, Estonia, Germany, Hungary, Italy, Slovenia, Slovakia; *Kadner Graziano*, 73 RabelsZ (2009) 1, 46 fn. 154; for a comparative report see *Fach Gómez*, 6 YbPIL (2004) 291, 296-303.

of the environment.[12] The principle of ubiquity and the victim's option to choose the law of the country in which the event giving rise to the damage occurred is equally criticised by some legal scholars. Following them, the "polluter pays" principle only requires that the polluter has to remedy the cost of the environmental harm; it does not require that the claimant has a choice of law and can therefore maximise recovery. It is said that the outcome of the case is "less predictable, thereby frustrating the settlement of claims and makes it harder for the defendants to insure effectively against environmental liability."[13] Along this line, it is argued that applying the law of the state of emission discriminates against foreign operators compared to national operators. The foreign operator does not only have to comply with the law of the neighbouring country but also with the (stricter) rules of his own country. Applying the rule finally introduced by the European legislature means that the victim will profit from an unjustified **international bonus**.[14] And if he does so, the lack of consistency is criticised as the principle of ubiquity only applies to environmental harms: if, for example, a product causes damage to the environment, the question of applicable law will depend on the decision whether to apply Art. 5 or Art. 7.[15]

9 Furthermore, it is doubted that this rule leads to a higher level of environmental protection.[16] Finally, it is said that it is not the task of the Commission to use tort law in order to push countries with less stringent rules to set up a higher environmental standard.[17]

---

12 "... violations of the environment can be dealt with under Art. 3, as amended:" Report of 27 June 2005, A6-0211/2005, p. 23, Rapporteur: *Diana Wallis*.

13 *Petch*, J.I.B.L.R. 2006, 509, 511.

14 G. *Wagner*, IPRax 2006, 372, 380; *Kadner Graziano*, 73 RabelsZ (2009) 1, 46 and 9 YbPIL (2007) 71, 74 who nevertheless favours the principle of ubiquity.

15 *Leible/Lehmann*, RIW 2007, 721, 728. See below para. 24.

16 *Sonnentag*, 105 ZVglRWiss (2006) 256, 296.

III. Principle of Prevention

Other legal scholars justify the principle of ubiquity in environmental law, even if they oppose this idea in general.[18] The main reason lies in the protection of the environment. It is a matter of fact that there exist different levels of environmental protection and liability rules. Therefore, it matters what law has to be applied. In other words: if there were uniform substantive rules on environmental liability, legislation in the area of private international law would be superfluous, as the answer to the question of what law to apply would be of no relevance to the outcome of the case. The principle of ubiquity guarantees that the operator does not take advantage of the different levels of environmental protection. 10

It is criticised by some legal scholars that the principle of ubiquity makes liability less predictable. This unpredictability, however, depends to a large extent on the decision made by the person seeking compensation. Even though this is up to the Member States to decide, it is argued below that it is advisable to set up a very short **period of time** in which litigants must make this decision.[19] The period of unpredictability can therefore be limited to a minimum. As far as insurance matters are concerned, the operator must take into account all the places of injury which can be reached with the toxic substances produced or emitted – including the place of conduct. 11

In the case of environmental damage, conflict of law rules are used openly by the European legislature to make liability more severe. If the conflict of law rule pointed only in one direction, be it the place of injury *or* the place of conduct, there would be the risk that the operator could take advantage of the different 12

---

17 G. *Wagner*, IPRax 2006, 372, 380.

18 *von Bar*, 268 Rec. des Cours (1997) 291, 367ss.; *Kropholler*, Internationales Privatrecht, p. 525.

19 See below para. 31.

protection levels by operating in or close-by a low-protection country. The proposed exclusive application of the law of the place where the damage is sustained will result in the establishment of facilities in border regions in order to benefit from the lower levels of the victim's home state.[20] The principle of **prevention** therefore requires that the principle of ubiquity applies in international environmental cases. The principle of prevention, and not sympathy for the victim,[21] is the reason for setting up a special rule for environmental liability. To give the victim a choice is simply the means to achieve this result. The decision for the principle of ubiquity and the victim's option to choose the law of the place of conduct strengthens the effectiveness of EU environmental law[22] and gives a clear example of the regulatory function of conflict rules within the European Union.

C. Content of the Provision

I. Civil and Commercial Matters

13 The Rome II Regulation only applies in situations involving civil and commercial matters; it does not apply to *acta iure imperii* (Art. 1 (1) and Recital 9). The term "civil and commercial mat-

---

20 *Betlem/Bernasconi*, 122 LQR (2006) 124, 141; *von Hein*, VersR 2007, 440, 449 and in: Das Günstigkeitsprinzip im Internationalen Privatrecht, p. 124.

21 *Kegel/Schurig*, Internationales Privatrecht, p. 725: "die Sympathie mit dem Opfer ist im allgemeinen größer als die mit dem Täter".

22 *Symeonides*, 56 AmJCompL (2008) 1, 46 and FS Jayme, 935, 951; *Ofner*, ZfRV 2008, 13, 18; *von Hein*, VersR 2007, 440, 449: "Favor naturae" and in: Calliess, Rome Regulations, Art. 7 para. 2; *Freigang*, Grenzüberschreitende Grundstücksimmissionen (2008) 255; *Junker*, in: Münchener Kommentar BGB, Art. 7 paras. 1, 4; *Dicey, Morris & Collins*, para. S 35-225; *Cheshire, North & Fawcett*, p. 814; *Bogdan*, in: Liber Fausto Pocar, p. 95, 97 and in: Ahern/Binchy (eds.), The Rome II Regulation, p. 219, 220; *Kadner Graziano*, 73 RabelsZ (2009) 1, 47.

ters" is not defined in the Regulation; it will be given an **autonomous interpretation** according to the jurisprudence of the ECJ concerning Art. 1 of the Brussels Convention or the Brussels I Regulation (see Recital 7 of the Rome II Regulation).

Following the jurisprudence of the ECJ, it must be determined whether, by reason of the legal relationship between the parties to the action or of the subject matter of the action, the legal claim falls within the scope of the Regulation.[23] Litigation involving a state or a public authority falls within the scope of the Brussels I Regulation where the public authority has acted in a private law capacity. Claims are outside the scope of Art. 1 if the state is acting as sovereign or in accordance with public law powers.[24] The same is then true for the interpretation of the Rome II Regulation. 14

In cases of environmental liability, public authorities, including states, are often involved against private parties, be it as claimant or defendant. A typical example is the **recovery of clean-up costs** after an oil pollution incident.[25] 15

---

23 A case involving cross-border pollution was decided under the Brussels I Regulation: Art. 22 of the Brussels I Regulation was held not applicable to an action brought by a State (Province of Upper Austria) for cessation of a nuisance caused by the activities of a nuclear power plant on the territory of a neighbouring State (Czech Republic); in the end it remained undecided whether the case involved a "civil and commercial matter" under Art. 1, ECJ Case C-343/04 – *Land Oberösterreich v ČEZ as* [2006] ECR I-4557 para. 22/23. Please note that non-contractual obligations arising out of nuclear damage are excluded from the scope of the Rome II Regulation, Art. 1 para. 2 (f); see below paras. 43-52.

24 ECJ Case 29/76 - *LTU v Eurocontrol* [1976] ECR 1541; ECJ Case 814/79 – *Netherlands State v Rüffer* [1980] ECR 3807; ECJ Case C-292/05 – *Lechouritou* [2007] ECR 2007 I-1519.

25 E.g. oil spill of the tanker Amoco Cadiz, see *Kloss*, IPRax 1989, 184; *Eskenazi*, 24 J.M.L.C. (1993) 371.

16 It is a matter of *characterisation* to decide whether a State acts in a given case as a sovereign *(acta iure imperii)* or according to the rules of private law *(acta iure gestionis)*. Decisive to the issue is whether the state is exercising public authority powers. In cases of lawmaking, mistakes in planning, permitting or supervising, the defendant State acts as sovereign; in cases in which the State uses private forms of organisation or private law instruments, private law will apply to liability issues. The State as claimant will usually act as sovereign when it carries out a societal task and claims compensation for ecological damages; it grounds its claim on private rights if a private person could claim compensation on the basis of the same reasoning.

17 Going one step further, it was suggested to apply a "green" interpretation of "civil and commercial matters" in Brussels I.[26] The argument of interpreting "civil and commercial matters" in the light of EU environmental law seems to be even more valid in the context of the Rome II Regulation, and Recital 25 explicitly refers to Art. 174 of the EC Treaty (Art. 191 TFEU), which includes the **polluter pays principle**. It is therefore consistent to contend that Art. 7 should be construed so as to contribute to this fundamental principle of environmental protection. Following the argument that Art. 7 (with regard to Recital 24) covers not only damage to private property, but also damage to the environment itself, it was argued that claims for pure environmental harm, mainly claims brought by public authorities, are to be regarded as "civil matters."[27]

18 However, the concept of "civil and commercial matters" in Art. 1 is set out not only for the Rome II Regulation, but also for other

26 *Betlem/Bernasconi*, 122 LQR (2006) 124, 136; in the same sense: *Kadner Graziano*, 73 RabelsZ (2009) 1, 55 and 9 YbPIL (2007) 71, 85; arguing against this approach: *Dickinson*, para. 7.05.

27 *Kadner Graziano*, 9 YbPIL (2007) 71, 86 and 73 RabelsZ (2009) 1, 54; *von Hein*, in: Callies, Rome Regulations, Art. 7 para. 6 who argues on the basis of Directive 2004/35/EC.

instruments regarding civil justice (*e.g.* Brussels I Regulation). Therefore, it should not be given a broader interpretation for matters falling within one single provision than for other matters.[28] Whether the subject matter falls within the scope of application of the Rome II Regulation must be answered positively before a special conflict of law rule of the Regulation applies. In other words: while Recital 25 refers to Art. 7, which should certainly be interpreted in the light of the objectives set out in Art. 191 TFEU, it does not influence the interpretation "civil and commercial matters" in Art. 1. Having said that, the recovery of preventive and remedial measures (including the recovery of clean-up costs after an oil pollution incident through the State authorities), is to be characterised as being *acta iure imperii*, and therefore falls outside the scope of the Brussels I and the Rome II Regimes.[29]

II. Environmental Damage *et al*

Art. 7 applies in cases of a non-contractual obligation arising out **19**
of environmental damage or damage sustained by persons or property as a result of such damage. Following the European Parliament's proposal, the notion "environmental damage" is defined in Recital 24: it should be understood as meaning "adverse change in a natural resource, such as water, land or air, impairment of a function performed by that resource for the benefit of another natural resource or the public, or impairment of the variability among living organisms." A more detailed definition can be found in Art. 2 of the **Directive on environmental liability**, which focuses on public law and does not address issues of conflict of laws.[30] It is readily apparent that Recital 24 was drafted

---

28 *Dickinson*, para. 7.06.

29 *Dickinson*, para. 7.06; *Thorn*, in: Palandt, Art. 7 para. 4.

30 Directive 2004/35/EC of the European Parliament and of the Council of 21 April 2004 on environmental liability with regard to the prevention and remedying of environmental damage, OJ L 143/56 of 30 April 2004.

with regard to this Directive.[31] If further clarification on the notion of "environmental damage" is needed, Art. 2 of the Directive should be taken into account.

20 Noise immissions do not fall within the scope of Art. 7.[32]

21 Art. 7 Rome II covers two types of damages: first, it covers **damage to the environment** itself, and second, it covers both **damage to persons and property** if they are the result of the damage to ecology and consequence of human activity.[33] The latter is to say, that personal injuries, damages to property and private economic losses[34] are included in Art. 7 if, and only if, they result from damages to the environment.

22 When the applicable law is determined under Art. 7 and Art. 4(1), it is decisive where the environmental damage occurred; that law will also govern the damage to persons and property.[35] It may, of course, be possible that the environmental damage occurs in several countries ("*Streudelikt*") and that one incident will be subject to several different laws. Unless the claimant(s) opts in favour of the law of the place of conduct, each damage is judged according to the law of the place of injury (mosaic principle).

23 The Rome II Regulation does not provide for a special conflict of law rule for environmental damages involving interference with **real property**. Those claims should be considered tortious in nat-

---

31 More details on drafting Recital 24: *R. Wagner*, in: FS Kropholler, p. 715, 730.

32 *Junker*, in: Münchener Kommentar BGB, Art. 7 para. 14.

33 Proposal for a Regulation of the European Parliament and the Council on the law applicable to non-contractual obligations ("Rome II"), 22 July 2003, COM(2003) 427 final, p. 19.

34 *Garcimartín Alférez*, EuLF 3-2007, 77, 87; *Thorn*, in: Palandt, Art. 7 para. 2; *Dickinson*, para. 7.13.

35 *Bogdan*, in: Liber Fausto Pocar, p. 95, 99 and in: Ahern/Binchy (eds.), The Rome II Regulation, p. 219, 223.

ure.[36] The same result is reached under Art. 44 of the German EGBGB[37] and Art. 99 (2) of the Swiss PIL Act, which both provide that claims for nuisance originating from real property are governed by the conflict rule on tort (and not by the *lex rei sitae*). Thus, all cases of environmental liability fall under the same conflict rule. The advantages of this solution are twofold: first, all (delictual or property-based) claims of the injured party arising in a cross-border pollution case will be treated according to the same conflict rule, precluding difficult issues of characterisation from arising. Second, actions for damage caused to property are characterised as tortious by the ECJ in the context of Art. 5 (3) Brussels I Regulation.[38] Thus, the provision on jurisdiction and the conflict rule concerning environmental liability are consistent (see Recital 7 Rome II Regulation).

In cases where a **faulty product** causes environmental damage, it must be decided whether the rule for "damage caused by a product" (Art. 5) or "environmental damage" (Art. 7) will apply. The Regulation does not provide for a solution for this conflict.[39] It is suggested here that in cases in which both provisions are applicable, Art. 7 should take priority over Art. 5.[40] The rule on product liability in Art. 5 provides for escape clauses, whereas Art. 7 leaves no room for weakening the principle of ubiquity. 24

36 *Thorn*, in: Palandt, Art. 7 para. 3; *Hohloch*, in: Erman, Kommentar zum Bürgerlichen Gesetzbuch, Art. 40 EGBGB para. 50b; *Kadner Graziano*, 73 RabelsZ (2009) 1, 48; *von Hein*, in: Calliess, Rome Regulations, Art. 7 para. 15.

37 See on the now revised Art. 44 EGBGB: *R. Wagner*, IPRax 2008, 314, 318.

38 ECJ, Case 21/76 – *Mines de potasses d'Alsace* [1976] ECR-1735.

39 *Rushworth/Scott*, LMCLQ 2008, 274, 298: the Regulation yields "no obviously correct answer;" *Bogdan*, in: Liber Fausto Pocar, p. 95, 105 considers it possible that the claimant will be given the choice between the provisions.

40 *Junker*, in: Münchener Kommentar BGB, Art. 5 para. 20; *von Hein*, in: Callies, Rome Regulations, Art. 7 para. 10; cf. Art. 5 para. 13.

Only if Art. 7 takes priority over Art. 5 it can fulfill its preventive function aimed for by the legislator.

III. Reference to the General Rule in Art. 4(1)

25 Art. 7 is not subject to any exceptions; the law of the place of injury applies unless the claimant opts for the law of the country of the event giving rise to damage. In order to guarantee the principle of ubiquity, Art. 7 only refers to Art. 4(1); it does not cross-refer to paragraphs (2) and (3). A special proximate relationship to another legal system because of the habitual residence of both the tortfeasor and the victim (common habitual residence rule in paragraph 2) or a closer connection with another country (general escape clause in paragraph 3) will not be taken into consideration for the purposes of determining the applicable law in environmental liability cases.

26 Applying the proper law of tort because of a special proximate relationship would weaken the *lex loci delicti commissi*.[41] In transboundary pollution cases, the polluter should not get an opportunity to avoid the application of the *lex loci*. Especially when damage to real property arises, neither the application of the common habitual residence nor the general escape clause would justify a deviation from the *lex loci*.

27 Finally, a referral to Art. 4(2) and (3) would also derogate from the *principle of ubiquity*. The central reason for introducing the principle of ubiquity in Art. 7 is the high level of **environmental protection** sought. The fundamental principle of environmental protection is given priority over the conflict of laws interest in applying the so-called proper law of the tort. To deviate from the principle of ubiquity and to remove the victim's option to

41 *von Bar*, 268 Rec des Cours (1997) 291, 375; *Fach Gómez*, 6 YbPIL (2004) 291, 301.

choose the law of the place of conduct would lower the level of environmental protection strived for with the help of conflict of law rules.

However, it should be noted that Art. 7 does not restrict the parties' freedom to choose the applicable law under Art. 14.[42] 28

IV. The Victim's Right to Choose the Law of the Place of Conduct

According to Art. 7, it is for the victim (rather than the court) to elect the law of the State in which the event giving rise to the damage occurred. It is upon him to decide which law is most favourable to him. The law chosen will apply to **all the aspects** of the claimant's liability; there is no room for cherry-picking and *dépeçage*.[43] Equally, the claimant cannot choose different laws for different parts of the damage (*e.g.* one law for personal damage and another law for damage to property), as the wording of Art. 7 does not offer this possibility.[44] 29

This option right constitutes a unilateral choice of law or *facultas alternativa*, as the law of the place of conduct will replace the law of the place of injury once the choice is made.[45] 30

Recital 25 adds that the "question of when the person seeking compensation can make the choice of law applicable should be determined in accordance with the law of the Member State in which the court is seised." It is the *lex fori* that decides when the 31

---

42 Cf. fn. 1, 2.

43 *Dickinson*, para. 7.24; *Thorn*, in: Palandt, Art. 7 para. 8; *von Hein*, ZEuP 2009, 6, 30; *Bogdan*, in: Liber Fausto Pocar, 95, 98.

44 The term "the law" is used in the singular, not in the plural. For a different approach: *Bogdan*, in: Liber Fausto Pocar, p. 95, 98 and in: Ahern/Binchy (eds.), The Rome II Regulation, p. 219, 222.

45 *Junker*, in: Münchener Kommentar BGB, Art. 7 para. 27; *von Hein*, in: Callies, Rome Regulations, Art. 7 para. 20.

choice must be made. It is advisable for the lawmakers in the Member States to keep the **period for decision** relatively short. The costs of the legal process can be kept lower if the applicable law is known at an early stage. A change of the applicable law at a late stage of the process will produce unnecessary costs for the parties and court alike. It is not possible to revoke the choice once made.[46]

32 Member States that have rules on the choice of law in international tort law will apply them if and as long as the national conflict rules continue to be applicable despite Rome II.[47] In Germany, for example, Art. 46a EGBGB, according to which the choice has to be made in first instance within certain time limits, will apply.[48]

V. Scope of the Applicable Law

33 The applicable law determined according to Art. 7 governs, as for any other tort (cf. Art. 15), in particular the following issues:[49] conditions (*e.g.* strict or fault-based, causation) and extent of liability (*e.g.* limitation of liability), liability for others, compensation, prevention or termination of damage or injury, and remedies such as injunctions[50] (*e.g.* injunctive relief, prohibitory and mandatory injunctions), damages and the assessment of damages.

---

46 *Junker*, in: Münchener Kommentar BGB, Art. 7 para. 31; *Thorn*, in: Palandt, Art. 7 para. 8.

47 For the rules of English law on the proof of foreign law, see: *Dickinson*, para. 7.26; *Dicey, Morris and Collins*, rule 18.

48 German Official Journal (BGBl) 2008 I 2401; *R. Wagner*, IPRax 2008, 314, 318.

49 *Betlem/Bernasconi*, 122 LQR (2006) 124, 147.

50 *Kadner Graziano*, 73 RabelsZ (2009) 1, 73 and 9 YbPIL (2007) 71, 76; *Bogdan*, in: Ahern/Binchy (eds.), The Rome II Regulation, p. 219, 221.

D. Rules of Safety and Conduct (Art. 17)

A major problem results if the operator's conduct is authorised and legitimate in State A, but not authorised according to the laws of State B, where it causes damage. Art. 17 provides that "account shall be taken, as a matter of fact and in so far as is appropriate, of the rules of safety and conduct which were in force at the place and time of the event giving rise to the liability." The term **"rules of safety and conduct"** should be interpreted broadly according to Recital 34. 34

For purposes of environmental liability, one has to distinguish between **different scenarios**: if the victim has chosen the law of the place of conduct (State A), then this law will also decide on the effects of the rules of safety and conduct. Only one law will apply in this alternative; if there is a public authorisation, the claim will be precluded. 35

If, however, the law of the place of the injury applies (State B), it will have to be decided by the courts whether the rules of safety and conduct or an administrative authorisation in State A will be taken into account. Two situations are possible: if the court in State A has to decide, it will certainly take into account its own laws irrespective of the fact that the law of the place of injury is applicable to the case. This follows from the principle of unity of the legal system of the *lex fori*.[51] 36

The legal situation is more complicated if the court in State B has to decide on the issue of environmental liability according to the law of State B (place of injury): whether the permit from State A's agencies is effective must be judged according to the law of State A.[52] The private law effects of A's permit on the 37

---

51 *von Hein*, in: Callies, Rome Regulations, Art. 7 para. 26.

52 *von Bar*, 268 Rec des Cours (1997) 291, 384.

liability of the operator in a cross-border situation are dealt with in Art. 17.[53]

38 The wording of Art. 17 must be regarded as an evidentiary instruction: first, Art. 17 provides that "account shall be taken" of foreign safety rules, *i.e.* the court will not necessarily *apply* those rules.[54] Second, it states that the rules are taken into account "as a matter of fact" (not: as a matter of law). Third, taking into account the rules of safety and conduct lies in the court's discretion ("in so far as appropriate"). The purpose of Art. 17 is to "strike a reasonable balance between the parties" (Recital 34).

39 In the case mentioned above, where the activity is authorised and legitimate in State A but not in State B (where the damage is caused), "the court must then be able to have regard to the fact that the perpetrator has complied with the rules in force in the country in which he is in business."[55] This is to say, that the operator's conduct that leads to the damage had to comply with the administrative authorisation granted; if this is not the case, the issue of taking into consideration foreign rules of conduct and safety will not arise.

---

[53] Unless there is no special rule in an international convention such as Art. 4 para. 3 sentence 2 of the Bilateral Agreement of 19 December 1967 between Germany and Austria on the effects of the establishment of the Salzburg Airport. – For a different approach see however: *Mankowski*, IPRax 2010, 389-395 who proposes *(de lege ferenda)* a detailed solution by way of recognition.

[54] Proposal for a Regulation of the European Parliament and the Council on the law applicable to non-contractual obligations ("Rome II"), 22 July 2003, COM(2003) 427 final, p. 25: "Taking account of foreign law is not the same thing as applying it (...)."; *Betlem/Bernasconi*, 122 LQR (2006) 124, 150; *Cheshire, North & Fawcett*, p. 814.

[55] Proposal for a Regulation of the European Parliament and the Council on the law applicable to non-contractual obligations ("Rome II"), 22 July 2003, COM(2003) 427 final, p. 20.

40 The approach favoured in Art. 17 is a flexible one, but it also provides the court with little guidance. The court will therefore have to decide on its own if and how it will take account of foreign rules of safety and conduct. It will be of crucial importance whether the **principle of equivalence of the authorisations** is fulfilled (shared values). Possible criteria might be:[56]

- participation of individuals residing abroad in the authorisation procedure (= right to be heard)
- compliance with general rules of international law/EU law on environmental protection
- comparable environmental standard and authorisation procedure
- compliance with public policy

41 There is little case law on the effects of the authorisation for other Member States. The ECJ decided an action for **cessation of nuisance** by the activities of a **nuclear power plant** situated on the territory of another Member State.[57] The Land Oberösterreich is the owner of land used for agriculture, situated about 60 km from Temelín, a Czech power plant. According to Austrian law, actions for cessation of a nuisance emanating from installations which have been granted official authorisation, are precluded. However, according to a judgment of the Oberster Gerichtshof, this is only true for authorisations granted by Austrian authorities.

---

56 *Thorn*, in: Palandt, Art. 7 para. 9; *Schaub*, in: Prütting/Wegen/Weinreich, Art. 7 para. 4; *Hohloch*, in: Erman, Kommentar zum Bürgerlichen Gesetzbuch, Art. 40 EGBGB para. 50b; *Kadner Graziano*, 73 RabelsZ (2009) 1, 50; *Pfeiffer* in: Jahrbuch des Umwelt- und Technikrechts (2000) 263, 295; in favour of comparable conditions for the recognition of authorisations: *Mankowski*, IPRax 2010, 389, 391. But see for a different approach: *Bach*, Art. 17 para. 16.

57 ECJ, Case C-115/08 – *Land Oberösterreich v. ČEZ* [2009] OJ C 312/5 of 19 December 2009.

42 Based on the principle of prohibition of discrimination on grounds of nationality, the ECJ declares this interpretation of the Oberster Gerichtshof as non-compatible with the requirements of European Law. It therefore precludes the application of the legislation of a Member State, under which an undertaking in possession of the necessary official authorisation for operating a nuclear power plant situated in the territory of another Member State, may be the subject of an action for an injunction to prevent an actual or potential nuisance, whereas undertakings having an industrial installation in the Member State where the action is brought and in possession of an official authorisation may not be subject of such an action and may only be the subject of a claim for damages for harm caused to a neighbouring country. There is no justification for such a difference in treatment. The reason for this is that on the level of the European Union, there are uniform safety standards which are regularly evaluated and supervised. As union law guarantees the "consistent and effective protection of health of the general public against the dangers arising from ionising radiations" (para. 112), the action for an injunction cannot succeed. This judgment is not directly applicable to issues under the Rome II Regulation. However, it should certainly be taken into account when considering environmental liability.

E. Excluded from the Scope: Nuclear Damage

43 Art. 1(2)(f) Rome II expressly excludes "non-contractual obligations arising out of nuclear damage" from the scope of the Regulation.[58] The reason for excluding nuclear damage from the scope of application is "the importance of economic and State interests at stake" and the existing international scheme of nuclear liability.[59]

---

58 The issue of civil liability for nuclear damages was still included in the Commission's draft proposal of 2002.

Several conventions dealing with the question of civil liability in the field of nuclear energy are currently in force. In this context, the Paris Convention of 1960 and the Vienna Convention of 1963 are at the centre of attention. **44**

The **Paris Convention** (Convention on Third Party Liability in the Field of Nuclear Energy) was drafted under the auspices of the OECD and adopted on 29 July 1960.[60] It has been amended three times by Protocols adopted in 1964, 1982 and 2004; the need to increase the amounts paid out of public funds led to another instrument, the Brussels Supplementary Convention of 1963. **45**

The parallel instrument to the Paris Convention is the **Vienna Convention** (Convention on Civil Liability for Nuclear Damage),[61] which was drafted under the auspices of the International Atomic Energy Agency (IAEA) and adopted on 21 May 1963. Several provisions of the Vienna Convention were amended by the 1997 Protocol.[62] The Vienna Convention aims at global participation. **46**

---

59 Proposal for a Regulation of the European Parliament and the Council on the law applicable to non-contractual obligations ("Rome II"), 22 July 2003, COM(2003) 427 final, p. 10.

60 The Convention is in force in Belgium, Denmark, Finland, France, Germany, Greece, Italy, Netherlands, Norway, Portugal, Slovenia, Spain, Sweden, Turkey and the United Kingdom (www-oecd-nea.org). On the reform of the Paris Convention and of the Brussels Supplementary Convention, see *Dussart Desart*, in: IAEA, Handbook on Nuclear Law (2006) 215.

61 As of January 2011, the Convention had 36 parties (www.iaea.org). The nine European Contracting States are Bulgaria, Czech Republic, Estonia, Hungary, Latvia, Lithuania, Poland, Romania, and Slovakia.

62 Six States ratified the 1997 Protocol (www.iaeo.org); *Lamm*, in: IAEO, Handbook on Nuclear Law (2006) 169-185.

47 Both conventions are linked by a **Joint Protocol** of 21 September 1988.[63] Its aim is to treat parties to one convention and the Protocol as if they were parties to both conventions.

48 The existing conventions apply if a nuclear incident occurs in the territory of a Contracting Party (in a nuclear installation or in the course of carriage of nuclear substances to or from nuclear installations) and any damage to persons and any loss of goods are suffered on the territory of the Contracting States. They set up a special system of third party liability in the field of nuclear energy. This system is characterised by the objective (without fault) and exclusive liability of the operator of the nuclear installation, who is bound to pay compensation up to a certain amount and is obliged to have insurance or other financial security to cover this liability.

49 The entry into force of the **2004 Protocol** of the Paris Convention[64] will lead to major changes, mainly concerning the scope of application, the definition of nuclear damage and the amount of liability.

50 The revised Convention will not only apply to nuclear damage suffered in the territory of a Contracting State (including maritime zones), but also to nuclear damage suffered in a Non-Contracting State if that State is a party to the Vienna Convention and the Joint Protocol, has no nuclear installation, or has a nuclear installation and its nuclear liability legislation provides for equivalent reciprocal benefits (Art. 2 of the 2004 Protocol).

---

63 Joint Protocol Relating to the Application of the Vienna Convention and the Paris Convention; *von Busekist*, in: IAEA, Handbook on Nuclear Law (2006) 129-153. The Protocol entered into force on 27 April 1992; 26 States are now parties to the Protocol (www.iaea.org).

64 The 2004 Protocol has not yet entered into force. OJ L 338/32 of 23 December 2003; cf. *Schwartz*, in: IAEA, Handbook on Nuclear Law (2006) 37, 53-55; *Blobel*, Natur und Recht 2005, 137-143.

Contracting Parties can provide for an even broader scope of application of the revised Convention.[65]

51 For the first time ever, the Convention will contain a definition of the term "nuclear damage" (Art. 1(a)). It not only applies to "loss of life or personal injury; loss of or damage to property" and the economic loss arising therefrom, but it also includes "the costs of measures of reinstatement of impaired environment" and "the costs of preventive measures."

52 Furthermore, the Protocol will effect an important increase in the nuclear operator's liability amount while (instead of having a maximum level of liability) introducing a new minimum amount of EUR 700 million (Art. 7(a)); accordingly, the amount of required insurance or other financial security has been raised to this minimum amount.

F. Other Instruments

53 Several directives and international conventions concerning civil liability resulting from environmental damage are currently in force. They include inter alia:

I. Directive 2004/35/EC

54 Directive 2004/35/EC of 21 April 2004 on environmental liability with regard to the prevention and remedying of environmental damage[66] does not contain any provisions on private international law. Furthermore, liability for damages is excluded from the

---

65 For example § 25 para. 4 of the German Atomhaftungsgesetz, German Official Journal (BGBl) 2008 I 1793, 1794, according to which the Paris Convention will also apply if the Non-Contracting State has nuclear installation and its nuclear liability legislation does not provide for equivalent reciprocal benefits.

66 OJ L 143/56 of 30 April 2004.

scope of the Directive (Art. 3 (3) and Recital 14). In cases of transfrontier pollution, the cooperation of Member States is required (Art. 15).

II. International Conventions

55 1. Nuclear Energy

- Convention on Third Party Liability in the Field of Nuclear Energy (Paris Convention) of 29 July 1960
  - Supplementary Convention on Third Party Liability in the Field of Nuclear Energy of 31 January 1963 (Brussels Supplementary Convention)
  - Protocols of 1964, 1982 and 2004 (the latter not yet in force)
- Convention on Civil Liability for Nuclear Damage (Vienna Convention) of 21 May 1963
  - Optional Protocol Concerning the Compulsory Settlement of Disputes of 24 April 1963
  - Protocol of 12 September 1997
- Joint Protocol to the Application of the Vienna Convention and the Paris Convention of 21 September 1988
- Convention Relating to Civil Liability in the Field of Maritime Carriage of Nuclear Material of 17 December 1971
- Convention on the Liability of Operators of Nuclear Ships of 25 May 1962 (not in force)
- Convention on Supplementary Compensation for Nuclear Damage of 12 September 1997 (not in force)

56 2. Oil Pollution

- International Convention on Civil Liability for Oil Pollution Damage of 29 November 1969
  - Protocols of 1976, 1984, and 1992, and Amendments of 2000
  - The Protocol of 27 November 1992 replaces the 1969 Convention

- International Convention on the Establishment of an International Fund for Compensation for Oil Pollution Damage of 18 December 1971
  - Protocols of 1976, 1984 and 1992
  - The Protocol of 27 November 1992 replaces the 1971 Convention
  - Amendment of 18 October 2000 and Protocol of 16 May 2003
- Convention on the Civil Liability for Oil Pollution Damage from Offshore Operations of 17 December 1976 (not in force)
- International Convention on Civil Liability for Bunker Oil Pollution of 23 March 2001

3. Maritime Claims **57**

- Convention on Limitation of Liability for Maritime Claims of 19 November 1976

4. Carriage of Dangerous Goods **58**

- Geneva Convention on Civil Liability for Damage Caused during Carriage of Dangerous Goods by Road, Rail, and Inland Navigation Vessels of 10 October 1989 (not in force)
- Basel Convention on the Control of Transboundary Movements of Hazardous Wastes and Their Disposal of 22 March 1989
- Basel Protocol on Liability and Compensation for Damage Resulting from Transboundary Movements of Hazardous Wastes and Their Disposal of 10 December 1999 (not in force)
- International Convention on Liability and Compensation for Damage in Connection with the Carriage of Hazardous and Noxious Substances by Sea of 3 May 1996 (not in force)
  - amended by the 2010 Protocol (not in force)

59 5. Wrecks

- International Convention on Salvage of 28 April 1989
- Nairobi International Convention on the Removal of Wrecks of 18 May 2007 (not in force)

60 6. Activities Dangerous to the Environment

- The Council of Europe's Convention of 21 June 1993 on Civil Liability for Damage resulting from Activities Dangerous to the Environment (Lugano Convention) (not in force)

61 The Hague Conference on Private International Law has on its agenda an instrument on "the conflict of jurisdictions, applicable law and international judicial and administrative co-operation in respect of civil liability for environmental damage."[67]

62 See on the relationship of Rome II with existing international conventions: Art. 28.

Article 8
Infringement of intellectual property rights

1. The law applicable to a non-contractual obligation arising from an infringement of an intellectual property right shall be the law of the country for which protection is claimed.
2. In the case of a non-contractual obligation arising from an infringement of a unitary Community intellectual property right, the law applicable shall, for any question that is not governed by the relevant Community instrument, be the law of the country in which the act of infringement was committed.
3. The law applicable under this Article may not be derogated from by an agreement pursuant to Article 14.

---

[67] HCCH Annual Report 2009, p. 25.

A. Overview

I. Legislative History and Background

The Commission's preliminary draft proposal for a Rome II Regulation in 2002 did not contain a special conflict rule regarding infringement of intellectual property rights, while at the same 1 time not excluding this field from its material scope. Consequently, the general rule of Art. 4 would have governed such infringements. However, in reaction[1] to the Comments by the Hamburg Group for Private International Law,[2] the Commission adopted a rule in its initial proposal of 2003.[3] This rule remained largely unchanged in the subsequent legislative process. It was amongst those rules that were not seriously contested[4] although the relationship of intellectual property with the conflict of laws is far from settled.[5]

II. Structure

2 The rule in Art. 8 is a further ***lex specialis*** to the general conflict rule in Art. 4. It consists of two sub-rules distinguishing between intellectual property rights in general (sub-section 1) and unitary Community intellectual property rights (sub-section 2). A choice of law is explicitly excluded according to sub-section 3.[6]

---

1 *Hahn/Tell*, in: Basedow/Drexl/Kur/Metzger (eds.), Intellectual Property in the Conflict of Laws (2005) 7, 14; *Dickinson*, para. 8.01; *Plender & Wilderspin*, para. 22-007.

2 See *Hamburg Group for Private International Law*, 67 RabelsZ (2003) 1, 21 et seq.

3 It should be noted, however, that while the general rule in Art. 8(1) clearly picks up the proposal of the Hamburg Group, the special rule for unitary Community rights in Art. 8(2) considerably differs from the rule proposed by the Hamburg Group (Art. 8(2) refers to the law of the country where the act was committed rather than the law of the country where the IP right is affected as proposed by the Hamburg Group).

4 For further details see *Heinze*, in: jurisPK BGB, Art. 8 para. 3.

5 See in particular *Basedow/Drexl/Kur/Metzger*, Intellectual Property in the Conflict of Laws (2005); *Drexl/Kur*, Intellectual Property and Private International Law (2005); *Leible/Ohly*, Intellectual Property and Private International Law (2009); *Metzger/Basedow/Kono*, Intellectual Property in the Global Arena (2010).

6 For the problems surrounding this exclusion see *infra* paras. 42 et seq.

Art. 8(1) is the **general rule**. It establishes the *lex loci protectionis* instead of the *lex loci delicti commissi* in relation to all types of intellectual property rights, whether registered or not.[7] This accords with the predominant trend towards the *lex loci protectionis* in the conflict of laws regarding intellectual property rights.[8] And, what is more, it is the logical, although not mandatory consequence on the level of conflict of laws of the fundamental principle of territoriality governing intellectual property rights on the level of substantive law.[9] While this holds true for registered in- 3

7 See Recital 26 listing (non-exhaustively) copyright, related rights, database rights and industrial property rights such as patents and trademarks.

8 *Brière*, 135 Clunet (2008) 31, 48 ("un principe universellement reconnu"); *Basedow/Metzger*, in: FS Boguslavskij (2004) 153, 156 ("weltweit anerkannte kollisionsrechtliche Grundregel"); *Fezer/Koos*, in: Staudinger, Internationales Wirtschaftsrecht para. 843; for domestic applications of the *lex loci protectionis* see for Germany *Drexl* in: Münchener Kommentar BGB, IntImmGR paras. 6 et seq.; *Kropholler*, Internationales Privatrecht, § 53 VI. 2.; for England *Pearce v Ove Arup Partnership Ltd.* [1999] I.L.Pr. 442 paras. 59 seq.; *Lucasfilm v Ainsworth* [2008] EWHC 1878 paras. 235 et seq., 259 et seq.; for France see *Batiffol/Lagarde*, Droit international privé, paras. 532 et seq.

9 *Basedow/Metzger*, in: FS Boguslavskij (2004) 153, 155 seq.; *Buchner*, GRUR Int. 2005, 1004, 1006; *Leistner*, in: Leible/Ohly (eds.), Intellectual Property and Private International Law (2009) 97, 99; *Heinze* in: jurisPK BGB, Art. 8 para. 4; *Grünberger*, 108 ZVglRWiss (2009) 134, 144 et seq.; *Drexl*, in: Münchener Kommentar BGB, IntImmGR, para. 14; *Fentiman*, in: Drexl/Kur (eds.), Intellectual Property and Private International Law (2005) 129, 134 et seq.; in this direction also ECJ, Case C-9/93 – *Ideal Standard* [1994] ECR I-2789 para. 22 (concerning trademark law) and ECJ, Case C-192/04 – *Lagardère* [2005] ECR I-7199 para. 46 (acknowledging the principle of territoriality in copyright law as recognized in international law and the EC Treaty); see also the Commission's Explanatory Memorandum (p. 20), although the Commission wrongly equates the principles of *lex loci protectionis* and of territoriality; while the former is one of private international law, the latter concerns the territorial limits of IP rights as a matter of substantive law.

tellectual property rights such as patents and trademarks, the *lex loci protectionis* is equally justified in relation to copyright, whether it is based on the *droit d'auteur* concept pursued by most continental European laws or on the *copyright* concept of the Anglo-American legal systems.[10]

4 Art. 8(2) concerns **unitary Community intellectual property rights**. However, not all conflict issues with regard to such unitary rights are governed by Art. 8(2). One has to distinguish: The application of the Community instruments in relation to third states is governed by Art. 8(1) whereas the determination of the Member State law applicable to the gaps left by the Community instruments is governed by Art. 8(2);[11] they are governed by the *lex loci delicti*,[12] *i.e.* the law of the country in which the act of infringement was committed. Art. 8(2) acknowledges three facts: First, not all matters of substantive law regarding infringement claims in relation to unitary Community intellectual property rights are governed by the respective Community instruments themselves. Secondly, the conflict rules of the respective instruments are unsatisfactory in that they do not comprehensively de-

10 *Drexl*, in: Münchener Kommentar BGB, IntImmGR paras. 15 et seq.; *Basedow/Metzger*, in: FS Boguslavskij (2004) 153, 156; *Plender & Wilderspin*, para. 22-003; *Obergfell*, IPRax 2005, 9, 11 seq.; critical: *Schack*, in: Leible/Ohly (eds.), Intellectual Property and Private International Law (2009) 79, 91 et seq.; *Leistner*, in: Leible/Ohly (eds.), Intellectual Property and Private International Law (2009) 97, 100 correctly notes, the matter is mainly disputed with regard to the existence of the right and most importantly initial ownership (regarding the latter several European countries apply the *lex originis* instead of the *lex loci protectionis*, eg. Portugal, Greece, France; for further details on the national solutions prior to Rome II see *Boschiero*, 9 YbPIL (2007) 87, 99 et seq.).

11 *Drexl*, in: Münchener Kommentar BGB, IntImmGR para. 134.

12 *Metzger*, in: Drexl/Kur (eds.), Intellectual Property and Private International Law (2005) 215, 217; *Leistner*, in: Leible/Ohly (eds.), Intellectual Property and Private International Law (2009) 97, 107.

termine the national law filling those gaps. Thirdly, in case of unitary Community rights the territory for which protection is claimed according to Art. 8(1) is the entire EU so that the *lex loci protectionis* would be incapable of determining a national law.

B. Scope of the Conflict Rule

I. Material Scope

1. Intellectual Property Rights

5 The term "intellectual property rights" which is not defined by Art. 8 Rome II requires an **autonomous interpretation**[13] as it defines the material scope of a uniform European conflict rule. However, since this uniform conflict rule operates against the background of, and in relation to, substantially different national intellectual property rights, the autonomous interpretation has to take account of the variety of the national laws' concepts and their range of protected rights.[14] This implies a wide and flexible understanding which is supported by Recital 26 Rome II. This recital contains an explicitly non-exhaustive ("for instance") list of rights that are covered by Art. 8: copyright, related rights, the sui generis right for the protection of databases and industrial property rights.

6 An autonomous interpretation of copyright for the purposes of Art. 8 Rome II can be built on the concurrent **definitions and understanding in the respective international conventions** since all Member States and the EU itself are contracting states (or

13 *Grünberger*, 108 ZVglRWiss (2009) 134, 136 seq; *Heinze* in: jurisPK BGB, Art. 8 para. 9.

14 *Plender & Wilderspin*, para. 20-011; *Grünberger*, 108 ZVglRWiss (2009) 134, 137.

have to adhere to them via TRIPS[15]). This is foremost the Berne Convention[16] (Arts. 2 and 2bis) on which the interpretation of intellectual property rights in the TRIPS Agreement and the WIPO Copyright Treaty are based.[17]

7 **Copyright** includes the personal rights vested in the author such as moral rights in English law, *le droit moral* in French law and the *Urheberpersönlichkeitsrecht* under German law[18] as well as monetary claims for lawful use.[19]

8 **Industrial property rights** are characterised by an element of exclusivity.[20] They encompass patent rights (including rights derived from supplementary protection certificates), design rights, utility model rights, plant variety rights, rights of the creator of the topographies of a semiconductor product, geographical indications and designations of origin,[21] trademark rights and trade names in so far as these are protected as exclusive property rights in the national law concerned.[22] Likewise, rights in sports events

15 Agreement on Trade-Related Aspects of Intellectual Property Rights (Annex 1C of the Marrakesh Agreement Establishing the World Trade Organization).

16 Berne Convention for the Protection of Literary and Artistic Works of September 9, 1886 as revised and amended.

17 *Grünberger*, 108 ZVglRWiss (2009)134, 137 seq.; *Heinze* in: jurisPK BGB, Art. 8 para. 10; for further details see *Hilty/Henning-Bodewig*, Leistungsschutzrechte von Sportveranstaltern (2007) 57 et seq.

18 *Sack*, WRP 2008, 1405, 1406; *Grünberger*, 108 ZVglRWiss (2009) 134, 173 seq.

19 For details see *infra* para. 55.

20 *Peukert*, Güterzuordnung als Rechtsprinzip (2008) 56 et seq.; approving this definition for the purpose of Art. 8 Rome II *Grünberger*, 108 ZVglRWiss (2009) 134, 141.

21 For details see *infra* para. 16.

22 See in particular the Statement by the Commission concerning Article 2 of Directive 2004/48/EC of the European Parliament and of the Council on the enforcement of intellectual property rights, OJ 2005 L 94/37.

are industrial property rights if they are protected as exclusive property rights in the respective national law (as for example under French law).[23]

Unitary Community intellectual property rights are currently Community trademarks,[24] Community designs,[25] Community plant variety rights[26] as well as geographical indications and designations of origin.[27] National intellectual property rights harmonized by EU Directives do not constitute unitary Community rights since they are still based on the national laws.[28] Likewise, the European patent as it currently exists is nothing more than a bundle of national patents. 9

Trade secrets do not belong to intellectual property rights for the purpose of Art. 8 Rome II although they are protected under Art. 39 TRIPS since they are referred to as competitor-related acts of unfair competition under Art. 6(2) in the Commission's Explanatory Memorandum.[29] 10

Supplementary protection of technical innovations, ideas or other achievements not protected as patents, trademarks or other 11

23 *Grünberger*, 108 ZVglRWiss (2009) 134, 141.

24 Council Regulation (EC) No 207/2009 of 26 February 2009 on the Community trade mark (codified version), OJ 2009 L 78/1.

25 Council Regulation (EC) No 6/2002 of 12 December 2001 on Community designs, OJ 2002 L 3/1.

26 Council Regulation (EC) No 2100/94 of 27 July 1994 on Community plant variety rights, OJ 1994 L 227/1.

27 Council Regulation (EC) No 510/2006 of 20 March 2006 on the protection of geographical indications and designations of origin for agricultural products and foodstuffs, OJ 2006 L 93/12; for details on the relationship between Art. 6 and 8 in that regard see Art. 6 paras. 19 et seq.

28 *Heinze*, in: jurisPK BGB, Art. 8 para. 10; *Dickinson*, para. 8.15.

29 Commission's Explanatory Memorandum COM(2003) 427 final 16; concurring *Wadlow*, EIPR 2008 309, 310; *Plender & Wilderspin*, para. 22-020; *Heinze*, in: jurisPK BGB, Art. 8 para. 10.

industrial property rights by unfair competition law is not governed by Art. 8, but by Art. 6.[30]

12 **Personality rights** are likewise no intellectual property rights for the purpose of Art. 8 as Art. 1(2) lit. g Rome II excludes them from the Regulation's material scope.

2. Relevant Act

13 The issue of the relevant act affects the material scope as well as the connecting factor when determining the applicable law.[31] As regards the material scope, both Art. 8(1) and Art. 8(2) apply irrespective of an actual infringement of an intellectual property right. For Art. 8 to apply it is sufficient that the plaintiff alleges the infringement of an intellectual property right,[32] usually in the country or countries for which he claims protection.[33]

3. Comprehensive Coverage

14 By virtue of Art. 13, the material scope of application of the conflict rule in Art. 8 is extended beyond claims in tort/delict (chapter II of the Regulation) to claims for the infringement of intellectual property rights based on unjust enrichment, *negotiorum gestio* and *culpa in contrahendo* (chapter III of the Regulation). The purpose of this extension is to apply one single law to all non-contractual claims arising out of an infringement of an intellectual property right. It is particularly relevant with regard to

---

30 For details see Art. 6 paras. 17 seq.

31 For a detailed analysis of the different connecting factors of Art. 8 see *infra* paras. 28 et seq.

32 *Sack*, WRP 2008, 1405, 1410 seq.; *Grünberger*, 108 ZVglRWiss (2009) 134, 152 et seq.; *Heinze*, in: jurisPK BGB, Art. 8 para. 12; *Dickinson*, para. 8.25; a different view is taken by *Weller*, ZEuP 2008, 252, 287.

33 This is due to the fact that Art. 8(1) applies as the external conflict rule even with regard to unitary Community intellectual property rights (see *infra* para. 25).

claims based on unjust enrichment since a number of laws grant restitutionary remedies in case of an infringement of intellectual property rights, *e.g.* German law *(Eingriffskondiktion)* and English law.[34]

4. Relationship with Other Conflict Rules of the Regulation

a) Relationship between Art. 8 and Art. 4

Art. 8 supersedes the general conflict rule of torts/delicts in Art. 4 comprehensively. Particularly, one may neither have recourse to the common habitual residence connection under Art. 4(2) nor to the escape clause of Art. 4(3).[35] **15**

b) Relationship between Art. 8 and Art. 6(1)

The relationship between Art. 8 and Art. 6(1) is problematic particularly in relation to two areas of law: supplementary protection of ideas, innovations, technical solutions and the like which are not protected by an intellectual property right under unfair competition law[36] on the one hand and geographical indications and designations of origin on the other hand.[37] **16**

5. Relationship with Conflict Rules in Other EU Regulations

According to its wording, the conflict rule in Art. 8(2) Rome II is limited to questions that are not governed by the respective Community instruments on unitary Community intellectual property rights. Hence, the concurrent conflict rules contained in those instruments, namely Art. 102(2) Community Trademark Regula- **17**

---

34 *Thorn*, in: Palandt, Art. 13 para. 2; G. *Wagner*, IPRax 2008, 1, 11; *Dicey, Morris & Collins*, para. S 35-230; *Plender & Wilderspin*, para. 22-009.

35 *Basedow/Metzger*, in: FS Boguslavskij (2004) 153,161; *Sack*, WRP 2008, 1405, 1406.

36 For instance, under German law, this is referred to as "ergänzender wettbewerbsrechtlicher Leistungsschutz", codified in § 4 No. 9 UWG.

37 For a detailed analysis of the issue see Art. 6 paras 17 et seq.

tion, Art. 89(1) lit. d Community Designs Regulation and Art. 97(1) Community Plant Variety Rights Regulation, prevail.[38] However, the conflict rules of these instruments provide for the law of the country in which the acts of infringement are committed, *including the private international law.* This amounts to a reference back to Art. 8(2) Rome II since the Rome II Regulation is directly applicable in all Member States replacing the domestic private international law and thus constitutes the private international law of each Member State.[39] Consequently, the law is eventually determined by Art. 8(2) Rome II.

18 The relationship with the country of origin-principle of Art. 3 E-Commerce Directive[40] does not present a problem since intellectual property rights are excluded from the scope of the country of origin-principle by Art. 3(2) E-Commerce Directive in connection with its Annex, first indent.

19 There is no clash with the Intellectual Property Enforcement Directive,[41] the Resale Rights Directive[42] and the Satellite Broadcasting Directive[43] since those directives do not contain conflict rules overlapping with Art. 8 Rome II.

---

38 On the precedence of the Regulation's substantive rules see *infra* para. 27.

39 *Heinze*, in: jurisPK BGB, Art. 8 para. 6; *Sack*, WRP 2008, 1405, 1408.

40 Directive 2000/31/EC of the European Parliament and of the Council of 8 June 2000 on certain legal aspects of information society services, in particular electronic commerce, in the Internal Market (Directive on electronic commerce), OJ 2000 L 178/1.

41 Directive 2004/48/EC of the European Parliament and of the Council of 29 April 2004 on the enforcement of intellectual property rights, OJ 2004 L 195/16 (including the corrigendum).

42 Directive 2001/84/EC of the European Parliament and of the Council of 27 September 2001 on the resale right for the benefit of the author of an original work of art, OJ 2001 L 272/32.

43 Council Directive 93/83/EC of 27 September 1993 on the coordination of certain rules concerning copyright and rights related to copyright ap-

6. Relationship with EU Primary Law

There is neither an overlap nor a conflict between Art. 8 Rome II and the law of the European treaties. On the one hand, the principle of non-discrimination under Art. 18 TFEU and the basic freedoms of the TFEU neither amount to a conflict rule nor prescribe a particular conflict rule in relation to the infringement of intellectual property rights.[44] On the other hand, the conflict rule in Art. 8 Rome II is compatible with the aforementioned principles of the TFEU. 20

7. Relationship with International Conventions

Intellectual property rights are the subject of various international conventions. They may easily cross borders so that issues of existence, content and infringement frequently arise in a number of countries. It is fiercely debated whether those conventions, particularly the Berne Convention, the Paris Convention,[45] WTO/TRIPS and, to a lesser extent, also the WIPO conventions either directly contain a conflict rule or indirectly require a specific conflict rule to be adopted by its contracting states as a consequence of its substantive law principles (territoriality, national treatment).[46] If they directly contained conflict rules, these conflict rules would, according to Art. 28(1) Rome II, prevail over 21

---

plicable to satellite broadcasting and cable retransmission, OJ 1993 L 248/15; but see in this regard also *infra* para. 33.

44 *Drexl*, in: Münchener Kommentar BGB, IntImmGR paras. 121 seq.

45 Paris Convention for the Protection of Industrial Property of March 20, 1883 as revised and amended.

46 For further discussion and references see in particular *Ulmer*, Intellectual Property Rights and the Conflict of Laws (1978); *Fentiman*, in: Drexl/Kur (eds.), Intellectual Property and Private International Law (2005) 129; *Drexl*, in: Drexl/Kur (eds.), Intellectual Property and Private International Law (2005) 151; *Dinwoodie*, Conflicts and International Copyrights Litigation: The Role of International Norms (2005) 195, 200 et seq.; *Drexl*, in: Münchener Kommentar BGB, IntImmGR paras. 66 et seq.;

Art. 8 Rome II, but not materially differ from Art. 8 Rome II so that the matter is of little practical relevance. If they indirectly require a specific conflict rule to be adopted, the conflict rule in Art. 8 Rome II accords with the underlying principles of the respective conventions, in particular with the territoriality principle.[47]

II. Personal Scope

22 The personal scope of Art. 8 Rome II is unrestricted. In particular, it is not a matter for the conflict rule to determine the range of potential plaintiffs. Rather, the applicable substantive law will determine whether the plaintiff is the owner of the allegedly infringed intellectual property right[48] and whether the person claimed to be liable has actually infringed the respective right.

III. Territorial Scope

23 As the other provisions of Rome II, Art. 8 is a *loi uniforme*.[49]

C. Determination of the Applicable Law

I. Operation and Interplay with Unitary Community Instruments

24 Based on the structure of Art. 8,[50] the applicable law is determined in several steps.

Schricker-Katzenberger, Urheberrecht, Vor §§ 120 ff., paras. 120 et seq.; *Boschiero*, 9 YbPIL (2007) 87, 94 et seq.

47 *Heinze*, in: jurisPK BGB, Art. 8 para. 5; *Grünberger*, 108 ZVglRWiss (2009) 134, 144.

48 Whether the aspect of ownership, particularly first ownership, is governed by the law determined by Art. 8 is contested and will be dealt with *infra* paras. 51 seq.

49 See Art. 3 para. 1.

As a first step, one has to determine according to Art. 8(1) **for which territory protection is claimed**[51] (not for which territory protection exists since that is a matter for the substantive law), even in relation to unitary Community intellectual property rights (Community Trademarks, Designs, Plant Variety Rights as well as Geographical Indications and Designations of Origin) since they require that protection is claimed at least for the territory of one Member State.[52] Hence, Art. 8(1) applies comprehensively in order to determine the reach of the Member States's laws including the Community instruments concerned with unitary Community rights in relation to third states' laws (from the Community's perspective one may call this the external conflict rule).[53] If a national (even Non-Member State) intellectual property right constitutes the basis of the claim, Art. 8(1) directly leads to the applicable substantive law. In contrast, if a unitary Community intellectual property right constitutes the basis of the claim, **further steps** are required to determine the applicable law according to Art. 8(2): 25

First, to the extent that the **respective Community instrument directly provides for the protection sought** by the plaintiff, no recourse to any conflict rule is required. The protection directly conferred by these instruments is, however, generally limited. For instance, the Community Trademark Regulation provides only for injunctive relief (prohibition of the trademark's use)[54] whereas it lacks provisions on damages, removal of the signs used, elimination of the goods or services to which the sign is attached and/or disclosure in relation to the trademark infringement. 26

---

50 See *supra* paras. 2 et seq.

51 *Heinze*, in: jurisPK BGB, Art. 8 para. 8.

52 *Sack*, WRP 2008, 1405, 1408; *Heinze*, in: jurisPK BGB, Art. 8 para. 8.

53 *Drexl*, in: Münchener Kommentar BGB, IntImmGR paras. 132, 134; *Sack*, WRP 2008, 1405, 1408; *Grünberger*, 108 ZVglRWiss (2009) 134, 149.

54 See Art. 9 Community Trademark Regulation.

27 Secondly, as far as the **Community instruments themselves provide for conflict rules** in relation to the sanctions for infringement of a unitary Community right or general issues not addressed by the Community instruments,[55] those conflict rules formally prevail over Art. 8(2) Rome II. They provide either for the *lex fori*[56] or the law of the country in which the acts of infringement are committed,[57] including the respective private international law. This amounts to a reference back to Art. 8(2) Rome II since the Rome II Regulation is directly applicable in all Member States, thereby replacing their domestic private international laws.[58] Therefore, the law applicable to the gaps left in the Community instruments is practically determined by Art. 8(2) Rome II which, according to Art. 24 Rome II, leaves no room for *renvoi* (from the Community's perspective one may call this the internal conflict rule).[59] Issues of procedure are according to the unitary Community instruments[60] as well as Art. 1(3) Rome II governed by the *lex fori*.[61]

---

55 See Art. 101(2), 102(2) Community Trademark Regulation, Arts. 88(2), 89(1) lit. d Community Design Regulation and Art. 97(1) Community Plant Variety Rights Regulation; the Regulation on Geographical Indications and Designations of Origin (Regulation 510/2006 of 20 March 2006, OJ 2006 L 93/12) does not contain any conflict rules.

56 Art. 101(2) Community Trademark Regulation and Art. 88(2) Community Design Regulation with regard to general issues; Art. 97(1) Community Plant Variety Rights Regulation with regard to restitutionary sanctions.

57 Art. 102(2) Community Trademark Regulation and Art. 89(1) lit. d Community Design Regulation with regard to sanctions.

58 *Fayaz*, GRUR Int. 2009, 566, 572; *Heinze*, in: jurisPK BGB, Art. 8 para. 6; *Sack*, WRP 2008, 1405, 1408.

59 *Drexl*, in: Münchener Kommentar BGB, IntImmGR paras. 134 seq.; *Sack*, WRP 2008, 1405, 1408.

60 Art. 101(3) Community Trademark Regulation, Art. 88(3) Community Design Regulation and Art. 103 Community Plant Variety Rights Regulation; the Regulation on Geographical Indications and Designations of Origin does not contain any conflict rules.

II. Different Connecting Factors

While an alleged infringement of an intellectual property right is sufficient to enter the material scope of application of Art. 8, the connecting factors of Art. 8(1) and 8(2) differ in that regard. 28

1. The General (External) Conflict Rule (Art. 8(1))

a) Single State Scenarios

According to the principle of *lex loci protectionis*, the connecting factor of Art. 8(1) is not the actual infringement of an intellectual property right but the **claim for protection**: the law of the country or countries applies for which (not in which!) the plaintiff claims protection.[62] Hence, the plaintiff determines the applicable law(s) by his statement of claim (**subjective connecting factor**). It is then a matter for the applicable substantive law(s) to determine whether an actual infringement of the alleged intellectual property right has occurred under the respective law(s).[63] The issue of actual infringement includes the question whether minimal effects, unintended consequences, preparatory and partial acts amount to actual infringements of the alleged intellectual property right.[64] The conflict rule itself does neither rule out preparatory or partial acts (as do Arts. 4 and 6(1) Rome II) nor does it contain a substantiality threshold or a mechanism for spillover protection (as does Art. 6(3) lit. b Rome II). 29

---

61 The same should apply to matters of evidence which are explicitly mentioned in Art. 1(3) Rome II but not in the respective provisions of the unitary Community instruments (though one may regard evidence as a subcategory of procedure).

62 *Sack*, WRP 2008, 1405, 1410 seq.; *Grünberger*, 108 ZVglRWiss (2009) 134, 152 seq.; *Heinze*, in: jurisPK BGB, Art. 8 para. 12; *Dickinson*, para. 8.25; a different view is taken by *Weller*, ZEuP 2008, 252, 287.

63 *Leistner*, in: Leible/Ohly (eds.), Intellectual Property and Private International Law (2009) 97, 100; *Grünberger*, 108 ZVglRWiss (2009) 134, 149 and 151 et seq.; *Heiss/Loacker*, JBl 2007, 613, 636 seq.

64 *Sack*, WRP 2008, 1405, 1413; *Heinze*, in: jurisPK BGB, Art. 8 para. 12.

30 The system of the connecting factor of Art. 8(1) which **shifts most, if not all relevant issues to the level of the substantive law**[65] is foremost owed to the underlying principle of territoriality[66] and the corresponding subjective connecting factor of Art. 8(1) under the *lex loci protectionis*. Furthermore, the issue of infringement is by its nature a matter of substantive law[67] which cannot consistently be incorporated into the preceding issue of determining the applicable law under the respective conflict rule.[68]

31 The subjective connecting factor **does not result in a multiplication of claims**. It may open the door to several applicable laws but this is not tantamount to several claims actually lying under the respective laws.[69] In fact, the plaintiff is well advised to carefully consider for which countries he claims protection under Art. 8(1) since he will otherwise risk a partial dismissal of the claim on the merits.[70] Double recovery of damages or other forms of compensation will hardly ever be an issue since each of the applicable laws may provide for its own remedies including compensatory claims regarding the infringements that took place in relation to intellectual property rights existing under the respective law.[71]

---

65 *Leistner*, in: Leible/Ohly (eds.), Intellectual Property and Private International Law (2009) 97, 101 refers to it as a "non-solution" (at least with regard to multistate scenarios).

66 See *Grünberger*, 108 ZVglRWiss (2009) 134, 146 and 152 et seq.

67 *Kur*, in: Basedow/Drexl/Metzger/Kur (eds.), Intellectual Property in the Conflict of Laws (2005) 175, 179; *Sack*, WRP 2008, 1405, 1411.

68 *Grünberger*, 108 ZVglRWiss (2009) 134, 151 seq. and *Heinze*, in: jurisPK BGB, Art. 8 fn. 65 point additionally at the practical difficulty since there is no uniform European standard for determining the issue of infringement (apart from the unitary Community rights).

69 *Drexl*, in: Münchener Kommentar BGB, IntImmGR para. 12; *Grünberger*, 108 ZVglRWiss (2009) 134, 153; *Heinze*, in: jurisPK BGB, Art. 8 para. 12; *Sack*, WRP 2008, 1405, 1413.

70 *Heinze*, in: jurisPK BGB, Art. 8 para. 12; *Grünberger*, 108 ZVglRWiss (2009) 134, 153.

While the subjective connecting factor allows the plaintiff to choose the range of applicable laws, the flipside of this coin is that he **has to make use of that choice**. The court seized will only apply the law(s) of the country or countries for which the plaintiff claims protection. If he simply pleads the infringement of an intellectual property right without specifying the countries for which he claims protection (reference to foreign intellectual property rights may suffice in that regard), the court will not engage in any conflict of laws analysis but simply apply the *lex fori* to the claim.[72] It will take the plaintiff's limited pleading as claiming protection only for the country of the court seized. In effect, the subjective connecting factor of Art. 8(1) is similar to the common law requirement of pleading foreign law.[73] 32

b) Multi-State Scenarios

In multi-state scenarios, *i.e.* an act of infringement affecting intellectual property rights in a number of countries, particularly via print media, radio or television broadcasting[74] and the inter- 33

71 Similar *Sack*, WRP 2008, 1405, 1413.

72 Concurring: *Heinze*, in: jurisPK BGB, Art. 8 para. 14 as regards the position under German law, but this result is actually implied by Art. 8 itself.

73 For details on the issue of pleading and proof of foreign law see in particular *Gruber/Bach*, 11 YbPIL (2009) 157, 161 et seq.; for a comparative report of the law in all member states on the issue cf. *Palao Moreno/Iglesias Buhigues/Esplugues Mota* (eds.), Application of Foreign Law (forthcoming 2011); *Trautmann*, Europäisches Kollisionsrecht und ausländisches Recht im nationalen Zivilverfahren (2010); *Hartley*, Pleading and Proof of Foreign Law – The Major European Systems Compared, 45 ICLQ (1996) 271; the Commission will have to consider this peculiarity of Art. 8 when reviewing the effects of the different treatment of foreign law in the European jurisdictions under Art. 30(1)(i) Rome II.

74 For the specific considerations in case of terrestric and satellite radio or television broadcasting including the effect of the Satellite Broadcasting Directive and the so called "Bogsch theory" see *Sack*, WRP 2008, 1405, 1415 et seq.; *Drexl*, in: Münchener Kommentar BGB, IntImmGR paras. 242 et seq.

net, the connecting factor of Art. 8(1) inevitably leads to the **mosaic approach.**[75] This results in the applicability of the laws of all countries for which the plaintiff claims protection so that one single act of infringement may be judged differently by different applicable laws.

34 There is **no appreciability filter or spillover protection on the level of conflict of laws** under Art. 8(1).[76] This clearly follows from the parallel structure in Art. 8 and Art. 6. The general rule in Art. 6(3) lit. a which is comparable to Art. 8(1) in that regard does not contain any filter. An equivalent to the special rule in Art. 6(3) lit. b providing for a limited choice of one law in multistate scenarios which contains two filters to prevent abusive forum shopping is, however, missing in Art. 8. Rather, it is a matter for the substantive laws for which the plaintiff claims protection to determine whether they apply to the infringing act and/or its effects on an intellectual property right on its territory.[77]

35 Due to the principle of territoriality, the **sanctions** imposed by the laws of the countries for which protection is claimed, are **limited to infringements of intellectual property rights in the respective country under the respective law.**[78] While this split into several

---

75 *Sack*, WRP 2008, 1405, 1414; *Leistner*, in: Leible/Ohly (eds.), Intellectual Property and Private International Law (2009) 97, 101 (welcoming it as an act of political self-restraint in an area where the way forward is still disputed in an ongoing debate); *Plender & Wilderspin*, para. 20-024; *Dickinson*, para. 8.27; *Heinze*, in: jurisPK BGB, Art. 8 para. 15; *Basedow/ Metzger*, in: FS Boguslavskij (2004) 153, 163 and 171 seq.; with regard to internet infringement see in particular *Drexl*, in: Münchener Kommentar BGB, IntImmGR paras. 251 et seq.; *Sack*, WRP 2008, 1405, 1417 seq.

76 *Heinze*, in: jurisPK BGB, Art. 8 para. 15; *Sack*, WRP 2008, 1405, 1415; in relation to German law see already Bundesgerichtshof (Germany), 13 October 2004 – I ZR 163/02, NJW 2005, 1435, 1436 – *Hotel Maritime*; in favour of an appreciability threshold, however, *Buchner*, GRUR Int. 2005, 1004, 1007 (though not explicitly with regard to Art. 8 Rome II).

77 *Drexl*, in: Münchener Kommentar BGB, IntImmGR para. 298.

mosaic pieces works with regard to compensatory sanctions, it poses difficulties when it comes to injunctive relief:[79] since one single act infringes intellectual property rights under several national laws, a prohibitory injunction under one law will regularly have the (extraterritorial) effect of prohibiting the act altogether.[80] This holds particularly true for infringements via the internet which may potentially infringe intellectual property rights worldwide. For reasons of comity, national courts granting injunctive relief should avoid such extraterritorial effect as far as possible by trying to limit their prohibitory orders to the national territories of the countries under the laws of which the alleged intellectual property right is actually infringed.[81] The ability to do so depends on a large extent on the level of control of the defendant regarding the territorial reach of the act of infringement which will be higher in case of print media, while lower in case of radio/television broadcasting and acts commited via the internet.

2. The Special (Internal) Conflict Rule (Art. 8(2))

a) Single State Scenarios

Under the principle of *lex loci delicti*, the connecting factor of Art. 36
8(2) requires localisation of an actual or impending[82] infringement in one or more countries. This clearly follows from the

---

78 *Drexl*, in: Münchener Kommentar BGB, IntImmGR para. 234.

79 *Heinze*, in: jurisPK BGB, Art. 8 para. 15.

80 *Sack*, WRP 2008, 1405, 1414 approves of this possibility and even recommends to apply for injunctive relief in the country which grants such relief on the easiest terms by granting the highest degree of protection for the right holder.

81 *Drexl*, in: Münchener Kommentar BGB, IntImmGR paras. 234, 261 seq. and 279 (who also considers that a law may declare itself inapplicable on the level of the substantive law if the effects of the infringement on its territory are so neglectable that it would be unjustified to apply the respective law, in particular with an extraterritorial effect).

82 See Art. 2 Rome II.

wording "in which the act of infringement was committed" providing for an **objective connecting factor**. The issue of infringement as a legal issue[83] and as a matter of substantive law is imported into the conflict rule, more specifically into its connecting factor. While this incorporation of substantive law aspects into the conflict rule runs counter to the preferable separation of conflict issues from those of substantive law, its consequences are acceptable in case of unitary Community rights: First, the relevant infringement is uniformly defined by the respective Community instruments for all Member States.[84] The court seized with the claim is put into a position to determine and locate acts of infringement irrespective of the applicable law. Secondly, the issue of infringement is in any event not governed by the national law(s) determined by virtue of Art. 8(2) but by the respective Community instrument itself.

37 The act of infringement does not refer to the damage or effects on the market but solely to the actual act that constitutes the infringement of the intellectual property right.[85]

---

83 This is the relevant difference compared to the objectice connecting factors of Art. 4 and 6, damage and effects which are rather factual issues that can be determined without reference to a national law.

84 This aspect is also noted by *Dickinson*, para. 8.37; *Heinze*, in: jurisPK BGB, Art. 8 para. 13.

85 See Council Document No. 9009/04; *Basedow/Metzger*, in: FS Boguslavskij (2004) 153, 169; *Grünberger*, 108 ZVglRWiss (2009) 134, 149; *Heinze*, in: jurisPK BGB, Art. 8 para. 16; G. *Wagner*, IPRax 2008, 1, 10; *Schack*, in: Leible/Ohly (eds.), Intellectual Property and Private International Law (2009) 79, 84; a different view is taken by *Fayaz*, GRUR Int. 2009, 566, 572 who favours a ubiquity connection as advocated by the ECJ for Art. 5 No 3 Brussels I; as *Heinze*, in: jurisPK BGB, Art. 8 fn. 90 rightly points out, the EU legislator abstains from the principle of ubiquity in relation to conflict rules on tort/delict (see only the general rule in Art. 4 Rome II) unless explicitly stated (as in Art. 7 Rome II) while keeping it only for jurisdiction issues (with regard to which other considerations apply) – see ECJ, Case C-68/93 – *Shevill* [1995] ECR I-415 para. 20; Case C-167/00 –

b) Multi-State Scenarios

Multi-state scenarios under Art. 8(2) differ from those under Art. 8(1) since multiple connections resulting in a multi-state scenario require several different acts due to the objective connecting factor attaching to the countries in which acts of infringement were committed or are impending. Those different acts may form part of a single activity by the defendant, *e.g.* producing, marketing and selling a product in violation of a Community design, or be replicated in each Member State by its very nature, *e.g.* the use of a sign that is protected as a Community trademark for consulting services offered throughout the Community. 38

The **solutions proposed for these multi-state scenarios differ considerably.**[86] First, it has to be determined whether Art. 8(2) mandates the mosaic approach or whether it is *de lege lata* possible to judge all acts according to one single law. *E contrario* Art. 6(3) lit. b, the former view has something to commend it even though it may appear undesirable and infeasible. The appeal of the latter solution has, however, led several authors to propose "single law solutions" even under the framework of Art. 8(2) Rome II. They range from (1) the law of the defendant's domicile provided that the claim is also brought there[87] over (2) the law in which the economically most important acts of infringement were com- 39

Verein für Konsumenteninformation [2002] ECR I-8111 paras. 42 et seq.; Case C-168/02 – *Kronhofer* [2004] ECR I-6009 para. 16; Case C-189/08 – *Zuid Chemie* [2009] ECR I-6917 para. 23.

86 For an overview see *Leistner*, in: Leible/Ohly (eds.), Intellectual Property and Private International Law (2009) 97, 115 et seq.; *Fayaz*, GRUR Int. 2009, 566, 572 et seq.; *Metzger*, in: Drexl/Kur (eds.), Intellectual Property and Private International Law (2005) 215, 219 et seq.

87 *Metzger*, in: Drexl/Kur (eds.), Intellectual Property and Private International Law (2005) 215, 223; *Basedow/Metzger*, in: FS Boguslavskij (2004) 153, 171; *Schack*, in: Leible/Ohly (eds.), Intellectual Property and Private International Law (2009) 79, 87.

mitted[88] and – close to the second proposal – (3) the law of the country in which the final act resulting in the respective sanction was committed, *i.e.* regularly marketing and distribution,[89] to (4) the *lex fori*. *De lege ferenda*, the first proposal (the "defendant's domicile solution") deserves support for several reasons: it is feasible (unlike the mosaic approach), it provides legal certainty (unlike the most important infringement approach) and it achieves concurrence with the jurisdiction rule under Art. 5 No. 3 Brussels I as interpreted by the ECJ (unlike the *lex fori* approach). *De lege lata*, however, the "defendant's domicile solution" like the two other "single law solutions" are incompatible with the structure of Art. 8 under the framework of the Rome II Regulation. The "defendant's domicile solution" replicates Art. 6(3) lit. b Rome II for the purposes of Art. 8 which contradicts the systematic structure of the Regulation in a way that appears to be insuperable even by teleological considerations.[90] As a result, there is **no way around the mosaic approach** under the current state of the law. Depending on the experiences with Art. 6(3) lit. b, one may consider extending it to Art. 8(2) in the course of the Regulation's reform.[91]

3. Escape Clause and Choice of Law

40 Both conflict rules of Art. 8 lack any flexibility since they neither provide for escape clauses nor for a choice of law.

---

88 In that direction Hanseatisches Oberlandesgericht Hamburg (Germany), 27 January 2005 – 5 U 36/04, 152/04, GRUR-RR 2005, 251, 255 – Home Depot; *Mühlendahl/Ohlgart*, Die Gemeinschaftsmarke (1998) 214 seq.

89 *Heinze*, in: jurisPK BGB, Art. 8 para. 16.

90 A different view is taken by *Leistner*, in: Leible/Ohly (eds.), Intellectual Property and Private International Law (2009) 97, 115 et seq. who regards functional solutions compatible with the given statutory rule in Art. 8.

91 G. *Wagner*, IPRax 2008, 1, 8 already favours an extension of Art. 6(3) lit. b to Art. 6(1).

Art. 8 itself **does not contain an escape clause**, and it follows *e contrario* by comparison with Arts. 5(1), 6(2) and 9 that the escape clauses in Art. 4(2) and 4(3) forming part of the general conflict rule on tort/delict are inapplicable in the context of Art. 8: they are neither repeated (as in Art. 5(2) Rome II) nor incorporated by reference (as in Arts. 5(1), 6(2) and 9 Rome II).[92] These systematic reasons appear to be insuperable, although an escape clause attaching to a manifestly closer connection, *e.g.* in the context of a licensing agreement, has strong arguments to commend it, particularly in relation to unitary Community intellectual property rights in so far as they are governed by Art. 8(2).[93] 41

A **choice of law is explicitly and comprehensively excluded by Art. 8(3)**. As convincing as the exclusion may be in relation to Art. 8(1) based on the territorial limits of intellectual property rights and the public interests involved,[94] the **less convincing it is in relation to the law applicable under Art. 8(2)**.[95] The terri- 42

92 *Basedow/Metzger*, in: FS Boguslavskij (2004) 153, 161; *Sack*, WRP 2008, 1405, 1406; *Leistner*, in: Leible/Ohly (eds.), Intellectual Property and Private International Law (2009) 97, 105 seq. and 113 seq. (although regretting the inapplicability of the escape clause of Art. 4(3) following *Metzger*, in: Drexl/Kur (eds.), Intellectual Property and Private International Law (2005) 215, 219 and *Schaper*, in: Drexl/Kur (eds.), Intellectual Property and Private International Law (2005) 201, 212).

93 *Basedow/Metzger*, in: FS Boguslavskij (2004) 153, 170; *Leistner*, in: Leible/Ohly (eds.), Intellectual Property and Private International Law (2009) 97, 112 seq.

94 *Basedow/Metzger*, in: FS Boguslavskij (2004) 153, 169; *Dickinson*, para. 8.54; *Sack*, WRP 2008, 1405, 1406; *Boschiero*, 9 YbPIL (2007) 87, 107 et seq. and *Leistner*, in: Leible/Ohly (eds.), Intellectual Property and Private International Law (2009) 97, 105 seq. regard the exclusion in relation to Art. 8(1) as acceptable, although they favour a limited choice as regards remedies and compensation following the recent approaches in Art. 5 CLIP principles and § 302 ALI principles).

95 *Boschiero*, 9 YbPIL(2007) 87, 107 et seq.; *Leistner*, in: Leible/Ohly (eds.), Intellectual Property and Private International Law (2009) 97, 111 et

torial limits are not national since the unitary rights grant protection for the entire common market, so that the connecting factor of *lex loci delicti* lacks the public interest link to the country of protection.[96] Furthermore, it would have strengthened the uniform character of the unitary Community intellectual property rights and fostered their attractiveness to allow at least the choice of a Member State's law in relation to remedies and sanctions as the core area not regulated by the respective Community instruments themselves. This would have allowed the parties to choose one national law to govern the consequences of an infringement, namely remedies and sanctions, in commonly arising multi-state scenarios (since the territory of protection is the entire common market).[97] Art. 6(3) lit. b Rome II could have served as a model: the infringement issue (of the statutory prohibition in Arts. 101, 102 TFEU) is also regulated uniformly by EU law while private law sanctions and remedies lack such uniform regime so that the national laws have to fill the gap. However, even against this backround of a missing rationale for the exclusion of a choice of law in relation to unitary Community rights, the clear wording of Art. 8(3) bars any restrictive interpretation of Art. 8(3), limiting it to Art. 8(1).[98]

---

seq.; *Heinze*, in: jurisPK BGB, Art. 8 Rom II-VO para. 21; *Dickinson*, para. 8.54; see in that direction during the legislative process already *Metzger*, in: Drexl/Kur (eds.), Intellectual Property and Private International Law (2005) 215, 218 seq. and *Schaper*, in: Drexl/Kur (eds.), Intellectual Property and Private International Law (2005) 201, 211 seq.; approving of the comprehensive exclusion *Buchner*, GRUR Int. 2005, 1004, 1007 seq.; *Grünberger*, 108 ZVglRWiss (2009) 134, 153 and 175 seq.; *Plender & Wilderspin*, para. 20-035 (though rather undifferentiated).

96 *Leistner*, in: Leible/Ohly (eds.), Intellectual Property and Private International Law (2009) 97, 112.

97 See *supra* paras. 38 seq.

98 Such a restrictive interpretation is, however, advocated by *Leistner*, in: Leible/Ohly (eds.), Intellectual Property and Private International Law (2009) 97, 113.

Overall, it would be the best solution to establish a uniform system of sanctions for unitary Community intellectual property rights (which would render Art. 8(2) superfluous).[99] The second best solution would be to allow at least a choice of one law to govern those aspects in order to efficiently enforce those rights. The currently applicable mosaic approach, however, is only the third best solution. 43

There are possibilities for the parties to **circumvent the exclusion of a choice of law**. They are, however, rather burdensome and are outside the context of non-contractual claims for the infringement of an intellectual property right. For instance, the parties may conclude a licencing agreement after the infringement has occurred, covering the infringing use of the intellectual property right which provides for a licensing fee instead of damages.[100] Alternatively, the parties may agree on a settlement providing for a payment in the amount of the compensation that would be due for the infringement of the intellectual property right under the law whose application they would favour if a choice of law were allowed. 44

III. Scope of the Applicable Law

1. General Considerations

a) The General (External) Conflict Rule (Art. 8(1))

The statutory basis for the scope of the law applicable under the general conflict rule is Arts. 8(1) and 15 Rome II. Problems arise with regard to several issues since the scope of the applicable law has been contested for a long time, while neither Art. 8(1) nor Art. 15 Rome II provide clear answers: Art. 8(1) itself does not address the issue of scope, and Art. 15 is very generally and 45

---

99 Concurring *Heinze*, in: jurisPK BGB, Art. 8 fn. 97; *Fayaz*, GRUR Int. 2009, 566, 577.

100 *Heinze*, in: jurisPK BGB, Art. 8 para. 21; *Grünberger*, 108 ZVglRWiss (2009) 134, 168 seq. and 175 seq.

broadly drafted so as to potentially cover all conflict rules of Arts. 4 to 13 Rome II; in fact, however, Art. 15 is designed in light of classic torts/delicts affecting physical property (Art. 4 and 5) rather than special torts such as Arts. 6, 8 and 9. Nevertheless, Recital 26 as well as Arts. 8, 13 and 15 Rome II provide several indications for determining the scope of the applicable law in relation to the various aspects of a claim arising from the infringement of an intellectual property right: First, Recital 26 in conjunction with Art. 8(1) indicates that all intellectual property rights, whether copyright and related rights or industrial property rights, shall be uniformly governed by the same principles under Art. 8(1). This bars any caveats and exclusions of specific aspects in relation to special types of intellectual property rights.[101] Secondly, Art. 8(1) in conjunction with Arts. 13 and 15[102] create a conflict rule with comprehensive coverage as regards all aspects of the infringement claim from the existence of the intellectual property right via different bases of the claim to the range of remedies and sanctions.[103] Thirdly, the interdependence of most aspects of an infringement claim, *e.g.* infringement and content of an intellectual property right, strongly militates in favour of submitting all these aspects to one single law.

46 Against this background, the **scope of the *lex loci protectionis* under Art. 8(1) is wide**. Nearly all relevant aspects of an infringement claim are governed by it.

47 According to Art. 15 lit. a, the basis and extent of liability, including the determination of persons who may be held liable for their acts are governed by the applicable law. This covers formal

---

101 *Schack*, in: Leible/Ohly (eds.), Intellectual Property and Private International Law (2009) 79, 91 et seq., however, argues for a differentiation between registered and unregistered intellectual property rights in relation to the scope of the applicable law.

102 Note the wording of Art. 15 "in particular"; for details see Art. 15 para. 1 and *Illmer*, 28 CJQ (2009) 237.

103 Concurring *Sack*, WRP 2008, 1405, 1408.

(in particular all registration/application/filing issues) and material prerequisites for the creation and existence of the intellectual property right,[104] the relevant acts of infringement, questions of causation and fault as well as issues of joint liability,[105] and according to Art. 15 lit. g issues of third party liability by inducement as well as contributory negligence.[106]

According to Art. 15 lit. b, the grounds for exemption from liability as well as any limitation or division of liability are governed by the applicable law. This covers in particular the term of protection (including a comparison of terms under the Berne Convention and other international conventions), issues of exhaustion of rights and all sorts of limitations of liability owed to public interest,[107] particularly in copyright law.[108] 48

According to Art. 15 lit. c and lit. d, the existence, the nature and the assessment of damage or the remedy claimed as well as the measures which a court may take, within the limits of powers conferred on the court by its procedural law, to prevent or terminate injury or damage or to ensure the provision of compensation are governed by the applicable law. This covers all sanctions in terms of measures to prevent impending and to prohibit actual infringements as well as remedies to compensate damage that 49

---

104 *Basedow/Metzger*, in: FS Boguslavskij (2004) 153, 162; *Sack*, WRP 2008, 1405, 1409; *Grünberger*, 108 ZVglRWiss (2009) 134, 171; *Heinze*, in: jurisPK BGB, Art. 8 para. 19; a different view is taken by *Leistner*, in: Leible/Ohly (eds.), Intellectual Property and Private International Law (2009) 97, 103; *Schack*, in: Leible/Ohly (eds.), Intellectual Property and Private International Law (2009) 79, 92 seq.; *Dickinson*, para. 8.18.

105 *Grünberger*, 108 ZVglRWiss (2009) 134, 172; *Heinze*, in: jurisPK BGB, Art. 8 para. 19; *Sack*, WRP 2008, 1405, 1409.

106 *Leistner*, in: Leible/Ohly (eds.), Intellectual Property and Private International Law (2009) 97, 104; *Sack*, WRP 2008, 1405, 1410.

107 *Sack*, WRP 2008, 1405, 1409; *Heinze*, in: jurisPK BGB, Art. 8 para. 19.

108 Cf., for instance, section 6 (§§ 44a to 63a) of the German Copyright Act *(Urheberrechtsgesetz)*.

has occurred (including the claims incorporated by Art. 13). In particular, the availability of injunctive relief (in particular the preconditions of interim injunctive relief[109]), claims for disclosure, cease and desist orders as well as orders for the elimination of infringing goods are governed by the applicable law.[110] The *caveat* "within the limits of powers conferred on the court by its procedural law" merely means that a court is not obliged to order measures that are so alien to its system that they cannot be tailored so as to fit into it.[111] General procedural issues such as requirements of pleading, evidence and rather technical matters are governed by the *lex fori* according to Art. 1(3) Rome II.[112]

50 According to Art. 15 lit. e, the question whether a right to claim damages or a remedy may be transferred, including by inheritance, is governed by the applicable law.[113] The transfer itself as a contractual obligation will usually be governed by the law determined under the Rome I Regulation.[114]

51 According to Art. 15 lit. f, the range of persons entitled to compensation for damage personally sustained is equally governed by

---

109 *Leistner*, in: Leible/Ohly (eds.), Intellectual Property and Private International Law (2009) 97, 105; *Heinze*, in: jurisPK BGB, Art. 8 para. 19.

110 *Basedow/Metzger*, in: FS Boguslavskij (2004) 153, 162; *Grünberger*, 108 ZVglRWiss (2009) 134, 172.

111 *Heinze*, in: jurisPK BGB, Art. 8 para. 19.

112 See *Illmer*, 28 CJQ (2009) 237 for the dichotomy of substance and procedure under Rome II; slightly inaccurate *Leistner*, in: Leible/Ohly (eds.), Intellectual Property and Private International Law (2009) 97, 105.

113 *Grünberger*, 108 ZVglRWiss (2009) 134, 164; *Sack*, WRP 2008, 1405, 1409; *Heinze*, in: jurisPK BGB, Art. 8 para. 18; the opposite view is taken by *Leistner*, in: Leible/Ohly (eds.), Intellectual Property and Private International Law (2009) 97, 103; *Dickinson*, para. 8.18; *Schack*, in: Leible/Ohly (eds.), Intellectual Property and Private International Law (2009) 79, 95 (at least with regard to unregistered intellectual property rights).

114 For a detailed analysis see *Grünberger*, 108 ZVglRWiss (2009) 134, 165 et seq.

the *lex loci protectionis* as the applicable law. It is argued that this includes (possibly in conjunction with Art. 15 lit. a) the highly contested issue of first ownership.[115] Others take the view that neither lit. a nor lit. f are clear in that respect but that it follows from the overall structure and conjoined effect of Recital 26, Arts. 8, 13 and 15 Rome II that the issue of first ownership is governed by the *lex loci protectionis* under Art. 8(1).[116] A third group of authors favours the *lex loci originis* as regards first ownership. They take the view that the issue of first ownership is outside the scope of the law applicable under Art. 8(1).[117] One should, however, note that this approach does not automatically result in the application of the *lex loci originis* under Rome II but merely in the application of national conflict rules, some of which follow the *lex loci protectionis* while others apply the *lex loci originis*. In any event, one should check the *lex fori's* conflict rule on the issue: if it also applies the *lex loci protectionis*, the dispute is practically irrelevant in the given case.

Overall, the arguments for the *lex loci protectionis* prevail at least **52**
under Art. 8(1) Rome II. Considering the implications to be drawn from the conjoined effect and structure of Recital 26, Arts. 8, 13 and 15 Rome II, the issue is *de lege lata* covered by the connection of Art. 8(1) Rome II. Furthermore, the issue of first ownership is not a preliminary question justifying a different

115 *Sack*, WRP 2008, 1405, 1409 seq.

116 *Basedow/Metzger*, in: FS Boguslavskij (2004) 153, 162; *Grünberger*, 108 ZVglRWiss (2009) 134, 161 et seq.; *Sack*, WRP 2008, 1405, 1409 seq.; *Heinze*, in: jurisPK BGB, Art. 8 paras. 18 seq.

117 *Metzger*, JZ 2010, 929, 933 (explicitly revoking his position taken in the previous paper together with Basedow), *Leistner*, in: Leible/Ohly (eds.), Intellectual Property and Private International Law (2009) 97, 103; *Schack*, in: Leible/Ohly (eds.), Intellectual Property and Private International Law (2009) 79, 93 seq.; *Dickinson*, para. 8.18; *Klass*, GRUR Int. 2008, 546, 547; *Pertegás Sender*, in: Malatesta (ed.), The unification of choice of law rules on torts and other non-contractual obligations in Europe – the Rome II Regulation (2006) 221, 239.

connecting factor. Rather, it is part of the main issue of infringement, intertwined with its other aspects so that it should be governed by the same law.[118]

53 According to Art. 15 lit. h, the rather general issues of extinction of an obligation and the rules of prescription and limitation, including rules relating to the commencement, interruption and suspension of a period of prescription or limitation are governed by the applicable law.

b) The Special (Internal) Conflict Rule (Art. 8(2))

54 The scope of the *lex loci delicti* under Art. 8(2) is foremost set by its own caveat under which it only applies to "any question that is not governed by the relevant Community instrument". This leaves mainly sanctions to be governed by the *lex loci delicti*.[119] Consequently, Art. 15 plays only a minor role. According to its lit. c, remedies and the assessment of damages and, according to lit. d, the range of sanctions (within the limits of the *lex fori's* procedural law) are governed by the *lex loci delicti*.

2. Unlawful and Lawful Acts

55 According to its wording and as a matter of course, Art. 8 governs the law applicable to unlawful acts, *i.e.* infringements of intellectual property rights. The conflict rule should, however, equally apply to compensatory claims that are granted by several domestic laws for specific types of lawful acts in relation to intellectual property rights.[120] Art. 13 indicates that all non-contractual claims shall be governed by the same law according to the *lex loci*

---

118 Convincingly against the proposition of a separable preliminary question *Grünberger*, 108 ZVglRWiss (2009) 134, 157 et seq.

119 For details on the interplay of Art. 8(2) with the unitary Community instruments see *supra* paras. 25 et seq.

120 *Grünberger*, 108 ZVglRWiss (2009) 134, 138, 175; *Heinze*, in: jurisPK BGB, Art. 8 para. 17, against an analoguous application, however, *Dickinson*, para. 8.18; *Sack*, WRP 2008, 1405, 1410.

protectionis under Art. 8(1).[121] Hence, the **scope of Art. 8 should be extended to lawful acts** such as artists' resale rights *(droit de suite)*, claims for remuneration in case of private use of copyrighted material[122] and claims for compensation in relation to the use of a sign during the period between the publication of registration and the actual registration as a Community trademark according to Art. 9(3)2 Community Trademark Regulation. In any event, the matter is of little practical relevance since most national conflict rules which would apply if the matter was not covered by Art. 8, equally provide for the *lex loci protectionis* in relation to lawful acts.[123]

3. Contractual versus Non-Contractual Obligations

Claims based on contractual obligations in relation to intellectual property rights, such as licencing agreements and agreements for the transfer of intellectual property rights, are governed by the Rome I Regulation[124] since they are even outside the material scope of Art. 8 altogether.[125] The transferability of the intellectual property right as such and its effect on third parties is, however, governed by the *lex loci protectionis* under Art. 8(1) Rome II.[126] 56

---

121 *Heinze*, in: jurisPK BGB, Art. 8 para. 17.

122 See *e.g.* §§ 53, 54 lits. a-h German Copyright Act *(Urheberrechtsgesetz)*.

123 This is rightly pointed out by *Sack*, WRP 2008, 1405, 1410.

124 As regards unitary Community intellectual property rights under Art. 8(2) only apart from the issues governed by the Community instruments itself (see Arts. 16 et seq. Community Trademark Regulation, Arts. 27 et seq. Community Design Regulation and Arts. 22 et seq. Community Plant Variety Rights Regulation).

125 *Heinze*, in: jurisPK BGB, Art. 8 para. 18; *Grünberger*, 108 ZVglRWiss (2009) 134, 165 et seq. with a detailed analysis.

126 In that direction also *Grünberger*, 108 ZVglRWiss (2009) 134, 164; see generally: *Metzger*, in: Basedow/Drexl/Kur/Metzger (eds.), Intellectual Property in the Conflict of Laws (2005) 61, 72 seq.

D. Jurisdiction Issues

57 Apart from the special rules on jurisdiction with regard to unitary intellectual property rights provided by the respective Community instruments,[127] jurisdiction in cross-border cases is, as a general rule, governed by the **Brussels I Regulation** if the defendant has his domicile or seat within the EU, and by the national regimes of jurisdiction if his domicile or seat are located in a Non-Member State (cf. Art. 4 Brussels I).

58 Relevant heads of jurisdiction as regards non-contractual infringement claims under the Brussels I Regulation are Art. 2, 5 No. 3, 22 No. 4, 23 and 24 with respect to the main proceedings, Art. 6 in relation to joint co-defendants, and Art. 31 with regard to interim relief which is frequently sought in intellectual property infringement cases.

59 Exclusive jurisdiction under Art. 22 No. 4 (which is, however, limited to registered intellectual property rights) supersedes any other head of jurisdiction (save Art. 31 regarding interim relief) whatever the form of proceedings in which the validity of the registered intellectual property right is raised, be it by way of an action or a defence, be it at the time of filing the case or at a later stage in the proceedings.[128] If aspects of validity are not at stake, and failing a jurisdiction clause (which is rather rare in relation to non-contractual infringement claims) or a submission to the jurisdiction of the court, the plaintiff may choose between the general jurisdiction at the defendant's domicile according to Art. 2

[127] See Arts. 94 et seq. Community Trademark Regulation, Arts. 79 et seq. Community Design Regulation and Arts. 101 seq. Community Plant Variety Rights Regulation; all three special jurisdiction regimes refer to the Brussels I and Lugano regime but provide for several modifications; for details see special literature on the respective Community instruments.

[128] ECJ, Case C-4/03 – *GAT* [2006] ECR I-6509, paras. 25 et seq. (dealing with Art. 22(4)'s identical predecessor Art. 16(4) Brussels Convention).

and the special jurisdiction under Art. 5 No. 3. In that regard, the plaintiff has to consider two aspects: First, as regards intellectual property infringement, both the place where the damage occurred and the place where the event giving rise to the damage took place under Art. 5 No. 3 coincide in the country for which protection is claimed.[129] Hence, Art. 5 No. 3 does not amount to a choice between two jurisdictions in those cases. Secondly, in multi-state scenarios the mosaic principle may influence the plaintiff's choice between Art. 2 and Art. 5 No. 3. An action in relation to infringements in different countries (even under different laws according to the mosaic principle[130]) may only lie at the defendant's domicile whereas the jurisdiction under Art. 5 No. 3 may be limited to the infringement in the respective country.[131]

Article 9
Industrial action

Without prejudice to Article 4(2), the law applicable to a non-contractual obligation in respect of the liability of a person in the capacity of a worker or an employer or the organisations representing their professional interests for damages caused by an industrial action, pending or carried out, shall be the law of the country where the action is to be, or has been, taken.

129 Concurring: *Heinze*, in: jurisPK BGB, Art. 8 para. 7.

130 See *supra* paras. 33 et seq.

131 The ECJ has not decided the issue so far, but such a view would accord with the principles the ECJ laid down with regard to cross-border media torts in ECJ, Case C-68/93 – *Shevill* [1995] ECR I-415, para. 33; concurring *Grünberger*, 108 ZVglRWiss (2009) 134, 156 seq.; *Heinze*, in: jurisPK BGB, Art. 8 para. 7; for further details see *Heinze*, Einstweiliger Rechtsschutz im europäischen Immaterialgüterrecht (2007) 224 et seq.

A. Introductory Issues

I. Legislative History

1 Neither the Commission's preliminary draft proposal for a Rome II Regulation in 2002 nor its initial proposal of 2003[1] contained a special conflict rule regarding industrial action. Since the field was not excluded from the Regulation's material scope, the general conflict rule of Art. 4 would have governed non-contractual liability arising from industrial action. Upon an **initiative by Sweden**, the European Parliament, in its first reading in 2005, proposed a special rule for liability in tort/delict in relation to industrial action.[2] In the subsequent amended proposal of

---

[1] COM(2003) 427 final.

[2] See Art. 6 of the European Parliament's legislative resolution after the first reading (P6-TA(2005)0284 of 6 July 2005).

2006,[3] the Commission neither accepted the conflict rule suggested by Parliament nor did it provide for an alternative rule. After some initial hesitation, a majority in the Council supported a special conflict rule on industrial action. Making several amendments to Parliament's proposal, a special conflict rule on industrial action was adopted as part of the Council's Common Position.[4] Despite further debates in the Council[5] and a rather reluctant statement by the Commission,[6] the suggested conflict rule was finally adopted without any further amendments.[7]

II. Background

The conflict rule in Art. 9 has **no predecessor in the national conflict regimes of the Member States**. Rather, the determination of the applicable law was a matter for case law and academic discourse.[8] The Swedish initiative for a special conflict rule on industrial action was triggered in particular by the preceding judgment of the ECJ in the ***DFDS Torline*** *case*.[9] The case concerned jurisdiction under Art. 5 No. 3 Brussels I[10] in relation to 2

3 COM(2006) 83 final.

4 Common Position (EC) No 22/2006 of 25 September 2006, OJ 2006 C 289E/68.

5 Latvia and Estonia voted against the Common Position (and against the Regulation in its final form), Cyprus and Greece expressed their concern; see Council Document 12219/06 ADD 1 of 14 September 2006; see also the Statement of the Council's Reasons of 25 September 2006, OJ 2006 C 289E/68 at 77 (II.1.5.).

6 COM(2006) 566 final, p. 4.

7 For further details of the discussion in the Council see *Dickinson*, paras. 9.07 et seq.

8 For details on the different solutions see *Heinze*, 73 RabelsZ (2009) 770, 777 et seq. with further references.

9 ECJ, Case C-18/02 – *DFDS Torline* [2004] ECR I-1417.

10 Council Regulation (EC) No 44/2001 of 22 December 2000 on jurisdiction and the recognition and enforcement of judgments in civil and commercial matters, OJ 2001, L 12/1.

tortuous/delictual liability arising in the course of an industrial action. Polish sailors were employed by Danish shipowners on a cargo vessel (the Tor Caledonia) that served the route Harwich (England) to Gothenborg (Sweden). In the course of a dispute over the wages payed to the Polish sailors, a Swedish trade union initiated industrial action by instructing its members not to accept employment on the Tor Caledonia and by instructing another Swedish trade union to refuse harbour services, in particular loading and unloading, in relation to the Tor Caledonia (sympathy action). The Danish shipowners sued the Swedish trade union before a Danish labour court for damages in respect of the loss caused by the industrial action. Upon a reference for a preliminary ruling the ECJ applied its settled case law as expressed in the cases of *Mines de Potasse d'Alsace*[11] and *Shevill*[12] in holding that the plaintiff has a choice under the jurisdiction of Art. 5 No. 3 Brussels I whether to sue in the country where the damage occurred or in the country of the event giving rise to it.[13] On this basis, the ECJ held that under the given circumstances the damage consisted of the financial loss to the Danish shipowners caused by the withdrawal of the Tor Caledonia from its route to Gothenburg and the hire of a replacement ship to serve this route.[14] However, the ECJ left it to the national court to determine whether such damage occurred at the place of establishment of the Danish shipowners or elsewhere. The flag state was held to be only one factor in determining the place where the damage occurred save in cases where the damage occurred on board the vessel itself; in this latter case the flag state would be the place where the damage occurred.[15]

11 ECJ, Case 21/76 – *Mines de Potasse d'Alsace* [1976] ECR 1735 paras. 19 et seq.

12 ECJ, Case C-68/93 – *Shevill* [1995] ECR I-415 para. 20.

13 The reference in its question 2 (paras. 39 et seq.) concerned the role of the flag state when determining the place where the damage occurred.

14 ECJ, Case C-18/02 – *DFDS Torline* [2004] ECR I-1417 para. 42.

15 ECJ, Case C-18/02 – *DFDS Torline* [2004] ECR I-1417 para. 44.

Although the ECJ did not determine the place where the damage occurs in case of an industrial action, by accepting financial loss as the relevant damage it indicated that the damage may occur in another country than the one where the industrial action took place. Assuming a certain degree of synergy and concordance between the Brussels I and the Rome II Regulation, the application of Art. 4 Rome II to cases of industrial action could have led to the application of foreign law to an industrial action.[16] Given the substantial differences in the national labour law regimes concerning industrial action, this was regarded as inappropriate. 3

III. Policy Issues

As expressed by the Swedish initiative for the special conflict rule, the **law of industrial action is embedded in the national legal cultures and regulation of labour law relations** which differ significantly between the Member States. The area of law is sensitive and in many respects driven by strong public interests as well as protectionism of local customs and the respective regulation of economic and industrial relations.[17] Against this background, any conflict rule dissociated from the place where the industrial action takes place appears inappropriate and would face severe problems of acceptance. A likely response by the courts of the Member States would be regular recourse to Art. 16 Rome II (overriding mandatory provisions) and/or Art. 26 Rome II (public policy).[18] This would, however, be inconsistent with the system of Rome II: Arts. 16 and 26 are de- 4

16 *Garcimartín Alferéz*, EuLF 2007, I-77, 88; *Van Hoek*, in: Dorssemont/Jaspers/Van Hoek (eds.), Cross-Border Collective Actions in Europe – A Legal Challenge (2007) 425, 451 seq.

17 *Van Hoek*, in: Dorssemont/Jaspers/Van Hoek (eds.), Cross-Border Collective Actions in Europe – A Legal Challenge (2007) 425, 448; *Dicey, Morris & Collins*, para. S 35-238; *Morse*, in: Liber Fausto Pocar (2009) 723, 724; *Heinze*, 73 RabelsZ (2009) 770, 781.

18 Similar *Heinze*, 73 RabelsZ (2009) 770, 781.

signed as exceptions, not as the rule. Furthermore, both provisions have the structural disadvantage that they are only capable of enforcing the provisions and policy of the forum state. In case of industrial action taking place in another state (*e.g.* in case of a claim at the employer's seat), there is no connection to the forum state that would justify enforcing provisions or policy of that state.[19]

5 The special conflict rule in Art. 9 aims at avoiding this conflict between a law dissociated from the place where the industrial action takes place and the *lex fori* by simply providing for the law of the country where the industrial action is taken, *i.e.* where it is implemented and affects the labour relations between the parties.[20] In doing so, the special conflict rule puts an emphasis on behavioural regulation rather than restitutionary interests.[21] In effect, the special conflict rule **operates like a special mandatory rule in relation to industrial action** giving full effect to the regulation of industrial action at the place where such industrial action is implemented. This *ratio legis* has several implications for interpreting aspects of the conflict rule in Art. 9 such as the assessment of the reference to Art. 4(2),[22] the law relevant for interpretating the concept of industrial action[23] and the role of Arts. 16 and 26 in the context of industrial action.[24] Overall, it

19 Cf. in this regard also *Van Hoek*, in: Dorssemont/Jaspers/Van Hoek (eds.), Cross-Border Collective Actions in Europe – A Legal Challenge (2007) 425, 449.

20 *Fallon*, in: Basedow/Baum/Nishitani (eds.), Japanese and European Private Law in Comparative Perspective (2008) 261, 274 does not see any need for a special conflict rule in relation to industrial action but would regularly apply the escape clause of Art. 4(3) to apply the law of the place where the action is taken.

21 *Knöfel*, EuZA 2008, 228, 236; *Junker*, in: Münchener Kommentar BGB, Art. 9 para. 2.

22 See *infra* paras. 22 et seq.

23 See *infra* paras. 8 et seq.

24 See *infra* para. 41.

implies that the *lex fori* should be given minimal weight whereas the *lex causae*, *i.e.* the law of the country where the industrial action takes place should govern all aspects of liability caused by an industrial action as comprehensively as possible. Taking a practical stance, one should, however, note that under the most relevant jurisdiction of Art. 5 No. 3 Brussels I, the court seized is regularly in a position to apply its own law since *lex fori* and *lex causae* coincide in the law of the country where the industrial action is taken.[25]

IV. Structure

6 The rule in Art. 9 is a further ***lex specialis*** to the general conflict rule on tort/delict in Art. 4. In conjunction with other provisions of the Regulation, it establishes a straight-forward **ladder of three connections**. First, a choice of law pursuant to Art. 14 prevails over any of the objective connections contained in Art. 9 itself. Secondly, by explicit reference, the common habitual residence connection in Art. 4(2) takes precedence over the conflict rule provided by Art. 9 itself. Thirdly, covering the vast majority of cases, Art. 9 itself provides for the law of the country where the industrial action is to be, or has been, taken.

7 Art. 9 neither provides for an escape clause itself nor does it incorporate the escape clause of Art. 4(3) by way of reference. Considering that a choice of law prior to the industrial action is more of a theoretical nature and that a choice of law after the industrial action is equally rare, the conflict regime determining the law applicable to industrial action is rigid and inflexible to effectively protect the rights and obligations of workers and employers (Recital 27).

---

25 For details on jurisdiction and the interaction with the applicable law see *infra* paras. 42 et seq.

B. Scope of the Conflict Rule

I. Material Scope

1. The Concept of Industrial Action

a) Lex Causae

8 The conflict rule in Art. 9 applies to non-contractual liability caused by an industrial action. According to Recital 27, the exact scope of what constitutes an industrial action is to be determined by "each Member State's internal rules." Consequently, the concept of industrial action is ***not*** *to be interpreted autonomously as most other terms of the Regulation* (see e.g. Recital 11).[26] Attempts to argue despite the clear wording of Recital 27 in favour of an autonomous interpretation[27] are not convincing. The two sentences of Recital 27 cannot be regarded as a unit that merely explains the choice for a special conflict rule.[28] Rather, its two sentences concern different aspects. The first sentence is limited to the concept of industrial action by prescribing the way in which it shall be interpreted: according to internal, domestic rules. It does not address liability for damage caused by industrial action comprehensively. Otherwise it would simply duplicate the conflict rule in Art. 9. It is rather the recital's second sentence alone that provides an explanation for the connection chosen in Art. 9: protecting the rights and obligations of workers and employers.

---

26 *Morse*, in: Liber Fausto Pocar (2009) 723, 727; *Dicey, Morris & Collins*, para. S 35-240; *Dickinson*, para. 9.19; *Heinze*, 73 RabelsZ (2009) 770, 782 seq.; *Junker*, in: Münchener Kommentar BGB, Art. 9 para. 14; *Knöfel*, EuZA 2008, 228, 241; *Leible/Lehmann*, RIW 2007, 721, 731; *von Hein*, VersR 2007, 440, 450; *Guerchon/Piedelièvre*, Gazette du Palais 2007, 3106, 3120.

27 *Plender & Wilderspin*, paras. 23-008 et seq.; *van Hoek*, NIPR 2008, 448, 451.

28 This is the main argument of *Plender/Wilderspin*, para. 23-008.

The reference to "each Member State's internal rules" in Recital 27 is open to interpretation. For several reasons it is, however, not convincing to apply the *lex fori* to determine the scope of the concept of industrial action.[29] Such an approach would disregard the policy choice of Art. 9[30] to submit all aspects of liability for damage caused by industrial action to the law of the place where the action is taken, *i.e. lex causae*. Furthermore, applying the *lex fori* would undermine the uniform character of the conflict rule. One of its central aspects would be interpreted differently depending on the court seized.[31] Consequently, the **concept of industrial action has to be interpreted by the respective *lex causae***, *i.e.* the law of the country where the industrial action in question is to be, or has been, taken.[32] 9

It should be noted, however, that in practice the issue of *lex fori* vs. *lex causae* is often irrelevant. Both laws will regularly coincide at the place where the industrial action is to be, or has been, taken under the relevant heads of jurisdiction for interim relief, *i.e.* provisional or protective matters (Art. 31 Brussels I), as well as the main proceedings (Art. 5 No. 3 Brussels I).[33] 10

The relevant ***lex causae* is not restricted to a Member State law;** the respective wording in rectial 27 ("… by each Member State's internal rules.") disregards the universal character of the Regulation's conflict rules according to Art. 3. Therefore, even a Non-Member State's *lex causae* may govern the scope of industrial ac- 11

---

29 Such a *lex fori*-approach is favoured by *Knöfel*, EuZA 2008, 228, 241; *Spickhoff*, in: Bamberger/Roth, Anh. zu Art. 42 EGBGB para. 69; *Thorn*, in: Palandt, Art. 9 para. 2 (though with hesitation).

30 Cf. in that regard *supra* paras. 4 seq.

31 *Heinze*, 73 RabelsZ (2009) 770, 782.

32 See also *Heinze*, 73 RabelsZ (2009) 770, 782; *Dickinson*, para. 9.19.

33 For details on jurisdiction and the interaction with the applicable law see *infra* paras. 42 et seq.

tion in the individual case.[34] Recital 27 merely names two commonly arising incidents of industrial action: strike action (on the part of workers and/or unions) and lock-out (on the part of employers and/or employers' associations). Other examples include boycotts, work-to-rule, go-slow-action and secondary acts like sympathy or solidarity strikes.

b) Autonomous Delimitations

12 Despite the decentralised, heterogeneous interpretation according to the respective *lex causae*, one may infer from Art. 9 **limitations and delimitations of the concept of industrial action that apply regardless of the *lex causae's* concept**. One such limitation is to restrict the concept of industrial action to acts in furtherance of labour relations/conditions as opposed to political action such as the blocking of railway transports of radioactive waste, even if pursued by the employees of the railway company or the waste company.[35] One such delimitation is the explicit extension to both sides of a labour dispute: action by employees as well as employers and their respective organisations representing their professional interests.

13 Additionally, while Art. 28 of the Charter of Fundamental Rights of the European Union[36] in conjunction with Art. 6 TEU may not serve as the source of an autonomous interpretation or provide constituting elements of the concept of industrial action,[37] it

---

[34] *Dicey, Morris & Collins*, para. S 35-238, fn. 56; *Heinze*, 73 RabelsZ (2009) 770, 782; *Spickhoff*, in: Bamberger/Roth, Anh. zu Art. 42 EGBGB para. 69.

[35] *Dickinson*, para. 9.20; with some hesitation and rather against such a limitation *Heinze*, 73 RabelsZ (2009) 770, 783.

[36] Art. 28 reads: "Right of collective bargaining and action. Workers and employers, or their respective organisations, have, in accordance with Community law and national laws and practices, the right to negotiate and conclude collective agreements at the appropriate levels and, in cases of conflicts of interest, to take collective action to defend their interests, including strike action".

may well serve as a minimum standard of what the Member States (not third countries) have to accept as an industrial action for the purposes of Art. 9 Rome II.[38] Such a cautious approach to the Charter would take due account of its Art. 53 while still giving full effect to the Charter's fundamental rights given that these rights have to be respected by the Member States when applying a European Regulation.

2. Limitation to Tort/Delict

The material scope of the conflict rule in Art. 9 is limited to claims in delict/tort (chapter II of the Regulation). *E contrario* Art. 13, it does not extend to claims based on unjust enrichment, *negotiorum gestio* and *culpa in contrahendo* (chapter III of the Regulation).[39] A potential clash is most likely to arise with regard to unjust enrichtment claims based on industrial action. In this case, the law determined by Arts. 9 and 10 Rome II respectively is in the majority of cases the same, so that the issue may be of little practical relevance.[40] 14

3. Non-Contractual vs. Contractual Obligations

Art. 9 only covers non-contractual liability caused by an industrial action. Contractual liability is governed by the respective conflict rules of the Rome I Regulation[41] (Arts. 8 and 12(1)(b)- 15

37 *Heinze*, 73 RabelsZ (2009) 770, 783.

38 *Knöfel*, EuZA 2008, 228, 241.

39 *Junker*, in: Münchener Kommentar BGB, Art. 9 para. 11; in contrast: *Morse*, in: Liber Fausto Pocar (2009) 723, 733 favours a comprehensive application of Art. 9.

40 *Morse*, in: Liber Fausto Pocar (2009) 723, 732 seq.; *Heinze*, in: jurisPK BGB, Art. 9 para. 10.

41 Regulation (EC) No 593/2008 of the European Parliament and of the Council of 17 June 2008 on the law applicable to contractual obligations (Rome I), OJ 2008 L 177/6.

(d)).[42] Such contractual liability concerns in particular the effect of an industrial action on individual employment contracts (such as termination of the contract, suspension of wages) and contractual agreements between the persons involved in the industrial action (such as agreements to suspend the action or agreements in the course of an understanding to bring the industrial action to an end).[43]

II. Personal Scope

16 In relation to the personal scope of the conflict rule in Art. 9 one has to distinguish between the person(s) claimed to be liable on the one hand and the person(s) sustaining pending or actual damage on the other hand.

1. Person Claimed to be Liable

17 With regard to the **person(s) claimed to be liable**, Art. 9 contains an explicit limitation to (liability as) a person "in the capacity of a worker or an employer or the organisations representing their professional interests". According to Art. 15(a), in relation to organisations this covers personal liability of the individuals representing them.[44] Otherwise, the conflict rule could be evaded too easily by suing such individuals in respect of their individual acts in the course of the industrial action under the law determined by Art. 4.[45]

---

42 *Junker*, in: Münchener Kommentar BGB, Art. 9 para. 20; *Knöfel*, EuZA 2008, 228, 240; *Dickinson*, para. 9.17; *Brière*, 135 Clunet (2008) 31, 49; *Guerchon/Piedelièvre*, Gazette du Palais 2007, 3106, 3120.

43 *Knöfel*, EuZA 2008, 228, 240; *Heinze*, in: jurisPK BGB, Art. 9 para. 10.

44 *Dickinson*, para. 9.25; *Heinze*, in: jurisPK BGB, Art. 9 para. 6; the opposite view (application of Art. 4) is taken by *Junker*, in: Münchener Kommentar BGB, Art. 9 para. 25 (regarding this as a strange result so that he suggests connecting such liability via the escape clause of Art. 4(3)); *Knöfel*, EuZA 2008, 228, 239.

45 This is rightly pointed out by *Dickinson*, para. 9.25.

2. Person Sustaining Damage

With regard to the **person(s) sustaining damage**, Art. 9 is silent. The matter is practically relevant with regard to third persons suffering damage as a result of an industrial action in which they are not involved. A common scenario is personal injury to a third person or damage to the property of a third person at the occasion of an industrial action. Another possible scenario is that of a person who has entered into a sales contract with a contracting partner whose employees opt for industrial action, *e.g.* a strike, as a result of which the third person is not supplied with the sold goods. Just-in-time delivery of intermediate goods in a complex production process may serve as an example: if parts required for the brake system at the production line of a car manufacturer are not delivered in time, the entire production process is interrupted. 18

Two options are at hand: an application of the special conflict rule in Art. 9[46] versus an application of the general conflict rule in Art. 4.[47] 19

In the first scenario of personal injury or damage to property of the third person it appears to be rather clear from the *ratio legis* of Art. 9 that it does not apply. Rather, Art. 4 as the *lex generalis* applies instead. The tort/delict towards the third person may be a (usually remote) consequence of the industrial action. It is, however, not characterised by the industrial dispute. Rather, the damage sustained by the third person is comparable with harm to a bystander in the course of any other tort/delict such as personal injury to a bystander caused by a defective product (which is also not governed by the regular connections under Art. 5(1), but by 20

---

46 *Leible/Lehmann*, RIW 2007, 721, 731; *Junker*, in: Münchener Kommentar BGB, Art. 9 para. 24.

47 *Knöfel*, EuZA 2008, 228, 243; *Guerchon/Piedelièvre*, Gazette du Palais 2007, 3106, 3120; *Morse*, in: Liber Fausto Pocar (2009) 723, 731; *Heinze*, 73 RabelsZ (2009) 770, 784; left open by *Dickinson*, para. 9.26.

the escape clause of Art. 5(2), regularly providing for the place where the damage occurs[48]). There is no causal link between the industrial action and the damage as it is required under Art. 9.[49] It appears unjustified from the bystander's point of view to apply a foreign, unexpected and unpredictable law governing an industrial dispute to a delict/tort towards him. Furthermore, the application of the same law to all claims somehow linked with the industrial action is not even required to achieve systematic stringency or efficiency: both claims are not related to each other, they are based on different grounds and they will often be brought in different fora.[50] In practice of course, Art. 4 and Art. 9 will usually provide for the same law in the scenario of direct, physical damage to person or property which will regularly occur at the *locus actus* of the industrial action.

21 In the second scenario of interference with a contractual relationship, the matter is more complicated. While Art. 9 would regularly point at the law of the *locus actus* of the industrial action, Art. 4(1) would regularly point at the law of the country where the manufacturing process or the like is interrupted (which may or may not be at the seat of the third person). There are arguments for both propositions. On the one hand, the employees or unions engaging in the industrial action usually know or at least accept that the industrial action will affect the position of contracting partners of the employer. This, in connection with the arguments raised in relation to the first scenario, militates in favour of an application of Art. 4. On the other hand, the third person is aware of the risk that industrial action might be directed towards its contracting partner. This aspect rather militates for an application of Art. 9. In the present author's opinion, the position and legitimate expectations of the employees or unions are more rather of protection on the level of conflict of laws (substantive law may well provide otherwise). Thus, Art. 9 should determine

---

48 See Art. 5 para. 44.

49 See *infra* para. 40.

50 Similar *Knöfel*, EuZA 2008, 228, 243.

the applicable law for non-contractual claims of the third person against the employees or unions. The industrial action may affect various contractual relationships and it would seriously undermine the right to industrial action if the person(s) engaging in it had to anticipate and consider the effects under several laws which they could not even foresee. In contrast, the third person faces only one, foreseeable risk: that there will be a strike or other industrial action by the employees of its contracting partner which he is free to choose. If, however, one favours the application of Art. 4, the escape clause of Art. 4(3) should not apply in so far as it could enable the application of the law applicable to the contract between the third person and the employer to the non-contractual claim against the employees or unions.[51] The striking employees or unions are not parties to the contractual relationship and the application of the law governing the contractual relationship would constitute an undue burden for them since they are not in a position, and cannot reasonably be expected, to anticipate the laws of all contracts between the employers and third parties that may be affected by their industrial action.

In practice, the second scenario is of little relevance since the third person has a direct contractual claim against the employer as its contracting partner for breach of contract which will usually provide compensation for the damage he has suffered. Only if this claim fails for reasons that do not also affect the non-contractual claim or if the employer becomes insolvent, a claim based on tort/delict against the employees or unions becomes may become relevant. 22

III. Territorial Scope

As the other provisions of Rome II, Art. 9 is a *loi uniforme*.[52] 23

---

51 Such a solution via the escape clause of Art. 4(3) is proposed by *Knöfel*, EuZA 2008, 228, 243.

52 See Art. 3 para. 1.

C. Determination of the Applicable Law

I. Choice of Law

24 Although the possibility of a choice of law is **hard to reconcile with the policy pursued by the special conflict rule in Art. 9** to avoid the application of a law dissociated to the place of the industrial action, it is *e contrario* Arts. 6(4) and 8(3) not excluded. In any event, a choice of law will govern industrial liability cases only rarely. Neither workers nor unions or other organisations representing the workers' professional interests are pursuing a commercial activity[53] so that a choice prior to the industrial action under Art. 14(1)(b) is not possible. A subsequent choice of law under Art. 14(1)(a) once the industrial dispute has arisen and the action has taken place will, however, hardly ever occur. It appears therefore as a rather theoretical consideration that the parties may, by way of a concurring choice of law after the industrial action, align the laws applicable to non-contractual and contractual liability stemming from the same industrial action. In any event, Art. 14(1)2 sets a rather high threshold for an implied choice of law by way of pleading a certain law.[54]

II. Common Habitual Residence

25 The application of the common habitual residence rule in the context of industrial action is often criticised.[55] Even more than a choice of law, the automatic application of the law of the common habitual residence appears to be irreconcilable with the pol-

53 *Wagner*, IPRax 2008, 1, 10; *Junker*, in: Münchener Kommentar BGB, Art. 9 para. 35.

54 See prior to the Regulation *e.g.* Rechtbank Amsterdam (Netherlands), 30 November 1978, Nederlandse Jurisprudentie 1981, No. 65 p. 162.

55 *Morse*, in: Liber Fausto Pocar (2009) 723, 726 seq.; *Dickinson*, para. 9.32; *Dicey, Morris & Collins*, para. S 35-239; *Junker*, in: Münchener Kommentar BGB, Art. 9 para. 31.

icy choice in Art. 9 to avoid the application of a law dissociated to the place of the industrial action.

26 An important area of application of Art. 4(2) may be the **posting of workers**. Industrial action in the context of such posting is usually pursuing two alternative purposes: either it aims to generally change the labour relations of the posted workers or it aims to integrate the posted workers into the labour law system of the place of posting (*e.g.* payment of equivalent wages, minimum insurance coverage etc.).

27 Under the first alternative, the closest connection appears to be with the country of origin. The industrial action is not linked to the posting of the workers. Often it will be combined with concurrent action by workers in the country of origin. If the industrial action by the posted workers is initiated by a union from the country of origin against the employer in the same country (the cross-border effect is met by the involvement of the posted workers), Art. 4(2) in conjunction with Art. 23 Rome II may allow for the law of their concurrent seats to govern the liability issues arising in the course of the industrial action. Under the second alternative, however, the closest connection appears to be with the country of posting. If a local union is organising the industrial action, Art. 4(2) in conjunction with Art. 23 Rome II may allow for the law of their concurrent seats to govern the liability issues arising in the course of the industrial action.

28 The problems are obvious. The two examples given are model examples. Reality may not be this clear-cut and the circumstances may be more complex. Art. 4(2) is, however, inflexible and may therefore lead to unsatisfactory results. Two examples may illustrate that: If a union in the country of origin initiates an industrial action in the country of posting, Art. 4(2) applies (providing for the law of the country of origin where both union and employer have their seats) although the industrial action bears no relevance to the labour relations in the country of origin. Likewise, if posted workers organise industrial action against their

employer in the country of posting, their concurrent "personal" home law may apply although the labour relations are only related to the country of posting. The matter is further complicated if the posted workers come from different countries so that liability may be governed by Art. 9 with regard to some of them but by Art. 4(2) with regard to others.[56]

III. Country Where the Action Is to Be, or Has Been, Taken

29 The characteristic connection of Art. 9 provides for the law of the country where the industrial action is to be, or has been, taken. This connection covers the vast majority of cases and is straight-forward. The place where the industrial action is to be, or has been, taken refers to the **place where such action is to be, or has been, implemented**, *i.e.* where the interests of the parties to the industrial dispute collide.[57] This is not tantamount to the place where the persons involved in the industrial action acted since such acts may only be of a preparatory nature. Likewise, the place where the industrial action was planned, coordinated and/or approved is irrelevant.[58]

30 In the maritime context, the law of the flag alone will determine the place where the action was taken only if such action was taken aboard the ship while in transit. If, however, as in the majority of cases, the industrial action is undertaken while the ship is docked in a harbour, the law of the country where the harbour is located applies.[59]

---

56 *Van Hoek*, in: Dorssemont/Jaspers/Van Hoek (eds.), Cross-Border Collective Actions in Europe – A Legal Challenge (2007) 425, 455 (with further criticism).

57 *Morse*, in: Liber Fausto Pocar (2009) 723, 728; *Dickinson*, para. 9.31.

58 *Heinze*, in: jurisPK BGB, Art. 9 para. 8; *Dickinson*, para. 9.31; *Knöfel*, EuZA 2008, 228, 244.

59 *Heinze*, in: jurisPK BGB, Art. 9 para. 8; for further details see *Knöfel*, EuZA 2008, 228, 244 et seq.; *Van Hoek*, in: Dorssemont/Jaspers/Van

IV. Multi-State Scenarios

Whether a multi-state industrial action gives rise to private international law issues depends on the circumstances of the individual case, more precisely on the **question whether the multi-state circumstances give rise to a cross-border element**. 31

A cross-border element is lacking if each industrial action takes place within the borders of the respective state and involves only the local workforce and/or local unions vis-à-vis a local subsidiary of the mother corporation.[60] In this scenario, multi-state industrial action takes the form of a bundle of national industrial actions, even if implemented in different countries as part of a concerted plan within a multinational corporation. Art. 9 Rome II does not come into play. Rather, each of the parallely undertaken industrial actions is governed by local law with regard to its lawfulness and liability issues. The multi-state does not result in a cross-border scenario. Even in large, international corporations multi-state industrial action often takes such form of a bundle of national actions involving no cross-border element. 32

Multi-state industrial action may, however, take other forms that give rise to a cross-border element, hence requiring the application of Art. 9 to determine the applicable law(s). If, for example, in the scenario just described the concerted industrial actions in different countries are organised by a single cross-border union or a foreign union, *e.g.* ITF[61] or ETUC,[62] or if the concerted industrial actions are directed at the multinational corporation itself which has its headquarters in one of the countries targeted by the 33

Hoek (eds.), Cross-Border Collective Actions in Europe – A Legal Challenge (2007) 425, 456 seq.

60 *Van Hoek*, in: Dorssemont/Jaspers/Van Hoek (eds.), Cross-Border Collective Actions in Europe – A Legal Challenge (2007) 425, 427 and 450.

61 International Transport Workers' Federation (see http://www.itfglobal.org/language-selector.cfm).

62 European Trade Union Confederation (see http://www.etuc.org).

industrial actions, the multi-state scenario is at the same time a cross-border scenario. Like most other conflict rules of the Rome II Regulation, Art. 9 does not contain a special rule for such multi-state scenarios. Rather, the **mosaic principle**, as adapted to industrial action, applies: each industrial action is governed by the law where the respective action took place. In particular, Art. 9 does not allow to connect the different industrial actions implemented in several countries to one single law, *e.g.* the law of the country where the centre of gravity of the industrial action is located.[63] Neither the wording nor the purpose of Art. 9 leave room for such a possibility.

V. Scope of the Applicable Law

1. Liability and Legality

34 According to its wording, the law determined by Art. 9 is limited to the issue of liability, not covering the legality of the industrial action as such. In addition, Recital 28 explicitly states that the conflict rule in Art. 9 does not prejudice the conditions for the exercise of industrial action under national law. Although it may generally be desirable to apply one single law to matters of liability and legality, it appears to be impossible to extend the scope of the applicable law to matters of legality. The wording bars such an extension. Further, the ECJ's judgment in the *DFDS Torline* case is of no avail in that regard. The fact that the ECJ applied Art. 5 No. 3 Brussels I also to a claim on the legality of the industrial action as being a matter of tort/delict[64] does not mean that it

---

63 *Knöfel*, EuZA 2008, 228, 237; *Heinze*, in: jurisPK BGB, Art. 9 para. 8.

64 ECJ, Case C-18/02 – *DFDS Torline* [2004] ECR I-1417 para. 28 ("It follows from the foregoing, that the answer to Question 1(a) must be that Article 5(3) of the Brussels Convention must be interpreted as meaning that a case concerning the legality of industrial action, in respect of which exclusive jurisdiction belongs, in accordance with the law of the Contracting State concerned, to a court other than the court which has jurisdiction to try the claims for compensation for the damage caused by that

regarded this issue also as one of industrial action. The application of Art. 5 No. 3 Brussels I does not require such a finding. The ruling in *DFDS Torline* is therefore entirely consistent with applying a national conflict rule (which will be one of tort/delict) to the legality of an industrial action.

35 Consequently, the **legality of the industrial action is governed by the law determined by the respective national conflict rules**, regardless of whether it becomes relevant in the course of a claim based on non-contractual liability under Art. 9 Rome II or contractual liability under Art. 8 Rome I.[65]

36 In practice, the matter is irrelevant if the national conflict rules concerning the legality of industrial action provide for the same connection as Art. 9 (although they may not incorporate a common habitual residence connection).[66] Hence, in a considerable number of cases, the issues of liability and legality will be governed by one single law despite different conflict rules.

37 According to Recital 28, a further area not prejudiced by the law determined under Art. 9 Rome II is the legal status of trade unions and of the representative organisations of workers which is equally a matter solely for the national laws.

2. Damages Claims and Injunctive Relief

38 Despite the reference to "damages" in the English language version, actions under Art. 9 are **not limited to damages claims.**

---

industrial action, falls within the definition of tort, delict or quasi-delict.").

65 *Knöfel*, EuZA 2008, 228, 234 seq.; *Junker*, in: Münchener Kommentar BGB, Art. 9 para. 20; the opposite view is taken by *Heinze*, 73 RabelsZ (2009) 770, 786 seq.

66 According to *Van Hoek*, in: Dorssemont/Jaspers/Van Hoek (eds.), Cross-Border Collective Actions in Europe – A Legal Challenge (2007) 425, 448 this appears to be the case in many Member States.

Rather, the law determined by Art. 9 also governs preventative injunctive relief, *a majore ad minus* interim and final injunctive relief (once the damage has already started to materialise) as well as declaratory relief proceedings concerned with pending industrial action that is likely to cause damage.[67] This already follows from a comparison with other language versions. With "*Schäden*" (instead of "*Schadensersatz*") in the German version, "*dommages*" (instead of "*dommages-intérêt*" or "*indemnité*") in the French version or "*Schade*" in the Dutch version, they use a much more open term, not linked to a specific type of remedy but rather equivalent to the English term "loss" or "damage" (without "s").[68] Furthermore, Art. 9 itself refers to "damages caused by an industrial action, pending or carried out, …" While this could still be limited to actual damage caused by the imminent threat of an industrial action, Art. 2(2) and (3) leave no room for doubt: Art. 9 covers non-contractual obligations that are likely to arise, *i.e.* also scenarios where an actual damage has not yet occurred. In addition, pursuant to Art. 15(c) and (d), the availability of remedies is generally not governed by the conflict rule itself but by the *lex causae*. Finally, practical considerations require that the applicable law governs injunctive relief.[69] The majority of cases concerning non-contractual liability arising out of industrial action do not trigger damages claims but call for injunctive relief; this is exemplified by two important recent cases before the ECJ regarding industrial action, *Viking Line*[70] and *Laval*[71] (although not concerning the issue of the applicable law).

---

67 *Dicey, Morris & Collins*, para. S 35-241; *Dickinson*, para. 9.27; *Heinze*, in: jurisPK BGB, Art. 9 para. 10; *Knöfel*, EuZA 2008, 228, 242; *Junker*, in: Münchener Kommentar BGB, Art. 9 para. 22; with some hesitation *Morse*, in: Liber Fausto Pocar (2009) 723, 729 seq. ("a highly speculative conclusion").

68 Concurring *Dickinson*, para. 9.27.

69 *Morse*, in: Liber Fausto Pocar (2009) 723, 730; *Junker*, in: Münchener Kommentar BGB, Art. 9 para. 22.

70 ECJ, Case C-438/05 – *Viking Line* [2007] ECR I-10779.

71 ECJ, Case C-341/05 – *Laval* [2007] ECR I-11767.

In effect, **three scenarios** may occur in which liability and the availability of the respective remedy are governed by the law determined by Art. 9: (1) Pending industrial action that has not yet caused any damage but is likely to cause future damage; the regular remedy will be preventative injunctive relief.[72] (2) Pending industrial action that has in itself (by way of its threat) already caused actual damage;[73] the regular damage will be a damages claim. (3) Current industrial action that has already caused damage; the regular remedies will be injunctive relief to immediately stop the allegedly unlawful industrial action (with a view to the future) and a damages claim (with a view to the damage that has already occurred). 39

3. Causal Link between Industrial Action and Damage

The law determined by Art. 9 only covers claims or injunctive relief in respect of damage *caused* by the industrial action. This requirement of a causal link excludes damage to persons or property at the occasion of an industrial action.[74] Such torts/delicts have no connection with, and are not part of, the industrial action. Consequently, they are governed by the law determined by the general conflict rule in Art. 4. Examples for such occasional torts are injuries to bystanders in the course of a demonstration, or damage to personal property of persons involved in the industrial action (such as damage to a worker's car at the occasion of a lock-out). 40

---

72 The preconditions of such relief, *e.g.* the requirement of an imminent threat or the interdependence of a prohibition of the industrial action and the likely damage, are determined by the *lex causae*.

73 *Knöfel*, EuZA 2008, 228, 242 states two examples: damage to goodwill and damage by taking precautionary measures, *e.g.* hiring replacement workers on the verge of a forthcoming strike action.

74 *Junker*, in: Münchener Kommentar BGB, Art. 9 para. 20; *Palao Moreno*, 9 YbPIL (2007),115, 119; *Heinze*, in: jurisPK BGB, Art. 9 para. 6.

4. Mandatory Rules and Public Policy

41 In light of the policy pursued by the connection of Art. 9[75] mandatory rules of the forum (Art. 16) as well as the public policy of the forum (Art. 26) will hardly ever be able to restrict the application of the law of the place of the industrial action under Art. 9. Both Art. 16 and Art. 26 are limited to the respective law of the forum. Hence, they may only play a role if the place of the industrial action and the forum state differ. In such a case, however, it is difficult to imagine a constellation in which mandatory laws or the public policy of the forum could prevail over the applicaton of the law of the place of the industrial action.[76]

D. Jurisdiction Issues

42 Jurisdiction in relation to non-contractual liability claims in cases of industrial action is closely intertwined with Art. 9 Rome II and its legislative history. In the European cross-border context, jurisdiction may be based on Arts. 2 and 5 No. 3 Brussels I with regard to the main proceedings as well as Art. 31 Brussels I with regard to injunctive relief. In Non-Member State scenarios, jurisdiction will be based on the respective national heads of jurisdiction (which are in that regard in many countries similar to those of Brussels I).

43 A **concentration of claims in one forum by virtue of Art. 6(1) Brussels I** may be possible if several unions (*e.g.* a European-wide one like ITF or ETUC and several national ones) are involved in a single industrial action.[77] In contrast, the prerequisites of Art. 6 Brussels I are usually not met in case of parallel local industrial

---

75 See *supra* paras. 4 et seq.

76 *Heinze*, 73 RabelsZ (2009) 770, 787 et seq. (considering only a violation of European fundamental rights); see also *Van Hoek*, in: Dorssemont/Jaspers/Van Hoek (eds.), Cross-Border Collective Actions in Europe – A Legal Challenge (2007) 425, 448 seq.

actions and with regard to claims against unions and individual employees. In this context, the common conflict rule in Art. 9 Rome II significantly reduces existing incentives for forum shopping created by Art. 6(1) Brussels I. In particular, increased predictability and legal certainty are likely to foster cross-border collective action.

With regard to interim injunctive relief, Art. 9 regularly enables the competent court under Art. 31 Brussels I to apply its own law.[78] This accords with the need for speed in such interim relief proceedings and renders them an effective weapon against allegedly unlawful industrial action. 44

With regard to the main proceedings, **Art. 5 No. 3 Brussels I** is the practically most relevant jurisdiction. The plaintiff may choose between the country where the event giving rise to the damage took place and the country where the damage occurred.[79] 45

As a result of the combined effect of the ECJ's judgment in the *DFDS Torline* case[80] and the conflict rule in Art. 9 Rome II, the 46

---

77 *Van Hoek*, in: Dorssemont/Jaspers/Van Hoek (eds.), Cross-Border Collective Actions in Europe – A Legal Challenge (2007) 425, 442; lacking a rule comparable to Art. 6(3)(b) Rome II, the court will, however, have to apply different national laws under the mosaic principle (see *supra* para. 33).

78 Under Art. 31 Brussels I it will regularly be the courts at the place where the industrial action is to be taken that have a real connecting link with the case when applying the *van Uden* criteria (see ECJ, Case C-391/95 – *Van Uden* [1998] ECR I-7091 para. 40).

79 See in particular ECJ, Case 21/76 – *Mines de Potasse d'Alsace* [1976] ECR 1735 paras. 19 et seq.; Case C-68/93 – *Shevill* [1995] ECR I-415 para. 20; Case C-167/00 – *Verein für Konsumenteninformation* [2002] ECR I-8111 paras. 42 et seq.; Case C-168/02 – *Kronhofer* [2004] ECR I-6009 para. 16; Case C-18/02 – *DFDS Torline* [2004] ECR I-1417 para. 40; Case C-189/08 – *Zuid Chemie* [2009] ECR I-6917 para. 23.

80 For details see *supra* paras. 2 seq.

country where the event giving rise to the damage took place is the country where the industrial action is to be, or has been, taken.

47 The **country where the damage occurred** is, however, unclear. Art. 9 Rome II is of no help since it does not address the place where the damage occurred.[81] In the *DFDS Torline* judgment, the ECJ held that the relevant damage under the second alternative of the jurisdiction rule in Art. 5 No. 3 Brussels I (country where the damage occurred) is the financial loss incurred by the employer as a result of withdrawing a ship from its normal route. The ECJ did not determine whether it regarded such financial loss as the direct damage (as opposed to indirect consequences) resulting from the industrial action. Furthermore, the ECJ left it to the respective national court to determine the place where such financial loss has occurred. It is submitted that the direct damage resulting from the industrial action in the *DFDS Torline* case was not the financial loss arising from the withdrawal but the obstruction of loading and discharging the ship at the harbour of its normal route.[82] The withdrawal was only the reaction to that obstruction. Consequently, the *DFDS Torline* judgment, in effect regarding the place of indirect financial consequences as the place where the damage occurred, is difficult to reconcile with several other judgments by the ECJ. In those judgments, the ECJ stressed that the place where the plaintiff suffered financial

---

81 According to *Garcimartín Alferéz*, EuLF 2007, I-77, 88 the special conflict rule in Art. 9 Rome II is no exception to the general conflict rule in Art. 4 Rome II. Rather, it is a clarification of the place where the damage occurred for the purposes of industrial action. Most other commentators regard Art. 9 Rome II as an exception to Art. 4 Rome II, providing for the law of the place where the event giving rise to the damage occurred, see *e.g. Junker*, in: Münchener Kommentar BGB, Art. 9 para. 2; *Knöfel*, EuZA 2008, 228, 237; *Joubert*, in: Corneloup/Joubert (eds.), Le règlement communautaire "Rome II" sur la loi applicable aux obligations non contractuelles (2007) 55, 78.

82 Concurring *Heinze*, 73 RabelsZ (2009) 770, 776.

loss constitutes the place where the damage occurred within the meaning of Art. 5 No. 3 Brussels I only if the financial loss is the direct damage resulting from the tort/delict.[83] Furthermore, the understanding in *DFDS Torline* appears to be irreconcilable with the concept of the place where the damage occurred as expressed in Art. 4 Rome II: according to its wording (in conjunction with Recitals 16 and 17), indirect consequences, the classic example of which is financial loss, are irrelevant for determining the country where the damage occurred.[84] Consequently, it is submitted that little weight should be attributed to the respective statements of the ECJ in the *DFDS Torline* judgment, although it is the only case specifically concerning industrial action. The issue in question is independent of the field of application. Rather, damage for the purposes of Art. 5 No. 3 Brussels I should be limited to the direct damage suffered by the plaintiff. In case of an industrial action this is the obstruction of work and labour at the place where the industrial action is taken. As a result of the view taken by the present author, even the place where the damage occurred for the purposes of Art. 5 No. 3 Brussels I will regularly coincide with the connecting factor of Art. 9 Rome II. Hence, either of the two alternatives under Art. 5 No. 3 Brussels I will put the court seized in a position where it can regularly apply its own law to the case.

---

83 ECJ, Case C-364/93 – *Marinari* [1995] ECR I-2719 paras. 14 seq. ("… that term [place where the harmful event occurred] cannot be construed so extensively as to encompass any place where the adverse consequences can be felt of an event which has already caused damage actually arising elsewhere. Consequently, that term cannot be construed as including the place where, […], the victim claims to have suffered financial damage following upon initial damage arising and suffered by him in another Contracting State."); ECJ, Case C-168/02 – *Kronhofer* [2004] ECR I-6009 paras. 20 seq. ("… that the expression 'place where the harmful event occurred' does not refer to the place where the claimant is domiciled or where 'his assets are concentrated' by reason only of the fact that he has suffered financial damage there …").

84 See Art. 4 paras. 17 et seq.

48 Interpreting the place where the damage occurred as the place where the industrial action was taken, one may wonder whether the law applicable to non-contractual liability for damages caused by an industrial action was not left to the general conflict rule of Art. 4. It is the *DFDS Torline* decision by the ECJ that rendered such an approach not viable. The decision created the risk that, for the purposes of industrial action, the place where the damage occurred would have been different from the place where the industrial action was taken. To rule out this risk, a special conflict rule explicitly providing for the law of the place where the industrial action is to be, or has been, taken was regarded as necessary (regardless of whether this place is understood as the place where the damage occurred or as the place of the event giving rise to it). Whereas the *DFDS Torline* decision created the risk that the understanding of Art. 5 No. 3 Brussels I would have been imported into the Rome II Regulation, namely Art. 4, it should now be *vice versa*: the understanding in the Rome II Regulation of the place where the damage occurred should be imported into Art. 5 No. 3 Brussels I, in effect overruling the possible consequences of the *DFDS Torline* ruling.

Chapter III
Unjust Enrichment, *Negotiorum gestio* and *Culpa in contrahendo*

Article 10
Unjust Enrichment

1. If a non-contractual obligation arising out of unjust enrichment, including payment of amounts wrongly received, concerns a relationship existing between the parties, such as one arising out of a contract or a tort/delict, that is closely connected with that unjust enrichment, it shall be governed by the law that governs that relationship.

2. Where the law applicable cannot be determined on the basis of paragraph 1 and the parties have their habitual residence in the same country when the event giving rise to unjust enrichment occurs, the law of that country shall apply.
3. Where the law applicable cannot be determined on the basis of paragraphs 1 or 2, it shall be the law of the country in which the unjust enrichment took place.
4. Where it is clear from all the circumstances of the case that the non-contractual obligation arising out of unjust enrichment is manifestly more closely connected with a country other than that indicated in paragraphs 1, 2 and 3, the law of that other country shall apply.

A. Scope

I. The Term Unjust Enrichment

1. General

1 The concept of unjust enrichment is interpreted differently throughout EU member states. In some its reach is broad while in others it is rather narrow; some states have clearly defined the

concept while others have left it undeveloped.[1] Recital 11 of Rome II requires integrating these divergent approaches into an autonomous European concept of unjust enrichment. An autonomous, unitary definition of unjust enrichment – while not an end in itself – is indispensible for distinguishing unjust enrichment actions from claims in tort, contract, and *negotiorum gestio*. Unfortunately, neither the Regulation's language nor its drafting history provide clear guidance for this complex task – except that Art. 10(1) provides that "payment of amounts wrongly received" constitute an obligation arising out of unjust enrichment.

2. Distinction between Unjust Enrichment and Tort

2 Distinguishing unjust enrichment claims from claims for tort/delict can raise difficult questions.[2] When neighbour A steals strawberries from neighbour B's garden and makes jam out of them, neighbour A obviously commits a tort. On the other hand, the fact that he now owns several glasses of fresh strawberry jam may be regarded as unjust enrichment. In this context, two questions arise: can claims for tort and claims for unjust enrichment co-exist? If so, what criteria denominate a claim as sounding in tort or unjust enrichment?

3 The domestic systems of member states answer the first question in differing fashion: while, *e.g.*, French law allows claims for unjust enrichment only when no tort claims exist, German law offers plaintiffs the possibility to frame claims for tort and claims for unjust enrichment concurrently. The Regulation does not address this issue at all, neither explicitly nor implicitly, thus leaving the question to be answered by national substantive law. Allowing such a diffuse approach may result in inconsistent outcomes if, for example, the law applicable to tort claims follows the French

---

1 For a comparative analysis see *Visser*, in: Reimann/Zimmermann (eds.), The Oxford Handbook of Comparative Law (2006), 969 et seq.; – cf. Commission's Explanatory Memorandum, COM(2003) 427, p. 21.

2 See already Art. 4 paras. 2 et seq.

model while the law applicable to unjust enrichment claims follows the German model (or *vice versa*).[3]

With regard to the second question, scholars have proposed two possible starting points for distinguishing between tort and unjust enrichment: the cause of action or the legal consequences of a claim.[4] 4

The consequence-based approach asks whether the plaintiff claims reimbursement for his loss or whether he seeks to recoup the defendant's gain: loss-based claims would be regarded as tortious, whereas gain-based claims would fall under the concept of unjust enrichment. However, such a distinction is likely to cause great difficulties in practice. Often, a plaintiff's loss will equal the defendants profit, thus rendering a claim for reimbursement identical to one for disgorgement. What is more, when calculating damages, courts may resort to principles of reimbursement as well as disgorgement in crafting their damage awards.[5] 5

By contrast, the cause of action approach does not look to the consequences of the claim, but rather to its prerequisites, more precisely to the defendant's behaviour. Claims that require wrongdoing[6] by the defendant would be considered tortious, while claims that exist independently of wrongdoing would qualify as unjust enrichment claims. 6

---

3 For this reason it seems desirable to apply the same law to tort and unjust enrichment claims. If Art. 4 and Art. 10 call for the application of different laws, courts should try to apply the escape clause of either provision to the largest extent possible.

4 For an overview on the debate, see *Dickinson*, paras. 4.11-4.19; *Chong*, 57 ICLQ (2008) 863, 890 et seq.

5 Cf. *Dickinson*, para. 4.14.

6 *Dickinson*, para. 4.13 defines such wrongdoing as "an act or omission of or attributable to the defendant or other event for the consequences of which the defendant is responsible to the claimant."

7 It is submitted that both approaches should be applied in a cumulative manner. In other words, a claim may be regarded a claim for unjust enrichment only when it aims at disgorgement of the defendant's gain **and** the imposition of liability does not require wrongdoing by the defendant.[7]

3. Distinction Between Unjust Enrichment and *Negotiorum Gestio*

8 As mentioned above, the Rome II Regulation does not provide whether claims for tort, unjust enrichment and *negotiorum gestio* may be framed concurrently. Instead, it leaves this question to be answered by the substantive law(s) it deems applicable.[8] Thus, when the enrichment is the result of a *negotiorum gestio*, a court may properly apply Art. 10 to determine applicable law. However, the Art. 10-designated substantive law should govern *only* those claims that arise independently from the intervener's unrequested (yet altruistic) behaviour. In contrast, claims under that law that are based on the intervener acting predominantly out of altruistic motives should not be governed by Art. 10-designated law. Such claims should instead fall under the purview of the law designated by Art. 11.

4. Distinction between Unjust Enrichment and Contractual Obligations

9 When a person performs a contractual payment obligation although the contract is invalid, the other person is unjustly enriched. Nevertheless, Art. 10 does not apply in this scenario: according to Art. 12(e) Rome I, courts must determine the conse-

---

7 *Rushworth/Scott*, LMCLQ 2008, 274, 286; *Plender & Wilderspin*, 24-085; contra: *Cheshire, North & Fawcett*, p. 825; *Thorn*, in: Palandt, Art. 10 para. 2 (arguing that gain-based remedies should as a rule be classified as unjust enrichment, even if they result from a wrongdoing); cf. ECJ, Case C-47/07 P – *Masdar*, [2008] ECR I-9761 para. 49.

8 See *supra* para. 3.

quences of nullity of a contract under the law made applicable by the Rome I Regulation. Thus, Rome I must be considered a *lex specialis* that overrides Art. 10's general provisions in cases involving void(ed) contracts.[9]

This exception may result in different laws being applied to the restitution of a payment. When a buyer pays 1,000 € under a void contract which – if valid – would have called for a payment of only 800 €, his claim for restitution must be classified as a contractual claim governed by Rome I in so far as 800 € are concerned. However, the buyer's demand for restitution of the remaining 200 € constitutes an unjust enrichment claim because it arises without regard to the contract or its validity. 10

5. Distinction between Unjust Enrichment and Property Law

As laid down in the commentary to Art. 1, the Regulation does not apply where the *existence* of a property right is in question (*e.g.* to questions of title) but does apply where an extrinsic interference with an existing property right is at issue. In the strawberry example given above (para. 2), the question of whether B became the owner of the strawberry jam falls outside the Regulation's scope, whereas the question of whether B must restitute the jam or pay damages to A is covered by the Regulation. 11

Applying the Regulation to extrinsic interferences with an existing property right generates the follow-up question of whether claims to remedy such interference are governed by Art. 4, Art. 10 or Art. 11. Generally, violations of property rights are governed by Arts. 4 et seq. However, where the claim does not depend on wrongful behavior by the defendant and requests dis- 12

9 *Spickhoff*, in: Bamberger/Roth, Anh. zu Art. 42 EGBGB para. 76; *Junker*, in: Münchener Kommentar BGB, Art. 10 para. 14; *Dickinson*, para. 10.16.; *Thorn*, in: Palandt, Art. 10 para. 4.

gorgement rather than damages, Art. 10 applies.[10] Such cases may arise where the defendant has gained possession of another's property through the act of a third person that is not attributable to him.

13 Further, Art. 10 (and in certain circumstances Art. 11[11]) determines what law governs the expenses incurred during an exercise of control over foreign property.

II. Excluded Matters

14 Even if they qualify as unjust enrichment, claims that arise out of areas of law that **Art. 1(2)** excludes from the Regulation's scope are not governed by Art. 10. Instead, domestic conflict-of-law rules determines the law applicable to such claims.

15 Further, **Art. 13** excludes obligations arising out of an **infringement of an intellectual property** right from Art. 10's scope. Instead, Art. 8 determines applicable law – even if the claim must be classified as unjust enrichment rather than tort.[12]

B. Rule

I. Structure of Art. 10

16 The system found in Art. 10 mirrors the general rule of Art. 4 – and although the connecting factors are listed in a different order, their hierarchy remains the same.[13] Subsection (1) provides for a primary connection to an existing relationship. If there is no such relationship, but the parties have a common residence, then sub-

---

10 Cf. *supra* para. 7.

11 For the distinction between unjust enrichment and negotiorum gestio, see *supra* para. 9.

12 See in more detail the commentary on Art. 13.

13 See Art. 4 para. 12.

section 2 provides that the *lex domicilii communis* governs their unjust enrichment obligations. If there is neither an existing relationship nor a common residence, subsection 3 looks to the place of enrichment. Finally, the escape clause in subsection 4 allows courts to apply the law of another country if they find their case to be "manifestly more closely connected" with that other country.

II. Accessory Connection to an Existing Relationship (Subsection 1)

Where the enrichment concerns a relationship existing between the parties that is closely connected with the unjust enrichment, subsection 1 demands the law that governs this relationship apply to the unjust enrichment claim as well. The reason behind this rule lies in expediency: it is "preferable for the entire legal situation to be governed by the same law."[14] Thus, to a certain extent, Art. 10(1) mirrors the second half of Art. 4(3)'s escape clause (the first half can be found in subsection 4). By placing the accessory connection at the top of Art. 10's connection cascade, the legislature probably intended to highlight its particular importance in the field of unjust enrichment. This would also comport with one marked difference between Art. 4(3) and Art. 10(1): while the language of Art. 4(3) ("may") leaves to the court's discretion whether it applies the escape clause, Art. 10(1)'s accessory connection is of mandatory character.[15] 17

Article 10 offers **relationships arising out of contract or tort** as an example of such a pre-existing relationship. Thus, when A owes 1,000 € in contractual or tort damages to B but pays 18

14 Commission's Explanatory Memorandum, COM(2003), 427, p. 21 (on Art. 9); cf. *Garcimartín Alférez*, EuLF 2007 I 77, 88.

15 *Huber/Bach*, IPRax 2005, 73, 80; critical: *Heiss/Loacker*, JBl. 2007, 613, 642 fn. 365.

1,500 €, his claim for restitution of the excess sum of 500 € is governed by the same law that applies to the pre-existing contractual or tort liability.

19 Since contractual and tort-based relationships are listed as mere examples, **other relationships**, such as, *e.g.*, pre-contractual relationships and family relationships, may be taken into account as well.[16] Note, however, that purely factual relationships are not relevant under Art. 10(1), simply because there is no law governing such a factual relationship.[17]

20 Art. 10(1) requires a certain **temporal separation** of the unjust enrichment obligation and the relationship to which it is closely connected.[18] Specifically, the relationship must have been in existence before the event that gave rise to the unjust enrichment occurred. Admittedly, when compared to Art. 4(3)(2) (which expressly requires the relationship to be *pre*-existing), Art. 10's language ("a relationship existing between the parties") appears rather unclear in this regard. However, legislative history corroborates the requirement of a temporal separation: the prefix "pre-" had been affixed to the word "existing" in the Commission's initial proposal but was deleted during the legislative process.[19] Since no reasoning for an intentional deletion can be found within the legislative documents, it can be asumed that the prefix was accidently lost – and that the legislature did not intend to alter the term's meaning.[20]

---

16 Cf. Art. 4 para. 91.

17 Cf. Art. 4 para. 92.

18 *Dickinson*, paras. 10.25 and 4.15; *Huber/Bach*, IPRax 2005, 73, 81; – contra: *Cheshire, North & Fawcett*, p. 827; *Backmann*, in: jurisPK BGB, Art. 10 para. 13. The provision thus cannot be employed when to create parallelism of applicable law between unjust enrichment claims and other contractual or non-contractual claims when a single act gives rise to both claims; cf. *Dickinson*, para. 10.23 (but see also para. 10.26).

19 The prefix is missing for the first time in the Joint text dated 22 June 2007; cf. *Plender & Wilderspin*, para. 24-091 fn. 122.

It is subject to some debate whether (and if so, how) subsection 1 applies when an unjust enrichment obligation has **close connections to two or more relationships**. When, for example, a defendant overpays on a judgment which is based on both a contractual damages claim[21] and a claim for torts, how should the law applicable for the restitution claim be determined? Some scholars have argued that subsection 1 does not apply to such cases based firstly on the provision's language (that speaks of "*a* relationship"), and based secondly on the fact that subsection 1 does not provide a mechanism for determining which of the relations should be considered dispositive.[22] It is submitted, however, that a solution should rather be found by looking to whether one of the relationships can be regarded as the "main" relationship in the concrete case. If such a main relationship can be discerned, Art. 10(1) should be applied (and the law that governs this "main relationship" should govern the entire restitution claim); if not, Art. 10(1) cannot be applied.[23] 21

III. *Lex Domicilii Communis* (Subsection 2)

When there is no pre-existing relationship between the parties, Art. 10(2) provides for the application of the *lex domicilii communis*, *i.e.* the law of the country in which both parties – *i.e.* the debtor and the creditor of the unjust enrichment obligation[24] – have their habitual residence. Article 10(2) is almost identical to 22

---

20 *Dickinson*, para. 10.23; *Thorn*, in: Palandt, Art. 10 para. 8; cf. *Garcimartín Alférez*, EuLF 2007 I-77, 88.

21 Note that Art. 12(e) Rome I would not apply in this case because it determines only the law applicable to "consequences of nullity of a contract".

22 *Plender & Wilderspin*, para. 24-090; *Spickhoff*, in: Bamberger/Roth, Anh. zu Art. 42 EGBGB para. 75.

23 This approach is in line with the ECJ's jurisprudence in regard to Art. 5(1) Brussels I; cf. ECJ Case C-386/05 – *Color Drack*, [2007] ECRI-3699 para. 40; ECJ, Case C-19/09 – *Wood Floor Solutions*, para. 43.

24 *Dickinson*, para. 10.28.

Art. 4(2), thus permitting reference to the commentary on Art. 4(2) in interpreting Art. 10(2).[25]

23 One difference should be noted, though: in determining whether the parties habitually reside in the same country, Art. 10(2) and Art. 4(2) rely on different points in time.[26] While Art. 4(2) requires a common residence at the time of damage, Art. 10(2) looks to the time "when the event giving rise to unjust enrichment occurs." Thus, under Art. 10(2), the time of action that led to the enrichment is dispositive rather than the time when this action actually enriched the defendant.[27] As an example, imagine that A mistakenly transfers money from his bank account to the bank account of B. If A and B both have their habitual residence in the same country when A orders the bank transfer, Art. 10(2) applies irrespective of whether B moves to another country before the money is credited to his account.

IV. Place of enrichment (Subsection 3)

24 When neither a pre-existing relationship nor a common residence link the parties, Art. 10(3) provides that "the law of the country in which the unjust enrichment took place" shall apply. While the European Parliament advocated relying on the place "where the *events* giving rise to the enrichment occurred,"[28] the

---

[25] In particular, Art. 10(2) faces the same policy criticism as Art. 4(2); see Art. 4 para. 64 and 66 et seq.; cf. *Pitel*, NIPR 2008, 456, 457. Again, however, practical consideration support the *lex domicilii communis* rule: it allows the court seized of the action to apply its hometown law, cf. *Chong*, 57 ICLQ (2008) 863, 882.

[26] *Dickinson*, para. 10.28.

[27] Apparently contra: *Cheshire, North & Fawcett*, p. 828.

[28] European Parliament legislative resolution on the proposal for a regulation of the European Parliament and of the Council on the law applicable to non-contractual obligations ("Rome II"), P6_TA(2005)0284, p. 13 (Art. 9) – emphasis added.

Commission succeeded in setting the place where the enrichment itself occurred as dispositive.[29]

Relying on the place of enrichment will often result in different laws being applicable to tort and unjust enrichment claims.[30] While the main tort rule in Art. 4(1) focuses on the place of damages – and thus on the aggrieved party – Art. 10(3) tends to concentrate on the party that benefits from an asset transfer.[31] Therefore, if the Italian resident A mistakenly transfers money from his Italian bank account to B's bank account in Spain, Art. 10(3) requires that Spanish law govern the unjust enrichment claim. However, if B had fraudulently induced A to effect the bank transfer, Art. 4(1) would require that Italian law govern all tort claims. 25

The difficulties that occur in locating the place of enrichment correspond to those in regard to the place of damages – in particular when the damages are of purely financial character. Most of the solutions found in regard to Art. 4(1) can be projected onto Art. 10(3). 26

First, for localising the situs of the enrichment, courts should **focus on the discrete asset**, rather than on the "center of wealth" of the enriched person.[32] Therefore, in the example given above, the place of enrichment is Spain even if B lives in Portugal and maintains all other assets there. 27

---

29 Proposal for a regulation of the European Parliament and of the Council on the law applicable to non-contractual obligations ("Rome II"), COM (2003) 427, p. 35.

30 Cf. *Huber/Bach*, IPRax 2005, 73, 81.

31 *Cheshire, North & Fawcett*, pp. 829 et seq.; *Backmann*, in: jurisPK BGB, Art. 10 para. 26; – sceptical: *Kadner Graziano*, 73 RabelsZ (2009) 1, 65.

32 Cf. ECJ, Case C-168/02 – *Kronhofer*, [2004] ECR I-6009 paras. 13 et seq. on the equivalent question of determining the location of damages.

28 Second, only the **immediate enrichment** is relevant for determining the applicable law; indirect consequences of the enrichment are of no relevance.[33] Therefore, in the example given above, the place of enrichment is Spain even if B withdraws the money from an ATM in Germany. Allowing indirect consequences, such as the place of withdrawal, to influence the law applicable to enrichment claims results in uncertainty and – what is more – would allow the enriched person to manipulate the connecting factor.[34] Further, indirect consequences will often lead to difficulties in practice: if B withdraws a certain sum from his bank account, this sum can be allocated to the transfer that caused the enrichment (and thus constitute a "place of enrichment") only if the bank account had no money in it prior to the transfer or if B withdraws all money in the account.

29 If the enrichment consists in saving a party from expenditure, the situs of the enrichment should be located at the place where this expenditure would have been incurred.[35]

30 Both rules fail in attempting to localize the place of enrichment in cases of **payment on a third party's debt**. When A owes a certain sum to B and C satisfies this obligation, A is enriched because his obligation towards B is terminated – but where does this termination take place? Two locations seem possible: from a practical point of view, it seems desirable to locate all "incorporeal" enrichments at the habitual residence of the enriched person. From a doctrinal point of view, an obligation (and therefore also its termination) should be located at the place of performance.[36] In the light of the ECJ's rulings on the place of damages, it seems

---

33 *Chong*, 57 ICLQ (2008) 863, 885 et seq.; *Dickinson*, para. 10.34; cf. ECJ Marinari on the equivalent question of determining the location of damages.

34 *Chong*, 57 ICLQ (2008) 863, 887.

35 *Cheshire, North & Fawcett*, p. 830.

36 Therefore, a payment obligation may generally be located at the place of the creditor's bank account.

preferable to follow the latter option: given that the ECJ refuses to locate financial damages at the habitual residence of the aggrieved person, it would be inconsistent to apply the habitual residence rule in regard to the enrichment.

Where an enrichment is **scattered over different countries**, the same solution should apply as proposed for Art. 4: when courts can easily identify a "center of enrichment", the law at this place should govern the entire unjust enrichment claim (*i.e.* also in respect to enrichments that occurred in other countries); when no such center of enrichment exists, courts should apply the mosaic principle.[37] 31

V. Escape Clause (Subsection 4)

Article 10(4) mirrors the first half of Art. 4(3)'s escape clause (the second half has been promoted to the top of Art. 10's connection cascade in subsection 1): where it is clear from all the circumstances of the case that the unjust enrichment obligation is "manifestly more closely connected with another country", that country's law applies. Article 10(4) sets a high standard: the unjust enrichment obligation must be *manifestly* more closely connected with another law than with the law deemed applicable by subsections 1 through 3.[38] As unjust enrichment claims are unlikely to generate particular problems in this regard, reference can be made to the commentary on Art. 4 (paras. 79 et seq.) for a detailed analysis. 32

VI. Three-Party-Relationship

When more than two persons are involved in an enrichment case, courts will very likely face difficulties in determining *who* may claim restitution from whom. Conflict of law rules may further complicate the courts' task when calling for different laws 33

---

[37] See in detail, Art. 4 paras. 59 et seq.

[38] *Chong*, 57 ICLQ (2008) 863, 889.

to be applied to the different "two-person-relations". Imagine that the law applicable to the A-B relationship provides that A has a claim against C rather than against B – while the law applicable to the A-C relationship provides for the opposite (claim against B but not against C). Of course courts may resolve such a dilemma by *praeter legem* solutions – which most domestic conflict rules acknowledge and which may and must be allowed under European conflict rules as well. However, it seems preferable to prevent such a dilemma in the first place by having a single law apply to the entire multiple-person relationship. For this aim, either subsections 1 and 2 must be applied restrictively – *i.e.* only when *all* parties involved meet the requirements (all parties share a pre-existing relationship or a common residence) – or the escape clause in Art. 10(4) must be employed to overcome inconsistent results that derive from subsections 1 and 2.

Article 11
Negotiorum gestio

1. If a non-contractual obligation arising out of an act performed without due authority in connection with the affairs of another person concerns a relationship existing between the parties, such as one arising out of a contract or a tort/delict, that is closely connected with that non-contractual obligation, it shall be governed by the law that governs that relationship.
2. Where the law applicable cannot be determined on the basis of paragraph 1, and the parties have their habitual residence in the same country when the event giving rise to the damage occurs, the law of that country shall apply.
3. Where the law applicable cannot be determined on the basis of paragraphs 1 or 2, it shall be the law of the country in which the act was performed.
4. Where it is clear from all the circumstances of the case that the non-contractual obligation arising out of an act performed without due authority in connection with the affairs of another person is manifestly more closely connected with a country other than that indicated in paragraphs 1, 2 and 3, the law of that other country shall apply.

A. Scope

I. The Term *Negotiorum Gestio*

1. General

1 The concept of *negotiorum gestio* is unknown to the legal systems of several member states.[1] However, since the remaining legal systems share a more or less common understanding of *negotiorum gestio*,[2] Recital 11's task of establishing an autonomous concept is not as difficult as it is in regard to unjust enrichment. Moreover, Art. V. – 1:101 DCFR may serve as guidance. This provision looks to whether a person (the intervener) acts with the **predominant intention of benefiting another** (the principal). The relevant question in determining whether an intervention in another's affairs constitutes a *negotiorum gestio* is therefore whether the intervener acts on altruistic or egoistic motives.[3]

---

1 Cf. Commission's Explanatory Memorandum, COM(2003) 427, p. 21; for a comparative overview see *Study Group on a European Civil Code/Acquis Group*, Comment on Art. V. – 1:101 DCFR notes I. 1 et seq.

2 *Study Group on a European Civil Code/Acquis Group*, Comment on Art. V. – 1:101 DCFR note I. 2.

3 Cf. ECJ, Case C-47/07 P – *Masdar*, [2008] ECR I-9761 para. 67.

2 If the intervener does not know that his behavior may intervene in a third person's affairs, courts may not classify his conduct as *negotiorum gestio* – even if it actually results in a benefit for the principal. The same is true when the intervener knows that he is intervening in a third person's affairs but intervenes for egoistic reasons (or with intent to cause damage to the principal). Still, some member states – such as Germany[4] – classify as *negotiorum gestio* situations in which the intervener acts on behalf of the principal, but does so for egoistic reasons (or with intent to harm the principal). It is submitted that such a classification should not be transferred to the autonomous concept of Art. 11 Rome II.[5]

3 Article V. – 1:101 DCFR limits the concept of *negotiorum gestio* to cases in which the intervener – from a reasonable person's understanding – has good grounds for acting. Where it would be clear to a reasonable person in the intervener's shoes that the principal will not benefit from the intervention, no *negotiorum gestio* may be presumed. It is submitted that this limitation should be transferred to the conflict-of-law level.[6] Doing so frees courts from the difficult and often subjective task of evaluating the intervener's allegation that he acted with benevolent intent.

4 Note that *negotiorum gestio* refers both to claims brought by the principal for damages and restitution as well as to claims framed by the intervener for reimbursement of expenditure, for remuneration or for damages.[7]

4 See § 687(2) German Civil Code (BGB).

5 *Thorn*, in: Palandt, Art. 11 para. 2; *Backmann*, in: jurisPK BGB, Art. 11 para. 6.

6 Contra: *Plender & Wilderspin*, para. 25-019.

7 *Rushworth/Scott*, LMCLQ 2008, 274, 289; *Spickhoff*, in: Bamberger/Roth, Anh. zu Art. 42 EGBGB para. 85; *Ofner*, ZfRV 2008, 13, 20; cf. Arts. V. – 2:102 through V. – 3:103 DCFR.

2. Distinction between *Negotiorum Gestio* and Contractual Obligations

Certain situations may render it difficult to draw the line between contractual obligations and obligations arising out of *negotiorum gestio*. As an example, imagine that a plumber is contractually required to install a new bathtub. In the course of performing this task, he notices that one of the water pipes that leads to the tub is leaking and repairs the defect. Do the plumber's claims for reimbursement of expenditures for repairing the pipe (*e.g.* for materials used) arise out of the installation contract or out of *negotiorum gestio*? It is submitted that a general answer cannot be given, but that the answer rather depends on whether the terms contract can be interpreted to include the repair of the water pipe in the individual case. The same is true, of course, for the "principal's" claim for damages, when, *e.g.*, the plumber further exacerbates the leak. 5

However, the distinction between contractual claims and claims arising out of *negotiorum gestio* is unlikely to have much practical relevance: when courts classify an obligation as arising out of *negotiorum gestio* rather than out of contract, Art. 11(1) submits those claims to the law that governs the contract. 6

3. Distinction between *Negotiorum Gestio*, Unjust Enrichment and Tort

The Rome II Regulation does not decide the question of whether claims for tort, claims for unjust enrichment and claims for *negotiorum gestio* can be framed concurrently; instead, this question is left to be answered by the designated substantive law(s).[8] Therefore, on the level of conflict of laws, it is necessary to determine all laws that potentially provide claims for the plaintiff. 7

8 See Art. 10 para. 3.

8 Claims that are based on a tort (of the Regulation's autonomous understanding) should be taken from the law designated by Art. 4; claims that are based on a *negotiorum gestio* (of the Regulation's autonomous understanding) should be taken from the law designated by Art. 11; and claims for unjust enrichment (also of the Regulation's autonomous understanding, *i.e.* claims for restitution of a benefit that are based neither on a tort nor on a *negotiorum gestio*) should be taken from the law designated by Art. 10.

9 Thus, when a *negotiorum gestio* results in an **enrichment,** the substantive law applicable under Art. 11 may provide the plaintiff with claims that allow for restitution solely on the basis that the intervener acted predominantly out of altruistic motives. Claims under this law that do not require predominantly altruistic behavior should be disregarded. Instead, such claims should be brought under and governed by the law designated applicable by Art. 10. When the *negotiorum gestio* results in a loss for the plaintiff, the same principles should be followed when deciding whether Art. 4 or Art. 11 applies.

II. Excluded Matters

10 Even if they qualify as *negotiorum gestio*, claims that arise out of areas of law which **Art. 1(2)** excludes from the Regulation's scope are not governed by Art. 11. Instead, domestic conflict-of-law rules determine the law applicable to such claims.

11 Further, **Art. 13** excludes obligations arising from an **infringement of an intellectual property** right from Art. 11's scope. Instead of Art. 11, Art. 8 determines the law applicable to such claims even if they must be classified as *negotiorum gestio* rather than tort.[9]

12 Further, where **international conventions** contain conflict-of-law rules for obligations arising out of *negotiorum gestio*, these conven-

9 See in more detail the commentary on Art. 13.

tions displace Art. 11.[10] Such international conventions exist in particular in the field of maritime law (1989 IMO Convention on Salvage[11]) and maintenance law (1973 Hague Convention on Maintanance Obligations[12]).

B. Rule

I. Structure of Art. 11

As is true for Art. 10, the structure of Art. 11 mirrors the general rule of Art. 4 – and although the connecting factors are listed in a different order, their hierarchy remains the same.[13] Subsection (1) provides for a primary connection to an existing relationship. If there is no such pre-existing relationship, but if the parties have their habitual residence in the same country, subsection 2 provides that the *lex domicilii communis* governs their obligations. If there is neither a relationship nor a common state of residence, subsection 3 holds the place of action to be dispositive. Finally, the escape clause in subsection 4 allows the courts to apply the law of another country if it finds the case to be "manifestly more closely connected" with that country. 13

II. Accessory Connection to an Existing Relationship (Subsection 1)

Where the *negotiorum gestio* concerns a relationship between the parties that is closely connected with that *negotiorum gestio*, subsection 1 requires the law that governs this relationship to govern the *negotiorum gestio* claim as well. The reason for this rule lies in expediency: it is "preferable for the entire legal situation to be 14

---

10 See Art. 28 Rome II.

11 International Convention on Salvage of 28 April 1989.

12 Convention of 2 October 1973 on the Law Applicable to Maintenance Obligations; see Art. 10(3) of the Convention.

13 See Art. 4 para. 12.

governed by the same law."[14] Article 11(1) thus mirrors the second half of Art. 4(3)'s escape clause (the first half can be found in subsection 4). By placing the accessory connection at the top of Art. 11's connection cascade, the legislature probably intended to highlight its particular importance in the field of *negotiorum gestio*. Such prioritisation would comport with one marked difference between Art. 4(3) and Art. 11(1): while the language of Art. 4(3) ("may") leaves it to a court's discretion whether it applies the escape clause, Art. 11(1)'s accessory connection is of mandatory character.[15]

15 As an example of an "existing relationship," Art. 11 offers the **example of relationships arising out of contract or tort** – although a pre-existing relationship arising from a tort is hardly imaginable Article 11(1)'s accessory connection rule is not, however, restricted to pre-existing contracts and torts. Instead, **other relationships** may be taken into account as well, such as pre-contractual relationships or family relationships.[16] Therefore, when a father benevolently intervenes in his son's affairs, the law that governs the father-child-relationship will also govern all claims for *negotiorum gestio*. Purely factual relationships are not relevant under Art. 11(1) – for the simple reason that there is no law governing such a factual relationship.[17]

16 Article 11(1) requires a **temporal separation** of the *negotiorum gestio* obligation and the relation to which it is closely connected[18] – the relationship must have been in existence before

---

[14] Commission's Explanatory Memorandum, COM(2003), 427, p. 21 (on Art. 9); cf. *Garcimartín Alférez*, EuLF 2007 I 77, 88.

[15] *Huber/Bach*, IPRax 2005, 73, 80; critical: *Heiss/Loacker*, JBl 2007, 613, 642 fn. 365.

[16] Cf. Art. 4 para. 91.

[17] Cf. Art. 4 para. 92.

[18] *Dickinson*, para. 10.25 and 4.15; *Huber/Bach*, IPRax 2005, 73, 81; – contra *Backmann*, in: jurisPK BGB, Art. 11 para. 12. The provision thus cannot be employed to create parallelism of applicable law between unjust en-

the act of intervention. Admittedly, compared to Art. 4(3)(2) – which explicitly demands the relationship to be *pre*-existing – Art. 11's language appears rather unclear in this regard. However, legislative history corroborates the requirement of a temporal separation: the prefix "pre-" was contained in the Commission's initial proposal but was deleted during the legislative process.[19] Since no reasoning for an intentional deletion can be found within the legislative documents, it can be asumed that the prefix was accidently lost – and that the legislature did not intend to alter the term's meaning.[20]

It is subject to some debate whether (and if so, how) subsection 1 applies when the *negotiorum gestio* obligation has close connections to two or more relations. Some scholars argue that in such cases, subsection 1 should not be applied, based firstly on the provision's language that speaks of "*a* relation", and secondly on the fact that subsection 1 does not provide a mechanism for determining which of the relations should be considered dispositive.[21] It is submitted, however, that a solution should instead be found by looking to whether one of the relationships can be regarded as the "main" relationship in the concrete case. If such a main relationship can be discerned, Art. 11(1) should be applied (by designating as applicable the law that governs this main relationship to the entire *negotiorum gestio* claim); if not, Art. 11(1) cannot be applied.[22] **17**

richment claims and other contractual or non-contractual claims when a single act gives rise to both claims; cf. *Dickinson*, para. 10.23 (but see also para. 10.26).

19 The prefix disappears for the first time in the Joint text dated 22 June 2007; cf. *Plender & Wilderspin*, para. 24-091 fn. 122.

20 *Dickinson*, para. 10.23; *Thorn*, in: Palandt, Art. 11 para. 8; cf. *Garcimartín Alférez*, EuLF 2007 I 77, 88.

21 *Plender & Wilderspin*, para. 24-090.

22 This approach is in line with the ECJ's jurisprudence in regard to Art. 5(1) Brussels I; cf. ECJ Case C-386/05 – *Color Drack*, [2007] ECRI-3699 para. 40; ECJ, Case C-19/09 – *Wood Floor Solutions*, para. 43.

18 When the *negotiorum gestio* consists of a payment of a third party's debt, a pre-existing relationship between the parties (*i.e.* the intervener and the debtor) may not exist.[23] There is some debate as to whether Art. 11(1) permits an accessory connection to the law that governs the obligation that the intervener has satisfied. In this author's opinion, such an interpretation is in conflict with Art. 11(1)'s language. Instead, courts should employ the escape clause in Art. 11(4). This approach has the benefit of offering a flexible solution, since there may be cases in which the law applicable to the satisfied debt is completely unforeseeable to the intervener.[24]

III. *Lex Domicilii Communis* (Subsection 2)

19 When there is no pre-existing relationship between the parties, Art. 11(2) provides for an application of the *lex domicilii communis*, *i.e.* the law of the country in which both parties – the debtor and the creditor of the *negotiorum gestio* obligation[25] – have their habitual residence. Since Art. 11(2) is almost identical to Art. 4(2), the commentary to Art. 4 may be referenced in interpreting Art. 11(2).[26]

20 There is, however, one difference between the two provisions: in determining whether the parties have a common residence in a certain country, Art. 11(2) and Art. 4(2) rely on different points in time. While Art. 4(2) requires a common residence at the time of damage, Art. 11(2) requires a common residence at the time

---

23 Cf. *Sonnentag*, ZVglRWiss 2006, 256, 305.

24 *Thorn*, in: Palandt, Art. 11 para. 6; G. *Wagner*, IPRax 2008, 1, 12; – sceptical *Sonnentag*, ZVglRWiss 2006, 256, 305.

25 *Dickinson*, para. 10.28.

26 In particular, Art. 10(2) faces the same policy criticism as Art. 4(2); see Art. 4 para. 64 and 66 et seq.; cf. *Pitel*, NIPR 2008, 456, 457. Again, however, practical considerations support the *lex domicilii communis* rule: it allows the court seized of the action to apply its hometown law, cf. *Chong*, 57 ICLQ (2008) 863, 882.

"when the event giving rise to the damage occurs." Thus, Art. 11(2) sets the time of action as dispositive to determining applicable law instead of the time at which this action leads to a loss or to an enrichment. In this regard, it should also be noted that Art. 2 expands the term "damages" to cover all consequences that may result from a *negotiorum gestio*.[27]

IV. *Lex Loci Gestionis* (Subsection 3)

When neither a pre-existing relationship nor a common residence link the parties, Art. 11(3) provides that "the law of the country in which the act was performed" shall apply. While the Commission proposed relying on the place where "the beneficiary has his habitual residence" *(lex domicilii gestoris)*,[28] the European Parliament succeeded with its demand to rely on the *lex loci gestionis*.[29] 21

When the **act is performed in more than one country**, the solution proposed for Art. 4 should also apply to Art. 11(3): when courts can easily identify a "center of action" the law at this place should govern the entire *negotiorum gestio* claim (*i.e.* also in respect to actions that occurred in other countries).[30] If the act consists in the transport of a person or a good, courts should as a rule presume the starting point of this transport to be the center of action.[31] When no center of action exists, courts should apply the mosaic principle.[32] 22

27 *Junker*, in: Münchener Kommentar BGB, Art. 11 para. 15; *Thorn*, in: Palandt, Art. 11 para. 7; *Kadner Graziano*, 73 RabelsZ (2009) 1, 65, fn. 236.

28 COM(2003) 427, pp. 35 et seq.

29 European Parliament legislative resolution on the proposal for a regulation of the European Parliament and of the Council on the law applicable to non-contractual obligations ("Rome II"), P6_TA(2005)0284, p. 14 (Art. 10).

30 *Plender & Wilderspin*, paras. 25-032 et seq.; *Spickhoff*, in: Bamberger/Roth, Anh. zu Art. 42 EGBGB para. 87; *Thorn*, in: Palandt, Art. 11 para. 8; apparently contra: *Heiss/Loacker*, JBl. 2007, 613, 623.

23 If the act was performed **onboard a ship or airplane**, the same difficulties arise as under Art. 4(1), and again the solutions proposed in regard to Art. 4(1)[33] should be transferred to Art. 11(3). Therefore, when the act was performed while the vessel was **in territorial waters or airspace**, but no other connection to this country exists, courts should readily employ the escape clause of Art. 11(4): such cases most likely have a closer connection to the law of the vessel's flag or the port of departure or destination. When the act was performed while the vessel was **in international waters or airspace**, Art. 11(3) is inapplicable. Instead, courts should apply the law of the flag or the part of departure or destination under the escape clause of subsection 4.

V. Escape Clause (Subsection 4)

24 Article 11(4) mirrors the first half of Art. 4(3)'s escape clause (the second half has been promoted to the top of Art. 11's connection cascade in subsection 1): where it is clear from all the circumstances of the case that the *negotiorum gestio* obligation is "manifestly more closely connected with another country", that country's law applies. Article 11(4) sets a high standard for resort to the escape clause: the *negotiorum gestio* obligation must be "manifestly" more closely connected with another law than with the law deemed applicable by subsections 1 to 3.[34] As *negotiorum gestio* claims are unlikely to generate particular problems in this regard, reference may be made to the commentary on Art. 4 (paras. 79 et seq.) for a detailed analysis.

---

31 *Junker*, in: Münchener Kommentar BGB, Art. 11 para. 18; *Spickhoff*, in: Bamberger/Roth, Anh. Art. 42 EGBGB para. 87; *Thorn*, in: Palandt, Art. 11 para. 8.

32 See in detail, Art. 4 paras. 54 et seq.; – contra: *Rushworth/Scott*, LMCLQ 2008, 274, 289 proposing to choose either country in which the act was commenced or completed.

33 See Art. 4 paras. 102 et seq.

34 *Chong*, 57 ICLQ (2008) 863, 889.

Article 12
Culpa in contrahendo

1. The law applicable to a non-contractual obligation arising out of dealings prior to the conclusion of a contract, regardless of whether the contract was actually concluded or not, shall be the law that applies to the contract or that would have been applicable to it had it been entered into.
2. Where the law applicable cannot be determined on the basis of paragraph 1, it shall be
   (a) the law of the country in which the damage occurs, irrespective of the country in which the event giving rise to the damage occurred and irrespective of the country or countries in which the indirect consequences of that event occurred; or
   (b) where the parties have their habitual residence in the same country at the time when the event giving rise to the damage occurs, the law of that country; or
   (c) where it is clear from all the circumstances of the case that the non-contractual obligation arising out of dealings prior to the conclusion of a contract is manifestly more closely connected with a country other than that indicated in points (a) and (b), the law of that other country.

A. Scope

I. The Term *Culpa in Contrahendo*

1. General

1 Obligations that arise out of dealings prior to the conclusion of a contract are neither purely contractual nor purely non-contractual, but are instead situated somewhere between contract and tort claims. When faced with this dilemma under the Brussels I regime, the ECJ held that, in the absence of "an obligation freely entered into by the parties," damages for an unjustified breaking off of contractual negotiations constituted a non-contractual claim.[1] The legislature refined the ECJ's holding in deciding that pre-contractual obligations do not fall under the Rome I regime (see Art. 1(2)(i) Rome I) but are governed by Art. 12 Rome II.

2 However, while one question is thus answered, a second question arises: which obligations are to be considered "pre-contractual"? As obligations situated between contractual obligations and "regular" non-contractual obligations, pre-contractual obligations require two lines of demarcation: one between contractual and pre-contractual, and another between pre-contractual and "regular" non-contractual. While the first distinction is important in deciding whether Rome I or Rome II applies,[2] the latter is necessary to determine whether Art. 12 or Art. 4 applies.

3 The answer provided by the Regulation is only of limited help. First, the legislature decided to designate pre-contractual obligations encompassed by Art. 12 as "*culpa in contrahendo*" claims. This term is known in several national legal systems, but these systems interpret the term differently.[3] Comparative recourse to

---

1 ECJ, Case C-334/00 – *Tacconi*, [2002] I-ECR 7357.

2 For a detailed discussion of this question see Art. 1 paras. 19 et seq.

3 See *von Bar/Drobnig*, The interaction of contract law and tort and property law in Europe, paras. 343 et seq.

national laws therefore seems unfeasible. What is more, Recital 30 explicitly demands that "*culpa in contrahendo* for the purposes of this Regulation is an **autonomous concept** and should not necessarily be interpreted within the meaning of national law". Second, the legislature decided that pre-contractual obligations may arise "regardless of whether the contract was actually concluded or not". When a contract has been concluded, it will most likely be difficult to distinguish *culpa in contrahendo* claims from contractual claims (*i.e.* Rome II or Rome I); when no contract has been concluded, the difficulty shifts to the destinction between *culpa in contrahendo* and "regular" non-contractual obligations (*i.e.* Art. 12 or Art. 4).

2. Distinction between *Culpa in Contrahendo* and Tort

Regarding the distinction between *culpa in contrahendo* and regular non-contractual obligations, Recital 30 provides some concrete examples: "the violation of the duty of disclosure and the breakdown of contractual negotiations"[4] should be considered *culpa in contrahendo*, while one party's personal injury during negotiations should not. In addition to these concrete examples, Recital 30 also procides a more general guideline: "Article 12 covers only non-contractual obligations presenting a **direct link** with the dealings prior to the conclusion of a contract." (emphasis added) 4

With the concrete examples of Recital 30 in mind, it is submitted that such a "direct link" regularly requires that the obligation in question either a) serves the purpose of protecting the other party's interest in the conclusion of the contract or b) exists solely due to the close relationship of the negotiating parties.[5] Therefore, **duties to protect the integrity** of the other party lack such a "direct link:" contractual negotiations mereley provide the con- 5

4 Cf. Art. II.–3:301(3) DCFR.

5 Similar *Lüttringhaus*, RIW 2008, 193, 197.

text in which a party violates obligations towards the other party that also exist outside the negotiations.[6]

6 By contrast, all **duties that require a party to work towards the conclusion of a (valid) contract** can be subsumed under the term *culpa in contrahendo*. These can include the duty to disclose information the other party needs to ensure validity of the contract: where one party knows that exchange control regulations invalidate contracts unless the parties have obtained official approval and those regulations obligate him to inform the other party about the need for official approval, his disclosure obligation falls under Art. 12. For the same reason, a claim for the costs of preparing a bid or participating in a public procurement procedure will generally qualify as *culpa in contrahendo* where the claimant has not been awarded the project or contract.

3. Distinction between *Culpa in Contrahendo* and Contractual Obligations

7 Neither Rome I nor Rome II offer guidance in distinguishing between *culpa in contrahendo* and contractual obligations. The command of Recital 30 – that violations of the duty of disclosure should be considered as a *culpa in contrahendo* – applies only in regard to the distinction between Art. 12 and Art. 4 (pre-contractual or regular non-contractual). While it is therefore clear that disclosure violations are *not* governed by Art. 4, it is not clear whether they fall under Art. 12 or are governed by Rome I. According to Art. 12(1) Rome I, the law applicable to contractual obligations should govern "the consequences of a total or partial breach of obligations" (lit. c) "the various ways of extinguishing obligations" (lit. d), and the "consequences of nullity of the contract"(lit. e). Thus, where a violation of the duty of disclosure entitles the other party to terminate the contract, it seems preferable to apply the law designated by Rome I.[7] Even further, any

6 *Dickinson*, para. 12.02; *Backmann*, in: jurisPK BGB, Art. 12 para. 8.

7 *Dickinson*, para. 12.09; – contra: *Cheshire, North & Fawcett*, pp. 833 seq.

demand to rescind a concluded contract and restitute the performances that have already been made must be considered contractual.

In this Author's opinion, there remains only little room under Rome II for claims that arise out of a **violation of the duty of disclosure**. Stated briefly, Rome II governs disclosure violations only where a) a party claims damages for being led to conclude a contract under disadvantageous terms or b) due to the disclosure violation, a contract has not been concluded. For example: a seller has concealed that the painting for which the buyer has shown interest was not painted by Rubens himself but by one of his students. When the buyer finds out, he loses interest and refuses to buy the painting. A claim for recovery of expenses incurred in the course of the negotiations clearly qualifies as *culpa in contrahendo*. By contrast, when the buyer finds out after the parties have already concluded their contract, his claim for restitution of the purchase price and even a claim for damages will be subject to Rome I. 8

4. Claims against Third Parties

Most legal systems allow for damages against third persons that are not party to the contract but in some way take part in or at least influence the negotiations. Typically, **three categories of liability** regulate the participation of such third parties: a) liability of the other party's agent for misrepresentation or lack of authority *(falsus procurator)*, b) liability of an expert retained by the other party to render an opinion on the object of purchase;[8] c) prospectus liability for the issuer of securities that the buyer has purchased on the market. 9

Whether such claims against third parties are governed by Art. 12 is subject to some debate amongst scholars. One group of com- 10

---

8 *E.g.* § 311(3) German Civil Code; cf. von *Bar/Drobnig*, The interaction of contract law and tort and property law in Europe, para. 344.

mentators deny that Art. 12 applies – based on the argument that pre-contractual obligations can only exist between potential parties to the contract.[9] In contrast, another group of authors finds that *close proximity* of the liable party to the (contemplated) contract justifies the application of Art. 12.[10]

11 **Comparative analysis** of the scope of *culpa in contrahendo* in different domestic legal systems seems to support the first group's opinion: most legal systems allow *culpa in contrahendo* claims exclusively against the potential contracting party.[11] Provisions such as § 311(3) German BGB, which allows for *culpa in contrahendo* claims against third parties that have substantially influenced the pre-contractual dealings, are rare.

12 However, excluding third parties from the scope of Art. 12 does not find support in the **provision's language**: a *culpa in contrahendo* claim exists whenever an obligation merely "arise[s] out of dealings prior to the conclusion of a contract". The liability of a *falsus procurator*, for example, may well be subsumed under this definition.

13 In determining whether Art. 12 should govern the liability created by third party participation in negotiations, the dispositive question should be the one imposed by Recital 30: does the liability present a **"direct link"** to the concrete dealings? As stated above, such a direct link exists only if the obligation in question either serves the purpose of protecting the other party's interest in the conclusion of the contract or, at least, exists *exclusively* because of the close relationship of the negotiating parties. As regards third parties, it should further be necessary that the third party actively participated in the concrete negotiations.[12] Other-

9 *Dickinson*, para. 12.07.

10 *Thorn*, in: Palandt, Art. 12 para. 3; *Spickhoff*, in: Bamberger/Roth, Anh. zu Art. 42 EGBGB para. 92; *Lüttringhaus*, RIW 2008, 193, 198.

11 *von Bar/Drobnig*, The interaction of contract law and tort and property law in Europe, paras. 345 et seq.

wise, one of the main goals of the regulation – to provide foreseeable results[13] – would be undermined: the application of the law that governs the contract will most likely be unforeseeable to any person who did not participate in the negotiations. For example, when an expert is retained by the seller of a real estate to render a written opinion and the seller uses this written opinion to convince potential buyers of the real estate's value, the expert has no opportunity to foresee which law will govern his liability towards a buyer. If the buyer is a consumer, applicable law depends entirely on the buyer's habitual residence – and no expert can foresee from which countries potential buyers may hail.

Concretely applying this understanding of the direct link requirement results in the following resolutions of the scenarios listed above: **14**

(a) An **agent's personal liability** for misrepresentation or lack of authority (*falsus* procurator) will generally fall under Art. 12.[14] The claim is one of *culpa in contrahendo* because it protects the other party's interest in the conclusion of the contract. **15**

(b) The same is true for the **liability of an expert** that is retained by one party and relied on by the other.[15] However, a direct link to the concrete dealings is necessary: Art. 12 governs the expert's liability only when the expert has taken an active part in, or at least (at the time of rendering his opinion) had sufficient knowledge of the concrete negotiations. **16**

---

12 *Spellenberg*, in: Münchener Kommentar BGB, Art. 12 paras. 19 et seq.

13 See Art. 4 para. 16.

14 For the general question of whether the Rome II regulation applies to the liability of a *falsus procurator* see Art. 1 para. 23; cf. *Bach*, IPRax 2011, 116 et seq.; – contra: *Spellenberg*, in: Münchener Kommentar BGB, Art. 12 para. 23.

15 *Schinkels*, JZ 2008, 272, 279 f.; *Lüttringhaus*, RIW 2008, 193, 198.

17 (c) **Prospectus liability** does not fall under Art. 12.[16] The issuer of securities most likely will not have any knowledge of who purchases its securities or the negotiations that lead thereto.

18 In practice, the question of whether Art. 12 encompasses third party liability will often be irrelevant. When Art. 4 is applied rather than Art. 12, the escape clause of Art. 4(3)(2) permits courts to presume an accessory connection to the law governing the relationship between the negotiating parties.[17] Therefore, in cases to which this Author suggests applying Art. 12, an application of Art. 4(3)(2) would produce substantially similar results.

5. Concurrent Liability

19 Where the behavior of one party may lead to *culpa in contrahendo* liability as well as to tort claims, the same principles that are used to determine the applicable law for concurrent contractual and non-contractual claims apply.[18] The law designated by Art. 12 will determine whether *culpa in contrahendo* claims arise while the law designated by Arts. 4 et seq. will decide whether torts claims exist.

II. Excluded Matters

20 Even if they qualify as *culpa in contrahendo*, claims that arise out of areas of law which **Art. 1(2)** excludes from the Regulation's scope, are obviously not governed by Art. 12. Rather, domestic conflict-of-law rules apply.

21 Further, **Art. 13** excludes obligations arising from an **infringement of an intellectual property** right from Art. 12's scope. Instead, Art. 8 applies even if the claim must be classified a claim for *culpa in contrahendo* rather than tort.[19]

---

16 *Wurmnest*, in: jurisPK BGB, Art. 1 para. 46.

17 See *Dickinson*, para. 12.08.

18 See Art. 1 para. 18.

B. Rule

I. Structure of Art. 12

The "main principle" of Art. 12 is laid down in subsection 1: the law that applies to the contract (or would have applied had the contract been validly concluded) also governs any *culpa in contrahendo* obligations. Only where the law applicable to the contract cannot be determined does Art. 12(2) permit another law to apply. The system found in subsection (2) **mirrors the general rule of Art. 4**: if the parties have a common residence, the *lex domicilii communis* governs their obligations (lit. b); if not, the *lex loci damni* applies (lit. a); and lit. (c) provides an escape clause if there exists a manifestly closer connection to a country other than those under lit. (a) or (b). The escape clause in Art. 12(2)(c), unlike its counterpart in Art. 4(3), cannot refer to an existing (contractual) relationship, since Art. 12(2) only applies where the law governing such a relationship cannot be determined.[20] 22

While under Art. 14 the parties may freely agree on the law applicable to *culpa in contrahendo* claims, a **choice of law clause** seems unlikely in practice. Still, where the parties have agreed on a choice of law regarding contractual claims, their agreement is relevant in determining applicable law under Art. 3 Rome I and is thus indirectly relevant to determining the law applicable to *culpa in contrahendo* claims under Art. 12(1) Rome II.[21] 23

II. Accessory Connection to the Law Which Governs the Contract (Subsection 1)

The law that applies to the contract also governs obligations that arise out of pre-contractual dealings. This "accessory connection" to the law governing the contract minimizes the uncertainties 24

19 See in more detail the commentary on Art. 13.

20 *Plender & Wilderspin*, para. 26-018.

21 See in detail *infra* para. 27.

that derive from the difficulties in distinguishing contractual and pre-contractual obligations as described *supra*, para. 7.

25 Where a contract – be it for *culpa in contrahendo* or for other reasons – has not been (validly) concluded, an accessory connection nevertheless exists. On the clear words of Art. 12(1), the court must simply determine the law that would govern the contract if it were in existence.

26 When determining the law applicable to the contract, the court must give consideration to all rules relevant under the Rome I regime.

27 First, a **choice of law agreement** that sets forth what law governs parties' contractual obligations, so long as it is valid under Art. 3 Rome I, governs *culpa in contrahendo* obligations under Art. 12 as well.[22] In determining the formal and material validity of that agreement, courts need to look only to the requirements set out in the Rome I Regulation: the criteria provided in Art. 14 Rome II do not apply; accordingly, the court may not resort to the restrictions in Art. 14(2) and (3) Rome II (however, the absence of these restrictions is ameliorated through similar provisions contained in Art. 3(3) and (4) Rome I).

28 **Where a contract has not been concluded**, the court may evaluate the prospects for such an agreement.[23] If, *e.g.*, within their business dealings, two parties have always agreed on the same choice of law clause, the court might assume that this clause would have been incorporated in the particular contract for which the parties had negotiated in the concrete case. Similarly,

22 A choice of law agreement that whose terms affect the law applicable to contractual claims as well as non-contractual, or at least to pre-contractual obligations, is governed by Art. 14 Rome II and thereby displaces Art. 12.

23 *Thorn*, in: Palandt, Art. 12 para. 5; *Backmann*, in: jurisPK BGB, Art. 12 para. 14

where only one party has already submitted its General Terms and Conditions, a choice of law agreement may be assumed if a) these conditions contain a choice of law clause and b) the other parties' General Terms and Conditions are silent in this regard.

Second, in the **absence of a choice of law agreement**, the general rule of Art. 4 Rome I (including the escape clause in subsection 3) applies. Where the unconcluded contract would have been subject to one of the special rules contained in Arts. 5 through 8 Rome I, these provisions override the general rule of Art. 4 Rome I. 29

III. Art. 4 Cascade (Subsection 2)

1. Scope of Application

Subsection 2 applies only when the *lex contractus* cannot be determined. Thus, its scope remains rather marginal.[24] Where a contract has been concluded, the law applicable to that contract is usually easily determined.[25] However, where – be it due to *culpa in contrahendo* or for another reason – the contractual negotiations have ended at an early stage, cases are imaginable where it may be impossible to determine the law that would have been applicable to the contract. For example, where more than two parties are involved in the negotiations or where the contract would have comprised complex contractual issues, such as in joint ventures,[26] or simply where the seller of a potential purchase contract moved from one country to another and it is unclear whether the contract would have been concluded before or after moving – in any of these situations, section 2 may find applica- 30

24 *Garcimartín Alférez*, EuLF 2007 I 77, 89; *Wagner*, IPRax 2008, 1, 12, *Ofner*, ZfRV 2008, 13, 21, *Kadner Graziano*, 73 RabelsZ (2009) 1, 64.

25 *Cheshire, North & Fawcett*, p. 836; *Rushworth/Scott*, LMCLQ 2008, 274, 291; *Heiss/Loacker*, JBl 2007, 613, 640.

26 Cf. *Plender & Wilderspin*, para. 26-019.

tion. In addition, courts may refuse to apply the *lex contractus* if one party alleges that a certain choice of law clause would have been concluded.

2. Cascade System

31 Where the law applicable to the contract cannot be determined, subsection 2 provides for a cascade system similar to that in Art. 4. Although the language that links the three steps of the cascade with the word "or" seems to indicate that courts may view the "cascade" as mere alternatives instead of progressive steps, the **cascade hierarchy** explicitly provided in Art. 4 should also apply to Art. 12(2).[27] Thus, as a general rule, the *lex loci damni* applies (lit a). If the parties' habitual residences lie in the same country, this country's law *must* be applied (*lex domicilii communis*, lit. b). If there is a country to which the case is more closely connected than to the countries of lit. (a) or (b), the court *may* apply this country's law (escape clause, lit.c).

32 Regarding the details of Art. 12(2)'s connection cascade, reference can be made to the commentary on Art. 4. As a rule, the damage that results from *culpa in contrahendo* is primarily of a pecuniary nature. Therefore, the difficulties that arise in applying Art. 4(1)[28] will also likely arise in applying Art. 12. In the case of a *culpa in contrahendo* claim for the break-off of negotiations, the **damage consists in the lack of contract**. At first glance, such damage seems to occur at the place at which the contract would have been concluded. However, one may also conclude that the real damage to the aggrieved party lies in the lack of performance by the other party rather than in the lack of contract. Such a paradigm would result in setting the place of hypothetical performance as dispositive in determining applicable law.[29] However, where contractual negotiations have been broken off at such

---

27 *Garcimartín Alférez*, EuLF 2007 I 77, 89; – contra: *Lüttringhaus*, RIW 2008, 193, 197.

28 See Art. 4 paras. 26 et seq.

an early stage as to prevent the *lex contractus* from being determined, courts may face difficulties to predict with any certainty the hypothetical place of contracting or the hypothetical place of performance. If neither place is predictable, courts should escape to Art. 12(2)(c).[30]

Article 13
Applicability of Article 8

For the purposes of this Chapter, Article 8 shall apply to non-contractual obligations arising from an infringement of an intellectual property right.

Art. 13 is merely an **annex to Art. 8**. It extends the material scope of application of the conflict rule in Art. 8 beyond claims in tort/delict (chapter II of the Regulation) to claims for the infringement of an intellectual property right based on unjust enrichment, *negotiorum gestio* and *culpa in contrahendo* (chapter III of the Regulation). The purpose of this extension is to **apply the same law to any non-contractual claim arising out of an infringement of an intellectual property right**. It is particularly relevant with regard to claims in unjust enrichment since a number of laws grant restitutionary remedies in case of infringements of intellectual property rights, *e.g.* German law under the *Eingriffskondiktion* or English law.[1] 1

---

29 This rule comports with the principles that govern determining the law applicable to the tort of procurement to breach of contract, see Art. 4 para. 47.

30 Although the plain language of Art. 12(2)(c) requires that an applicable law can be determined under lits. (a) and (b), it is submitted that the provision should be applied analogously when the determination under lits (a) and (b) fails, cf. for a similar problem Art. 4 para. 82.

1 *Thorn*, in: Palandt, Art. 13 para. 2; G. *Wagner*, IPRax 2008, 1, 11; *Dicey, Morris & Collins*, para. S 35-230; *Plender/Wilderspin*, para. 22-009.

Chapter IV
Freedom of choice

Article 14
Freedom of choice

1. The parties may agree to submit non-contractual obligations to the law of their choice:
   (a) by an agreement entered into after the event giving rise to the damage occurred;
   or
   (b) where all the parties are pursuing a commercial activity, also by an agreement freely negotiated before the event giving rise to the damage occurred.
   The choice shall be expressed or demonstrated with reasonable certainty by the circumstances of the case and shall not prejudice the rights of third parties.
2. Where all the elements relevant to the situation at the time when the event giving rise to the damage occurs are located in a country other than the country whose law has been chosen, the choice of the parties shall not prejudice the application of provisions of the law of that other country which cannot be derogated from by agreement.
3. Where all the elements relevant to the situation at the time when the event giving rise to the damage occurs are located in one or more of the Member States, the parties' choice of the law applicable other than that of a Member State shall not prejudice the application of provisions of Community law, where appropriate as implemented in the Member State of the forum, which cannot be derogated from by agreement.

A. General

I. Scope of Application

1 Article 14 establishes a qualified freedom of contract in the field of non-contractual obligations. Art. 14's positioning within the Rome II Regulation makes it generally applicable to all types of non-contractual obligations: torts as well as unjust enrichment, *negotiorum gestio* and *culpa in contrahendo* fall within its scope.[1] This broad scope is not altered by the language in subsections (1)(a) and (1)(b) that permits choice-of-law agreements before or after an "event giving rise to … damage." Such language is *not* a restriction of Art. 14 to torts/delicts only; instead, it constitutes an attempt to maintain uniform terminology within the Regulation and is defined in Art. 2(1) as comprising any consequence arising out of the different types of non-contractual obligations listed above.[2]

---

1 *Heiss/Loacker*, JBl. 2007, 613, 622; *Junker*, in: Münchener Kommentar BGB, Art. 14 para. 11; G. *Wagner*, IPRax 2008, 1, 14.

2 See Art. 2 para. 6.

2 However, the provision's scope is **limited in three ways**:

3 First, parties are precluded from choosing the law applicable to **certain types of torts**. Under Art. 6(4), parties may not derogate from the law applicable to unfair competition torts.[3] Similarly under Art. 8(3), parties may not contractually alter the law applicable to claims of infringement of intellectual property rights. By virtue of Art. 13, Art. 8(3)'s prohibition on party choice of law extends to all other non-contractual obligations regarding intellectual property rights as well. The restrictions on party choice of law of Art. 6(4) and 8(3) are criticised in legal literature for being unjustified and incomprehensible.[4] Since restrictions on parties' choice of law are only justified as a protection of third party rights and/or common interests, scholars have proposed (counter)exceptions to the restrictions of Arts. 6 and 8 when a dispute does not threaten third party or common interests.[5]

---

3 Whether this comprises cases where the act of unfair competition exclusively affects the interest of a specific competitor is the object of some debate. In this regard, Art. 6(2) refers to the "main rule" of Art. 4; thus, it is argued that applicable law is found under the latter rather than under the former article, as required by Art. 6(4).

4 *Leible*, RIW 2008, 257, 259; *Wurmnest*, in: jurisPK BGB, Art. 14 para. 7. In fact, the Commission in its Explanatory Memorandum on the initial proposal merely stated that freedom of choice "would not be appropriate" in the field of intellectual property COM(2003) 427, p. 22 (on Art. 10) – a thesis that the Committee on Legal Affairs of the European Parliament rightfully contested (see Report on the proposal for a regulation of the European Parliament and of the Council on the law applicable to non-contractual obligations ("Rome II") (Wallis-Report), A6-0211/2005, p. 17: "There also seems to be no reason why such agreements cannot be concluded in relation to intellectual property".

5 *Leible*, RIW 2008, 257, 259; similarly *Wurmnest*, in: jurisPK BGB, Art. 14 para. 8.

Second, in certain circumstances, sections (2) and (3) of Art. 14 provide that **mandatory provisions** of another country's law will prevail over the parties' chosen law (see in detail *infra* paras. 32 et seq and 37 et seq.). 4

Third, the **rules contained in chapters IV and V** of the Regulation take priority over the parties' choice of law. Therefore, overriding mandatory provisions (Art. 16) and the public policy (Art. 26) of the *lex fori*, as well as the rules of safety and conduct at the place of action (Art. 17), will override a choice of law by the parties. 5

II. Differentiation between Consumer Contracts and Commercial Contracts

Parties enjoy full autonomy to choose the law applicable to their non-contractual obligations only when they "are pursuing a commercial activity" (lit. b). Thus, as soon as one party qualifies as a consumer, party autonomy is restricted: the parties may not agree on applicable law before the "event giving rise to the damage" has occurred (lit. a).[6] 6

The consumer restriction has been criticised as being too severe and not severe enough at the same time because it relies on the formal aspect of the "pursuance of business activities", rather than allowing a flexible judgment on whether one party is weaker than the other and thus in need of protection.[7] On the one hand, consumers are deprived of autonomy – even if a relationship between 7

6 For special requirements on anterior choices of law see in detail *infra* paras. 22 et seq.

7 According to Recital 32, "protection should be given to weaker parties" in general, *i.e.* not be bound to the parties' status as businesspersons or consumers; cf. *Symeonides*, 56 Am.J.Comp.L. (2008) 1, 44, naming the examples of franchise, licensing, and insurance contracts.

two consumers is concerned[8] – while on the other, imbalances of power are likely even among commercial actors.

8 While the latter scenario can be adequately dealt with by interpreting subsection (1)(b)'s requirement of "free negotiation" narrowly,[9] consumer's loss of autonomy most likely presents no appreciable danger. Whenever the parties agree on an applicable law before the "event giving rise to the damage" occurs, a contractual relationship will almost always exist.[10] In such cases, the law governing the existing contractual relationship may be applied to non-contractual obligations by virtue of the applicable escape clause under Art. 4(3), 10(4), 11(4), or 12(2)(c)[11]. However, returning autonomy to consumers through escape clauses – which courts *may* but need not apply[12] – does increase the legal uncertainty connected to consumer choices of law: when a choice of law agreement must not be "directly" considered under Art. 14 courts may see good grounds not to allow an "indirect" effect under Art. 4(3)(2).[13]

---

8 *Sonnentag*, 105 ZVglRWiss (2006) 256, 277 et seq.; *Leible*, RIW 2008, 257, 258; *de Boer*, 9 YbPIL (2007) 19, 28; *von Hein*, 64 RabelsZ (2000) 595, 612 et seq.

9 *Rugullis*, IPRax 2008, 319, 322.

10 *De Boer*, 9 YbPIL (2007) 19, 27; *Mankowski*, IPRax 2010, 389, 402. In exceptional cases, including relationships between consumers, scenarios may exist in which no contractual relationship exists and yet the parties have a legitimate interest in fixing the law applicable to damages claims, *e.g.* if a car driver (residing in country A) gives another person (not residing in country A) a lift into another country free of charge; cf. *Kadner-Graziano*, Gemeineuropäisches Internationales Privatrecht, pp. 185 et seq.

11 Cf. *Cheshire, North & Fawcett*, p. 838; *Mankowski*, IPRax 2010, 389, 402.

12 See Art. 4 para. 79.

13 *Leible/Lehmann*, RIW 2007, 721, 726; *Leible*, in: Reichelt (ed.), Europäisches Gemeinschaftsrecht und Internationales Privatrecht, 2007, 31, 45; *von Hein*, 102 ZVglRWiss (2003) 528, 548.

III. Selectable Law

Article 14 permits the parties to submit non-contractual obligations to "the law of their choice". Thus, the parties are free to choose the law of any country of the world irrespective of whether the chosen country is related to the case. However, by using the term "law" instead of "rules" (or "rules of law"), Art. 14 restricts the parties' choice to law that is *in force* in any country. The restriction receives further support in the language of Art. 14(2) that speaks of "the country" whose law has been chosen. Thus regrettable though it may be, **non-national law**, such as, *e.g.*, the (Draft) Common Frame of Reference,[14] may not be chosen.[15] The same is true for **international conventions**: the parties may not choose to apply directly any of the numerous Hague Conventions to their non-contractual obligations. However, they are free to choose the law of a country that is a signatory to a convention they desire, thus making the convention applicable (if its requirements as to scope are fulfilled) – in other words, the parties may indirectly choose the rules of a convention. 9

IV. Partial Choice of Law (*dépeçage*)

Article 14 is silent as to whether parties may restrict their choice of law to certain non-contractual obligations while leaving other non-contractual obligations to be governed by the law made applicable under the Regulation's default provisions in chapters II and III. For contractual obligations, Art. 3(1)(3) Rome I expressly allows such a partial choice of law, which has generated two arguments with regard to Rome II. On one side, one can con- 10

14 *Study Group on a European Civil Code v Research Group on EC Private Law (Aquis Group)*, Principles, Definitions and Model Rules of European Private Law, Draft Common Frame of Reference (DCFR), Outline Edition, 2009. Cf. *Stürner/Brinkmann*, IPRax 2008, 366 et seq.

15 *Dickinson*, para. 13.20; *Leible*, RIW 2008, 257, 261; *Rühl*, in: FS Kropholler, 187, 190; *Junker*, in: Münchener Kommentar BGB, Art. 14 para. 15; *Wurmnest*, in: jurisPK BGB, Art. 14 para. 5.

clude that Art. 3 Rome I expresses a general principle of the Rome regime in favour of partial choices of law. On the other, one could argue *e contrario* that the lack of a partial choice provision in Art. 14 Rome II argues against allowing partial choices of law for non-contractual obligations. The majority of legal writers seem to favour the first conclusion.[16]

B. Prerequisites

I. Common Prerequisites for Both Types, Art. 14(1)(2)

1. Consensus

11 Regardless of whether the parties make their choice of law before or after the "event giving rise to the damage" occurs, a mutual agreement between them is required, be it express or implied. According to subsection (1)(2), the parties' choice of applicable law must be "expressed or demonstrated with reasonable certainty by the circumstances of the case." It is submitted that this **standard of "reasonable certainty"** calls for a restrictive interpretation.

12 An implicit choice of law agreement may be given where the parties, in their contract, make **reference to legal provisions** of a certain jurisdiction. Courts may conclude "with reasonable certainty" from such a reference that the parties intended to subject their contract to the law whose provisions they expressly cited.[17]

13 By contrast, a choice of law agreement cannot be implied from the mere fact that, within a dispute proceeding, both parties base

16 *Thorn*, in: Palandt, Art. 14 para. 4; *Spickhoff*, in: Bamberger/Roth, Anh. zu Art. 42 EGBGB para. 96; *Heiss/Loacker*, JBl. 2007, 613, 623; *Junker*, in: Münchener Kommentar BGB, Art. 14 para. 37; – contra: *Dickinson*, para. 13.20.

17 *Plender & Wilderspin*, para. 29-024.

their **arguments on a certain law** otherwise not applicable under chapters II and III. Instead, the parties may simply be under the same misapprehension in regard to the applicable law. Therefore, arguments based on a certain country's law should be considered a choice of this law only if the parties know that the law is not designated by the rules of chapters II and III.[18]

A **choice of forum clause** should not, as a rule, be regarded as an implicit choice of law clause. If parties have the legal background to know that they may choose a forum, their silence concerning applicable law should rather be considered as a lack of agreement.[19] 14

Generally, the inclusion of a choice of law clause in one party's **general conditions** may constitute a choice of law agreement if it satisfies the requirements for formation and validity imposed by the law applicable to these questions[20], – *i.e.* in particular the requirements for validly including general conditions into a contract. There is some debate, however, as to whether a clause contained in one party's general conditions may suffice for an anterior choice of law (see *infra* para. 28). 15

---

18 *Dickinson*, para. 13.36; *Junker*, in: Münchener Kommentar BGB, Art. 14 para. 32; *von Hein*, 102 ZVglRWiss (2003) 528, 548; *Leible*, RIW 2008, 257, 261, who argues that if both parties base their arguments on law that is neither their hometown law nor the *lex fori*, it may be presumed that they have chosen that law.

19 But see Recital 12 Rome I: "An agreement between the parties to confer on one or more courts or tribunals of a Member State's exclusive jurisdiction to determine disputes under the contract should be *one of the factors* to be taken into account in determining whether a choice of law has been clearly demonstrated." (emphasis added); *cf. Leible*, RIW 2008, 257, 261; *Wurmnest*, in: jurisPK BGB, Art. 14 para. 16 (both arguing that only an exclusive choice of forum may be regarded as a implicit choice of law).

20 For the applicable law see *infra* paras. 16 et seq.

2. Formation and Validity

16 Except for providing that the parties must (expressly or implicitly) agree to a choice of law, Art. 14 remains silent on questions of formation and validity. It neither provides substantive requirements nor does it specify the law from which such requirements should be taken. Due to the absence of any substantive provisions to provide a basis for interpretation, an autonomous approach to formation and validity is unlikely to be a practicable solution.[21] Admittedly, this is inconsistent with the approach taken by the ECJ in regard to choice of forum agreements under Art. 23 Brussels I.[22] However, European legislators have already rejected consistency in their approaches to choice of forum and choice of law clauses: Articles 3(5) and 10 Rome I also reject an autonomous approach to choices of law applicable to contractual obligations. Instead, they provide for the "anticipatory application" of the chosen law – formation and validity of the choice of law agreement are governed not by an autonomous European standard, but rather by the *chosen law*.[23]

17 In the Author's opinion, Rome II should follow Rome I's **"anticipatory application"** scheme. Following the Rome I approach makes sense because, firstly, it provides a greater degree of legal certainty. Secondly, the fact that only one choice of law clause in a contract will govern both contractual and non-contractual obligations demands parallelism in judging the formation and validity of the agreement.[24] Dogmatically, the propriety of the "anticipatory application" approach may be deduced in two different ways: if one regards the choice of law agreement as a contractual

21 *Dickinson*, para. 13.18.

22 See *e.g.* ECJ, Case C-214/89 – *Duffryn v Petereit*, [1992] ECR I-1745, paras. 13 et seq. (on Art. 17 Brussels Convention).

23 *Dickinson*, para. 13.12.

24 *Dickinson*, para. 13.18.

agreement[25] the "closest connection" test in Art. 4(4) Rome I[26] may be applied with the dispute's closest connection existing to the law chosen by the parties[27] – if one does not, Arts. 3(5) and 10 Rome I should be applied analogously.

If **international conventions** form part of the chosen country's law (*e.g.* the CISG), the conventions are to be considered within their scope of application. **18**

The applicable law must not impose overly stringent requirements on the formation and validity of a choice of law agreement. Such requirements would substantially interfere with the effectiveness of Art. 14's freedom of choice provisions and would therefore be inapplicable under EC law.[28] **19**

3. Formal Requirements

It is submitted that formal requirements of a choice of law agreement are those of the law designated applicable under Art. 11 Rome I.[29] Therefore, in most cases the parties will be governed by the requirements of either the law they choose or the law of the country in which the choice of law agreement was concluded. **20**

---

25 The assumption that the choice of law agreement qualifies as a contract is doubted by *Plender & Wilderspin*, paras. 29-011 et seq.

26 As in regard to the choice of law neither party is required "to effect the characteristic performance," the applicable law is to be determined by way of the closest connection test under Art. 4(4) Rome I.

27 *Leible/Engel*, EuZW 2004, 7, 15; *Heiss/Loacker*, JBl, 2007, 613, 623. Still, certain dogmatic concerns arise from the fact that Art. 4(4) speaks of a close connection to a country rather than to a law.

28 *Dickinson*, para. 13.19; cf. ECJ, Case C- 453/99 – *Courage Ltd v Bernard Crehan*, [2001] ECR I-6297 para. 29.

29 *Thorn*, in: Palandt, Art. 14 para. 11; *Spickhoff*, in: Bamberger/Roth, Art. 42 EGBGB para. 97.

4. Alteration

21 The principle of party autonomy requires that the parties may mutually agree to modify their choice of law agreement at any time.[30]

II. Additional Prerequisites for an Anterior Choice of Law, Art. 14(1)(b)

1. … Before the Event Giving Rise to the Damage

22 Article 14(1)(b) sets out further restrictions when the parties conclude their choice of law agreement "before the event giving rise to the damage" occurs. As demonstrated above, this language must be interpreted in the light of Art. 2's catalogue of events that give rise to "damage." Therefore, the term "damage" refers to any consequence arising out tort/delict, unjust enrichment, *negotiorum gestio* or *culpa in contrahendo*. Further, if there is no event giving rise to damage – as is the case when negatory claims are filed – damage is considered to have "occurred" at the point in time when an event giving rise to damage becomes *likely* to occur (see Art. 2(3)(a)).

2. … Pursuing a Commercial Activity …

23 Article 14 allows an anterior choice of law only when the parties "are pursuing a commercial activity." Regrettably, the legislature refused to employ the term "professional" as used in the Rome I Regulation as well as in most EU consumer protection directives. This may be due to the fact that the usual definition given for a professional ("a person acting in the exercise of his trade or profession"[31]) at first glance seems to fit only awkwardly into the context of torts – a person rarely commits a tort within the ex-

---

30 *Junker*, in: Münchener Kommentar BGB, Art. 9 para. 24.

31 See *e.g.* Art. 6(1) Rome I.

ercise of his profession.[32] The same inaccuracy, however, inheres within the phrase "pursuance of commercial activity."

To hold that a choice of law was made "in pursuance of commercial activity," a court must find that (a) the choice of law was agreed upon in the course of the party's business,[33] and (b) the tort was somehow linked to this course of business, regardless of the terminology used to label the course of business. Case law interpreting the term "professional" under Rome I may be applied to the phrase "in pursuance of commercial activity" under subsection (1)(b). 24

3. … All Parties …

An anterior choice of law is only permissive if *all parties* are professionals. Therefore, consumers are barred from participating in an anterior choice of law agreement, be it with a professional or with another consumer. 25

Subsection (1)(b) does not, however, prevent two professionals from agreeing on the applicable law although consumers are in some way involved in a case.[34] While invalid with regard to consumers that participated in the agreement, the agreement may remain valid as between the (remaining) professionals. In other words, the participation of a consumer does not – without more – invalidate a choice of law in its entirety. 26

---

32 *Leible/Lehmann*, RIW 2007, 721, 726; *Leible*, RIW 2008, 257, 260; – contra: *Mankowski*, IPRax 2010, 289, 400 giving *inter alia* the examples of product liability and unfair competition which *per definitionam* occur in the exercise of a profession.

33 *Wagner*, IPRax 2008, 1, 13; *Ofner*, ZfRV 2008, 13, 22.

34 It is not necessary that all parties involved in the event giving rise to the damages claim agree on a choice of law. The rights and interests of other parties are sufficiently protected by subsection (1)(2).

4. … an Agreement Freely Negotiated …

27 An anterior choice of law is valid only when it was "freely negotiated" by the parties. This requirement pays regard to the fact that even between two professionals, a disparity in bargaining power is a likely occurrence. The requirement of free negotiations, as envisioned by Recital 31, thus serves as a tool to protect the weaker party.[35] However, a mere **disparity in bargaining power**, without more, does not entail a failure of free negotiations.[36] In order to invalidate a choice of law agreement the weaker party must show some evidence that the stronger party abused its greater bargaining power to force the weaker party to accept its choice of law.

28 Subsection (1)(b) remains silent regarding whether the inclusion of one party's **general terms and conditions** in a contract can constitute a valid agreement on applicable law.[37] Some scholars have argued that a choice of law clause contained in one party's general terms and conditions does not meet the requirements of subsection (1)(b).[38] Indeed, such a clause can hardly be labelled "freely negotiated," since general conditions are *per definitionem* "not individually negotiated".[39] Nevertheless, some scholars have taken the opposite position on the basis that choice of law clauses within general conditions constitute the "usual case" in commercial practice and that, therefore, not permitting a choice of law via general conditions would render (1)(b) meaningless.[40]

---

35 *Rugullis*, IPRax 2008, 319, 322.

36 G. *Wagner*, IPRax 2008, 1, 13.

37 *Hay*, EuLF 2007 I 137, 151; but see for the provision's drafting history *Rushworth/Scott*, LMCLQ 2008, 274, 293.

38 *Garcimartín Alférez*, EuLF 2007 I 77, I-82; *Heiss/Loacker*, JBl. 2007, 613, 623; *Rugullis*, IPRax 2008, 319, 322; *von Hein*, ZEuP 2009, 6, 20.

39 See Art. 3(2) Council Directive 93/13/EC of 5 April 1993 on unfair terms in consumer contracts; cf. *Leible*, RIW 2008, 257, 260; *Rugullis*, IPRax 2008, 319, 322; *Heiss/Loacker*, JBl. 2007, 613, 623; – differentiating: *Dickinson*, para. 13.41.

Further, there is a difference between *free* and *individual* negotiations: as long as the party whose general terms contain the choice of law clause, was not in a position to force the other party to accept such a clause, it may well be assumed that the other party *freely* accepted the choice of law clause, albeit it was not *individually* negotiated.[41] While tending to the latter view, in the Author's opinion the debate will rarely be relevant in practice – the use of General Conditions implies that there is a contract which can serve as the object of an accessory connection under the escape clause of Art. 4(3) (or Arts. 10(4), 11(4), 12(2)(c)).[42]

5. Choice of Law in Favour of the Weaker Party

As the reason for imposing additional prerequisites on an anterior choice of law agreement is to protect the consumer as the weaker party,[43] it stands to reason that these prerequisites are not meant to apply to the disadvantage of the consumer. However, if the consumer is the victim and the chosen law provides for damages while the law otherwise applicable does not, the invalidity of the choice of law agreement favors the professional rather than the consumer. The same is true if – assuming a reversal of circumstance – the consumer must indemnify a professional and is exempt from liability under the chosen law only. **29**

This disadvantage could be avoided by applying the additional requirements of subsection (1)(b) only upon objection by the **30**

---

40 *Hay*, EuLF 2007 I 137, 151; *Wagner*, IPRax 2008, 1, 13; *Thorn*, in: Palandt, Art. 14 para. 9; cf. *Rushworth/Scott*, LMCLQ 2008, 274, 292: "In so far as carefully drafted choice of law agreements are rarely individually negotiated, Art. 14(1)(b) is cause for commercial concern".

41 *Plender & Wilderspin*, para. 29-023; stricter: *Mankowski*, IPRax 2010, 389, 400 demanding that the clause must have been up for discussion; *Wurmnest*, in: jurisPK BGB, Art. 14 para. 11 demanding that the clause must be seperately signed.

42 Cf. *Mankowski*, IPRax 2010, 389, 402.

43 See Recital 31; cf. *supra* paras. 7 et seq.

consumer. However, this solution does not find any support within the wording of Art. 14 or the structure of the Regulation. Rather, a comparison with Art. 3(2)(2) Rome I[44] shows that the legislature did not intend to codify a solution that solely favours the consumer under subsection (1)(b). While Rome I expressly assures that its 'weaker party' provisions function exclusively for the benefit of consumers, Rome II contains no such provision. Regrettable as this may be, therefore, subsection (1)(b)'s restriction will apply even if this is to the benefit of the stronger party and at the expense of the weaker party.

C. Restrictions

I. Rights of Third Parties

31 Under subsection (1)(2), a choice of law may not "prejudice the rights of third parties." The scenario the legislature had in mind when drafting this provision was insurance: subsection (1)(2) ensures that a choice of law clause does not obligate the tortfeasor's insurer to pay a sum greater than what it would pay under the law that would be applicable if not for the choice.[45] Also covered by subsection (1)(2) are cases in which two or more tortfeasors have acted in concert. If the victim and tortfeasor 1 agree upon the applicability of a law that does not entitle the victim to damages, the agreement may not preclude tortfeasor 2 from recourse against tortfeasor 1. It is true that such protection already exists under Art. 20, which provides that the law under which the victim proceeds against tortfeasor 2 applies to tortfeasor 2's claims

44 Art. 3(2)(2) Rome I reads: "Such a choice may not, however, have the result of depriving the consumer of the protection afforded to him by provisions that cannot be derogated from by agreement by virtue of the law which, in the absence of choice, would have been applicable on the basis of paragraph 1".

45 COM(2003) 427, p. 22 (on Art. 10); cf. Art. 18 para. 10.

against tortfeasor 1. Article 20, however, does not protect against the opposite scenario: if the victim and tortfeasor 1 agree to apply a law under which tortfeasor 1 (but *not* tortfeasor 2) is liable, subsection (1)(2) instead of Art. 20 protects tortfeasor 2 against claims by tortfeasor 1.

II. National Mandatory Provisions, Art. 14(2)

Under subsection (2) the parties may not, through their choice of 32
law, depart from the mandatory provisions of a country's law that would be applicable if not for their choice. The term mandatory as used in subsection (2) is obviously broader then the term "overriding mandatory provisions" in Art. 16. While under Art. 16 national provisions are only "overriding mandatory provisions" if they apply irrespective of which law Rome II deems applicable, Art. 14(2) precludes parties from opting out of any provisions from which the parties could not deviate were they in a purely domestic context.[46]

The restriction of subsection (2) applies only when "all elements 33
relevant to the situation" occur within the country seeking to apply its mandatory provisions. Subsection (2) does not define the term "**relevant elements**." Since case law is also lacking, scholars have proposed classifying all Rome II "connecting factors" – elements listed throughout the Regulation that connect a country's law to a particular dispute – as "relevant elements." However, since all imaginable factual circumstances are relevant "connecting factors" under the escape clauses of Arts. 4(3), 10 (4), 11(4), and 12(2)(c), equating "relevant elements" with "connecting factors" is largely unworkable.

The fact that section (2) overrides the parties' chosen law only 34
when "*all* relevant elements" of a claim occur in another country

---

46 *Plender & Wilderspin*, paras. 29-033.

potentially lessens section (2)'s importance in practice.[47] Moreover, section (2)'s restriction on party choice is open to misuse. When a court and/or the parties wish to avoid the application of mandatory provisions under section (2), an "element relevant to the situation" located in a third country is easy to find.

35 With these difficulties in mind, a reasonable approach would appear to lie in either a) teleologically limiting the requirement that "all" relevant elements be located in the same country, or b) applying section (2) analogously if the mandatory rules of countries in which all "relevant elements" are located are substantially similar. Unfortunately, in the Author's opinion, neither approach is permissible because each disregards the express wording of the provision and thus the intent of the legislature. Moreover, interpreting a narrow scope into section (2) protects party autonomy. Since every application of mandatory law overrides parties' freedom to choose the applicable law – and some member states have classified their *entire* tort law as "mandatory"[48] – a narrowly-interpreted section (2) is more in harmony with parties' autonomy.

36 Parties cannot circumvent section (2) by choosing a different forum because it is not the mandatory provisions of the forum that are granted effect, but rather those of the law that would be applicable if not for the parties' choice.[49]

III. European Mandatory Provisions, Art. 14(3)

37 Under section (3), the "mandatory law" scheme of section (2) is projected from the national to the European level. In short:

---

47 Cf. *Dickinson*, para. 13.30 with reference to an English decision on the parallel provision in Art. 3(3) Rome Convention (*Caterpillar Financial Services Corp v SNC Passion* [2004] EWHC 569; [2004] 2 Lloyd's Rep 99).

48 G. *Wagner*, IPRax 2008, 1, 14.

49 *Sonnentag*, 105 ZVglRWiss (2006) 256, 279; *von Hein*, VersR 2007, 440, 445; *Leible*, RIW 2008, 257, 262; *Huber/Bach*, IPRax 2005, 73, 75.

where all relevant elements are located within the European Union, the parties may not derogate from mandatory standards of European law by choosing the law of a Non-Member-State. Despite its clear general rule, section (3) creates two difficulties upon closer scrutiny.

First, the wording of section (3) does not speak of the "European Union" but instead uses the term "member states," which, as defined in Art. 1(4), do not include **Denmark.** For the purposes of section (3) however, excluding Denmark makes no sense[50] and must be regarded as a mistake by the legislature. This becomes evident when one considers that the parallel provision of Rome I, Art. 1(4)(2), expressly *abrogates* the exclusion of Denmark. The same should apply under Rome II as well.[51] 38

Second, as most provisions regarding non-contractual obligations are contained in directives rather than regulations, slight differences between different member states may arise from differing approaches to implementing the directives. Therefore, the legislature had to specify which country's **national implementation rules** should apply under section (3), and it decided on the rules of the *lex fori*. From a dogmatic point of view, the more appropriate approach would have been to apply the rules *as implemented* by the law that had to be applied if not for the choice. The reason behind the legislature's decision to back the implementation rules of the *lex fori* is a practical one: the court will be best familiar with its own rules. This decision – although heavily criticized in legal literature[52] – must *de lege lata* be followed. Relying on the *lex fori*, however, will be impossible if Art. 14 is applied by a judge of a 39

50 The absurd consequences are displayed by *Leible*, RIW 2008, 257, 263; *Junker*, in: Münchener Kommentar BGB, Art. 14 para. 43.

51 For the different dogmatic approaches to reach this result, cf. *Heiss/Loacker*, JBl. 2007, 613, 623; – contra: *Dickinson*, para. 13.32.; *Junker*, in: Münchener Kommentar BGB, Art. 9 para. 43.

52 *Leible/Lehmann*, RIW 2007, 721, 727; *Leible*, RIW 2008, 257, 263; *Sonnentag*, 105 ZVglRWiss (2006) 256, 280.

non-member state, *e.g.* in the course of *renvoi*. It is submitted that in such cases the implementation rules of the country whose rules would apply to the present case if not for the choice should govern.

D. Consequences of an Invalid Choice of Law Agreement

40 If a choice of law agreement does not meet the requirements set out under Art. 14, it may still have some effect. It may constitute a contractual agreement to incorporate the rules of the chosen law, which results in such rules forming a (or multiple) term(s) of the parties' contract. The difference between such a contractual "incorporation" and a "regular" choice of law agreement lies in the fact that parties may not escape mandatory provisions by way of contractual incorporation, while a choice of law agreement – subject to the narrow exception of Art. 14(2) – allows them to do so.

Chapter V
Common rules

Article 15
Scope of the law applicable

The law applicable to non-contractual obligations under this Regulation shall govern in particular:

(a) the basis and extent of liability, including the determination of persons who may be held liable for acts performed by them;

(b) the grounds for exemption from liability, any limitation of liability and any division of liability;

(c) the existence, the nature and the assessment of damage or the remedy claimed;

(d) within the limits of powers conferred on the court by its procedural law, the measures which a court may take to prevent or terminate injury or damage or to ensure the provision of compensation;
(e) the question whether a right to claim damages or a remedy may be transferred, including by inheritance;
(f) persons entitled to compensation for damage sustained personally;
(g) liability for the acts of another person;
(h) the manner in which an obligation may be extinguished and rules of prescription and limitation, including rules relating to the commencement, interruption and suspension of a period of prescription or limitation.

A. General/Overview/System

1 In some Member States, the law made applicable by domestic conflict of law rules does not decide issues such as limitation periods, the burden of proof and the measure of damages. Instead, these questions are answered by the *lex fori*, in most cases because they are considered procedural.[1] Such exceptions, on the one hand, invite litigants to engage in forum shopping;[2] on the other hand, they generate a measure of legal uncertainty, the prevention of which is one of the main purposes of the Rome II Regula-

1 COM(2003) 427, p. 23 (on Art. 11); cf. *Turner*, 156 NLJ (2006) 1666 et seq.
2 *Weintraub*, 43 Texas Intl. L. J. (2008) 401, 410 et seq.

tion. For these reasons, the law designated as applicable under Rome II shall apply to as many issues connected with the non-contractual obligation as possible.[3] Against this background, the enumeration of issues contained in **Art. 15 must be regarded as non-exclusive:** the law Rome II designates as applicable governs all issues listed in Art. 15's subsections, but not all issues potentially governed by applicable law are listed. The wording of Art. 17 ("in particular") further underscores its non-exclusive nature.[4] Where the Rome II-designated law governs an issue, it governs the issue exclusively: the *lex fori* may not be applied, not even subsidiarily. If, *e.g.*, the applicable foreign law does not provide for a maximum extent of liability but the *lex fori* does, the cap of the *lex fori* must nevertheless remain unapplied.

2 The goal of deciding all aspects of a non-contractual obligation under the same law, however, is undermined when mandatory provisions of the *lex fori* (Art. 16) or the *ordre public* of the forum-state (Art. 26) can override the application of foreign law. It is further undermined by states that treat foreign law as a matter of fact in their proceedings: the courts of these states impose the obligation to plead and prove the content of foreign law on the plaintiff and apply the *lex fori* if the plaintiff fails to do so.[5]

B. Particular Governed Aspects

I. Basis and Extent of Liability, Lit. (a)

3 It goes without saying that the applicable foreign law must, as a rule, govern the requirements for as well as the extent of the tortfeasor's liability, *i.e.* all positive requirements or intrinsic factors.

---

[3] *Plender & Wilderspin*, para. 16-015.

[4] *Dickinson*, para. 14.04.

[5] See in detail Art. 1 para. 62 and Art. 30 paras. 2 et seq.; cf. *Gruber/Bach*, 11 YbPIL (2009) 157 et seq.

These factors include *inter alia* whether tort liability is fault-based, the criteria for fault[6], and the question of causality.[7]

With regard to the **extent of liability**, the relationship between subsection 15(a)'s term "extent of liability" and subsection 15(b)'s reference to "limitation[s] of liability" is unclear. Some scholars suggest that the term "extent" refers to rules that prevent liability from arising, while the term "limitation" implies rules that influence an existing liability.[8] The distinction seems to be etymologically correct. However, in practice it will often be difficult to distinguish between a rule that prevents the existence of liability and one that merely limits an existing liability. Since, however, it is of no significance for the purposes of Rome II whether foreign law applies through Art. 15(a) or (b), a distinction between "extent" and "limitation" is unnecessary. 4

As regards **which persons may be held liable**, the applicable foreign law governs both natural and legal[9] persons' capacity to incur liability.[10] Article 1(2)(d) does not exempt the legal persons' capacity to incur liability from the scope of the regulation. Article 1(2)(d) exempts only *obligations arising out* of the law of companies from the purview of applicable foreign law,[11] and a person's capacity to incur liability is not such an obligation, but rather a preliminary question. 5

It should be noted that lit. (a) subjects only "the determination of persons who may be held liable *for acts performed by them*" to the applicable foreign law. The question of whether a person is **liable** 6

---

6 But see Art. 17.

7 COM(2003) 427, p. 23 (on Art. 11); cf. *Plender & Wilderspin*, para. 16-009.

8 *Plender & Wilderspin*, para. 16-012.

9 *Cheshire, North & Fawcett*, pp. 848 seq. *Dickinson*, paras. 14.11 et seq.; *Dicey, Morris & Collins*, para. 35-040; *Plender & Wilderspin*, para. 16-010.

10 Cf. Recital 12.

11 See Art. 1 para. 43.

for acts of another is subjected to the applicable foreign law under lit. (g).

7 If **two or more persons are liable** to a plaintiff, the applicable foreign law governs the question of whether the plaintiff can demand only partial payment or whether he may collect the entire judgment from any tortfeasor.[12] Where the applicable law provides the latter solution, contribution claims between the debtors are governed by Art. 20.

II. Exemption, Limitation, and Division of Liability, Lit. (b)

8 While lit. (a) brings the positive requirements for liability under the purview of Rome II-applicable law, lit. (b) subjects exemptions from, limitations of, and the division of liability – so to say the negative requirements or extrinsic factors of liability – to the law applicable under Rome II.[13] These negative requirements include *inter alia* hardship, *force majeure*, necessity, third party fault and fault by the victim (*i.e.* contributory negligence).[14]

9 According to the Commission's Explanatory Memorandum, even "the inadmissibility of actions between spouses and the exclusion of the perpetrator's liability in relation to certain categories of persons" – generally speaking, a person's **capacity to incur liability towards a particular victim**[15] – must be evaluated under Rome II-applicable law[16].

10 Whether the parties may **exclude or limit their liability by an agreement** is, pursuant to lit. (b), also governed by Rome II-ap-

---

12 *Cheshire, North & Fawcett*, p. 842.

13 *Cheshire, North & Fawcett*, p. 842.

14 COM(2003) 427, p. 23 (on Art. 11).

15 The capacity to incur liability in general is covered by (a).

16 COM(2003) 427, p. 23 (on Art. 11).

plicable law. However, lit. (b) remains silent on questions of "how" such agreement may be reached, *i.e.* on manifestations of assent and formal and material validity. Since such agreement may be seen as a separate contract, better reasons argue in favour of applying the *lex contractus* as determined under the Rome I regime.[17] Practical aspects corroborate such a rule: if the agreement is invalid under the law applicable to the tort but valid under the *lex contractus*, successfully suing the tortfeasor may constitute a breach of contract which entitles the tortfeasor to damages.[18]

Defences, such as the **lapse of a limitation period**, are governed by Rome II-designated law as well, albeit pursuant to lit. (h) instead of lit. (b). 11

Applicable foreign law governs the **division of liability** only as between a plaintiff and tortfeasors – the relationship between the tortfeasors is subject to the special provisions of Art. 20. Thus, Rome II-applicable law governs whether tortfeasors are jointly and severally liable, or whether their liability is merely several. If tortfeasors are jointly and severally liable, claims for contribution between tortfeasors are governed by Art. 20.[19] 12

III. Existence, Nature, and Assessment of the Remedy Claimed, Lit. (c)

Whereas lit. (a) addresses the question of liability, lit (c)'s terms "existence and nature of the remedy" refer to the question of which damages are compensable – *e.g.* personal injury, damage to property, moral damage, environmental damage, purely economic loss or even loss of opportunity.[20] 13

17 *Plender & Wilderspin*, para. 16-029; – contra: *Dickinson*, para. 14.15; *Cheshire, North & Fawcett*, p. 865.

18 Cf. *Dickinson*, para. 14.15.

19 Cf. Art. 20 para. 1.

20 COM(2003) 427, p. 23 (on Art. 11).

14 The term "assessment of the remedy" refers to the **quantification of damages,**[21] thus subjecting damages calculations to applicable foreign law. This represents a "radical change"[22] for English law, which treats the quantification of damages as a procedural rather than substantive matter.[23]

15 In some cases, Rome II seems to alter the damages calculations under lit. (c): Recital 33 provides that, when **calculating personal injury damages for traffic accidents** that occurred outside the victim's state of habitual residence, a court must consider "all relevant circumstances of the specific victim, including in particular the actual loss and costs of after-care medical attention." However, it is more likely that Recital 33 aim to ensure that courts consider factual instead of legal circumstances, and thus Recital 33 likely does not interfere with lit. (c).[24]

IV. Prevention of Injury, lit. (d)

16 Besides questions of compensation for loss already suffered, the applicable law also decides on measures to prevent further injury, *e.g.* **disclosure and injunctive relief** – even interlocutory injunctive relief.[25] However, the court is not obliged to order measures that exceed the powers conferred on it by the (procedural law of the) *lex fori*.[26] Therefore, whether a measure can be taken in gen-

---

21 *Dickinson*, paras. 14.19 et seq.; *Dicey, Morris & Collins*, para. S 35-257; *Cheshire, North & Fawcett*, p. 844; *Plender & Wilderspin*, para. 16-056; *Stone*, 4 Ankara L. Rev. (2007) 95, 127; *Weintraub*, 43 Texas Intl. L. J. (2008) 401, 411; – contra: *Hay*, EuLF 2007 I 137, 148.

22 *Illmer*, CJQ 2009, 237, 242.

23 *Harding v Wealands* [2006] UKHL 32, reversing the contrary decision of the Court of Appeal (2005) 1 All ER 415 (CA). Thus, under Rome II, the decision of the Court of Appeal is "revived." For an overview on the decisions see *Plender & Wilderspin*, paras. 16-046 et seq.

24 *Dickinson*, para. 14.31; *Thorn*, in: Palandt, Art. 17 para. 5; – contra: *Symeonides*, 56 Am.J.Comp.L. (2008), 173, 183.

25 Critical: *Plender & Wilderspin*, para. 16-067.

eral is a question to be answered by the *lex fori*, whereas whether the requirements of such a measure are satisfied under the concrete circumstances is to be answered by Rome II-applicable law.[27]

V. Transfer of Remedies, Lit. (e)

Under lit. (e), the question of whether a right to claim damages or 17
to invoke another remedy may be **assigned** is subject to the applicable foreign law. According to the provision's wording, however, the applicable law governs only the question of *whether* a remedy is assignable, not *how* such a assignment must be made. Therefore, the designated law decides all questions as to whether a claim is assignable as well as those that relate to the relationship between the assignor and debtor.[28] It does not, however, govern the relationship between assignor and assignee, which is subject to the law made applicable by Art. 14(1) Rome I.[29]

Lit. (e) also regulates **survivorship actions**: the applicable foreign 18
law governs "whether an action can be brought by the victim's heir to obtain compensation for damage sustained by the victim."[30] In contrast, aspects of *cessio legis* are not governed by the applicable foreign law, but are instead subject to the law designated by Art. 19.

VI. Persons Entitled to Compensation for Damage Sustained Personally, Lit. (f)

While lit. (a) governs which persons may be held liable for a tort, 19
lit. (f) governs whether "a person other than the 'direct victim'

26 COM(2003) 427, p. 24, Art. 11; cf. *Stone*, 4 Ankara L. Rev. (2007) 95, 128.

27 *Cheshire, North & Fawcett*, p. 847.

28 COM(2003) 427, p. 24 (on Art. 11).

29 *Plender & Wilderspin*, para. 16-072; *Dickinson*, para. 14.39.

30 COM(2003) 427, p. 24 (on Art. 11).

can obtain compensation for damage sustained on a 'knock-on' basis, following damage sustained by the victim"[31] Such losses include suffering caused by bereavement, loss of alimony, or financial consequences that the third person must bear as a consequence of his relationship to the victim (*e.g.* if the parents of an injured minor are responsible for a hospital's bill or if a parent company is detrimentally affected by a tort against its subsidiary).[32]

20 In the author's opinion, lit. (f) must be **interpreted broadly**. Despite the fact that the Commision in its Explanatory Memorandum lists only non-material and financial damages as allowable "knock-on" damages, indirect physical damage sustained on a knock-on basis should come under lit. (f)'s purview as well.[33] It is often arbitrary whether or not pain caused by bereavement has a physical or a mere psychological effect – let alone that the border between the two is poriferous.

VII. Liability for the Acts of another Person, Lit. (g)

21 The question of whether and to what extent a person other than the tortfeasor can be held liable for the tortfeasor's acts is also governed by the applicable foreign law. The question of **vicarious liability** includes the liability of parents for children, of principals for their agents, of employers for employees.[34] However, Art. 1(2)(d) excludes from applicable foreign law the question of whether a company's director can be held liable for torts of the company.[35]

22 As a result of lit. (g), different laws may apply to the person acting and to a third person to which these acts are attributable. If, *e.g.*,

---

31 COM(2003) 427, p. 24 (on Art. 11).

32 Cf. Art. 4 paras. 107 et seq.

33 Cf. Art. 4 para. 108.

34 *Dicey, Morris & Collins*, para. S 35-261.

35 See Art. 1 para. 45.

the employee of a French enterprise lives in Belgium and in the course of its work (in France) causes a traffic accident with another Belgian resident, the latter's claim for damages against the enterprise is governed by French law while the claim against the employee is governed by Belgian law. This may at times lead to the result that the employee is liable while the enterprise is not (or vice versa). As a consequence, difficulties may arise with regard to questions of recourse.[36]

Still, the law made applicable by Rome II governs only the requirements for holding one person liable for another's conduct, **23**
in particular (a) the necessary relationship between the person sought to be held liable and the third person and (b) the connection of this relationship to the non-contractual obligation in question. **Preliminary questions**, such as whether the relationship that serves as the basis for imputing liability (parent-child or employer-employee) exists are not governed by the Rome II-designated law, but by the law made applicable under domestic conflicts of law principles.[37]

VIII. Defences, Lit. (h)

Whether and when a claim becomes ineffective for lapse of time **24**
is governed by the law made applicable under Rome II.[38] **Limitations periods** do not therefore constitute a procedural question to which the *lex fori* is applicable. The same is true for other defences

36 For a detailed analysis of possible difficulties see, Art. 4 paras. 66 et seq. and Art. 20 paras. 13 et seq.

37 *Dickinson*, para. 14.47.

38 Critical: *Kadner Graziano*, 73 RabelsZ (2009) 1, 68 et seq. analyzing the immense differences in limitation periods in the domestic laws of the Member States (*e.g.* from 1 year in Spain to 10 years in France) that can surprise unsuspecting victims by confronting them with a far shorter limitation period under the *lex loci damni* than the period of the victims' hometown law.

(such as satisfaction, forfeiture, release or waiver by the entitled party)[39] and the consequences of a settlement by the parties.[40]

25 As regards set-offs, the law deemed applicable under Rome II governs the question of whether the **right to set-off** exists but does not govern the existence of the counter-claim.[41]

Article 16
Overriding mandatory provisions

Nothing in this Regulation shall restrict the application of the provisions of the law of the forum in a situation where they are mandatory irrespective of the law otherwise applicable to the non-contractual obligation.

A. Introduction

1 For decades, the recognition of mandatory rules *(lois de police, lois d'application immédiate, Eingriffsnormen)* has been a **complex issue** and controversially discussed in the conflict of laws. In European conflict of laws rules, a concurrent approach is now taken in both the Rome I and Rome II Regulations.

---

39 *Thorn*, in: Palandt, Art. 17 para. 5.

40 *Spickhoff*, in: Bamberger/Roth, Anh. zu Art. 42 EGBGB para. 113.

41 *Plender & Wilderspin*, para. 16-079.

Art. 16 Rome II provides that nothing in the Regulation "shall restrict the application of the provisions of the law of the forum in a situation where they are mandatory irrespective of the law otherwise applicable to the non-contractual obligation." The wording is taken from Art. 7(2) of the Rome Convention[1] and similar to the wording of Art. 9(2) of the Rome I Regulation.[2] The provision allows the court to refuse to apply the normally applicable law to the extent that it violates the mandatory rules of the *lex fori*. When applying *lois de police*, the traditional theory of the neutrality of conflict of law rules is certainly not relevant.[3] Consequently, Art. 16 is one of the few rules in the Rome II Regulation which takes account of the content of the substantive laws of the involved countries.[4] 2

Article 16 allows the forum to impose its own mandatory rules. This is to say that the normally applicable law will be displaced in so far as it is necessary to take account of the forum's mandatory rules. Comparable to Art. 26, the provision on *ordre public*, Art. 16 allows *dépéçage*, *i.e.* the law applicable governs all issues of the non-contractual obligation and the *lex fori* applies insofar as it is necessary to comply with its mandatory rules. Contrary to the public policy provision which operates as a shield against the application of foreign law, Art. 16 gives overriding effect to a rule originating in national law and therefore acts as a sword.[5] 3

There is no (codified) rule on the application of internationally mandatory rules of a third country (which is not the forum state 4

---

1 Convention on the law applicable to contractual obligations, OJ C 27/36 of 26 January 1998.

2 Regulation (EC) No 593/2008 of the European Parliament and of the Council of 17 June 2008 on the law applicable to contractual obligations (Rome I), OJ L 177/6 of 4 July 2008.

3 *Pataut*, in: Fuchs/Muir Watt/Pataut, Les conflits de lois et le système juridique communautaire (2004) 117, 118.

4 *Symeonides*, 56 Am.J.Comp.L. (2008) 173, 182.

5 *Dickinson*, para. 15.13.

or the country whose law is the applicable law) in the Rome II Regulation. This issue has always been highly controversial (cf. paras. 24-30).

B. Overriding Mandatory Provisions

5 Article 16 does not refer to all rules which cannot be derogated from, but only to "overriding" mandatory provisions which must be applied regardless of the law applicable to the non-contractual obligation. The Regulation does not contain a definition of the term "mandatory provisions." The term was initially defined by the Court of Justice in *Arblade*: "national provisions compliance with which has been deemed to be so crucial for the protection of the political, social or economic order in the Member State concerned as to require compliance therewith by all persons present on the national territory of that Member State and all legal relationships within that State."[6] The decision as to whether a rule is considered to be an overriding mandatory rule must be made by the court in each individual case. An assessment has to be made whether the rule in question is not only internally mandatory but of international relevance **(*internationally* mandatory rules)**. In the *Ingmar* case, the ECJ did not hesitate to apply certain Community provisions as overriding mandatory law *(lois de police)*.[7]

6 A recurrent topic throughout the negotiations of the Rome I and Rome II Regulation was the intended harmonisation of the two legal acts. The wording and content of Art. 16 Rome II and Art. 9(2) Rome I are quite similar. It can therefore be argued that the

6 ECJ Case C-369/96 and Case C-376/96 [1999] ECR I-8453, quoted in the Proposal for a Regulation of the European Parliament and the Council on the law applicable to non-contractual obligations ("Rome II"), 22 July 2003, COM(2003) 427 final, p. 24.

7 ECJ, Case C-381/98 [2000] ECR I-9305; *Brière*, 135 Clunet (2008) 31, 66; *Pataut* in: Fuchs/Muir Watt/Pataut, Les conflits de lois et le système juridique communautaire (2004) 117, 120.

definition on "overriding mandatory provisions" included in the latter Regulation is equally valid in the context of the Rome II Regulation.[8] Thus, the relevant definition is to be found in Art. 9(1) of the Rome I Regulation: "Overriding mandatory provisions are provisions the respect for which is regarded as crucial by a country for safeguarding its public interests, such as its political, social or economic organisation, to such an extent that they are applicable to any situation falling within their scope, irrespective of the law otherwise applicable to the contract under this Regulation." Additionally, Recital 37 of Rome I clarifies that the concept of "overriding mandatory provisions" should be construed more restrictively than the expression "provisions which cannot be derogated from by agreement."

Consequently, overriding mandatory rules have to fulfil two cumulative requirements:[9] the **interest criterion** ("the respect for which is regarded as crucial by a country for safeguarding public interests") and the **overriding criterion** ("irrespective of the law otherwise applicable"). While the interest criterion was taken from the *Arblade* ruling, the overriding criterion had its place in the Rome Convention. Matching *both* criteria is the new element brought about by the definition in Art. 9 Rome I Regulation. 7

According to the interest criterion, an internationally mandatory rule which will apply irrespective of the law otherwise applicable must be regarded as crucial by the forum country for safeguarding public interests. In order to identify whether a given rule of the 8

---

8 According to Recital 7 of the Rome II Regulation, the substantive scope and the provisions of this Regulation should be consistent with the Brussels I and the Rome I Regulations; see also: *Dickinson*, para. 15.18; *Thorn*, in: Palandt, Art. 16 paras. 1, 4; *Junker*, RIW 2010, 257, 268 and in: Münchener Kommentar BGB, Art. 16 para. 13; *von Hein*, ZEuP 2009, 6, 24 and in: Callies, Rome Regulations, Art. 16 para. 12.

9 *Kunda*, Internationally mandatory rules of a third country in the European contract conflict of laws. The Rome Convention and the proposed Rome I Regulation (2007), 146-169.

lex fori is of such eminent importance, the court will rely to a large extent on the wording and interpretation of the relevant provision, the will of the national legislature when enacting the rule and the surrounding circumstances. **Examples** for internationally mandatory rules include provisions for the protection of competition, embargoes, exchange control rules and rules on the protection of the country's currency and export controls on art objects and national heritage.

9 Doubts may arise with regard to rules enacted to protect private interests, for example those of weaker parties such as consumers and workers. It has been put forward that the definition given in Art. 9(1) Rome I Regulation is too restrictive and might not include those rules.[10] The reference to the crucial importance of the provisions for the public interests of a country might on the one hand be regarded as an argument in favour of excluding provisions of private law which aim at balancing interests between private parties; on the other hand, these rules might be considered as internationally mandatory provisions if they aim at protecting the social and economic organisation of the State.

C. Scope of Application

10 The question and definition of overriding mandatory provisions is an issue dealt with extensively and controversially in the field of contractual obligations, *i.e.* in the context of the Rome I Regulation. While an abundance of case law and literature exists on the application of mandatory rules in contract law and examples to illustrate the problem are usually taken from the law of contract,[11] the topic is neglected in the field of non-contractual obligations.[12]

---

10 *Wilderspin*, ERA Forum 2/2008, 259, 272; *Heiss/Loacker*, JBl. 2007, 613, 644.

11 *Dicey & Morris*, para. 1-053 ss.; *Dickinson*, J. Priv. Int. L. 2007, 53; *Kunda*, Internationally mandatory rules of a third country in the European con-

It has hence been argued that in the field of non-contractual obligations, there will be no need for a provision on mandatory provisions; in any case, a public debate on the application of *lois de police* in the area of non-contractual obligations has not taken place. 11

Article 16 nevertheless found its way into the Rome II Regulation. The reason for including this provision was certainly to provide coherence between the two Regulations containing conflict of law rules in contractual and non-contractual obligations. However, the scope of application of Art. 16 Rome II Regulation will be much **more limited** than of its parallel provision in Art. 9 Rome I Regulation. This is due to the fact that there is virtually no case law on mandatory rules in international tort law. A major reason for this certainly is that choice of law plays a less important role in the area of non-contractual obligations compared to international contract law. Furthermore, the Rome II Regulation builds upon a system of subtly differentiated conflict of law rules. 12

Against the background of the Rome II Regulation, several examples will be examined. 13

I. Choice of Law

The freedom of choice of law permitted in the Rome II Regulation, particularly in Art. 14, might *prima facie* require application of overriding mandatory provisions in order to prevent parties from choosing the law of a third state, thereby circumventing (mandatory) rules applicable in the absence of choice.[13] Having 14

---

tract conflict of laws. The Rome Convention and the proposed Rome I Regulation, Rijeka (2007); *Kunda*, GPR 2007, 210; *Freitag*, IPRax 2009, 109.

12 But see *von Hoffmann*, FS Henrich, p. 283; on English overriding mandatory rules: *Cheshire, North & Fawcett*, pp. 849 et seq.; *Dickinson*, para. 15.15.

13 *Brière*, 135 Clunet (2008) 31, 66.

said that, it is to be noted that the choice of law to the non-contractual obligation is subject to a **number of restrictions**. Two aspects are relevant in this context: firstly, the *ex ante* choice of law agreement can only be entered into where all the parties are pursuing a commercial activity (Art. 14(1)(b)). The relevant rules on consumer protection will therefore continue to apply in B2C relations (see Recital 31). Secondly, where all elements relevant to the situation are located in one country, the parties' choice of law shall not prejudice the application of mandatory provisions of that law (Art. 14(2)). In case the parties have chosen the law of third state (Art. 14(3)), the same is true for the mandatory provisions of Union law, which cannot be derogated from by agreement.[14]

15 Two special rules for non-contractual obligations, Art. 6(4) on unfair competition and Art. 8(3) on infringement of intellectual property rights, exclude the freedom of choice in their domain. A derogation from the law of the country where competitive relations or collective interests of consumers are located (Art. 6(1)), or from the law of the country for which protection is claimed (Art. 8(1)), is therefore not possible.

16 In the context of choice of law, the application of Art. 16 can therefore only be of an essentially limited scope.

II. Compensation for Victims of Traffic Accidents

17 The compensation of victims after traffic accidents abroad was highly disputed when drafting Rome II. In order to prevent injustice done to the victims, the European Parliament suggested applying the rules of the individual **victim's place of habitual residence** for the purposes of determining the type of claim and

14 Please note that this provision refers to union rules which are mandatory in the domestic sense (zwingende Normen), but not to "overriding mandatory provisions" (international zwingende Normen); see on this difference Recital 37 of the Rome I Regulation.

calculating the quantum of damages.[15] This approach was not followed by the Council and the Commission. The compromise found was Recital 33, according to which the court should take into account all the relevant actual circumstances of the specific victim when quantifying damages for personal injury in cases of road traffic accidents.

This is to say that the law of the place of the habitual residence of the traffic accident victim will *not be applied* for quantifying damages; it will only be taken "into account." This Recital might also influence the decision whether national laws can be considered as overriding mandatory rules. To give an example: after the introduction of the French law on traffic accidents in 1985 (loi Badinter),[16] a vivid debate followed whether the *loi Badinter* could be considered as *loi d'application immédiate*. This was eventually denied by the French Cour de Cassation.[17] In the context of Rome II, national laws on the protection of traffic law victims will presumably not be interpreted as overriding mandatory rules. Following Recital 33, those national rules are only to be taken into account as *facts* when fixing the final amount of compensation.[18] 18

III. Rules of Safety and Conduct

The general rule in Art. 4 provides that the law applicable to a non-contractual obligation shall be the law of the country in which the damage occurs. This solution does not only strike "a fair balance between the interests of the person claimed to be liable and the person sustaining the damage" (Recital 16), but it underlines the connection with the country where the direct damage occurs 19

15 Report of 27 June 2005, A6-0211/2005, Rapporteur: *Diana Wallis*.

16 Loi no. 85-677 du 5 juillet 1985 tendant à l'amélioration de la situation des victimes d'accidents de la circulation et à l'accélération des procédures d'indemnisation.

17 Cour de Cassation (France), Cass. civ. 1er 12 July 2001, Rev. crit. dr. int. priv. 2002, 541.

18 *Symeonides*, 56 Am.J.Comp.L. (2008) 173, 205.

(place of injury). In cases in which the law of the place of injury will not apply (*e.g.* Art. 4(2) habitual residence), the rules of conduct and safety at the place of injury shall nevertheless be taken into account as a matter of fact according to Art. 17.

IV. Exchange Control

20 A major issue in the context of mandatory rules, not only in the area of contract law, but also in tort law, are foreign exchange control laws. Due to the free movement of capital, exchange control laws are not allowed in the Member States of the European Union; however, outside the European Union, restrictions on payments and transfers for current international transactions are used, mostly by developing countries. States which are members of the International Monetary Fund (IMF) may not impose such restrictions unless they are approved by the Fund, one major purpose of the Fund being to assist in the elimination of foreign exchange restrictions that hamper the growth of world trade. The Articles of Agreement of the IMF containing provisions that permit exchange control also include a provision on how members must react when a member applies exchange control consistently with the treaty. This is **Art. VIII, Section 2(b)**, first sentence:

21 "Exchange contracts which involve the currency of any member and which are contrary to the exchange control regulations of that member maintained or imposed consistently with this Agreement shall be unenforceable in the territories of any member."

22 According to this provision, exchange control regulations of another member must be treated as mandatory rules by the *lex fori*; the sanction for non-observance is unenforceability. Scope, content and interpretation of this provision are highly disputed in jurisprudence and literature worldwide.[19] In spite of the term "ex-

---

[19] *Gold*, The Fund Agreement in the Courts (vol. I-IV 1962, 1976, 1986, 1989); *Procter*, Mann on the Legal Aspect of Money, chap. 15; *Schefold* in:

change contracts," the provision was not held to be limited to contracts, but has in isolated cases been applied to claims for damages and torts.[20] This "unhappy result"[21] contradicts the wording of Art. VIII, Section 2(b) and is therefore not followed by courts in other Member States. Consequently, there is no room for applying this provision in the context of tort.

V. Miscellaneous

Further examples for internationally mandatory rules actually discussed include rules allowing victims of criminal offences to draw compensation from a public fund,[22] pertinent rules on industrial action,[23] exclusion or limitation of liability vis-à-vis third parties in contracts of employment,[24] provisions of the Product Liability Directive[25] and the liability for harm caused by medical products, *e.g.* section 84 of the German Arzneimittelgesetz.[26] 23

Kronke/Melis/Schnyder, Handbuch Internationales Wirtschaftsrecht, Teil I, p. 963.

20 This is the case according to some German judgements, see: *Fuchs*, Lateinamerikanische Devisenkontrollen (1995) p. 186.

21 *Procter*, Mann on the Legal Aspect of Money, para. 15.14 note 22.

22 Cour de Cassation (France), Cass., 2e 25 January 2007, D. 2007, 578; *von Hein*, in: Callies, Rome Regulations, Art. 16 para. 13.

23 See Recital 28. In favour: *Thorn*, in: Palandt, Art. 16 para. 5; *von Hein*, in: Callies, Rome Regulations, Art. 16 para. 17; sceptical: *Junker*, in: Münchener Kommentar BGB, Art. 16 para. 16.

24 *von Hoffmann*, in: FS Henrich, p. 283, 294; *Thorn*, in: Palandt, Art. 16 para. 5; for a comparative approach see *von Bar*, Gemeineuropäisches Deliktsrecht I (1996) para. 193.

25 In favour: *Dickinson*, para. 15.20; against: *von Hein*, in: Callies, Rome Regulations, Art. 16 para. 8: "merely *internally* mandatory substantive law".

26 In favour: *Thorn*, in: Palandt, Art. 16 para. 5; against: *von Hoffmann*, in: FS Henrich, p. 283, 294.

D. Third Country's Internationally Mandatory Provisions

24 With respect to contractual obligations, it was most disputed whether mandatory provisions which form neither part of the proper law of the contract *(lex causae)*[27] nor of the law of the forum *(lex fori)* have to be applied by the judge. A compromise between the diverging opinions of the Member States was found in Art. 9(3) Rome I Regulation. The judge may apply the rules of the country where the contract will be or has to be performed that render the contractual performance unlawful. This reflects the English law position in the light of the *Ralli Bros* decision.[28]

25 However, Art. 16 Rome II is silent on the issue of applying third country's internationally mandatory provisions. The Regulation does not restrain the judge from applying the internationally mandatory provisions of the forum independently from the law applicable to the non-contractual obligation, but whether the third country's internationally mandatory provisions will have to be applied is now a topic of discussion in legal literature. The silence of the European legislator on this question is interpreted differently.[29]

---

27 Rules of the law applicable *(lex causae)* apply irrespective of Art. 16 Rome II, whether or not they are mandatory in character.

28 *Ralli Bros. v. Cia Naviera Sota y Aznar* [1920] 2 KB 287.

29 In favour of applying third country's internationally mandatory rules: *Kadner Graziano*, 73 RabelsZ (2009) 1, 72; *Thorn*, in: Palandt, Art. 16 para. 3; *Junker*, RIW 2010, 257, 268 and in: Münchener Kommentar BGB, Art. 16 para. 25-28; *Schaub/Remien*, in: Prütting/Wegen/Weinreich, Art. 16 para. 5; *von Hein*, ZEuP 2009, 6, 24 and VersR 2007, 440, 446; *Garcimartín Alférez*, EuLF 2007 I-77, 90; *Leible/Lehmann*, RIW 2007, 721, 726; *Heiss/Loacker*, JBl. 2007, 613, 644.
Against: *Brière*, 135 Clunet (2008) 31, 66; G. *Wagner*, IPRax 2008, 1, 15; *Dickinson*, para. 15.25; *Ludwig*, in: jurisPK-BGB, Art. 16 para. 9; *Ofner*, ZfRV 2008, 13, 23; *Francq*, EJCL 3/2007-2008, 319, 340; *de Lima Pinheiro*, Riv. dir. int. priv. proc. 2008, 5, 32.

The first **drafts** on the Rome II Regulation provided for a provision similar or identical to Art. 16 as it stands now.[30] However, the Proposal for a Rome II Regulation of July 2003 opted for a much wider scope of the provision, including a paragraph on mandatory rules of third countries (Art. 12). The Commission did not see any reason for excluding foreign mandatory rules from the scope of the provision, especially as references to foreign mandatory rules have been "perfectly exceptional."[31] This approach was shared by the European Economic and Social Committee[32] and the European Parliament[33]; the wording of the provision was repeated in the amended proposal for a Rome II Regulation.[34] **26**

Following a Council meeting in 2006, Art. 16 was cut down to applying only the overriding mandatory provisions of the law of the forum. The draft statement of the Council's reasons only contains the following explanation: "the Articles on mandatory provisions (...) have further been simplified."[35] The subsequent Communication on the common position[36] adds that the deleted **27**

---

30 See Art. 7 (lois de police), Internal draft of the European Commission, in: *von Hoffmann*, in: Staudinger Vorbem. zu Art. 38 ff. EGBGB, para. 16; Art. 12 of the Pre-draft for a proposal on the law applicable to non-contractual obligations (April 2002).

31 Proposal for a Regulation of the European Parliament and the Council on the law applicable to non-contractual obligations ("Rome II"), 22 July 2003, COM(2003) 427 final, p. 25.

32 Opinion of 2 June 2004, CE 0841/2004, p. 7.

33 Report of 27 June 2005, A6-0211/2005, p. 30, Rapporteur: *Diana Wallis*, and Legislative Resolution of Parliament (1st reading) of 6 July 2005, P6_TA(2005)0284.

34 Amended Proposal for a European Parliament and Council Regulation on the law applicable to non-contractual obligations ("Rome II"), 21 February 2006, COM(2006) 83 final, Art. 13.

35 JUSTCIV 137, 11 September 2006, para. 7.

36 Communication concerning the common position of the Council on the adoption of a Regulation of the European Parliament and of the Council

provision on third countries' mandatory provisions "did not reflect any Community interest." According to the official documents, the scope of the provision on overriding mandatory provisions was not discussed again until the adoption of the Rome II Regulation on 11 July 2007.

28 The argument for introducing a broad provision on mandatory rules was to achieve uniform application of the Rome I and Rome II Regulation; at this stage, the Commission proposed to take over Art. 7 Rome Convention[37] into the Rome I Regulation. However, in accordance with its right under Art. 22 Rome Convention, the UK and six other Member States did not apply Art. 7(1) of the Rome Convention on third-countries' mandatory rules on the basis that to do so would give rise to an unacceptable degree of legal uncertainty.[38] Therefore, it did not come as a surprise that a wide provision on mandatory rules gave rise to **widespread concern** in commercial circles, particularly the City of London. In the light of these concerns and against the background that the majority of Member States applied Art. 7(1) Rome Convention, a compromise was found, which is Art. 9(3) of the Rome I Regulation. In the UK, the Rome I proposal is thus far considered to be an "acceptable outcome."[39]

29 Article 16 of the future Rome II Regulation was consequently reduced to its original version in order to reach again consistency

---

on the law applicable to non-contractual obligations ("Rome II"), 27 September 2006, COM(2006) 566 final, p. 4.

37 The first paragraph of Art. 7 of the Rome Convention states that when applying the law of a country, "effect may be given to the mandatory rules of the law of another country with which the situation has a close connection, if and in so far as, under the law of the latter country, those rules must be applied whatever the law applicable to the contract." It was neither implemented in the Rome I nor in the Rome II Regulation.

38 *Dicey Morris & Collins*, para. 35-120.

39 Ministry of Justice, Rome I – Should the UK opt in? Consultation Paper CP 05/08, published on 2 April 2008.

between the two Regulations. Article 16 Rome II thus corresponds to (the uncontroversial provision of) Art. 9(2) Rome I. Therefore, the **uniform application** of the two instruments should be aimed at.[40] Allowing a broader interpretation of the same rule in the Rome II Regulation runs against the principle of consistency between the two Regulations (Recital 7 of the Rome II Regulation) and it would certainly not be acceptable to all those Member States which had refused to apply Art. 7(1) Rome Convention.

To sum up, the effect of Art. 16 Rome II is to provide for the application of mandatory rules of the *law of the forum* that override the normal rules for choice of law. To permit the application of mandatory rules of a country that is neither the forum nor the country of applicable law contradicts the wording of the provision and the intention of the European legislator. Furthermore, this narrow interpretation of Art. 16 improves the certainty as to the law applicable and therefore the **predictability** of the outcome of litigation. 30

Article 17
Rules of safety and conduct

In assessing the conduct of the person claimed to be liable, account shall be taken, as a matter of fact and in so far as is appropriate, of the rules of safety and conduct which were in force at the place and time of the event giving rise to the liability.

40 Report on Rome I of 21 November 2007, A6-0450/2007, Rapporteur: *Cristian Dumitrescu*: "This amendment is designed to clarify the meaning of overriding mandatory provisions (…). It has also better-regulation aims as it will bring Rome I into line with Rome II. This would also facilitate the ultimate merger of Rome I and Rome II into a single instrument." (p. 33).

A. General/Overview/System

1 Article 17 codifies a principle that would have gone without saying:[1] where a person acts in a certain country, it may be more appropriate to judge his conduct according to the rules of that country even if Rome II makes the law of another country applicable. The most popular example of such a situation is the traffic accident that occurs in Germany but whose consequences are judged by English law (which would be the case if both parties have their habitual residence in England). If the accident was caused because both parties were driving on the same side of the road, the question of who was on the wrong side must obviously be answered under German rather than under English traffic regulations.

2 It should be noted that accounting for rules of safety and conduct of the place of action does not necessarily bar certain rules of otherwise applicable law from continuing to apply. If, *e.g.* the victim of a traffic accident was using his mobile phone at the time of the accident, his conduct may give rise to a contributory negligence defence even if he was not prohibited from doing so under the traffic rules of the place of damages, but only under the traffic rules of the *lex domicilii communis*.

---

1 According to the Commission's Explanatory Memorandum, "[t]here are equivalent principles in the conflict systems of virtually all the Member states." The provision is based on Art. 7 of the Hague Convention on traffic accidents and Art. 9 of the Hague Convention on product liability; COM(2003) 427, p. 25, Art. 13; cf. *Dickinson*, para. 15.33.

Article 17 should not be regarded as an exception to the rules contained in Chapters II, III, and IV. Instead of providing for an alternative applicable law, Art. 17 is **quasi-factual in nature**.[2] As applied to claims, this means that whether or not a claim's success depends on the tortfeasor acting negligently[3] will be answered by the Rome II-designated law.[4] However, the rules of safety and conduct at the place of action will be taken into account in determining whether the tortfeasor acted negligently (see in detail *infra* para. 6) 3

Article 17 is based on Art. 7 of the 1971 Hague Convention on the law applicable to traffic accidents and Art. 9 of the 1973 Hague Convention on the law applicable to products liability.[5] According to the Commission's Explanatory Memorandum, "[t]here are equivalent principles in the conflict systems of virtually all the Member states."[6] However, under *e.g.* German law, the Art. 17-equivalent (uncodified) rule has a narrower scope: if applied to the Rome II regime, it would permit deviation only from the law made applicable under Art. 4(2) rather than from the law applicable under the "main rule" of Art. 4(1) as well.[7] The broad scope of application of Art. 17 displays one of the **provison's main purposes**: to balance any inequity to the person liable that might result from the application of the *lex loci damni* rather than the *lex loci damni commissi*.[8] 4

2 Commission's Explanatory Memorandum, COM(2003) 427, p. 25 (on Art. 13).

3 Article 17 is not applicable when a person is accused of having caused damage intentionally – rules of safety and conduct apply only when negligent behaviour is to be judged.

4 *Junker*, in: Münchener Kommentar BGB, Art. 17 para. 17.

5 COM(2003) 427, p. 25 (on Art. 13).

6 COM(2003) 427, p. 25 (on Art. 13).

7 Cf. G. *Wagner*, IPRax 2008, 1, 6.

8 Cf. Recital 34.

B. Prerequisites

I. In Assessing the Conduct of the Person Claimed to be Liable …

5 The wording of Art. 17 suggests that it applies only in regard to the tortfeasor's obligations. However, in some cases, the conduct of the victim is relevant as well, particularly in cases of **contributory negligence**. In the example given above (para. 1), it is obvious that the behaviour of the victim should not be judged under English law. Therefore in the author's opinion, Art. 17 applies analogously to the victim's conduct.[9]

II. … Account Shall be Taken as a Matter of Fact …

6 The rules of safety and conduct do not "apply" in a strict sense, but are taken into account on a purely factual basis as so-called **local data**.[10] In determining whether behaviour was negligent, a court must decide what a reasonable person in the same situation would have done. Such a person would of course have obeyed the rules of safety and conduct in force at the place where he acted. Just like any other component of the concrete situation facing the actor, these rules thus become relevant as facts of the case rather than as applicable law.[11]

---

[9] *Dickinson*, para. 15.34; G. *Wagner*, IPRax 2008, 1, 7; *Ofner*, ZfRV 2008, 13, 17; cf. *Stone*, EuLF 2004 I 213, 219; *Junker*, in: Münchener Kommentar BGB, Art. 9 para. 25; *Wurmnest*, in: jurisPK BGB, Art. 4 para. 23; – contra: *Heiss/Loacker*, JBl. 2007, 613, 637; *Symeonides*, 56 Am.J.Comp.L. (2008) 173, 213.

[10] COM(2003) 427, p. 25 (on Art. 13); cf. *Betlem/Bernasconi*, 122 LQR (2006) 124, 150; *Dickinson*, para. 15.33; *Leible/Lehmann*, RIW 2007, 721 725; *von Hein*, VersR 2007, 440, 446; *Sonnentag*, 105 ZVglRWiss (2006) 256, 310 et seq.; *Cheshire, North & Fawcett*, p. 855; *Plender & Wilderspin*, paras. 18-110; – contra: *Symeonides*, 56 Am.J.Comp.L. (2008) 173, 212 et seq.

7 This entails two practically important consequences. First, as facts of the case, relevant rules of conduct must be **pleaded and proven** by the parties even if the procedural law of forum views foreign law through the principle of *iura novit curia*.[12] Second, parties may not **derogate** from the rules of conduct and safety in force in the country of action by virtue of Art. 14. Instead, the possibility to mutually deviate from these rules constitutes a question of exemption of liability – an issue to be decided under the law Rome II deems applicable.[13]

III. … Account Shall be Taken in so far as Is Appropriate …

8 In assessing whether it is "appropriate" to take into account the safety and conduct rules of the place of action, it is necessary to distinguish between two types of torts: torts in which the action and the injury take place in the same country *(Platzdelikt)*, and torts in which the action and the injury take place in different countries *(Distanzdelikt)*.[14]

9 In case of a *Platzdelikt*, Art. 17 allows consideration of local safety rules only when Rome II makes applicable the law of a country other than the place of both action and damage – *e.g.* through the habitual residence rule or an escape clause. In such cases, applying local safety rules under Art. 17 should generally be considered appropriate. Exceptions may have to be made, however, in exceptional cases, *e.g.* torts between persons travelling together in a foreign country when the the tort does not (even potentially)

---

11 The characterization of rules as factual circumstances is further supported in that non-national rules such as the FIS rules fall within the scope of Art. 17 as well, see *infra* para. 13.

12 *Staudinger*, EuLF 2005 I 61, 63; for the different national rules in regard to the ascertainment of foreign law see *Gruber/Bach*, 11 YBIPL (2009) 157, 161 et seq.

13 See Art. 15(b).

14 Critical in regard to the application of Art. 17 to a *Distanzdelikt*: *Hamburg Group for PIL*, 67 RabelsZ (2003) 1, 44.

affect any other person and has no (other) close connection to the country's safety and conduct rules.

10 In cases involving a *Distanzdelikt*, both the country of action and the country of damage have an interest in the application of their safety and conduct rules, especially if these are stricter than those of the other country.[15] Therefore, one could argue that the stricter rules should prevail. However, the purpose of Art. 17 is not to serve the interests of countries, but rather to protect the interests of the party alleged to be liable: the provision aims to eliminate any prejudice to the person liable that would result from applying the *lex loci damni* rather than the *lex loci delicti commissi*.[16] Countries' interest in having their rules of safety applied must (and can) instead be satisfied at the level of public law (*e.g.* criminal law).

11 In light of Art. 17's purpose, two scenarios must be differentiated. Scenario 1: safety and conduct rules are stricter in the country of damage than in the country of action. Sceanrio 2: the same rules are stricter in the country of action. In scenario 1, the defendant benefits from Art. 17. However, this benefit is justified only if the defendant did not foresee (and could not have foreseen) that his action would create effects in another country.[17] Therefore, when the defendant foresaw or should have foreseen the possible effects in another country, Art. 17 should remain unapplied. In scenario 2, the defendant suffers a disadvantage through Art. 17 – a result that is inconsistent with Art. 17's purpose of eliminating the unfair surprise to the defendant created by diverging (and thus potentially unforeseeable) safety rules at the place of damage. More-

---

15 The country of action has an interest in governing the behaviour of persons acting within its territory, while the country of damages has an interest in protecting those persons that habitually or temporarily reside in its territory.

16 See *supra* para. 4.

17 *Symeonides*, 56 Am.J.Comp.L. (2008) 173, 213 et seq.; *Ludwig*, in: jurisPK BGB, Art. 17 para. 7.

over, the aggrieved party has no interest in the application of the safety rules of any country other than the country in which it suffered harm – at least none worthy of protection. Therefore, as a rule, courts should not account for stricter rules in place in the country of action under Art. 17 in determining whether conduct was negligent.[18]

V. … To the Rules of Safety and Conduct …

Under Art. 17, courts should take account of all local standards of safety and conduct. In the context of traffic accidents, these local standards clearly include all relevant rules of traffic law such as DUI limits or the prohibition of telephoning while driving.[19] 12

What is more, the policy behind Art. 17 – determining whether persons acted reasonably under all relevant circumstances – calls for an extensive interpretation of the term "rules of safety and conduct." Courts should not only account for national law, but also for **private or organizational rules** to which an actor's conduct was subject.[20] Thus, on a ski slope, FIS rules are to be taken into account; in a Formula 1 race, the FIA rules must be considered; and on a shooting range, a court must account for rules or guidelines set forth by the (private) operator. Ethical standards may be taken into account as well.[21] 13

Whether courts should take account of **administrative or official permits** is subject to some debate. The question has particular relevance when environmental damage is at issue. It is submitted that the purpose of Art. 17 offers a solution: a person's behaviour will be influenced by administrative acts in the same manner as it 14

---

18 G. *Wagner*, IPRax 2008, 1, 6; *Ludwig*, in: jurisPK BGB, Art. 17 para. 7; – contra: *de Lima Pinheiro*, Riv. dir. int. priv. proc. 2008, 5, 33; *Symeonides*, 56 Am.J.Comp.L. (2008) 173, 214 et seq.

19 Cf. *Junker*, NJW 2007, 3675, 3681.

20 G. *Wagner*, IPRax 2008, 1, 6; *Ludwig*, in: jurisPK BGB, Art. 17 para. 6.

21 *Dickinson*, para. 15.32.

is influenced by national rules of law – the former mostly concretising the latter.[22] Therefore, courts should as a rule account for administrative permits[23] – unless doing so would be inappropriate because, for example, the person claimed to be liable could foresee his conduct causing damage in a third country that had safety rules stricter than those in the country that issued the permit (see *supra* para. 11).

15 However, this rule does not go without an exception. It is necessitated by the fact that states can use different approaches to prevent damages: they can ensure certain standards either by way of public law (*i.e.*, by setting high requirements for the issuance of permits) or – probably less bureaucratic – by way of private law (*i.e.*, by setting up low requirements for damages claims). Countries that follow the public law approach will often restrict damages claims to cases in which the operator has violated certain conditions set out in the permit. Countries that follow the private law approach will generally be less reluctant to issue permits since the risk of damages establishes sufficient incentive for the operator of facilities to meet high safety standards. Problems occur when an operator that runs facilities in state A (following the private law approach) causes damages in state B (following the public law approach). Should such an operator be entitled to rely on the administrative permit issued in state A? This could lead to the remarkable result that he would not be liable for damages in country B (because he did not violate any requirement set out in the permit) although he would be if the damages had occurred in country A (because he then would have been liable under the strict liability rule there).

16 Therefore, some scholars (among them Fuchs on Art. 7 in the present commentary[24]) propose to restrict Art. 17 to cases in

---

22 *Leible/Lehmann*, RIW 2007, 721, 725.

23 *Handig*, GRURInt 2008, 24, 30; *Leible/Lehmann*, RIW 2007, 721, 725; *Ofner*, ZfRV 2008, 13, 19; *Ludwig*, in: jurisPK BGB, Art. 17 para. 5 – contra: *Siems*, RIW 2004, 662, 666; *Mankowski*, IPRax 2010, 389, 390 f.

which the permit satisfies certain criteria (such as a right of individuals residing in other countries to be heard, or equivalence of standards).[25] Without doubt, Art. 17's language allows the introduction of such criteria when restricting the application of local data to cases where this is "appropriate".[26] In this author's opinion, however, this approach is in conflict with Art. 17's purpose, when the tortfeasor could not reasonably foresee that his conduct would cause damage in another country (or to be precise, in the very country where the damage occurred that is the subject of the particular claim).

Instead, it is submitted as a general proposition that this dilemma could be escaped by another control mechanism – for which, again, the appropriateness requirement offers a hook: permits should not be taken into account to reduce or even exclude a person's liability under the *lex loci damni* if it did not have this effect under the *lex loci delicti commissi*. In other words: if the tortfeasor is liable under the law of action, it cannot rely on rules of safety and conduct of this country to escape from liability under the law of the country of damages. There are, of course, a lot of details still to be discussed in that regard which are, however, beyond the scope of this book. **17**

VI. … Which were in Force at the Place and Time of the Event Giving Rise to the Liability

The wording of Art. 17 refers not only to the place but also to the time of the harmful act. Thus, if the action does not cause damage for a certain period of time, and if within that time the rules of safety and conduct change, courts should not take the alteration into account. Under Art. 17, the relevant point of time for determining whether conduct was negligent is the "time of the event **18**

24 Art. 7 paras. 34 et seq. (for environmental damage).

25 *Thorn*, in: Palandt, Art. 7 para. 9; *Kadner Graziano*, 73 RabelsZ (2009) 1, 50; cf. Art. 7 para. 4c.

26 See *supra* paras. 8 et seq.

giving rise to the *liability*," not the time of the event "giving rise to the *damage*." The action giving rise to the liability is, *e.g.*, the production or marketing of a defective product. Therefore, changes in the safety rules that occur later than the marketing should remain unconsidered.[27] Instead, the manufacturer's conduct should be judged under the rules in force at the time of production and/or marketing of the defective product.

Article 18
Direct action against the insurer of the person liable

The person having suffered damage may bring his or her claim directly against the insurer of the person liable to provide compensation if the law applicable to the non-contractual obligation or the law applicable to the insurance contract so provides.

A. Overview

1 Art. 18 has two purposes. First, it privileges the victim: under its alternative conflicts rule, the victim may bring a direct action against the tortfeasor's insurer if the law applicable to the tort

27 For this reason, criticism in legal literature (*Leible/Engel*, EuZW 2004, 7, 16; *Heiss/Loacker*, JBl. 2007, 613, 637) that worries about the producer being surprised by a tightening of safety rules which becomes effective between the marketing and the occurrence of a damage, is obsolete.

or the law applicable to the insurance contract permits such an action. Second, it avoids any dispute about whether the claim against the insurer constitutes a tort (as opposed to a contractual) claim and is therefore subject to the choice of law rules for non-contractual obligations.[1]

The law applicable to the insurance contract is determined under Art. 7 Rome I. The law governing the non-contractual obligation is provided by Arts. 4-9 and Art. 14 Rome II. As will be shown below, the victim and the tortfeasor may not, under Art. 14 Rome II, choose a law that would prejudice the insurer's interests, *i.e.* a law that is more beneficial to the victim than the law otherwise applicable.[2] 2

Art. 18 is closely connected with Art. 19. If the insurer has satisfied the victim's direct claim according to Art. 18, then Art. 19 determines the applicable law for the insurer's claim for reimbursement towards the tortfeasor. 3

The scope of Art. 18 is limited: it deals only with the question of *whether* the victim can directly claim compensation from the insurer. The *scope* of the insurer's obligations is subject exclusively to the law of the insurance contract.[3] 4

---

1 In English Law, the issue is heavily debated (cf. *Dicey, Morris & Collins*, para. 35-043). The majority of authority characterizes the direct action as a contractual claim (Court of Appeal (England and Wales) 2 December 2004, *Through Transport Mutual Insurance Association (Eurasia) Ltd v New India Insurance Co Ltd (The Hari Bhum)* [2005] 1 Lloyd's Rep. 67). For a similar discussion in German Law before 1999 cf.: *von Hoffmann*, in: Staudinger, Art. 40 EGBGB paras. 433-436. The majority of German courts characterized the direct action as a claim in tort (Bundesgerichtshof (Germany) 23 November 1971 – VI ZR 97/70, BGHZ 57, 265, 270).

2 See below para. 10.

3 COM(2003) 427 final, p. 26; *Stone*, Ankara L. Rev. (2007) 95, 129; *Junker*, JZ 2008, 169, 177.

5 According to the Commission's Explanatory Memorandum, the alternative conflict of laws rule contained in Art. 18 is not unreasonably burdensome to the insurer.[4] The insurer cannot only anticipate that the law applicable to the insurance contract will govern its conduct, but can also foresee the application of the law governing the non-contractual obligation.[5] It is submitted that the preferential treatment of victims is a legitimate goal. However, it is doubtful whether the insurer can really foresee the law governing the non-contractual obligation.[6]

B. Detailed Commentary

I. Who can Claim Direct Compensation against the Insurer?

6 Whereas some Rome II articles apply to any "person seeking compensation" (Art. 6(3)(b) and Art. 7), Art. 18 entitles only the "**person having suffered damages**" to bring a claim directly against the insurer. However, this difference in wording does not mean that Art. 18 excludes a victim's legal successors from its scope.[7] It is in the victim's and his successors' interest that the latter have recourse against the tortfeasor's insurer. If, for example, the tortfeasor as well as the victim have taken out insurance[8]

---

4 COM(2003) 427 final, pp. 25 et seq. For another example of an even more liberal alternative conflict of laws rule for direct actions against the insurer, see: Art. 9 Hague Convention on the law applicable to traffic accidents.

5 COM(2003) 427 final, pp. 25 et seq.; *Garcimartín Alférez*, EuLF, 2007 I 77, 90.

6 Art. 4 para. 16 and see below para. 14. The rule in Art. 18 Rome II was strongly criticized by the UK Government and the House of Lords' European Union Committee. It was argued that the rule caused considerable uncertainty and unduly favoured one party to the litigation over the other, House of Lords' European Committee, The Rome II Regulation, 8th Report of Session 2003-2004 (HL Paper 66), paras. 149-150.

7 *Dickinson*, para. 14.99.

and the victim has been satisfied by its insurer, the victim's insurer should have the same options as the victim to bring a direct claim against the tortfeasor's insurer.

II. Does the Victim have to Opt for the Law Governing the Insurance Contract?

7 The Commission's initial proposal required the person having suffered damage to exercise a **right of option** in favour of the *lex contractus*. In the absence of such choice, the law governing the non-contractual obligation was to be applied.[9] However, in its amended proposal, the Commission inserted the present Art. 18, albeit "without modifying [the original proposal] as to substance".[10] *Dickinson* therefore argues that despite the wording of the final version, the law of the tort is applicable subject to the right of the victim to opt for the law of the insurance contract.[11]

8 It is submitted that, in spite of the Commission's intention not to change the substance of Art. 18, this view has to be rejected. In contrast to other Rome II articles (*e.g.* Art. 7), the final version of Art. 18 contains a **genuine alternative conflict rule**. Art. 7, in contrast, is phrased differently: it sets as applicable law the law designated by Art. 4(1) "unless the person seeking compensation for damage chooses to base his or her claim on the law of the country in which the event giving rise to the damage occurred." Thus, the difference in wording between Art. 7 and Art. 18, in spite of the Commission's intent, reflects a difference in substance.

---

8 Eg. in Court of Appeal (England and Wales) 2 December 2004, *Through Transport Mutual Insurance Association (Eurasia) Ltd v New India Insurance Co Ltd (The Hari Bhum)* [2005] 1 Lloyd's Rep. 67.

9 COM(2003) 427 final, p. 26; advocating this solution for the benefit of procedural economy: *Fuchs*, GPR 2/03-04, 100, 104.

10 COM(2006) 83 final, p. 3.

11 *Dickinson*, para. 14.87; similar *Dicey, Morris & Collins*, para. S 35-265; *Garcimartín Alférez*, EuLF 2007 I 77, 90.

9 The effect of an alternative conflict rule depends on the *lex fori*.[12] In many Civil Law countries such as Germany and France, the court *ex officio* determines the applicable law. Under the final version of Art. 18, the court cannot simply apply the law of the non-contractual obligation in the absence of the victim's choice of the *lex contractus*. Instead, the court must compare the law of the tort and the law of the insurance contract, after which it must *ex officio* apply the law which is more beneficial to the victim.[13] In contrast, under English law, the parties must plead and prove foreign law.[14] The effect of an alternative conflict rule is that the victim must choose between the law of the non-contractual obligation and the law of the insurance contract. If the victim fails to plead and prove the content of foreign law to the satisfaction of the court, the court decides the case under English law.

III. What is the Law Applicable to the Non-Contractual Obligation in the Sense of Art. 18 Rome II?

10 Generally, the law applicable to the non-contractual obligation is the law governing the relationship between the tortfeasor and the victim. There is, however, a **limitation to that rule**: Art. 14(1)2 provides that a choice of law shall not prejudice the rights of third parties and applies to both substantive and procedural rights, *i.e.* the right not to be sued.[15] Thus, the victim and the tortfeasor cannot choose according to Art. 14 – at the expense of the insurer – a law which provides for a direct action if the law otherwise applicable does not provide for such a claim.[16] Art. 14(1)3 does,

12 *Von Hein*, ZEuP 2009, 6, 31.

13 *Spickhoff*, in: Bamberger/Roth, Anh. zu Art. 42 EGBGB para. 121; *Thorn*, in: Palandt, Art. 18 para. 3; *Junker*, in: Münchener Kommentar BGB, Art. 18 para. 12; *Junker*, JZ 2008, 169, 177; cf. for the identical German rule: *Wagner*, in: Anwaltskommentar BGB, Art. 40 EGBGB para. 53.

14 *Dicey, Morris & Collins*, paras. 9-001 et seq.

15 *Leible*, RIW 2008, 257, 262.

however, not prevent the tortfeasor and victim from choosing a law that is more beneficial to the insurer than the law otherwise applicable.

Some scholars argue that another exception to Art. 18 exists, 11
namely for cases in which Art. 4(3) applies:[17] if the law that governs the tort is determined by a "manifestly closer connection" between the victim and the tortfeasor, so it is argued, this law should not apply to the insurer. Three arguments are generally cited in favour of such an exception: first, Art. 14(1)2 notes that a choice of law between the tortfeasor and the victim shall not have any effect on the legal position of a third party, here the insurer. Art. 4(3), however, exists to account for the fact that the law applicable to the tort is frequently the law chosen by the parties to govern their contractual relationship.[18] Secondly, the "manifestly closer connection" that determines the applicable law under Art. 4(3) characterizes only the special relationship between the tortfeasor and the victim – there is no such close connection with the insurer.[19] Lastly, the law applicable pursuant to Art. 4(3) is not foreseeable for the insurer. Since the alternative conflict of laws rule in Art. 18 alone puts the insurer at a disadvantage, this disadvantage should not be aggravated by deviating from the standard rule of Art. 4(1).

In spite of these arguments, no exception should be made for 12
cases of Art. 4(3).[20] First, the *lex loci damni* that would govern the tort under Art. 4(1) may itself have no connection with the

---

16 See Art. 14 para. 31; *Spickhoff*, in: Bamberger/Roth, Anh. zu Art. 42 EGBGB para. 123; *Thorn*, in: Palandt, Art. 18 para. 4; *Junker*, in: Münchener Kommentar BGB, Art. 18 para. 10.

17 *Spickhoff*, in: Bamberger/Roth, Anh. zu Art. 42 EGBGB para. 123; *Staudinger*, EuLF 2005 I 61, 63; on German law: *v. Hoffmann*, in: Staudinger, Art. 40 EGBGB para. 443.

18 Art. 4 para. 86.

19 On German law: *von Hoffmann*, in: Staudinger, Art. 40 EGBGB para. 443.

20 On German law: *Gruber*, VersR 2001, 16, 20.

dispute either. By way of Art. 4(3), the victim's contractual as well as tort claims are governed by one and the same law, *i.e.* the law of the contractual relationship with the tortfeasor. This is the law with the closest connection and relevance to the dispute, and it should therefore be taken into account for purposes of Art. 18 as well.

13 Secondly, if the victim has contractual as well as non-contractual claims against the tortfeasor, the insurer might be directly liable for both claims (*e.g.* professional negligence insurance). An exception under Art. 4(3) would lead to the following result in such cases: the right to file a direct action for the contractual claims would be governed by the law of the contract between the tortfeasor and the victim, whereas the right to a direct action to remedy the tort would be subject to the *lex loci damni*.[21] It is submitted that the law governing the contract should govern the direct action for both the contractual and non-contractual claims in order to prevent inconsistent outcomes.[22] As a result, Art. 4(3) should be applied when determining the law of the non-contractual obligation within the meaning of Art. 18.

14 Thirdly, the foreseeability argument is largely irrelevant. It is true that the law applicable to a tort under Art. 4(3) is frequently not foreseeable to the insurer. However, the law applicable to a tort under Art. 4(1) or (2) is just as unforeseeable.[23]

IV. Which Questions are Governed by Art. 18 Rome II?

15 As already mentioned above, Art. 18 only answers *whether* the victim can directly claim compensation from the insurer. Ac-

21 *Gruber*, VersR 2001, 16, 20, fn. 42.

22 The prevention of such inconsistent outcomes is precisely the purpose of Art. 4(3) Rome II.

23 See above para. 5 and Art. 4 para. 16.

cording to the Commission's explanatory memorandum, the *scope* of the insurer's obligations is exclusively subject to the law of the insurance contract.[24]

According to some authors, in the interests of the victim, the more beneficial law – either the law of the non-contractual obligation or the law of the insurance contract – determines the **maximum amount covered** by the insurance policy.[25] However, this argument is misplaced: the question of the maximum amount covered does not concern *whether* the victim may bring a direct claim, but it is clearly a question of the direct claim's *scope*. Thus, it is not covered by Art. 18.[26] 16

However, it is submitted that the question of whether an insurer may raise against the victim the **defense that it is released** from its obligation to pay compensation on behalf of the tortfeasor is within the scope of Art. 18.[27] The reason for its inclusion is simple: it is a question of the existence of a claim rather than a question of scope. An example in that regard: an insurer agrees with the insured person under the law of state A that the insurer is not liable if the insured person negligently violated an obligation under the insurance contract. However, the law of state B, which governs the non-contractual obligation, allows a direct action against the insurer in spite of such a clause restricting liability.[28] If the victim initiates proceedings against the insurer and the in- 17

---

24 COM(2003) 427 final, p. 26.

25 *Staudinger*, EuLF 2005 I 61, 63; *Spickhoff*, in: Bamberger/Roth, Anh. zu Art. 42 EGBGB para. 123.

26 Under the identical German rule, predominant opinion is that the maximum coverage amount is determined exclusively by the law of the insurance contract: *Wagner*, in: Anwaltskommentar BGB, Art. 40 EGBGB para. 54; *Gruber*, VersR 2001, 16, 17.

27 *Spickhoff*, in: Bamberger/Roth, Anh. zu Art. 42 EGBGB para. 123; see for the opposite view *Junker*, in: Münchener Kommentar BGB, Art. 18 para. 14.

28 *E.g.* § 117(1) German VVG.

surer relies on its exclusion of liability under the law of state A, the victim may claim the protection of the law of state B by virtue of Art. 18.

18 Another example, which is cited by *Dickinson*[29] and *Plender and Wilderspin*,[30] occured in the English case of *Through Transport v New India.*[31] In this case, the insurance contract contained a so-called **"pay to be paid" clause**, which obliged the insured to first discharge the liability towards the person having suffered damages before claiming reimbursement from the insurer. Finnish law, which was applicable to the tort, allowed a direct claim of the victim against the insurer and contained an anti-avoidance provision that rendered void all terms and conditions which restricted this right.[32] The court held that Finnish law was of no relevance. A direct action against the insurer was nothing but a right of the victim to enforce a claim arising out of a contract concluded between the insurer and the insured. Since the contractual claim was subject to English law, the anti-avoidance provision in Finnish law could be ignored.[33] Today, the case would be decided differently. Art. 18 would be applicable because the "pay to be paid" clause constitutes a defence which concerns the existence of the direct claim and not merely its scope. Thus, the claimant could rely on Finnish law, disregard the "pay to be paid" clause, and directly claim compensation from the insurer.[34]

---

29 *Dickinson*, paras. 14.93-14.95.

30 *Plender & Wilderspin*, paras. 28-009 – 012.

31 Court of Appeal (England and Wales) 2 December 2004, *Through Transport Mutual Insurance Association (Eurasia) Ltd v New India Insurance Co Ltd (The Hari Bhum)*[2005] 1 Lloyd's Rep. 67.

32 *Ibid.* p. 72.

33 *Ibid.* pp. 82-83.

34 *Dickinson*, paras. 14.93-14.95.

V. Traffic Accidents

Art. 18 Rome II was certainly drafted against the background of traffic accidents. Unfortunately, its relevance to traffic accidents remains limited. 19

First, **Art. 9 Hague Convention on traffic accidents**, if it applies to an accident, supersedes Art. 18.[35] Art. 9 provides an even more liberal alternative conflict of laws rule: generally, the victim has a direct right of action if the law of the state of registration, the law of the state where the accident occurred or the law governing the insurance contract provides for such a right. 20

Secondly, the importance of Art. 18 Rome II is diminished by the so-called **Green Card System** that was established in 1949 by the International Conference of Motor Insurers in London.[36] The Green Card protects victims of road traffic accidents in cases in which the accident was caused by a visiting motorist. In case of an accident, the victim need not claim compensation from the foreign insurance company (*i.e.* the situation governed by Art. 18 Rome II). Rather, the victim can claim compensation directly from the "Bureau of the country of the accident."[37] The national Bureau handles claims under the same laws and regulations as a national insurance company.[38] All EU and EFTA states, as well as other states such as Russia, Belarus, Ukraine, Turkey, Iran, Morocco, Tunisia, Israel and the Balkan states, are members of the Green Card System. 21

---

35 See Art. 28 para. 10.

36 Cf. www.cobx.org.

37 See for the Green Card System: *Merkin & Rodger*, EC Insurance Law (1997), pp. 52 et seq.; *Merkin & Stuart-Smith*, The Law of Motor Insurance, (2004), paras. 1-18 et seq.

38 *Von Hoffmann*, in: Staudinger, Art. 40 EGBGB para. 465; *Junker*, in: Münchener Kommentar BGB, Art. 18 paras. 24-25.

22 Thirdly, no dispute arises under Art. 18 Rome II if the law governing the tort as well as the law governing the insurance contract provide for a direct action. This will be the case in most EC cases because **Art. 3 of the 4th Motor Insurance Directive**[39] obliged every Member State to provide for a direct right of action against the insurer in cases of accidents occurring in a Member State.[40]

Article 19
Subrogation

Where a person (the creditor) has a non-contractual claim upon another (the debtor), and a third person has a duty to satisfy the creditor, or has in fact satisfied the creditor in discharge of that duty, the law which governs the third person's duty to satisfy the creditor shall determine whether, and the extent to which, the third person is entitled to exercise against the debtor the rights which the creditor had against the debtor under the law governing their relationship.

A. Overview

1 Art. 19 addresses the rights of third persons against the tortfeasor (debtor) if those third persons (*e.g.* an insurer) had a duty to compensate the victim (creditor), more specifically the question

39 2000/26/EC.

40 *Thorn*, in: Palandt, Art. 18 para. 3; cf. also *Dickinson*, paras. 14.105-14.106 who illustrates the too narrow implementation of the directive in England.

whether the third party is subrogated to the creditor's claim against the debtor. Under Art. 19, the question of whether and the extent to which the third person is entitled to claim reimbursement is governed by the law which obliged the third person to compensate the victim. In the case of an insurer, this law is the law that governs the insurance contract. However, the content of the third person's claim against the debtor is determined by the law applicable to the non-contractual obligation (see *infra* paras. 6-7).[1]

Art. 19 must be distinguished from Art. 20. Both provisions deal with multiple debtors and the recourse of one debtor against the other. However, Art. 19 deals with the situation that the third person is only secondarily liable, whereas Art. 20 requires several persons to be jointly liable for the same claim towards the victim.[2] 2

Art. 19 Rome II must be further distinguished from Arts. 14 and 15 Rome I. Whereas Art. 14 Rome I determines the law that governs *contractual agreements* to subrogate any and all claims (*i.e.* also of non-contractual claims), Art. 19 Rome II only deals with the *legal* subrogation of a non-contractual claim,[3] *i.e.* the substitution of the creditor by operation of law.[4] Article 15 Rome I contains the same rule as Art. 19 Rome II for the legal subrogation of contractual claims. 3

---

1 *Spickhoff*, in: Bamberger/Roth, Anh. zu Art. 42 EGBGB para. 125; *Junker*, JZ 2008, 169, 177.

2 For further details see Art. 20 paras. 7-8; cf. *Garcimartín Alférez*, EuLF 2007 I 77, 91; *Junker*, JZ 2008, 169, 177; *Junker*, in: Münchener Kommentar BGB, Art. 19 para. 13.

3 This comprises situations in which the paying person acquires the creditor's rights *(cessio legis)* or is entitled to enforce the creditor's right (subrogation), cf. *Dornis*, JPIL 2008, 237, 242.

4 It is submitted in this regard, that Art. 19 Rome II should rather be titled identically to Art. 15 Rome I: *Legal* Subrogation.

B. Detailed Commentary

I. A Duty to Satisfy the Creditor

4 Article 19 first requires that the third person has a **duty** to satisfy the creditor. Therefore, the provision is not applicable if the third person **voluntarily** (or by mistake) compensates the victim. In such cases, Art. 19 is not applicable, not even by way of analogy.[5] Rather, it is submitted, the applicable law must be determined according to the following rules: if the third person claims repayment from the (supposed) creditor, this claim is subject to the rules on unjust enrichment in Art. 10.[6] If the third person seeks recourse against the person liable, this claim could be characterised both as an unjust enrichment and as *negotiorum gestio*.[7] Therefore, Arts. 10 and 11 determine the applicable law respectively.[8]

II. The Scope of the Law of the Subrogation

5 Art. 19 designates the law that creates the duty to satisfy the creditor as the law that governs the subrogation. The law of the subrogation determines the following issues: firstly, the **requirements** under which and the **time** at which the victim's (creditor's) claim against the tortfeasor (debtor) is transferred by operation of law;[9]

---

5 This was suggested by Guiliano & Lagarde Report, OJ 1980 C 282/11, Art. 13 para. 2: "the same rule applies to these situations, but the court has a discretion in this respect". Opposing this view: *Dickinson*, para. 14.113.

6 *Dickinson*, para. 14.113; *P. Huber*, in: Anwaltskommentar BGB, Art. 38 EGBGB para. 40.

7 For the distinction between unjust enrichtment (Art. 10) and *negotiorum gestio* (Art. 11) see Art. 10 para. 8 and Art. 11 para. 7.

8 Art. 10 para. 30; *P. Huber*, in: Anwaltskommentar BGB, Art. 38 EGBGB para. 40.

9 *Junker*, in: Münchener Kommentar BGB, Art. 19 para. 17; *Junker*, JZ 2008, 169, 177; *Spickhoff*, in: Bamberger/Roth, Anh. zu Art. 42 EGBGB para. 125.

secondly, **prohibitions of recourse** against the debtor (*e.g.* an insurer might not be allowed to exercise the acquired rights against a member of the household of the insured);[10] thirdly, the **extent** to which the third party is subrogated to the victim's (creditor's) rights against the tortfeasor (debtor).[11]

III. The Scope of the Law of the Non-Contractual Obligation

6 The tortfeasor's (debtor's) interests are protected under Art. 19 in that the **content** and the **scope** of the non-contractual claim are not influenced by the law of the subrogation, but are instead exclusively governed by the law of the non-contractual obligation.[12]

7 The law of the non-contractual obligation governs all issues that might result in prejudice to the debtor's legal position.[13] These issues include the following questions: can the debtor invoke against the third person the substantive and procedural defences (*e.g.* rights of set-off) which the debtor could have invoked against the original creditor?[14] Can the debtor fulfil his/her obligation by satisfying the original creditor so long as the debtor has not been informed of the subrogation?[15] The law of the non-

10 Cf. Art. 10:101(3) and (4) Principles of European Insurance Contract Law; *Martiny*, in: Münchener Kommentar BGB, Art. 33 EGBGB para. 40; *Hausmann*, in: Staudinger, Art. 33 EGBGB para. 74.

11 Cf. Art. 1252 French Code Civil; Art. 1205 Italian Codice Civile; Guiliano & Lagarde Report, OJ 1980 C 282/11, Art. 13 para. 2; *Stone*, Ankara L. Rev. (2007) 95, 129.

12 *Thorn*, in: Palandt, Rom I, Art. 15 para. 4; *Heiss*, JBl 2007, 613, 638; *Garcimartín Alférez*, EuLF 2007 I 77, 91.

13 *Junker*, in: Münchener Kommentar BGB, Art. 19 para. 18; *Spickhoff*, in: Bamberger/Roth, Anh. zu Art. 42 EGBGB para. 125; *Hausmann*, in: Staudinger, Art. 33 EGBGB para. 69; *Martiny*, in: Münchener Kommentar BGB, Art. 33 EGBGB para. 43.

14 Cf. Art. III. – 5:116 DCFR.

15 Cf. Art. III. – 5:118 DCFR.

contractual obligation also determines whether the third party may assign its subrogated claims (cf. Art. 15(e)).

IV. Other Claims than Subrogation Claims?

8 According to its plain language, Art. 19 covers only situations in which the secondary liable person exercises the creditor's rights against the first debtor. This leaves situations ungoverned where the secondarily liable person invokes other claims, such as in particular a regular claim for compensation. It is submitted that in these situations Art. 19 should be applied by way of analogy.[16]

V. Council Regulation (EEC) No. 1408/71

9 **Art. 93 of EEC Regulation No. 1408/71** on the application of social insurance schemes[17] provides a special rule on the subrogation of a non-contractual claim to a social insurance institution. As *lex specialis*, it takes precedence over Art. 19 Rome II (*see* Art. 27 Rome II). The Regulation applies to several branches of social insurance such as sickness and maternity benefits, invalidity benefits, old-age benefits, survivor's benefits, workers' compensation benefits and occupational diseases or unemployment benefits (cf. Art. 4 Regulation No. 1408/71). The persons covered by the Regulation are employed or self-employed persons, students as well as their family members and survivors (Art. 2 Regulation No. 1408/71). The Regulation is applicable only if the case at hand has connections to more than one Member State.[18]

---

16 See Art. 20 para. 4.

17 Full title: Council Regulation (EC) No. 1408/71 on the application of social security schemes to employed persons, to self-employed persons and to members of their families moving within the Community.

18 ECJ, Case C-95/99 – *Khalil*; ECJ, Case C-98/99 – *Nasser*; ECJ, Case C-180/99 – *Addou* [2001] ECR I-7413, para. 69.

Article 20
Multiple liability

If a creditor has a claim against several debtors who are liable for the same claim, and one of the debtors has already satisfied the claim in whole or in part, the question of that debtor's right to demand compensation from the other debtors shall be governed by the law applicable to that debtor's non-contractual obligation towards the creditor.

A. General/System/Overview

I. Relationship to Art. 15(a)

1 If two or more tortfeasors are responsible for the same injury, the victim may not receive full compensation from each tortfeasor separately, since the result would be an overcompensated victim. Therefore, some legal systems restrict the victim to receiving from each tortfeasor only a partial payment proportional to that tortfeasor's share of fault for the victim's injury (**several liability**). Most systems, however, subject joint tortfeasors to **joint (and several) liability**: each tortfeasor is jointly liable for the entire judge-

ment, and the victim may choose freely the tortfeasor from which he demands (full) payment.[1] As a result, the victim may (and often does) choose to sue the financially stronger tortfeasor. Under Art. 15(a), the law applicable to the non-contractual obligation between the victim and each tortfeasor determines whether liability is joint and several or merely several.[2] If the law applicable under 15(a) provides for joint liability, one tortfeasor will usually wish, after paying the full judgment for the victim, to claim contribution from the other tortfeasor. The question of what law decides the existence and extent of a contribution claim is governed by Art. 20.

2 Joint liabity of two debtors is most likely to occur in the field of torts/delicts (in particular in traffic accidents). Joint responsibility for an injury is less likely, but still possible, in the fields of *culpa in contrahendo* (*e.g.* if two business partners break off negotiations with the victim at the same time) and *negotiorum gestio* (*e.g.* if the party seeking compensation for its expenses acted in connection with the affairs of two persons). It is least likely to arise in claims for unjust enrichment. Throughout the remainder of this discussion, therefore, the explanations will focus on tort claims.

II. Relationship to Art. 19

3 The scope of Art. 20 must be distinguished from the scope of Art. 19. Both provisions have different scenarios in mind. **Art. 19** covers situations in which two elements are present: first, there is an (alleged) non-contractual claim by the creditor (C) against the debtor (B), with a third person (T) being bound (by law or by contract) to step in for the debtor[3] (secondary liability);

---

1 *Stoll*, FS Müller-Freienfels, 631, 640 et seq.; cf. Art. III. – 4:102(1) and Art. III. – 4:103(2) DCFR.

2 See Art. 15 para. 12.

3 Such as *e.g.* the tortfeasor's insurance company which the victim has sued directly under Art. 18 or the victim's health insurance that has paid a hospital bill.

and, secondly, the third person which has satisfied the claim now wants to exercise against the debtor the rights or the claim that the creditor (originally) had against him[4] (subrogation or cessio legis[5]). In contrast, **Art. 20** applies to situations in which two or more persons are directly and jointly (rather than successively with one being the primary and the other being only the secondary debtor) liable for the same claim[6] (*e.g.* in cases of multiple tortfeasors), irrespective of whether the paying person demands compensation or wants to exercise a subrogation right against the primary debtor.[7]

This leaves those situations ungoverned in which a secondarily liable person does not exercise the creditor's rights against the primary debtor (subrogation claim or *cessio legis*, as envisaged by Art. 19) but rather makes an independent compensation claim against the primarily liable person. On the basis of the assumptions made above, a purely technical analysis would lead to a gap: Art. 20 would not apply, as it requires joint direct liability, and Art. 19 – which generally does cover secondary liability – would not apply because it only applies if the remedy sought is subrogation or *cessio legis*. Three possibilities to deal with this dilemma may be considered: An analogous application of Art. 19, an analogous application of Art. 20 and an application of Arts. 10 or 11 (*i.e.* a classification of the claim as one for unjust enrichment or *negotiorum gestio*). It is submitted that an **analogous application of Art. 19** seems preferable as this prevents a fragmentation of law and the undesirable result that the law made applicable under the subrogation rule in Art. 19 does not actually provide for subrogation (but only for compensation) whereas the law applicable un- 4

4 *Dornis*, JPIL 2008, 237, 242; cf. Art. 19 para. 8.

5 This means that Art. 19 applies only for situations in which the paying person acquires the creditor's rights (*cessio legis*) or is entitled to enforce the creditor's right (subrogation), cf. Dornis, JPIL 2008, 237, 242.

6 See in detail *infra* para. 7; cf. *Garcimartín Alférez*, EuLF, 2007 I 77, 91; *Dornis*, JPIL 2008, 237, 242; *Junker*, JZ 2008, 169, 177.

7 *Dornis*, JPIL 2008, 237, 243.

der the compensation rule in Art. 20 – *vice versa* – only provides for subrogation, but not for compensation.[8]

III. Relationship to Art. 16 Rome I

5 Article 16 Rome I provides a rule that is equivalent, but not identical, to Art. 20 (for differences, see *infra* para. 18). Therefore, when one debtor is liable to a plaintiff under a non-contractual obligation while the other one is liable under a contractual obligation, a court must decide whether Art. 16 Rome I or Art. 20 Rome II governs their rights of contribution. In the Author's opinion, the general principle underlying both provisions requires that the nature of the obligation of the debtor who satisfies the creditor is dispositive of whether Art. 16 Rome I or Art. 20 Rome II applies. In short: if the debtor with a contractual obligation satisfies the creditor, Art. 16 Rome I applies; if the debtor with a non-contractual obligation does so, Art. 20 Rome II applies.

IV. Relationship to Arts. 10 and 11

6 A claim for contribution that one jointly liable tortfeasor pursues against another is governed exclusively by the law made applicable under Art. 20 – regardless of whether the claim arises from that law's actions for *negotiorium gestio* or unjust enrichment. Article 20 thus constitutes a *lex specialis* that prevails over the *lex generalis* provided in Arts. 10 and 11.[9]

---

8 Furthermore, an application of Art. 20 may be not feasible as there may not always be a claim of the creditor against the secondary debtor.

9 *Dornis*, JPIL 2008, 237, 244.

B. Detailed Commentary

I. Prerequisites

1. "… Several Debtors that Are Liable for the Same Claim …"

Article 20 requires that several debtors "are liable for the same claim." This language must not be interpreted too restrictively: it is not necessary for the application of Art. 20 that each tortfeasor is liable to a plaintiff under the same legal grounds. Especially considering that such a common legal ground does not exist where the tortfeasors are liable under the laws of different countries, a narrow interpretation of Art. 20 would render the provision meaningless.[10] Therefore, whether debtors are liable for the "same claim" should **depend on factual rather than legal factors**. To apply Art. 20, it suffices that both tortfeasors are liable for (*i.e.* have caused) the **same damage** – even if the debtors are liable on different legal grounds or under different domestic laws.[11] 7

Further, Art. 20 should apply – at least by way of analogy – even if the victim has **no claim against the second "debtor"** at all. Many legal systems allow the first debtor to claim contribution from the second debtor even if the latter is not liable to the victim in the first place.[12] For such cases, a court must determine the law applicable to the first debtor's contribution claim, and in the Author's opinion, governing law should be the law made applicable by Art. 20 (see for the legal consequences *infra* para. 13). Not to apply Art. 20 in such cases would require finding the law gov- 8

---

10 *Junker*, in: Münchener Kommentar BGB, Art. 20 para. 10. If both debtors are liable under the same law, contribution claims are unlikely to be subject to any conflict of laws unless the tortfeasors have a common habitual residence that is not shared by the victim.

11 *Dornis*, JPIL 2008, 237, 239. This is in line with the approach taken by Art. III. – 4:103(2) and (3) DCFR.

12 See for an example of such a scenario *infra* para. 15.

erning the first debtor's contribution claim against the second "debtor" in another rule of the Rome II Regulation – possibly under Art. 10 under the argument that the second debtor has been unjustly enriched.[13] Such a solution, however, is highly undesirable due to the fragmentation of law and legal uncertainty it would generate.

2. "... One of the Debtors Has Already Satisfied the Claim in Whole or in Part ..."

9 Article 20 designates as law applicable to contribution claims the law that governed the plaintiff's claim against the debtor who has paid him. Obviously, this law can be determined only after one tortfeasor has already (at least partially) satisfied the creditor. While in most legal systems applying this rule leads to no difficulties (because contribution is available only after the creditor has been satisfied), some legal systems (*e.g.* the English Civil Liability (Contribution) Act 1978) provide for a sort of "recourse in advance." Under such rules, an obligation of each co-debtor to contribute towards the common liability may arise before one of the debtors has undertaken to satisfy the creditor.[14] In the author's opinion, an analogy to Art. 20 lies as long as the debtor that demands contribution from the other debtors will most likely be the one that satisfies the creditor – *e.g.* because he is the tortfeasor being sued by the creditor.[15]

---

13 *Dicey, Morris & Collins*, para. 34-011.

14 See in more detail: *Dickinson*, paras. 14.119 et seq.

15 *Junker*, in: Münchener Kommentar BGB, Art. 20 para. 12; – contra: *Dickinson*, para. 14-119. It should be noted, that even if one was not to apply Art. 20, the English courts under the Rome II Regulation must not continue their practice (as *e.g.* in *Petroleo Brasiliero v Mellitus Shipping* [2001] 2 Lloyd's Rep 203; cf. *Dicey, Morris & Collins*, para. 34.011 and 34.051) to apply the Civil Liability (Contribution) Act whenever the defendant/respondent is within the jurisdiction of the (English) court: Not applying Art. 20 would lead to the consequence that the applicable law was to be found under another rule of the Rome II Regulation – a

II. Legal Consequences

1. General Outline

Article 20 provides that when one debtor fulfills his obligation towards the creditor, his contribution claim against the second debtor is governed by the same law that governed the obligation he fulfilled. This **"payer's law principle"** hopes to incentivize each tortfeasor to be the first to pay by ensuring that the tortfeasor's "own law" applies to his contribution claim.[16] However, it seems arguable whether a) the paying tortfeasor will actually benefit from an application of his "own law," and whether b) a tortfeasor will indeed care about the law applicable to a contribution claim when deciding whether he should pay the victim.[17] 10

When **three or more debtors** exist, Art. 20 applies to all contribution claims between the debtors. For example, assume that three debtors are equally at fault and one debtor satisfies the creditor in the full amount. When, under the law applicable to the contribution claim, the paying debtor may claim more than 1/3 of the total amount from the second debtor (*e.g.* because the third debtor is not able to pay), the second debtor may wish to claim contribution from the third debtor (*e.g.* after it again becomes solvent). This second contribution claim is also governed by the law that applied to the creditor's claim against the first debtor. The reasoning that allows extending the law that governs the first creditor-debtor claim to all debtor-debtor contribution claims is simple: if debtor 1 satisfies the creditor, he becomes creditor of a contribution claim against debtors 2 and 3. Under Art. 20, these contribution claims are governed by the same law that was applicable to the creditor-debtor 1-claim. If debtor 2 then satisfies 11

---

recourse to national conflict law is barred in any event. For possible alternatives to Art. 20 see *Dickinson*, para. 14-119.

16 Cf. *Hamburg Group for PIL*, 67 RabelsZ (2003) 1, 49 seq.

17 For elaborate criticism regarding the legislature's decision to follow the "payer's law principle," see *Dornis*, JPIL 2008, 237, 252 seq. and 264.

debtor 1's contribution claim, Art. 20 subjects his contribution claim against debtor 3 to the law that was applicable to debtor 1's contribution claim against debtor 2.

12 When **two out of three or more debtors** pay the creditor a sum that exceeds their fault- or causation-based share of liability, these debtors become independent 'first debtors' with contribution claims against all other debtors. The contribution claims of each excess-paying debtor must therefore be analysed independently under Art. 20, which may result in each debtor's contribution claims being governed by different national laws.[18]

2. Scope of the Law Applicable

2.1. Exclusion of Liability of the Second Debtor

13 Despite its straightforward wording, Art. 20 may lead to difficulties if the second "debtor" is exempt from liability under the law that is applicable to his obligation towards the creditor.[19] An example: on vacation, father and son, both residents of country A, are cycling on a curvy road on the coast of country B. The father makes a sudden mistake, causing a motorist (a resident of country B) who was attempting to pass the two cyclists to swerve, as a result of which the motorist loses control of his vehicle and crashes into the son. The son sues the motorist for damages and receives a judgment for 15,000 € under the law of country B. The motorist now claims contribution from the father. Under the law of country B, the father is jointly liable to his son for the full judgement of 15,000 €. However, if under Art. 4(2), a court applied the law of country A[20] the father has no liability towards his

---

[18] Cf. *Dornis*, JPIL 2008, 237, 266.

[19] For the question of whether Art. 20 is applicable in such cases see *supra* para. 8. For an elaborate analysis of the parties' expectations cf. *Dornis*, JPIL 2008, 237, 272 et seq., who *de lege feranda* demands the addition of a rule similar to that of Art. 16(2) Rome I (p. 277).

[20] For critical remarks in this regard see *supra* Art. 4 paras. 66 et seq.

son because the family law of country A excludes familial liability for negligence.[21]

14 A situation such as the one just illustrated may well occur also if only one country's law governs the son's claims against both father and motorist: one of multiple tortfeasors may not be liable towards the victim because of a legal or contractual exemption from liability.

15 Within domestic legal systems, three different options exist to resolve this problem at the contribution stage. Option 1 is to strictly enforce the exclusion of liability and thus bar contribution claims against the exempt debtor. This option clearly favours the debtor whose liability is exempted at the expense of the debtor that has satisfied the creditor. Option 2 is to ignore the exemption of liability at the contribution stage and consequently allow contribution claims as if the second debtor had been fully liable towards the creditor. As the direct opposite of option 1, this option clearly favours the debtor who has satisfied the creditor at the expense of the debtor whose liability is exempted. Option 3 is a variation of the second option: the non-exempt debtor maintains his contribution action against the exempt debtor, but the exempt debtor is granted a claim against the creditor in the amount he must pay his co-debtor. In this case, the benefit to the exempt debtor exists at the expense of the creditor. Option 3 also generates the same result as is reached under a regime of separate liability – a fourth option not situated at the contribution stage but possibly available under the law applicable to the obligation of the first debtor towards the creditor.[22]

---

21 Such an exclusion of liability is governed by the designated law, see Art. 15 para. 9.

22 See *supra* para. 1. The difference between options 3 and 4 – which may be essential in practice – lies in the different allocation of the insolvency risk: under option 3, the non-exempt debtor bears the risk of the exempt debtor's insolvency, and the exempt debtor bears the risk of the creditor's insolvency.

16 If the problem of an exempt co-tortfeasor occurs on an internatonal level, the first question that must be answered is whether a choice between options 1, 2, or 3 will be made at the level of conflict rules or whether the decision will be left to the applicable national law.

17 One could argue that the wording of Art. 20 already resolves the question: since it requires for its application that multiple debtors are liable for the same claim, it applies only when the creditor can maintain a claim against the second debtor. This approach, however, is not on point. Not applying Art. 20 to cases where one debtor is exempt does not bar a contribution claim against the second debtor. Article 20 is merely a conflict rule, not a material provision. Instead, a refusal to apply Art. 20 simply means that the law applicable to any contribution actions must be determined on another basis.

18 The Rome I Regulation, in contrast, appears to establish a solution to the exempt-debtor problem at the stage of conflict rules. **Article 16(2) Rome I** contains the same rule as Art. 20 Rome II, but with the following additive: "the other debtors may rely on the defences they had against the creditor to the extent allowed by the law governing their obligations towards the creditor." Such a rule clearly establishes option 1. As is always the case when a provision is set forth in one set of rules but not in another, the question arises whether, *e contrario*, mere absence in the latter rules entails exclusion of the provision or whether the provision expresses a general principle that should apply by way of analogy. In the author's opinion, neither argument fully convinces. The *e contrario* argument does not address why cases of multiple liability should be treated differently under the Rome Regulations. The general principle argument fails to answer why EU legislators prepared two *parallel* regimes but inserted *different* rules if they intended to treat contribution identically under the two regulations.[23]

[23] In particular when considering that the difference was pointed out and criticised in legal literature during the legislation process, see *e.g. Ham-*

19 If courts refuse to apply Art. 16(2) Rome I's solution under Art. 20, they will face the consequence that the problem of exempt debtors is not regulated at the level of conflict rules but is left to be solved by applicable domestic law. If the applicable law provides for option 3, the exempt debtor's 'claw-back' claim against the creditor should also be governed by the same law as the non-exempt debtor's contribution claim against the exempt debtor. This is the result of applying Art. 20 to this "second recourse" as well.[24]

2.2. Different Measurement of Damages

20 The same reasoning that governs exempt debtors also applies to situations in which a second debtor's liability is not excluded but, due to the application of a different law, is lower than his co-debtor's liability. In the cycling example from above, such a situation would arise if the two cyclists were unrelated but still residents of the same country. In such a case the law of country B (under which the motorist is liable) may provide 15,000 € as compensation for pain and suffering while the law of country A (under which the father is liable) merely offers statutorily-set compensation of 5,000 €.

21 Here, an analogous application of Art. 16(2) Rome I is confronted with another difficulty: the provision allows the second debtor to invoke the *defences* that it has against the creditor, against the first debtor; it is hard to argue that a lower measurement of damages constitutes such a defence.

---

burg Group for PIL, 67 RabelsZ (2003) 1, 49; cf. *Junker*, in: Münchener Kommentar BGB, Art. 18 para. 15; *Dornis*, JPIL 2008, 237, 241.

24 See *infra* para. 11.

3. Recourse and Choice of Law

22 The creditor and the first debtor cannot – at the expense of the second debtor – choose a law that would permit a contribution action against the second debtor when that debtor is not liable to the creditor in the first place.[25] Article 14(1)(2) prevents such a misuse of the freedom to choose applicable law: a choice of law may not "prejudice the rights of third parties."[26] In such cases, the law applies that would govern the creditor's claim against the first debtor if not for the choice of law agreement.

23 In contrast, a choice of law agreement that designates as applicable a law under which the first debtor must pay the creditor in full, but has no right of contribution, is effective under Art. 20.

24 The law that governs contribution claims is itself subject to Art. 14. Thus, joint tortfeasors may agree on what law governs questions of contribution. Again, however, Art. 14(1)(2) bars any choice of law to the extent that it prejudices the creditor's interests. Such prejudice may generally be presumed where the tortfeasors' chosen law allows for contribution prior to payment of the creditor while the law designated by Art. 20 follows the principle of *nemo subrogate contra se*. Allowing contribution before compensation risks that the second debtor's contribution payment exhausts his assets and that the creditor cannot enforce his claim against him – which the creditor may wish to do if he is not fully compensated by the first debtor.[27]

---

[25] *Dickinson*, para. 14.116.

[26] Cf. Art. 14 para. 31.

[27] Cf. *Dornis*, JPIL 2008, 237, 258.

Article 21
Formal validity

A unilateral act intended to have legal effect and relating to a non-contractual obligation shall be formally valid if it satisfies the formal requirements of the law governing the non-contractual obligation in question or the law of the country in which the act is performed.

A. Overview

Art. 21 is an alternative conflict of laws rule *in favorem negotii*: a unilateral act is legally valid if it satisfies the formal requirements of either the law of the non-contractual obligation or the law of the country where the act is performed *(lex loci actus)*. 1

The rule is inspired by Art. 9 Rome Convention[1] and is very similar to today's Art. 11(3) Rome I, which governs the formal validity of unilateral acts intended to have legal effect in relation to a contract. However, Art. 11(3) Rome I goes even further in promoting the formal validity of unilateral acts and provides a third alternative law: the law of the country where the person who has acted was resident at the time the act was performed. It is not quite clear why Art. 21 Rome II did not include this third alternative as well. 2

B. Unilateral Acts

Art. 21 is of little practical relevance.[2] It (theoretically) applies to unilateral acts which create, change, transfer, extinguish or bar the enforcement of a non-contractual obligation.[3] It should be noted that the term "unilateral act" is **interpreted autonomously** 3

---

1 COM(2003) 427 final, p. 26.

2 *Dicey, Morris & Collins*, para. S 35-268; COM(2003) 427 final, p. 26; *Junker*, in: Münchener Kommentar, Art. 21 para. 6.

3 *Spickhoff*, in: Bamberger/Roth, Anh. zu Art. 42 EGBGB para. 129.

and that legal acts can be considered "unilateral" even though domestic legal systems classify them as contractual.[4] The Giuliano & Lagarde Report on the Rome Convention – for example – treats the acknowledgement and remission of a debt as a unilateral legal act.[5] For all other legal acts that cannot be classified as unilateral but as contractual, Art. 11(1) and (2) Rome I determine the law that governs formal validity. These articles also apply to the formal validity of a choice of law under Art. 14 Rome II.[6]

C. Formal Validity

4 The alternative conflicts rule in Art. 21 is restricted to formal validity requirements, *i.e.* provisions that subject the legal effectiveness of an expression of will to a particular external manifestation.[7] In contrast, substantive validity requirements are governed solely by the law of the non-contractual obligation to which the unilateral act relates.[8]

Article 22
Burden of proof

1. The law governing a non-contractual obligation under this Regulation shall apply to the extent that, in matters of non-contractual obligations, it contains rules which raise presumptions of law or determine the burden of proof.

---

4 *Spickhoff*, in: Bamberger/Roth, Anh. zu Art. 42 EGBGB para. 129.

5 Guiliano & Lagarde Report, OJ 1980 C 282/11, Art. 9 para. I.A.1.; – *contra*: *Junker*, in: Münchener Kommentar BGB, Art. 21 para. 5.

6 Art. 14 para. 20.

7 Guiliano & Lagarde Report, OJ 1980 C 282/11, Art. 9 para. I.A.2.

8 Pursuant to the principle that all questions, from the creation to the extinction of an obligation, shall be governed by the same law (*statut unique*), *Magnus*, in: Staudinger, Einl. zu Arts. 27-37 EGBGB para. A 62.

2. Acts intended to have legal effect may be proved by any mode of proof recognised by the law of the forum or by any of the laws referred to in Article 21 under which that act is formally valid, provided that such mode of proof can be administered by the forum.

A. Overview

1 In principle, questions of evidence are matters of procedural law, *i.e.* matters governed by the *lex fori*.[1] This principle is expressed in Art. 1(3) which states that the Regulation does not apply to evidence and procedure. However, the general rule in Art. 1(3) applies "without prejudice" to Art. 22.

2 Art. 22(1) stipulates that not the *lex fori* but the law of the non-contractual obligation shall govern the burden of proof and presumptions of law. Even though rules which raise presumptions of law or determine the burden of proof are closely connected with questions of evidence, they are in truth questions of substance.[2]

---

1 COM(2003) 427 final, p. 26.

2 Guiliano & Lagarde Report, OJ 1980 C 282/11, Art. 14 para. A; *Dickinson*, para. 14.82; *Garcimartín Alférez*, EuLF 2007 I 77, 91. Note that procedural presumptions are not covered by Art. 22(1), see *infra* para. 7.

3 The significance of Art. 22(2) is twofold: Firstly, the provision stresses that the modes of proof are generally subject to the *lex fori*. Secondly, an exception is made with regard to the formal validity of acts according to Art. 21. The formal validity may also be proved by any mode of proof recognised under the law affirming the formal validity pursuant to Art. 21. Yet, the exception is subject to a counter-exception: the courts do not need to accept any mode of proof which they cannot administer.

4 Art. 22 Rome II is inspired by Art. 14 Rome Convention and is almost identical to today's Art. 18 Rome I.

B. Detailed Commentary

I. Rules which Raise Presumptions of Law or Determine the Burden of Proof (Art. 22(1) Rome II)

1. General

5 Rules on the burden of proof determine first who has to submit evidence concerning a fact and secondly who has to bear the failure to provide evidence. **Presumptions of law** relieve the party in whose favour they operate from the necessity of producing any evidence.[3] "Presumptions of law" in the sense of the provision are not merely codified presumptions but include those which have been developed in case law. Furthermore, Art. 22(1) applies to rebuttable as well as conclusive presumptions.[4] Whereas a conclusive presumption cannot be rebutted in spite of evidence to the contrary, a rebuttable presumption only leads to a shifting of the burden of proof. The question whether a rebuttable pre-

---

3 Guiliano & Lagarde Report, OJ 1980 C 282/11, Art. 14 para. A.

4 *Junker*, in: Münchener Kommentar BGB, Art. 22 para. 5; *Spickhoff*, in: Bamberger/Roth, Anh. zu Art. 42 EGBGB para. 131; *Thorn*, in: Palandt, Art. 18 para. 3.

sumption has indeed been rebutted is for the *lex fori* to decide because it is a question of the standard of proof.

An example for a presumption of law is section 2(1) of the UK Misrepresentation Act 1967.[5] According to this provision, the victim of a misrepresentation is relieved from the burden of proving fraudulent behaviour of the tortfeasor. He can recover the loss resulting from a misrepresentation unless the person who has made the misrepresentation can rebut the presumption of fraudulent behaviour and prove that he had reasonable ground to believe that the represented facts were true. An example from German law is § 831(1) BGB: an employer is liable for a tort committed by the employee unless the employer can prove that he did not act negligently in appointing and supervising the employee. Many more examples can be found in (medical) product liability laws[6] or in Environmental Liability Acts[7]. 6

2. Procedural Presumtions Are not Covered by Art. 22(1) Rome II

Art. 22(1) does not apply to **procedural presumptions**. This is expressed in the wording insofar as it only refers to presumptions "in matters of non-contractual obligations". Therefore, Art. 22(1) does not apply *e.g.* to a rule presuming an admission of facts by one party to a civil action in case of silence of the other party.[8] The same is true for an evidential rule that leads to a shifting of the burden of proof if a party suppresses or manipulates evidence and thereby precludes the other party from proving a certain fact (*Beweisvereitelung*/evidentiary frustra- 7

---

5 *Dickinson*, para. 14.83.

6 *E.g.* Art. 7 EC Products Liability Directive; Art. VI. – 3:204 DCFR.

7 *E.g.* § 6 German Environmental Liability Act.

8 Such rule can be for example found in Art. 11.4 ALI/UNIDROIT Principles of Civil Procedure or § 138(3) German ZPO.

tion).[9] Such procedural presumptions are only applicable if they are part of the *lex fori*.[10]

3. Presumtions of Fact Are not Covered by Art. 22(1) Rome II

8 Art. 22(2) is restricted to presumptions of law and thus subjects **presumptions of fact** to the *lex fori*.[11] Factual presumptions are based on the judge's experience of life or scientific rules.[12] They are closely connected to the evaluation of evidence which is undisputedly subject to the *lex fori*.[13] Presumptions of fact do not shift the evidential or legal burden but are nothing more than examples of circumstantial evidence.[14]

9 Sometimes it is difficult to decide whether a legal concept raises a presumption of law or a presumption of fact. In German Law, it is disputed how to characterize the so-called ***Anscheinsbeweis*** (*prima facie* evidence). This concept means that a judge takes into account his general experience of life and from fact A which has been proven assumes the existence of fact B which is disputed.[15] As an example, from a rear end collision German courts assume that the driver who hit the back of the car negligently caused the accident.[16] Some authors argue that *de facto* a *prima facie* evidence leads to a shifting of the burden of proof and that it is therefore to be treated

---

9 *Thole*, IPRax 2010, 285, 288.

10 Guiliano & Lagarde Report, OJ 1980 C 282/11, Art. 14 para. A; *Garcimartín Alférez*, EuLF 2007 I 77, 91.

11 *Morse*, Yearbook of European Law 1982, 107, 156.

12 *Schack*, Internationales Zivilverfahrensrecht (2010), para. 745.

13 *Spickhoff*, in: Bamberger/Roth, Anh. zu Art. 42 EGBGB para. 132; *Thorn*, in: Palandt, Art. 18 para. 4.

14 *Keane*, The Modern Law of Evidence (2008), pp. 655 et seq.

15 *Rosenberg/Schwab/Gottwald*, Zivilprozessrecht (2010), § 113 paras. 16 et seq.

16 Bundesgerichtshof (Germany) 18 October 1988 – VI ZR 223/87, NJW-RR 1989, 670, 671.

as a presumption of law.[17] In the example, the driver has to prove that he observed the inter-vehicle distance. Despite this similarity with presumptions of law, the German *Bundesgerichtshof* and many authors characterize a *prima facie* evidence as a presumption of fact.[18] The concept of *prima facie* evidence is based on the judge's experience of the typical history of events. There is a further difference between presumptions of law and *prima facie* evidence: The former pursue a certain policy, *i.e.* to benefit the party who is simply unable to prove a fact (*e.g.* in product liability cases). The concept of *prima facie* evidence is neutral in value, a certain fact is presumed because it is the most likely explanation.[19]

Further difficulties arise with regard to the Common Law notion 10
of ***res ipsa loquitur***. It provides that negligence on the part of the defendant is presumed if the cause of the harm belongs to the defendant's sphere of control.[20] There is, however, no consistency in classifying the notion as a presumption of fact or as a presumption of law, *i.e.* an evidential presumption or a persuasive presumption.[21] Support can be found for each category in case law.[22] Under Art. 22(1) an autonomous interpretation has to be

---

17 *Junker*, in: Münchener Kommentar BGB, Art. 22 paras. 8-9; *von Hoffmann*, in: Soergel, Art. 32 para. 77; *Magnus*, in: Staudinger, Art. 32 EGBGBG para. 107; *Spellenberg*, in Münchener Kommentar BGB, Art. 32 EGBGB para. 156; *Geimer*, Internationales Zivilprozessrecht (2009), para. 2290.

18 Bundesgerichtshof (Germany) 4 October 1984 – I ZR 112/82, NJW 1985, 554, 554; *Thole*, IPRax 2010, 285, 287; *Schack*, Internationales Zivilverfahrensrecht (2010), para. 746; *von Bar*, Internationales Privatrecht, Volume 2 (1991), para. 552; *Leible*, in: Anwaltskommentar BGB, Art. 32 EGBGB para. 53.

19 Cf. for details *Thole*, IPRax 2010, 285, 287.

20 Court of Exchequer Chamber (England and Wales) 7 Febrary 1865, *Scott v. London & St Katharine Docks Co* (1865) 3 H & C 596, 601.

21 *Keane*, The Modern Law of Evidence (2008), pp. 669 et seq.

22 *Res ipsa loquitur* as a presumption of fact: *Langham v The Governors of Wellingborough School and Fryer* [1932] 101 LJKB 513, 518; *res ipsa loquitur*

applied. Criteria for determining whether *res ipsa loquitur* constitutes a presumption of law or fact are: If the presumption is based on the judge's experience or scientific rules, this militates in favour of a presumption of fact. If the principle intends to benefit the party who is simply unable to prove a fact, this favours the assumption of a presumption of law.

II. Available Modes of Proof (Art. 22(2) Rome II)

11 Generally the modes of proof are subject to the *lex fori*. Art. 22(2) contains an exception **(1.)** and a counter-exception **(2.)** to this rule.

1. Applicable Laws

12 The formal validity of acts intended to have legal effect may be proved by any mode of proof recognised either by the *lex fori* or by any of the laws referred to in Art. 21. This liberalism originates from France and the Benelux countries where it is known as ***maximum des preuves***.[23] The reference to Art. 21 shows that Art. 22(2) only applies to unilateral acts. Art. 18(2) Rome I provides for the same rule for contracts. These rules intend to protect the parties' legitimate expectations that they can prove a legal act according to the law under which it is formally valid.[24] Moreover, Art. 22(2) Rome II is in conformity with the general tendency to restrict the formal invalidity of legal acts *(in favorem negotii)*.[25] All in all, there are three laws from which the admissible modes of

---

as an evidential presumption: High Court (England and Wales) 16 May 1933, *The Kite* [1933] P 154, 170; *res ipsa loquitur* as a persuasive presumption: Court of Appeal (England and Wales) 9 July 1948, *Barkway v South Wales Transport Co Ltd* [1948] 2 All E.R. 460, 471.

23 Guiliano & Lagarde Report, OJ 1980 C 282/11, Art. 14 para. B; Cour de cassation (France) 12 February 1963, *Ruffini v Sylvestre*, Rev. crit. dr. int. priv. 1964, 121.

24 Guiliano & Lagarde Report, OJ 1980 C 282/11, Art. 14 para. B.

25 See Art. 21 para. 1 and *Magnus*, in: Staudinger, Art. 32 EGBGB para. 108.

proof may result: the *lex fori* or any of the two laws designated by Art. 21. Under the latter provision, the law under which the act is formally valid is either the law of the non-contractual obligation *(lex causae)* or the law of the country in which the act is performed *(lex loci actus)*. If the legal act is only valid according to one of the laws, only the modes of proof of this law are available as an alternative to prove the formal validity.[26] The application of the law governing the formal validity of a legal act may lead to more liberal requirements with regard to the modes of proof but may never lead to stricter requirements compared to the *lex fori*.[27] It is difficult to think of a situation where Art. 22(2) will be of relevance. One might think of a recognition or remission of a debt which may only be proved by written evidence under the *lex fori* but may be proved by witnesses according to the *lex loci actus* or *lex causae*.

2. Administrable by the Forum

The courts of the Member States cannot be compelled to accept a mode of proof which they are unable to administer or are not allowed to administer for public policy reasons.[28] As examples for modes of proof which are not admitted in some Member States, *Giuliano* and *Lagarde* name affidavits, the testimony of a party or common knowledge.[29] A further example from German law is a summary proceeding which is exclusively based on documents *(Urkundenprozess)*. Here no oral evidence is permitted even if the *lex loci actus* or the *lex causae* provide for it.[30] 13

---

26 Guiliano & Lagarde Report, OJ 1980 C 282/11, Art. 14 para. B.

27 *Martiny*, in: Reithmann/Martiny (eds.), Internationales Vertragsrecht (2010), para. 289; *Magnus*, in: Staudinger, Art. 32 EGBGB para. 109.

28 *Spickhoff*, in: Bamberger/Roth, Anh. zu Art. 42 EGBGB para. 133.

29 Guiliano & Lagarde Report, OJ 1980 C 282/11, Art. 14 para. B.

30 *Magnus*, in: Staudinger, Art. 32 EGBGB para. 109; *Martiny*, in: Reithmann/Martiny (eds.), Internationales Vertragsrecht (2010), para. 290.

Chapter VI
Other Provisions

Article 23
Habitual residence

1. For the purposes of this Regulation, the habitual residence of companies and other bodies, corporate or unincorporated, shall be the place of central administration. Where the event giving rise to the damage occurs, or the damage arises, in the course of operation of a branch, agency or any other establishment, the place where the branch, agency or any other establishment is located shall be treated as the place of habitual residence.
2. For the purposes of this Regulation, the habitual residence of a natural person acting in the course of his or her business activity shall be his or her principal place of business.

A. Overview

Contrary to the Brussels I Regulation, the Rome II Regulation employs the concept of habitual residence instead of domicile. The former is the more flexible criterion and is generally accepted in conflict of laws matters (cf. Art. 4(2), 5(2), (3) Rome Convention).[1] 1

Habitual residence is used in several instances as a connecting factor for the law applicable to non-contractual obligations. Arts. 4(2), 10(2), 11(2) and 12(2) lit b Rome II point to the law of the common habitual residence *(lex domicilii communis)* as an exception to other general conflicts rules. In cases of product liability, the habitual residence of the victim is a primary connecting factor (Art. 5(1)1 lit (a) and Art. 5(1)2). 2

Contrary to what one might expect, Art. 23 does not offer a comprehensive definition of habitual residence. Instead, the provision states when the concept of habitual residence is replaced by the notion of central administration (Art. 23(1)1), location of an establishment (Art. 23(1)2) and principal place of business (Art. 23(2)). 3

B. Detailed Commentary

I. Habitual Residence of Companies and Other Bodies

1. Place of Central Administration (Art. 23(1)1 Rome II)

Companies and other bodies – corporate and incorporated – habitually reside at the place of their central administration. The notion of a "place of central administration" should be inter- 4

1 COM(2003) 427 final, p. 27. Describing the growing importance of habitual residence as a connecting factor in Private International Law: *Rogerson*, 49 ICLQ (2000) 86.

preted in accordance with **Art. 60(1)(b) Brussels I Regulation,**[2] under which the place of central administration constitutes one alternative for the domicile of a company. Under jurisprudence interpreting Art. 60(1)(b), the criteria for determining a person's "central administration" (in French: *administration centrale*, in German: *Hauptverwaltung*, in Dutch: *hoofdvestiging*)[3] are: where are the fundamental management decisions made, and where is control over the company exercised?[4] Art. 23(1)1 designates the so-called "real seat" of administration as a person's habitual residence, in contrast to the mere "statutory seat" or "place of incorporation/registration."[5]

5 In a German case on Art. 60 Brussels I, an English limited company with its registered office in Birmingham was held to have its central administration in Germany even though it only maintained a branch office there. For the court, the decisive fact was that the entire company was managed and controlled through the German branch.[6] In another German case, the court held that a company does not even need to have a registered branch or conduct its main business at the place of central administration.[7] As an example: a company with a registered office in Jersey that is *de facto* managed by its sole shareholder from his/her home in Rome has its central administration in Italy.

---

2 Cf. Recital (7); *Thorn*, in: Palandt, Rom I, Art. 19 para. 2.

3 *Vlas*, in: Mankowski/Magnus (eds.), Brussels I Regulation (2007), Art. 60 para. 5.

4 *Plender & Wilderspin*, para. 3-004; cf. for the very similar English concept *Dicey, Morris & Collins*, para. 30-005.

5 *Vlas*, in: Mankowski/Magnus (eds.), Brussels I Regulation (2007), Art. 60 para. 5.

6 Bundesgerichtshof (Germany) 27 June 2007 – XII ZB 114/06, EuZW 2007, 580.

7 Bundesarbeitsgericht (Germany), 23 January 2008 – 5 AZR 60/07, NJW 2008, 2797.

2. Location of a Branch, Agency or Other Establishment (Art. 23(1)2 Rome II)

Under Art. 23(1), a company's place of central administration may be replaced as a connecting factor by the location of a company's branch, agency or other establishment. This is the case if the event giving rise to the damage occurs, or the damage arises, in the course of operation of the branch, agency or other establishment. 6

a) Definition of "Branch, Agency or Other Establishment"

The terms "branch, agency or other establishment" were originally used in **Art. 5(5) Brussels I Regulation** and must therefore be interpreted consistently with Brussels I jurisprudence.[8] The ECJ in *Somafer v. Saar Fern Gas AG*[9] defined the terms as follows: "the concept of branch, agency or other establishment implies a place of business which has the appearance of permanency, such as the extension of a parent body, has a management and is materially equipped to negotiate business with third parties so that the latter, although knowing that there will if necessary be a legal link with the parent body, the head office of which is abroad, do not have to deal directly with such parent body but may transact business at the place of business constituting the extension."[10] 7

Examples of "branches" or "agencies" from ECJ decisions include: first, **the grantee of an exclusive sales concession** was not considered as the head of a branch, agency or other establishment because he/she was not subject to the control or direction of the grantor of the concession.[11] Secondly, because of a lack of control by the parent body, a **commercial agent/sales represen-** 8

8 Cf. Recital (7).

9 ECJ, Case C-33/78 – *Somafer SA v Saar Fern Gas* AG, [1978] ECR 2183, para. 12.

10 For more details, see *Mankowski*, in: Magnus/Mankowski (eds.), Brussels I Regulation (2007), Art. 5 paras. 273-295.

11 ECJ, Case C-14/76 – *De Bloos v Bouyer* [1976] ECR 1497, para. 23.

tative (a German *Handelsvertreter*) is no agent in the sense of Art. 5(5) Brussels I Regulation and thus Art. 23(1)2 Rome II. The court took three factors into account which showed a lack of dependency: the commercial agent was free to organize his/her own work and hours of work, was free to represent competitors and was in principle restricted to transmitting orders to the companies he represented.[12] Lastly, **a parent company** – even though legally independent – was considered the establishment of its subsidiary because it held itself out to third parties as acting on behalf of the subsidiary. The parent company took part in the negotiations as well as contract closings and was in charge of organizing deliveries and collecting invoices.[13]

b) Definition of "In the Course of the Operation of the Branch etc."

9 Furthermore, Art. 23(1)2 requires a specific type of connection between the non-contractual obligation and the branch, agency or establishment: the event giving rise to the damage must occur or the damage must arise *in the course of the operation* of the branch or agency. Authority in this regard is the English case *Anton Durbeck v. Den Norske Bank,*[14] which interpreted Art. 5(5) Brussels I Regulation. The Court of Appeal stated that it is undesirable to formulate a specific test for the nexus between a tort and the operations of a branch. Instead, whether damage arises "in the course of" a branch's operations depends on the facts of the individual case and a balancing exercise. The court compared the connection between the dispute and the state where the branch was established with the connection between the dispute and the state where the company had its domicile. For purposes of Art. 23(1)2, this would mean examining whether the non-contractual

---

12 ECJ, Case C-139/80 – *Blanckaert and Willems v Trost* [1981] ECR 819, paras. 12-13.

13 ECJ, Case C-218/86 – *SAR Schotte v Parfums Rothschild* [1987] ECR 4905, paras. 14-17.

14 Court of Appeal (England and Wales) 3 February 2003, *Anton Durbeck v Den Norske Bank* [2003] 2 WLR 1296.

obligation was more closely connected with the country of the branch than with the country of the central administration.[15] It is submitted that the following two criteria are likely to be decisive: firstly, if the company is the tortfeasor, do the employees whose actions give rise to the non-contractual obligation work for the branch, agency or establishment? Secondly, if the company is the victim, where is the *lex loci damni*, *i.e.* did the damage occur in the country of the branch or in the country of the company's central administration?

II. Habitual Residence of Natural Persons

1. Principal Place of Business, if the Person is Acting in the Course of His or Her Business Activity (Art. 23(2) Rome II)

For the purposes of the Rome II Regulation, a natural person who 10
is acting in the course of his or her business activity is presumed to be habitually resident at his or her principal place of business. Despite its broad wording, Art. 23(2), it is submitted, applies only to self-employed businesspersons and traders because others do not have a "principal place of business."[16] The term "principal place of business" is also used in Art. 4(2) Rome Convention and Art. 60(1)(c) Brussels I Regulation. It is a factual notion and refers to the place where the person conducts his/her primary business.[17] Factors in determining what location constitutes a person's "principal place of business" include the number of employees employed, the level of material expenses and the turnover generated in a specific country.

15 *Dickinson*, para. 3.56.

16 *Junker*, in: Münchener Kommentar BGB, Art. 23 para. 20.

17 *Vlas*, in: Mankowski/Magnus (eds.), Brussels I Regulation (2007), Art. 60 para. 6.

2. Habitual Residence of Natural Persons Who Are not Acting in the Course of Their Business Activities

11 Although the notion of "habitual residence" maintains an autonomous meaning, Art. 23 refrains from defining the term for natural persons who are not acting in the course of their business activities. Some guidance can be found in the ECJ case law on social insurance regimes and on the Brussels II *bis* Regulation.[18] The ECJ describes the habitual residence of persons as the "**habitual centre of their interests**".[19] The court then conducts a balancing exercise and takes into account all circumstances of the individual case, *e.g.* family situation, the degree of integration into the social environment, the reasons for the move to the new country, the length and continuity of the presence, whether the relevant person has stable employment and whether he/she intends to stay in the country.[20] It is submitted that the two main criteria a court should take into account are, firstly, the **period of presence** and secondly a **person's intention to make a country his or her home.**[21] A person who lived for over a year in Scotland but has always wanted to return to England is nevertheless habitually resident in Scotland.[22] In other words, presence in a country for a significant time outweighs the desire to move.[23] In con-

---

[18] Cf. also *Dickinson*, para. 3.50.

[19] ECJ, Case C-90/97 – *Swaddling v Adjudication Officer* [1999] ECR I-1075, para. 29; ECJ, Case C-372/02 – *Adanez-Vega v Bundesanstalt für Arbeit* [2004] ECR I-10761, para. 37; ECJ, Case C-452/93P – *Pedro Magdalena Fernández v Commission* [1994] ECR I-4295, paras. 22-23; ECJ, Case C-76/76 – *Silvana di Paulo v Office national de l'emploi* [1977] ECR 315, para. 17; cf. also *Borrás*, Explanatory Report on the Brussels II Convention, OJ 1998 C 221/27, para. 32.

[20] Cf. all cases mentioned at n. 17 above and ECJ, Case 523/07 – A, para. 44.

[21] *Lamont*, 3 JPIL (2007) 261, 263; *Rogerson*, 49 ICLQ (2000) 86, 94.

[22] Court of Appeal (England and Wales) M *v.* M [1997] 2 F.L.R. 263.

[23] *Rogerson*, 49 ICLQ (2000) 86, 94.

trast, a person who buys a one-way ticket from Bangladesh to England in order to start a new life is habitually resident in England from the day of arrival.[24]

Article 24
Exclusion of renvoi

The application of the law of any country specified by this Regulation means the application of the rules of law in force in that country other than its rules of private international law.

If a provision in the Rome II Regulation points to the law of country A, the judge must apply the *substantive* law of country A and must not apply its private international law rules which might refer him/her to the law of country B. The doctrine of *renvoi* is thus excluded.[1] The exclusion is in conformity with a trend in private international law to abolish *renvoi* (at least within the law of obligations).[2] It further corresponds to Art. 15 Rome Convention, Art. 20 Rome I Regulation and the Hague Conventions in the field of applicable law[3]. 1

24 *Plender & Wilderspin*, para. 3-027; *Kropholler*, Internationales Privatrecht (2006), p. 285; – *contra*: House of Lords (England and Wales) 21 October 1999, *Nessa v Chief Adjudication Officer* [1999] 1 WLR 1937, 1942.

1 Cf. for literature on the doctrine of *renvoi*: *Dicey, Morris & Collins*, Chapter 4; *Chesire, North & Fawcett*, pp. 57-73; *Loussouarn/Bourel/de Vareilles-Sommières*, Droit international privé (2007), pp. 257-282; *Kropholler*, Internationales Privatrecht, § 24; *Sonnentag*, Der Renvoi im Internationalen Privatrecht (2001).

2 *Von Hein*, 99 ZVglRWiss (2000) 251, 253 et seq.; *Mäsch*, 61 RabelsZ (1997) 285, 312; *Dicey, Morris & Collins*, paras. 35-151; – contra: *Briggs*, ICLQ (1998) 877.

3 *E.g.* Arts. 2-4 Hague Convention on the Law Applicable to International Sale of Goods (1955); Art. 3 Hague Convention on the Law Applicable to Traffic Accidents (1971); Art. 12 Hague Protocol on the Law Applicable to Maintenance Obligations (2009).

2 The objectives of the *renvoi* exclusion are threefold: firstly, it enhances – in conformity with Recital (6) – legal certainty and predictability.[4] The provisions of the Regulation constitute uniform rules whose application should not lead to inconsistent outcomes. Allowing *renvoi* would risk that the courts of different Member States apply different national laws to the same legal question.[5] Art. 24, as well as the principle that the Regulation is to be interpreted autonomously,[6] protect the uniform application of the Regulation. Secondly, the exclusion of *renvoi* facilitates and expedites the quest for applicable law.[7] Art. 24 releases the judge from the time-consuming and error-prone examination of foreign private international law rules. Thirdly, *renvoi* could jeopardize the values that underlie the conflict rules within the Regulation. The drafters of Rome II provided for a sophisticated set of rules which is intended to ensure a reasonable balance between state interests and the interests of the parties[8]. Two examples illustrate this: Art. 14 vests the parties with the freedom of choice regarding the applicable law. This freedom cannot be circumvented by invoking the private international law rules of country X, which might not permit a choice of law in non-contractual matters. Another striking example is Art. 5. The European legislature decided against the general application of the *lex loci damni* in cases of product liability. Instead, Art. 5 contains a detailed rule that tries to balance the interests of the victim with

---

4 COM(2003) 427 final, p. 28.

5 *Spickhoff*, in: Bamberger/Roth, Anh. zu Art. 42 EGBGB para. 138; *Thorn*, in: Palandt, Art. 24 para. 1.

6 *Dickinson*, para. 3.05-3.12.

7 *Leible*, in: Reichelt (ed.), Europäisches Gemeinschaftsrecht und IPR (2007) 31, 51.

8 Recital (16); *Symeonides*, 56 Am. J. Comp. L. (2007) 173, 183-184; *Fuchs*, GPR 2003-04, 100, 104; *Sonnentag*, 105 ZVglRWiss (2006) 256, 307; *von Hein*, 102 ZVglRWiss (2003) 528, 551.

those of the manufacturer.[9] The exclusion of *renvoi* prevents the application of the private international law rules of a third country which might designate as applicable a law that is unforeseeable to the parties involved.

As a rule, the exclusion of *renvoi* in practice makes a difference 3
only when the provisions of the Regulation point to the law of a Non-Member State.[10] It also has an impact beyond those cases if the Member State whose law is made applicable by the Regulation is a signatory to an international convention.[11] For example Finland, France, Luxembourg, the Netherlands, Slovenia and Spain are contracting states to the Hague Convention on the Law Applicable to Products Liability. If a German court were to decide a product liability case and Art. 5 designated Finnish law, Finnish substantive rules would apply directly even if the Hague Convention provided for another law.

---

9 Recital (20): The conflict-of-law rule in matters of product liability should meet the objectives of fairly spreading the risks inherent in a modern high-technology society, protecting consumers' health, stimulating innovation, securing undistorted competition and facilitating trade. Creation of a cascade system of connecting factors, together with a foreseeability clause, is a balanced solution in regard to these objectives.

10 *Huber/Bach*, IPRax 2005, 73, 81; critical towards the exclusion of *renvoi*: *De Lima Pinheiro*, Riv. dir. int. priv. proc. 2008, 5, 35 and *Leible/Engel*, EuZW 2004, 7, 16 criticize the exclusion of *renvoi* when the Regulation refers to the law of a Non-Member State. They argue that solution contained in Art. 24 Rome II contravenes the principle of international harmony of solutions.

11 *Thorn*, in: Palandt, Art. 24 para. 1; *Junker* NJW 2007, 3675, 3681; *Junker*, in: Münchener Kommentar BGB, Art. 24 paras. 4-5.

Article 25
States with more than one legal system

1. Where a State comprises several territorial units, each of which has its own rules of law in respect of non-contractual obligations, each territorial unit shall be considered as a country for the purposes of identifying the law applicable under this Regulation.
2. A Member State within which different territorial units have their own rules of law in respect of non-contractual obligations shall not be required to apply this Regulation to conflicts solely between the laws of such units.

A. Overview

1 What law applies if a conflict rule refers to the law of a country with several territorial units, each of which has its own domestic legal system? States with more than one legal system include, for example, the United Kingdom, Canada, the United States and Australia.[1] In such situations, two possible solutions exist for identifying the applicable legal system, both of which find support in private international law. The first option is to use the connecting factor provided by the conflict rule in order to determine which territorial unit's law is applicable. This approach was adopted by Art. 31 Hague Convention on Child Abduction 1980 and Arts. 19, 20 Hague Convention on the Law Applicable to Agency 1978. The second option is to leave it to the law of the designated country to identify which territorial unit's law is applicable. This is the option chosen in Art. 16 Hague Convention on the Law Applicable to Maintenance Obligations 1973 and Art. 26(a) European Convention on the Recognition and Enforcement of Decisions Concerning Custody of Children 1980.

2 Art. 25(1) Rome II adopts the first approach:[2] the provisions of the Rome II Regulation and their connecting factors designate

[1] COM(2003) 427 final, p. 28.

which territorial unit's law is to be applied. For these purposes, each territorial unit is considered a separate country. If, for example, damage is sustained in Scotland, Art. 4(1) points directly to Scots law.[3] Art. 25(1) is closely connected with Art. 24's exclusion of *renvoi*: whereas the latter provision releases the judge from examining foreign "international" conflict of law rules, Art. 25(1) releases the judge from taking into account "interstate" conflict of law rules. The objectives behind both articles are the same: providing legal certainty as well as predictability, expediting the determination of applicable law and upholding the policies embodied by the provisions of the Rome II Regulation.

Art. 25(2) points out that the provisions and connecting factors contained in the Regulation do not apply to purely domestic cases. If a court of a Member State has to choose the law of one territorial unit over the other, its decision must be guided by domestic conflict rules. 3

B. Detailed Commentary

I. Art. 25(1) Rome II

In the context of Art. 25(1), two questions may arise: firstly, when does a region constitute a "**territorial unit**" within the meaning of the provision? The concept of a "territorial unit" should not be interpreted too strictly: a separate court system or a legislature is not required to form a "territorial unit."[4] The essential and plain factor in evaluating whether a region constitutes an Art. 25 territorial unit is whether the region has its own laws 4

---

2 As does Art. 19 Rome Convention and Art. 22 Rome I.

3 *Ibid.*; for an example from the field of contractual obligations, cf.: Guiliano & Lagarde Report, OJ 1980 C 282/11, Art. 19.

4 *Junker*, in: Münchener Kommentar BGB, Art. 25 para. 6. See also *Dickinson*, para. 3.291; he requires at least a "degree of constitutional separation".

regarding non-contractual obligations – regardless of who enacted those laws.[5]

5 Secondly, a problem might arise if the **parties choose the law of a country with more than one legal system** (*e.g.* "United States Law") to govern their non-contractual obligations. One must then construe the agreement in order to determine whether the parties intended to designate the law of a certain state or region. The following facts might shed some light on the parties' actual intent: is one party habitually resident in a territorial unit of the designated country?[6] Has the event giving rise to the damage occurred *(lex loci actus)* within a territorial unit? Have the consequences of the tort been primarily felt in one territorial unit? If the law of one territory cannot be determined with reasonable certainty, the inter-territorial conflict of law rules of the chosen country determine the applicable law. If no inter-territorial conflict of law rules exist, the European judge must determine the law with the closest connection to the dispute, bearing in mind the choice of the parties and the connecting factors provided for in the Rome II Regulation.[7]

---

5 Frequently, territorial units also share a Common Law or Federal Law. Nevertheless, they are considered as separate territories in the sense of Art. 25(1) Rome II (on the German equivalent to Art. 19 Rome Convention: *Martiny*, in: Münchener Kommentar BGB, Art. 35 EGBGB para. 14; *Hausmann*, in: Staudinger, Art. 35 EGBGB para. 11).

6 The Higher Regional Court of Hamburg had to interpret the following choice of law clause in a contract between a Chinese producer of electronic parts and a German distributor: "the law governing this agreement as per European common market (EU)." The court held that it was the parties' clear intention not to apply Chinese but European law. Since there was no uniform law governing distribution contracts in the EU, the court presumed the parties' intention to choose the law which is most closely connected to the dispute. This was German law because the distributor had its place of business in Germany. (Oberlandesgericht Hamburg (Germany) 5 October 1998 – 12 U 62/97, IHR 1999, 37, 38).

II. Art. 25(2) Rome II

Under Art. 25(2), Member States with more than one legal system are not obliged to harmonize their rules on inter-territory conflict of laws with the provisions of the Regulation. However, this only holds true for purely domestic cases. As soon as a case evinces a connection to foreign law, it is a case of international conflict of laws governed by the Rome II Regulation.[8] Apparently, the UK – even though it is not obliged to do so – plans to apply the provisions of the Regulation to conflict of laws between the constituent territories of the UK.[9] 6

Article 26
Public policy of the forum

The application of a provision of law of any country specified by this Regulation may be refused only if such application is manifestly incompatible with the public policy (*ordre public*) of the forum.

7 *Hausmann*, in: Staudinger, Art. 35 EGBGB para. 13; – *contra*: *Leible*, in: Anwaltskommentar BGB, Art. 35 EGBGB para. 7; *von Bar*, Internationales Privatrecht, Volume 2 (1991), para. 464; *Magnus*, in: Staudinger, Art. 27 EGBGB para. 38.

8 *Dickinson*, para. 3.292.

9 *Ibid.*

A. Background

1 It is a general principle of the conflict of laws that a court will not apply the law of a foreign country if the application of this law would result in violating fundamental principles of the public policy of the forum.

2 Art. 26 Rome II Regulation provides for a general *ordre public* clause.[1] It departs both from the Commission's initial proposal and the European Parliament's legislative resolution, which also included a special rule on public policy provision on the non-application of *punitive damages*; the latter was rejected by the Council of the European Union.

3 The first **proposal** of the European Commission included two different provisions on public policy: first, the general rule on "Public policy of the forum" (Art. 22), which now has become Art. 26 Rome II Regulation; second, the European Commission proposed to introduce an additional provision on "non-compensatory damages"[2] which resembled Art. 40 (3) of the German EGBGB. The

---

1 The formulation has been taken from Art. 16 Rome Convention and is identical to Art. 21 Rome I Regulation. – Two more special *ordre public* clauses which formed part of the Proposal for a Regulation of the European Parliament and the Council on the law applicable to non-contractual obligations ("Rome II"), 22 July 2003, COM(2003) 427 final were later withdrawn. Art. 6 of the Proposal introduced a special *ordre public* clause in case of violations of privacy, an issue which is now excluded from the scope of application. Art. 23 (1) included a special Community public policy exception, which was widely considered to be superfluous: *von Hein*, VersR 2007, 440, 451.

2 Art. 24 of the Proposal for a Regulation of the European Parliament and the Council on the law applicable to non-contractual obligations ("Rome II"), 22 July 2003, COM(2003) 427 final: "the application of a provision designated by the Regulation which has the effect of causing non-compensatory damages, such as exemplary or punitive damages, to be awarded shall be contrary to Community public policy".

idea behind it was to refuse the application of the law of a third country providing for damages not calculated to compensate for damage sustained.[3] According to this Commission proposal, exemplary and punitive damages are contrary to Community public policy.

This proposal was heavily criticised, especially in England, for purporting to harmonise substantive rules of the Member States as opposed to conflict of law rules.[4] In spite of this criticism, the European Parliament followed the Commission's approach, but suggested a different wording of the provision. In the European Parliament **legislative resolution**, the general rule on *ordre public* was amended by two paragraphs according to which the application of a rule may be refused if such application would be in breach of fundamental rights and freedoms as enshrined in certain provisions (Art. 22(2)) or if exemplary or punitive damages are awarded (Art. 22(3)).[5] The Commission agreed to these changes.[6] 4

In order to clarify the concept of public policy, the **Common Position** by the Council[7] finally included one general provision on public policy of the forum, which is identical to the later Art. 26 Rome II Regulation. Reducing the provision to a general clause 5

---

3 Proposal for a Regulation of the European Parliament and the Council on the law applicable to non-contractual obligations ("Rome II"), 22 July 2003, COM(2003) 427 final, p. 29.

4 House of Lords (England and Wales), Paper 66 (2004) para. 46 and 164; *Stone*, EuLF 2004, 213, 224 ("Machtmissbrauch").

5 Art. 22, Legislative Resolution of Parliament (1st reading) of 6 July 2005, P6_TA(2005)0284; Report of 27 June 2005, A6-0211/2005, Rapporteur: *Diana Wallis*.

6 Amended Proposal for a European Parliament and Council Regulation on the law applicable to non-contractual obligations ("Rome II"), 21 February 2006, COM(2006) 83 final, p. 5.

7 Common Position (EC) No 22/2006 of 25 September 2006, OJ of 28 November 2006, C 289E/68; see also Council's Reasons, p. 80.

was not intended to reduce its scope of application, as there was "no disagreement that the public policy clause does offer sufficient guarantee and protection against potential negative effects of awards of extreme non-compensatory damages."[8] The European Parliament, however, still insisted in its second reading on introducing a special paragraph on punitive damages.[9] The Commission accepted this amendment made by Parliament,[10] but the Council decided not to approve all the European Parliament's amendments. In the following **Conciliation Procedure** the provision on public policy was not one of the main points of contention. A compromise was reached in the sense that Art. 26 is now drafted in the form of a general clause on public policy of the forum amended by Recital 32, which deals explicitly with non-compensatory or punitive damages.

6 This outcome is to be appreciated as the general *ordre public* clause is clearly sufficient to refuse the application of foreign punitive damages of an excessive nature.

B. Scope of Application

7 Art. 26 only concerns the application of **foreign substantive law** in the courts of a Member State. It must be distinguished from the

---

[8] Communication concerning the common position of the Council on the adoption of a Regulation of the European Parliament and of the Council on the law applicable to non-contractual obligations ("Rome II"), 27 September 2006, COM(2006) 566 final, p. 4.

[9] Art. 26, Legislative Resolution of Parliament (2nd reading) of 18 January 2007, T6-0006/2007, Legislative Report of 22 December 2006, A6-0481/2006.

[10] Commission Opinion on the European Parliament's amendments to the Council common position on the proposal for a Regulation of the European Parliament and of the Council on the law applicable to non-contractual obligations ("Rome II"), 14 March 2007, COM(2007) 126 final, p. 3.

procedural *ordre public*, relevant for the recognition and enforcement of foreign judgements (*e.g.* Art. 34 Brussels I Regulation), the latter only has attenuated effect *(effet atténué de l'ordre public)*. The reason for this is that applying laws may cause a stronger violation of the *ordre public* than enforcing a foreign judgment.

Art. 26 will be applied ***ex officio***, that is to say that courts may apply the *ordre public* clause without an application of one of the parties. During the negotiations the European Parliament suggested that "where, under this Regulation, the law specified as applicable is that of a Member State, the public policy exception may only be applied at the request of one of the parties" (Art. 22(4)). The justification given was that it appeared undesirable to have a public policy exception apply "automatically."[11] The Commission rightly rejected this proposal: it is for the courts to ensure compliance with fundamental values of the forum.[12] Therefore, the public policy exception clause must be applied *ex officio* (which is not the same as being applied automatically). 8

According to Art. 26, the following requirements have to be fulfilled: 9

I. Non-Contractual Obligation

Art. 26 applies within the scope of application of the Regulation ("law of any country specified by this Regulation"). Thus, it applies in situations involving a conflict of laws regarding non-contractual obligations in civil and commercial matters. Recital 32 makes it clear that **punitive damages** fall within the scope of application of the Regulation. This was contested by individual authors,[13] but the majority of scholars has always upheld the posi- 10

---

11 Report of 27 June 2005, A6-0211/2005, p. 33.

12 Amended Proposal for a European Parliament and Council Regulation on the law applicable to non-contractual obligations ("Rome II"), 21 February 2006, COM(2006) 83 final, p. 5.

13 *Mörsdorf-Schulte*, 104 ZVglRWiss (2005) 192, 249.

tion that punitive damages have to be characterised as "civil matters."

II. Exceptional Case

11 It becomes clear from the wording of Art. 26 that the *ordre public* clause is only to be invoked in exceptional cases. Additionally, this is highlighted by Recital 32 ("in exceptional circumstances"). Furthermore, the formula **"manifestly incompatible"** which is derived from the Hague Conventions, underlines that there must be special grounds for the application of public policy; *i.e.* the use of the public policy exception must be exceptional.[14]

12 It is certainly not enough to justify the exclusion of foreign law by arguing that there is a difference in content between the *lex fori* and applicable foreign law. A claim for compensation unknown to the *lex fori* should not be dismissed just because it is unknown. The application of a foreign law is manifestly incompatible with the public policy of the forum only if and in so far as its application violates fundamental principles of justice or basic ideas of public policy.[15]

III. Application of the Foreign Law

13 It should be noted that it is the **application of the foreign law** (and not the foreign law *per se*) which must be incompatible with the public policy of the forum. A foreign law can only be ex-

---

14 Proposal for a Regulation of the European Parliament and the Council on the law applicable to non-contractual obligations ("Rome II"), 22 July 2003, COM(2003) 427 final, p. 28; *Junker*, in: Münchener Kommentar BGB, Art. 26 para. 1.

15 ECJ Case C-38/98 – *Renault v Maxicar*, [2000] ECR I-2973, para. 30: "inasmuch as it infringes a fundamental principle." ECJ Case C-7/98 – *Krombach*, [2000] ECR I-1935, para. 37; confirmed in: ECJ Case C-394/07 – *Gambazzi v Daimler Chrysler*, [2009] OJ C 141/9 of 20 June 2009.

cluded if and in so far as the effect of its application is contrary to public policy in the particular case.

IV. Connection to the Forum

The rules of the forum are generally concerned only if the case has a connection to the forum. That could be case if the tortfeasor has his habitual residence in that country. However, according to the principle of **relativity of the *ordre public***, the connection to the forum may be weak if the violation of public policy is strong, and vice versa.[16] This is to say, that it is not necessary for the tort to have some strong connection to the forum where the application of foreign law violates an essential moral or legal interest. **14**

V. *Ordre public international*

Art. 26 cannot be applied whenever the application of foreign law would contradict the principles of the domestic law of the forum *(ordre public interne)*. Only if the court regards the principle in question as one expressing a basic public policy *(ordre public international)*, will it enforce the principle by refusing the application of the foreign law. **15**

It needs to be stressed that the **concept of public policy** remains a national one. As the ECJ held in a Brussels Convention case, "(…) it is not for the Court to define the content of the public policy of a Contracting State," but it must "review the limits within which the courts of a Contracting State may have recourse to that concept for the purpose of refusing recognition of a judgement emanating from another Contracting State."[17] **16**

The concept of *ordre public* is nevertheless influenced by the law of the European Union. When applying Art. 26 Rome II Regula- **17**

---

16 *Junker*, in: Münchener Kommentar BGB, Art. 26 para. 20.

17 ECJ Case C-38/98 – *Renault v Maxicar*, [2000] ECR I-2973; ECJ Case C-7/98 – *Krombach*, [2000] ECR I-1935.

tion, the national courts have to take into account the treaties, regulations, directives and the jurisprudence of the ECJ.[18]

C. Consequences

18 In the particular case, the liability of the tortfeasor and the amount of damages will, in a first step, be defined according to the rules of the foreign law designated by the conflict rule. In a second step, certain elements of the foreign law of tort will then be examined against the public policy of the forum. Consequently, the decision whether the application of a provision will be refused depends on the legal order of the forum and may vary accordingly. Whenever the application of foreign law violates the public policy of the forum, the court is allowed to **disregard the rules of the foreign law**. Whether the court will replace the foreign law with the *lex fori* or whether it will dismiss the claim depends on the national law, as Rome II is silent on this issue.[19]

19 Foreign law should not automatically be replaced by the *lex fori*, but modified in order to alleviate the existing concerns; however, in case this not possible the *lex fori* may serve as a substitute.[20] If the foreign national law grants damages of an excessive nature, the court has the discretion to diminish them to an acceptable amount *(Kappungsgrenze)*.

D. Punitive Damages

20 The award of punitive damages in the **United States** is heavily criticised in Europe, since punitive damage awards are often ex-

---

18 *Junker*, in: Münchener Kommentar BGB, Art. 26 para. 17.

19 *von Hein*, EuZW 2009, 624. But see *Weintraub*, in: Ahern/Binchy (eds.), The Rome II Regulation, p. 47, 52: "the court should dismiss the action without affecting the merits".

20 *Junker*, in: Münchener Kommentar BGB, Art. 26 para. 26.

cessive in nature and of an unreasonable amount. It its judgement *Exxon Shipping Co. v. Baker*,[21] the U.S. Supreme Court openly addresses this criticism. This decision discusses in detail purpose and limits of punitive damages. The case comes after several decisions[22] in which the Supreme Court interpreted the *Due Process Clause* as setting limits to punitive damages awards.

Punitive damages do not aim at compensation, but at retribution and deterring harmful conduct; they are limited to cases where the defendant's conduct is outrageous or showing wilful, wanton, and reckless indifference for the rights of others. 21

State regulation of punitive damages varies. In most American jurisdictions, the punitive award is determined by the jury in first instance and then reviewed by appellate courts. Many states have introduced limits or monetary caps on punitive awards. The Supreme Court points out that despite these limitations, punitive damages are overall higher and more frequent in the United States than they are anywhere else, the real problem being the stark unpredictability of punitive awards. The central question is how to limit best the amount of punitive damages. The Court held that, in maritime cases, a ratio of 1:1 of punitive to compensatory damages is a fair upper limit.[23] Generally, there seems to be a clear trend in American law of damages towards more reasonableness and predictability in this respect. 22

The award of damages which aim at **deterrence and punishment** is not limited to the United States. In European statutes, the ex- 23

---

[21] U.S. Supreme Court 25 June 2008 *(Exxon Shipping Co. v Baker)*, 128 S.Ct. 2605; 554 U.S. (2008).

[22] *E.g.* U.S. Supreme Court 20 May 1996 *(BMW of North America, Inc. v Gore)*, 517 U.S. 559, 568 (1996); U.S. Supreme Court 20 February 2007 *(Philip Morris USA v Williams)*, 127 S.Ct. 1057 (2007); 549 U.S. 346 (2007).

[23] U.S. Supreme Court 25 June 2008 *(Exxon Shipping Co. v Baker)*, 128 S.Ct. 2605; 554 U.S. (2008).

pression "punitive damages" is hardly ever used, but the award of non-compensatory damages is known in several states. Since the decision in *Wilkes v Wood*[24], there is little doubt that exemplary damages do form an independent type of damages in English tort law. It is clearly accepted that the purpose of these damages is to punish and deter the wrongdoer. In other words, exemplary damages are awarded whenever it is necessary to teach a wrongdoer that "tort does not pay."[25]

24 While the award of exemplary damages is limited to three kinds of cases according to English law, this limitation does not exist in the law of Australia,[26] New Zealand and Canada.

25 Especially in cases of **defamation**, courts in some EU Member States are open to award damages which go beyond compensation. This is certainly the case in England,[27] France,[28] Germany[29]

---

[24] *Wilkes v Wood* (1763) 98 E.R. 489, 498 per *Pratt* LCJ: "Damages are designed not only as a satisfaction to the injured person, but likewise as a punishment to the guilty, to deter from any such proceeding for the future, and as a proof of the detestation of the jury to the action itself."

[25] *Rookes v Barnard*, House of Lords (England and Wales) 21 February 1964, [1964] 1 All.E.R. 367, 411 per *Lord Devlin*.

[26] *Lamb v. Cotogno* (1987), ALJ 62 (1988) 249 quoting *Wilkes v Wood* (see above).

[27] *John v Mirror Group Newspapers Ltd*, Court of Appeal (England and Wales), [1996] 2 All E.R. 35, 57 per *Sir Bingham* MR.

[28] Cour d'Appel Paris (France) 4 January 1988, D. 1989 somm. 92 note *Amson*; Cour de Cassation (France), Cass.civ 1er 5 November 1996, D. 1997 jur 403 *Laulom; Jourdain*, D. 1997 somm. 289, 290: "Que la condamnation indemnitaire se charge d'un caractère punitif, cela est certain.": *Carval*, La responsabilité civile dans sa fonction de peine privée (Paris 1995), p. 25: "Il fait peu de doute, aux yeux de la doctrine française, que la responsibilité qui incombe aux auteurs d'atteintes aux droits de la personnalité n'est pas seulement compensatoire et qu'elle présente un fort caractère punitif.": *Brière*, 135 Clunet (2008) 31, 69: "(…) la notion de peine privée n'est pas étrangère à notre système juridique".

and Italy.[30] Furthermore, it is the European Court of Justice which underlines that "Member States must ensure in particular that infringements of Community law are penalised under conditions, (...) which, in any event, make the penalty effective, proportionate and dissuasive."[31]

Consequently, the theoretically clear line between compensation on the one hand and punishment tends to break down in practice.[32] Against this background, the Commission's proposal according to which exemplary and punitive damages are contrary to Community public policy could not be upheld.[33] 26

However, it is highlighted in the Rome II Regulation that punitive damages of an **excessive nature** are to be regarded as contrary to the *ordre public*. According to Recital 32, "the application of a provision of the law designated by this Regulation which would have the effect of causing non-compensatory exemplary or punitive damages of an excessive nature to be awarded may, depending on the circumstances of the case and the legal order of the Member State of the court seised, be regarded as being contrary to the public policy *(ordre public)* of the forum." 27

---

29 Bundesgerichtshof (Germany) 15 November 1994, BGHZ 128, 1, 16; *von Bar*, Gemeineuropäisches Deliktsrecht I, para. 609: "Dass hier Elemente des Gedankens der Privatstrafe wirksam werden, wird man nicht gut bestreiten können." Oberlandesgericht Hamburg (Germany) 30 July 2009, NJW-RR 2010, 624.

30 *Gallo*, Pene private e responsabilità civile (1996), p. 103.

31 ECJ Case C-387/02 – *Silvio Berlusconi* [2005] ECR I-3565, note 65.

32 *W.V.H. Rogers*, EC Tort Law and the English Law, in: *Koziol/Schulze*, Tort Law of the European Community (2008) 365, 388 note 112; *Junker*, in: Münchener Kommentar BGB, Art. 26 para. 24.

33 Cf. Cour de Cassation (France), Cass. civ. 1er 1 December 2010, Arrêt n° 1090: "le principe d'une condamnation à des dommages intérêts punitifs, n'est pas, en soi, contraire à l'ordre public, ..."

28 Compared to the original Commission's proposal to introduce a paragraph on "non-compensatory damages,"[34] the formulation in the Recital is much more cautious and leaves more discretion to the judge. While Art. 24 of the proposal would have, for example, prevented the application of English rules on exemplary damages in a foreign court as being contrary to Community public policy, this is certainly not the case under the Rome II Regulation (unless they are "of an excessive nature"). Whether non-compensatory damages are of an excessive nature depends "on the circumstances of the case and the legal order of the Member State" and must be decided under the *lex fori*.

Article 27
Relationship with other provisions of Community law

This Regulation shall not prejudice the application of provisions of Community law which, in relation to particular matters, lay down conflict-of-law rules relating to non-contractual obligations.

[34] Proposal for a Regulation of the European Parliament and the Council on the law applicable to non-contractual obligations ("Rome II"), 22 July 2003, COM(2003) 427 final.

A. General

I. Background

Art. 27 addresses the relationship between the conflict rules contained in the general regime of the Rome II Regulation and special conflict rules in relation to particular matters in other Community law provisions. To resolve such conflicts, Art. 27 opts for the ***lex specialis*-rule**: Special conflict rules in relation to particular matters prevail over those of the Rome II Regulation. The Rome I Regulation pursues the same approach in its Art. 23. 1

A far wider rule of precedence for other provisions of Community law was initially proposed by the Commission and the European Parliament. Precedence was not only given to special conflict rules in relation to particular matters but also to overriding mandatory provisions in other Community law instruments. And, most importantly, the country of origin-principle in other provisions of Community law would have replaced the respective conflict rule of the Rome II Regulation.[1] The Council rejected such a wide rule. It cut back the proposals to the *lex specialis*-rule limited to special conflict rules in relation to particular matters as it was finally adopted.[2] The relationship of the Rome II Regulation with the country of origin-principle contained in other Community law instruments, the E-Commerce Directive in particular, was transferred into a rather vague recital. 2

---

1 See in particular Art. 23(2) of the European Commission's initial proposal (COM(2003) 427 final of 22 July 2003) and similarly, though not entirely clear in that respect, Art. 1(3) of the European Parliament's legislative resolution after the first reading (P6-TA(2005)0284 of 6 July 2005); for a critical account see in particular *Wilderspin*, NIPR 2008, 408, 409 seq.

2 See Art. 27 and Recital 31 of the Common Position (EC) No 22/2006 of 25 September 2006.

II. Fragmentation

3 The *lex specialis*-rule in Art. 27 **interferes with one of the primary goals of the Rome II Regulation** to provide a single comprehensive conflict regime for non-contractual obligations striving for legal simplicity and certainty.[3] The first paragraph of Recital 35 is of little guidance in that respect as it simply stresses the tension between unanimity of conflict rules for non-contractual obligations in different legal instruments on the one hand and an alleged need for deviating special conflict rules beyond those of the Rome II Regulation on the other hand. In the end, the success and comprehensiveness of the Rome II Regulation in providing for a uniform regime throughout the European Union will amongst other aspects depend on the way the European Union itself is willing to adhere to the idea of a single uniform system by avoiding special conflict rules trumping the Rome II Regulation as far as possible.

B. The Operation of the Rule

I. Operation in General

4 The way in which conflict rules in relation to particular matters prevail over those of the Rome II Regulation is not entirely clear from the wording of Art. 27. Referring, however, to the application of the special conflict provisions ("... shall not prejudice the application of provisions ...") it appears that Art. 27 has the effect that the **respective conflict rule of the Rome II Regulation is replaced by the special conflict rule**: The special conflict rule applies while the otherwise applicable conflict rule of the Rome II Regulation disapplies.

---

[3] Rather critical in this respect also *Brière*, 135 Clunet (2008) 31, 70 et seq.; *Leible/Lehmann*, RIW 2007, 721, 734.

Disapplication does not automatically extend to the **common rules (Art. 15 to 22) and other provisions (Art. 23 to 25) of the Rome II Regulation**. Generally, those provisions will apply in conjunction with the special conflict rule. 5

Whether a provision of Community law does in fact constitute a conflict rule may be difficult to assess.[4] It has to be determined in relation to each provision individually without recourse to the Rome II Regulation.[5] 6

II. The Effect of the Country of Origin-Principle in Other Provisions of Community Law

While the country of origin-principle does not govern the determination of the applicable law under the Rome II Regulation,[6] it is embodied in several other Community law instruments laying down rules concerning the proper functioning of the internal market (third sentence of Recital 35) and the regulation of the free movement of goods and services, in particular the E-Commerce Directive (fourth sentence of Recital 35). Whether the country of origin-principle constitutes a conflict rule, is highly contested.[7] 7

---

4 *Cheshire, North & Fawcett*, p. 856.

5 Concurring *Garcimartín Alferéz*, EuLF 2007, I-77, 82; *R. Wagner*, in: FS Kropholler (2008) 715, 725.

6 *Leible*, in: Reichelt (ed.), Europäisches Gemeinschaftsrecht und Internationales Privatrecht (2007) 31, 47 seq.; *de Lima Pinheiro*, Riv. dir. int. priv. 2008, 5, 36.

7 See generally *Deinert*, 17 EWS (2006) 445; *Michaels*, 2 J. Priv. Int. L. (2006) 195; for further discussion of the matter and the relationship of Art. 6 Rome II Regulation with Art. 3 E-Commerce Directive and Art. 2(1), 3(2) of the Television Broadcasting Activities Directive see Art. 6 paras. 25 et seq. with further references.

8 **Neither Art. 27 Rome II nor Recital 35 settle the issue** by taking sides explicitly.[8] Rather, they ensure that the applicable law of a Member State determined by the conflict rules of the Rome II Regulation does not interfere with the country of origin-principle regardless of its nature as a conflict rule or not. If one regards the country of origin-principle as a conflict rule, Art. 27 applies directly: the provision containing the country of origin-principle replaces the respective conflict rule of the Rome II Regulation that would otherwise apply. If one regards the country of origin-principle with the prevailing view[9] not as a conflict rule, Recital 35 provides that the country of origin's provisions in the respective field covered by the other Community law instrument (which will mainly be those of public economic/regulatory law[10]) take precedence on the level of substantive law: once the applicable law is determined pursuant to the conflict rule of the Rome II Regulation, the respective provisions of the country of origin's substantive law prevail in case of incompatibility with the applicable substantive law.[11]

9 However, the wording of Recital 35, "… in so far as they cannot be applied in conjunction with the law designated by the rules of this Regulation." (third sentence) and "… application of provisions of the applicable law designated by the rules of this Regulation …" (fourth sentence), indicates quite clearly that the issue of compatibility relates to the substantive laws presupposing that the applicable law has been determined by applying the conflict rules of the Rome II Regulation.[12] This implies that the **country**

---

8 *Garcimartín Alferéz*, EuLF 2007, I-77, 82; *Heiss/Loacker*, JBl 2007, 613, 617; *von Hein*, 82 Tul.L.Rev. (2008) 1663, 1702.

9 For references see again Art. 6 para. 26.

10 *De Lima Pinheiro*, Riv. dir. int. priv. proc. 2008, 5, 37 with further references; in case of the E-Commerce Directive this is only provisions within the coordinated field pursuant to its Art. 2.

11 Rather critical with regard to this back-door for the country of origin-principle G. *Wagner*, IPRax 2008, 1, 3; *Wilderspin*, NIPR 2008, 408, 409 seq.; *Junker*, in: Münchener Kommentar BGB, Art. 27 para. 3.

of origin-principle is not regarded as a conflict rule so that it does not replace the respective conflict rule of the Rome II Regulation under Art. 27.[13]

Consequently, the relationship between Art. 6 Rome II and Art. 3 E-Commerce Directive as well as Art. 2(1), 3(2) of the Television Broadcasting Activities Directive is not governed by Art. 27 Rome II but rather to be solved on the level of the substantive law.[14] Beyond this conflict of the Rome II Regulation with the E-Commerce- and the Television Broadcasting Directive, an interference of the substantive law determined by the conflict rules of the Rome II Regulation with other provisions of Community law concerning the internal market and the basic freedoms as addressed by Recital 35 will be rather rare.[15] 10

III. Scope and Preconditions

Art. 27 applies with regard to other **provisions of community law.** This encompasses the law of the European treaties, the TFEU and the TEU in particular, as well as secondary Community law contained in Regulations and Directives. As regards Directives, it follows from their very nature[16] that Art. 27 does not only preserve the precedence of the Directive as such but also and foremost of the national legislative instruments implementing it. Otherwise, Art. 27 would not cover the most important incidents of conflicts and incompatibility addressed by Recital 35 since 11

---

12 *De Lima Pinheiro*, Riv. dir. int. priv. proc. 2008, 5, 36; *R. Wagner*, in: FS Kropholler (2008) 715, 725.

13 *von Hein*, ZEuP 2009, 1, 31; *R. Wagner*, in: FS Kropholler (2008) 715, 725; *Dicey, Morris & Collins*, paras. S 35-173.

14 For further details see also Art. 6 paras. 25 et seq.

15 *De Lima Pinheiro*, Riv. dir. int. priv. proc. 2008, 5, 38.

16 Cf. Art. 288 TFEU ("A directive shall be binding, as to the result to be achieved, upon each Member State to which it is addressed, but shall leave to the national authorities the choice of form and methods.").

most special provisions concerned with the internal market and the basic freedoms are contained in Directives. Systematically this may find support in an analogous application of Art. 14(3) Rome II ("... provisions of Community law, where appropriate as implemented in the Member State of the forum, ...").[17]

12 Art. 27 applies only with regard to provisions of Community law **in relation to particular matters**. Conflict rules in other Community law instruments covering the entire material scope of the Rome II Regulation do not benefit from the precedence under Art. 27. Currently, there are hardly any special provisions in relation to particular matters in force.[18] Art. 4 of the Insolvency Regulation[19] contains a conflict rule in relation to particular matters, but it appears to be the case that most insolvency issues are of a contractual nature so that a conflict of conflict rules may arise rather in relation to the Rome I Regulation which contains a *lex specialis*-rule (Art. 23) modelled after Art. 27 Rome II.

13 The rule in Art. 27 applies in relation to existing and future provisions in other Community law instruments. The rule is merely one of speciality, not of priority in time (as Art. 28).

Article 28
Relationship with existing international conventions

1. This Regulation shall not prejudice the application of international conventions to which one or more Member States are parties at the time when this Regulation is adopted and which lay down conflict-of-law rules relating to non-contractual obligations.

---

17 *Huber/Bach*, IPRax 2005, 73, 75; *Leible*, RIW 2008, 257, 263; *Junker*, in: Münchener Kommentar BGB, Art. 27 para. 8.

18 *Dickinson*, para. 16.32.

19 Regulation (EC) No 1346/2000 on Insolvency Proceedings, OJ 2000 L 160/1.

2. However, this Regulation shall, as between Member States, take precedence over conventions concluded exclusively between two or more of them in so far as such conventions concern matters governed by this Regulation.

A. Structure, Purpose and Background

1 Art. 28 addresses the conflict between international conventions laying down conflict rules and the Rome II Regulation. It distinguishes between international conventions to which Member States and third countries are parties and conventions to which only Member States are parties (dichotomy between Art. 28(1) and 28(2)) as well as between existing and future conventions (within Art. 28(1) supplemented by Recital 37). An identical rule governs the relationship of the Rome I Regulation with international conventions (Art. 25 Rome I).

2 The rule in Art. 28(1) resembles more or less the initial proposal by the Commission[1] while Art. 28(2) was introduced by the Council in its Common Position. The central issue, the European legislator was faced with in relation to existing international conventions and the Rome II Regulation were the two Hague Conventions on the law applicable to traffic accidents of 1971 and on the law applicable to products liability of 1973.[2]

1 See Art. 25 of the proposal COM(2003) 427 final; for a critical analysis of the initital proposal see *Brière*, 132 Clunet (2005) 677.

2 Both conventions are accessible at www.hcch.net.

3 There were **several options** at hand: (1) aligning the respective conflict rules of the Rome II Regulation with those of the Hague Conventions; (2) denunciation of the Hague Conventions by the Member States that are parties to it;[3] (3) distinguishing between intra- (Rome II Regulation applies in all Member States) and extra-community situations (Hague Conventions apply in their contracting Member States, Rome II Regulation applies in the Member States not party to them); (4) generally giving preference to the Hague Conventions over the Rome II Regulation in the contracting Member States. In choosing between those options the European legislator had to consider the primary goal of the Rome II Regulation as it is expressed in its Recital 6: a single Union-wide conflict of laws regime for non-contractual obligations striving for predictability of outcome and certainty of the applicable law. Option (1) was rejected since the conflict rules of the Hague Conventions are widely regarded as far too complex (following the grouping of contacts-model)[4] and since several non-contracting Member States were not willing to adopt the

---

[3] In total, the Convention on traffic accidents is currently ratified and in force in 19 states (12 of which are Member States: Austria, Belgium, Czech Republic, France, Latvia, Lithuania, Luxembourg, the Netherlands, Poland, Slovakia, Slovenia and Spain), the Convention on products liability is currently signed by 14, ratified and in force in 11 states (6 of which are Member States: Finland, France, Luxembourg, the Netherlands, Slovenia and Spain).

[4] For criticism on the complex regimes of the Hague Conventions see inter alia *Staudinger*, EuLF 2005, I-64 et seq.; *Kadner Graziano*, in: Basedow/Baum/Nishitani (eds.), Japanese and European Private International Law in Comparative Perspective (2008) 243, 245; *Kropholler*, Internationales Privatrecht, § 53 V. 3.; *Lorenz*, 37 RabelsZ (1973) 317, 328 et seq.; *von Hoffmann*, in: idem (ed.), European Private International Law, (1998) 88 and 102; but in favour of such alignment *e.g.* Stellungnahme der 2. Kommission des Deutschen Rates fur Internationales Privatrecht, p. 24 (accessible at http://ec.europa.eu/justice_home/news/consulting_public/rome_ii/deutscher_rat_internat_privatrecht_de.pdf).

Hague Rules via the Rome II Regulation.[5] Option (2) failed since the Member States which are party to the Hague Conventions were not willing to denounce them.[6] Option (3) was proposed by the European Parliament[7] and supported by the Commission in its amended proposal.[8] The Council, however, rejected the proposal for it would have resulted in a fragmented system of intra- versus extra-community constellations and in a considerable degree of legal uncertainty with regard to the applicable law resulting from the difficulty to distinguish intra- from extra-community situations.[9] Option (4) was finally chosen in Art. 28(1) for its clarity and the legal certainty it produces while also paying due respect to the international commitments of the Member States. It extends the principle of Art. 307 TFEU which respects international commitments by Member States with third countries that they have entered into prior to their accession to the Community to secondary Community legislation by establishing the principle of priority in time in relation to the date of adoption of the Rome II Regulation.[10]

4 Art. 28(1) puts international harmony over a comprehensive regional unification of conflict rules within the European Union. The result is a **fragmentation of the conflict regime** in case of existing international conventions, in particular in relation to the law applicable to traffic accidents and product liability which

---

5 *R. Wagner*, in: FS Kropholler (2008) 715, 726.

6 See again *R. Wagner*, in FS Kropholler (2008) 715, 726.

7 But only in relation to the Hague Convention on the law applicable to traffic accidents; see Art. 25(3) of the legislative resolution after the first reading (P6-TA(2005)0284 of 6 July 2005).

8 See Art. 24 of the amended proposal COM(2006) 83 final; the proposal finds support *inter alia* by the Hamburg Group for Private International Law, 67 RabelsZ (2003) 1, 56.

9 *Garriga*, 9 YbPIL (2007) 137, 140; *Brière*, 135 Clunet (2008) 31, 71; *R. Wagner*, in: FS Kropholler (2008) 715, 726.

10 See Recital 36; furthermore *Dickinson*, para. 16.40.

are two core areas of the law of non-contractual obligations.[11] The fragmentation is **aggravated by the exclusion of *renvoi*** in Art. 24 Rome II preventing external harmony of decisions between "Rome II States" and "Hague Convention States".[12] The combined effect of Art. 24 and 28(1) is an invitation to forum shopping. However, currently such fragmentation appears to be without viable alternative.[13] In particular, the uncertainty brought about by a differentiation of intra- versus extra-community situations is undesirable. The best solution would still be a denunciation of the Hague Conventions by the contracting Member States or at least a unification by way of a compromise in the course of the review of the Rome II Regulation under Art. 30 Rome II.[14] A study on the effect of Art. 28(1) in relation to the Hague Convention on the law applicable to traffic accidents is due on 20 August 2011 pursuant to Art. 30(1)(ii) Rome II and may pave the way for such a unification.

5 The rule in Art. 28(2) provides for an exception from the general rule of Art. 28(1) in relation to international conventions concluded exclusively amongst Member States. Since in this case international commitments exist only as between Member States, the European legislator was free to provide for the primacy of

---

11 This fragmentation is widely critizised; see *inter alia* Hamburg Group for Private International Law, 67 RabelsZ (2003) 1, 56; *Garriga*, 9 YbPIL (2007) 137, 143; *Joubert*, in: Corneloup/Joubert, Le règlement communautaire "Rome II" sur la loi applicable aux obligations non contractuelles (2007) 55, 62 et seq.; G. *Wagner*, IPRax 2008, 1, 3.

12 *Von Hein*, 73 RabelsZ (2009) 461, 474 and *idem*, in: Ahern/Binchy, p. 153, 158 (considering to achieve external harmony of decisions by applying the escape clauses of Art. 4(3) and 5(2) Rome II); *Junker*, in: Münchener Kommentar BGB, Art. 28 para. 9.

13 Concurring: R. *Wagner*, in: FS Kropholler (2008) 715, 726; G. *Wagner*, IPRax 2008, 1, 3; *Thorn*, in: Palandt, Art. 28 para. 6.

14 See in this regard also *Brière*, 135 Clunet (2008) 31, 73 et seq.; *Kadner Graziano*, 73 RabelsZ (2009) 1, 30; *von Hein*, in: Ahern/Binchy p. 153, 173.

Community law in that regard by giving preference to the Rome II Regulation. The exception of Art. 28(2) is, however, of little practical effect since there are currently no conventions exclusively between Member States in force containing conflict rules on non-contractual obligations.[15]

B. Operation and Prerequisites of the Rule

Art. 28 operates along the **dividing line** of international conventions to which Member States and third countries are parties (Art. 28(1)) and international conventions to which only Member States are parties (Art. 28(2)). In this regard due attention should be paid to Art. 1(4) Rome II according to which the term "Member State" means any other Member State than Denmark for the purposes of the Regulation. 6

I. Conventions between Member States and Third Countries

The relationship between conflict rules on non-contractual obligations in international conventions to which Member States and third countries are parties and the conflict rules of the Rome II Regulation is dealt with separately as regards existing and future conventions. 7

1. Existing Conventions – Art. 28(1)

Art. 28(1) addresses the relationship only in relation to conventions existing at the date of adoption of the Rome II Regulation, *i.e.* 11 July 2007. Whether a convention existed at that date, has to be determined in relation to each Member State separately: the priority rule of Art. 28(1) applies only in relation to those international conventions that were ratified (not only signed) by the forum Member State on the date of adoption of the 8

15 *Von Hein*, 73 RabelsZ (2009) 461, 473 seq.

Rome II Regulation, *i.e.* 11 July 2007; the date of entry into force of the respective convention is irrelevant.[16]

9 Art. 28(1) applies in relation to bilateral as well as multilatieral conventions as long as one of the contracting states is not a Member State of the European Union. This holds true even if the facts of the case are exclusively connected with the Community.[17] Furthermore, Art. 28(1) applies not only to conventions primarily concerning the conflict of laws but also in relation to single conflict rules forming part of an international convention that is foremost concerned with other aspects.[18] Uniform (substantive) law in international conventions is not governed by Art. 28(1). Rather, such uniform regimes are applied by the forum court on the basis of the regime's own rules of application (regularly if both parties are resident in contracting states or as part of the *lex causae* which would be determined by the Rome II Regulation).

10 The two main areas of application of Art. 28(1) are the **Hague Conventions on the law applicable to traffic accidents** of 1971 and on the **law applicable to products liability** of 1973.[19] Both conventions accept their precedence in Art. 15 respectively.[20]

---

16 *Junker*, in: Münchener Kommentar BGB, Art. 28 para. 13; *Kreuzer*, in: Reichelt/Rechberger (eds.), Europäisches Kollisionsrecht (2004) 13, 57; *Kreuzer*, in: FS Kropholler (2008) 129 et seq.; likewise the Explanatory Memorandum of the Commission COM(2003) 427 final, p. 14 uses the term "ratified" in relation to the then Art. 25.

17 Rather critical in this respect: *Thiede/Kellner*, VersR 2007, 1624, 1626; *Kadner Graziano*, 73 RabelsZ (2009) 1, 26; for this reason option (3) had been proposed by the European Parliament and the Commission.

18 *Junker*, in: Münchener Kommentar BGB, Art. 28 para. 22 (alternatively considering a precedence resulting from their annex function).

19 For details on the relationship to and the interplay with the respective conflict rules of the Rome II Regulation see Art. 4 paras. 91 et seq. and Art. 17 para. 4 (traffic accidents) as well as Art. 5 para. 7 (product liability).

20 *Guerchon/Piedelièvre*, Gazette du Palais 2007, 3106, 3112 seq.

The **Rome Convention** on the law applicable to contractual obligations[21] as the predecessor of the Rome I Regulation (but still applicable in Denmark and the United Kingdom) is another international convention falling under Art. 28(1) Rome II. The exception of Art. 28(2) Rome II does not apply since Denmark is a contracting state of the Rome Convention but not a Member State within the meaning of Art. 1(4) Rome II.[22] The rule in Art. 28(1) becomes relevant only in relation to Art. 10(1)(e) of the Rome Convention. It covers actions for unjust enrichment as a consequence of a nullity of contract that would otherwise be governed by Art. 10 Rome II. Since the Rome Convention has been replaced by the Rome I Regulation in all Member States apart from Denmark and the United Kingdom in relation to contracts concluded after 17 December 2009, Art. 10(1)(e) Rome Convention takes precedence only before Danish and UK courts. In all other Member States, Art. 12(1)(e) Rome I takes precedence over Art. 10 Rome II under Art. 27.[23] The matter is, however, of little practical relevance: since Art. 10(1) Rome II provides for the law governing the underlying relationship, in particular a contract, in the vast majority of cases application of all three conflict rules will result in the same applicable law. 11

2. Future Conventions

Future conventions between Member States and third countries in relation to conflict rules on non-contractual obligations are not addressed by Art. 28(1). Under the ECJ's case law[24] the EU acquires the exclusive competence to conclude international conventions where common rules have been adopted by the EU 12

---

21 OJ 1998 C 27/34 (consolidated version).

22 Concurring *Junker*, in: Münchener Kommentar BGB, Art. 28 para. 14; a different view is taken by *Thorn*, in: Palandt, Art. 27 para. 3 (conflict falls under Art. 28(2) so that Art. 27 should apply by way of analogy).

23 *Thorn*, in: Palandt, Art. 27 para. 3.

24 Opinion 1/03 – *Lugano* [2006] ECR I-1145 para. 116 building upon the earlier decision in ECJ, Case C-22/70 – *ERTA* [1971] ECR 263 para. 17.

that would be affected by conventions concluded by the Member States individually or even collectively. Since the material scope of the Rome II Regulation is rather comprehensive in relation to non-contractual obligations (subject only to the exclusions of Art. 1(2) Rome II) and since the Rome II Regulation claims universal application, nearly any international convention concerned with non-contractual obligations would affect the common rules of the Rome II Regulation. Consequently, with the adoption of the Rome II Regulation the Member States would have lost any competence to conclude international conventions in relation to conflict rules on non-contractual obligations.[25]

13 As this result seemed unsatisfactory to some Member States, **Recital 37** was inserted into the Rome II Regulation. It obliges the Commission to make a proposal for the conditions and procedure under which Member States would be entitled to negotiate and conclude agreements with third countries containing conflict rules on non-contractual obligations in individual and exceptional cases concerning sectoral matters. A **corresponding new Regulation** (applying to the Rome I and Rome II Regulations) was adopted on 13 July 2009.[26] It refers in particular to the amendment of existing agreements by the Member States as contracting parties (which still apply under Art. 28(1) Rome II), to the conclusion of new agreements, limited in time and scope and only in exceptional cases where the Community will not exercise its external competence,[27] and lastly to certain regional agreements addressing local situations.[28] The procedure consists of several stages: notification by the Member State(s) to the Commission (Art. 3), assessment by the Commission (Art. 4 setting out several conditions), authorisation to negotiate an agreement

---

[25] Concurring *Dickinson*, para. 16.43; *Garriga*, 9 YbPIL (2007) 137, 147; *Nourissat/Treppoz*, 130 Clunet (2003) 7, 20.

[26] Regulation (EC) No 662/2009 of 13 July 2009, OJ 2009 L 200/25; for a detailed analysis see: *Bischoff*, ZEuP 2010, 321.

[27] See Recital 8.

[28] See Recital 10.

(Art. 5; the authorisation may contain negotiating guidelines or even request the inclusion of specific clauses into the agreement ensuring the primacy of Community law once the Community makes use of its external competence), and finally authorisation to conclude an agreement (Art. 8). Furthermore, the Regulation provides for participation rights of the Commission in the negotiations between the Member State(s) and third countries (Art. 7) as well as confidentiality safeguards vis-à-vis other Member States (Art. 10, 11). The Regulation concludes with transitional provisions (Art. 12), a review clause (Art. 13: no earlier than 13 July 2017) and an expiry date (Art. 14: three years after the review). Overall, the Regulation is of a very technical nature. It sets out in great detail the conditions and procedure for conventions between Member States and third countries ensuring a comprehensive control by the Commission and the primacy of Community law in every respect.

II. Conventions Exclusively between Member States – Art. 28(2)

The relationship between conflict rules on non-contractual obli- 14
gations in international conventions to which only Member States are parties and the conflict rules of the Rome II Regulation is dealt with uniformly as regards existing and future conventions. Art. 28(2) applies as soon as its preconditions are fulfilled, whether on or after the Regulation's adoption on 11 July 2007 and disapplies as soon as a non-member state becomes party to the respective convention (from that moment in time Art. 28(1) applies).

The term "concluded" refers to the ratification (not to the signing 15
or entry into force) of the respective convention. As soon as the convention is ratified by one non-member state, Art. 28(1) applies. As a matter of course, the precedence of the Rome II Regulation is limited to its material scope of application (see Art. 1(2)). A relationship of the underlying facts to one or more Member States is not required although it will usually exist.

16 Art. 28(2) does not affect the binding effect of the respective international convention upon the contracting Member States as a matter of public international law.[29] It merely applies the principle of primacy of Community law over national law to the situation of intra-community conventions.[30] Mere primacy of the Rome II Regulation instead of a denunciation of the respective convention makes a difference if a third country ratifies a convention previously concluded exclusively amongst Member States: Art. 28(2) disapplies and the convention takes precedence over the Rome II Regulation by virtue of Art. 28(1).

Chapter VII
Final Provisions

Article 29
List of conventions

1. By 11 July 2008, Member States shall notify the Commission of the conventions referred to in Article 28(1). After that date, Member States shall notify the Commission of all denunciations of such conventions.
2. The Commission shall publish in the Official Journal of the European Union within six months of receipt:
   (i) a list of the conventions referred to in paragraph 1;
   (ii) the denunciations referred to in paragraph 1.

1 Art. 29 is an annex provision to Art. 28. Like Art. 28, it has a sibling in the Rome I Regulation (Art. 26 Rome I). According to Recital 36 it is the (sole) purpose of Art. 29 to facilitate the application of Art. 28 by making the conventions that take pre-

---

29 *Junker*, in: Münchener Kommentar BGB, Art. 28 para. 29.

30 *Garriga*, 9 YbPIL(2007) 137, 145; *Junker*, in: Münchener Kommentar BGB, Art. 28 para. 13.

cedence under Art. 28(1) easily accessible. Thus, it is a provision for the convenience of the users of the Rome II Regulation.

Art. 29(1) imposes a continuing obligation upon the Member States. By 11 July 2008 each Member State had to notify the Commission of all conventions covered by Art. 28(1) to which it is a contracting state. For the future, each Member State has to notify the Commission if it denounces any such convention since that will render the respective conflict rule(s) of the Rome II Regulation applicable in that Member State. 2

Art. 29(2) obliges the Commission to publish first a list with all existing conventions as notified by the Member States[1] and secondly any denunciation notified to it at a later stage. The list of conventions **neither claims to be correct nor complete** since the Commission merely has to put together and publish the conventions as notified by the Member States in one combined list without a duty to investigate itself any further.[2] 3

Article 30
Review clause

1. Not later than 20 August 2011, the Commission shall submit to the European Parliament, the Council and the European Economic and Social Committee a report on the application of this Regulation. If necessary, the report shall be accompanied by proposals to adapt this Regulation. The report shall include:
   (i) a study on the effects of the way in which foreign law is treated in the different jurisdictions and on the extent to which courts in the Member States apply foreign law in practice pursuant to this Regulation;
   (ii) a study on the effects of Article 28 of this Regulation with respect to the Hague Convention of 4 May 1971 on the law applicable to traffic accidents.

---

1 OJ 2010 C 343/7.

2 *Junker*, in: Münchener Kommentar BGB, Art. 29 para. 3.

2. Not later than 31 December 2008, the Commission shall submit to the European Parliament, the Council and the European Economic and Social Committee a study on the situation in the field of the law applicable to non-contractual obligations arising out of violations of privacy and rights relating to personality, taking into account rules relating to freedom of the press and freedom of expression in the media, and conflict-of-law issues related to Directive 95/46/EC of the European Parliament and of the Council of 24 October 1995 on the protection of individuals with regard to the processing of personal data and on the free movement of such data [7].

Commission Statement on the review clause (Article 30)
The Commission, following the invitation by the European Parliament and the Council in the frame of Article 30 of the "Rome II" Regulation, will submit, not later than December 2008, a study on the situation in the field of the law applicable to non-contractual obligations arising out of violations of privacy and rights relating to personality. The Commission will take into consideration all aspects of the situation and take appropriate measures if necessary.

Commission Statement on road accidents
The Commission, being aware of the different practices followed in the Member States as regards the level of compensation awarded to victims of road traffic accidents, is prepared to examine the specific problems resulting for EU residents involved in road traffic accidents in a Member State other than the Member State of their habitual residence. To that end the Commission will make available to the European Parliament and to the Council, before the end of 2008, a study on all options, including insurance aspects, for improving the position of cross-border victims, which would pave the way for a Green Paper.

Commission Statement on the treatment of foreign law
The Commission, being aware of the different practices followed in the Member States as regards the treatment of foreign law, will publish at the latest four years after the entry into force of the "Rome II" Regulation and in any event as soon as it is available a horizontal study on the application of foreign law in civil and commercial matters by the courts of the Member States, having regard to the aims of the Hague Programme. It is also prepared to take appropriate measures if necessary.

A. Background

1 Art. 30 contains a review clause as it is commonly found in EU Regulations.[1] It obliges the Commission to review, evaluate and report on the application of the Rome II Regulation to the European Parliament, the Council and the European Economic and Social Committee. In addition to the general review obligation, Art. 30 and three corresponding Commission Statements annexed to the Regulation in the Official Journal[2] address three specific issues to be reviewed and reported on. They all emanate from the legislative process and concern issues that were disputed between the European Parliament and the Council: treatment of foreign law (Art. 30(1)(i) and third Commission Statement), applicable law (Art. 30(1)(ii)) and compensation (second Commission Statement) in case of cross-border traffic accidents, and the violation of privacy and rights relating to personality (Art. 30(2) and first Commission Statement).

B. Specific Issues

1. Treatment of Foreign Law

2 The treatment of foreign law is characterized by two concepts within the European Union.[3] Under English law in particular, foreign law is regarded as a question of fact that must be pleaded

1 Cf. *inter alia* Art. 27 Rome I and Art. 73 Brussels I.

2 OJ 2007 L 199/49; although only one statement refers explicitly to Art. 30, all three statements must be examined in the context of the Regulation's future review.

3 For a thorough comparative analysis see *Gruber/Bach*, 11 YbPIL (2009) 157, 161 et seq.; for a comparative report of the law in all member states on the issue cf. Palao Moreno/Iglesias Buhigues/Esplugues Mota (eds.), Application of Foreign Law (forthcoming 2011); *Trautmann*, Europäisches Kollisionsrecht und ausländisches Recht im nationalen Zivilverfahren, 2010; *Geeroms*, Foreign Law in Civil Litigation: A Comparative

and proved by the party relying on it. If the parties do not plead the application of foreign law and/or if they cannot prove its content, the court will apply domestic law to the case despite its cross-border elements. In contrast, in most continental systems, particularly German law, foreign law is regarded as a question of law to which the principle of *iura novit curia* applies. The court must determine and apply foreign law *ex officio*.

3 The European Parliament had proposed specific rules on the treatment of foreign law in the Regulation obliging the plaintiff to notify the court of the applicable law according to the plaintiff's view while it remained with the court to finally determine the content of the foreign law.[4] The Council quite rightly rejected that approach from a systematic point of view. The treatment of foreign law is a matter of procedure (excluded from the material scope according to Art. 1(3) Rome II) and, what is even more, the treatment of foreign law is a cross-sectional matter. It affects not only the Rome II Regulation but the operation of all conflict rules set by the Community, *e.g.* also those in the Rome I Regulation and the Maintenance Regulation.[5] Therefore, the matter needs to be approached separately and with a view to Community conflict rules in general. The respective study by the Commission according to Art. 30(1)(i) is due no later than 20 August 2011 and may pave the way for a coherent approach on the level of Community law in the future.

2. Cross-Border Traffic Accidents

a) Applicable Law

4 The conflict regime determining the law applicable to cross-border traffic accidents is divided amongst the Member States due to

---

and Functional Analysis, 2004; for shorter accounts of the issue see *Trautmann*, ZEuP 2006, 283; *Hood*, 2 J. Priv. Int. L. (2006) 181.

4 See Art. 12, 13 of the European Parliament's legislative resolution after the first reading (P6-TA(2005)0284 of 6 July 2005).

5 *R. Wagner*, in: FS Kropholler (2008) 715, 728.

the rule in Art. 28(1). Depending on the forum where the action is brought, the law may be determined either by the conflict rules of the Rome II Regulation or by the conflict rules of the Hague Convention on the law applicable to traffic accidents of 1971.[6] The effect of this fragmentation shall be reviewed according to Art. 30(1)(ii) no later than by 20 August 2011 in order to consider a way out of this unsatisfactory *status quo* of the law.

b) Compensation for Personal Injuries

Compensation for personal injuries was of particular concern to **5**
the European Parliament during the legislative process. After the first reading, Parliament proposed a special conflict rule for traffic accidents in Art. 4(2) that modified the general rule of Art. 4(1): compensation was to be determined by the law of the habitual residence of the injured party unless inequitable to him, while all other aspects were governed by the law of the state where the accident occurred.[7] The Council rightly disagreed for a number of reasons (*inter alia* legal uncertainty, privilege of traffic accidents over other delicts/torts).[8] After the second reading, Parliament proposed another solution attaching to the substantive law: regardless of the applicable law, the court should apply the principle of *restitutio in integrum*, having regard to the victim's circumstances at his habitual residence, taking account of costs for after-care and medical attention in particular.[9] Again, Council rejected this proposal, foremost for a lack of competence of the Community to harmonize the substantive laws of the Member

---

6 For further details see Art. 4 paras. 91 et seq. and Art. 28 paras. 9 et seq.

7 See the European Parliament's legislative resolution after the first reading (P6-TA(2005)0284 of 6 July 2005); for a critical analysis see *inter alia von Hein*, VersR 2007, 440, 443 f.; G. *Wagner*, IPRax 2006, 372, 379; *Malatesta*, Riv. dir. int. priv. proc. 2006, 47, 59; *Adensamer*, ZVR 2006, 525; *Staudinger*, EuLF 2005, I-64.

8 See *R. Wagner*, in: FS Kropholler (2008) 715, 722.

9 See Recital 34 and Art. 22 of the European Parliament's legislative resolution after the second reading (P6-TA(2007)0006 of 18 January 2007.

States in this respect.[10] In the conciliation process, Parliament and Council finally agreed on Recital 33 (obliging the court to take account of all circumstances of the specific victim) and an obligation of the Commission to provide a preparatory study by the end of 2008[11] on the possible options to regulate the issue with the mid-term perspective of a Green Paper (see second Commission Statement).

3. Violation of Privacy and Rights Relating to Personality

6 Non-contractual obligations arising out of a violation of privacy and of rights relating to personality including defamation are excluded from the material scope of the Regulation pursuant to its Art. 1(2)(g). While the European Parliament and the Council agreed that the general rule of Art. 4(1) was not appropriate, particularly in mass media cases, they could not agree on a special rule. Parliament, however, insisted on a special rule providing for the law of the country in which the most significant element or elements of the loss or damage occured or are likely to occur.[12] The Council disagreed but could itself not agree on an alternative

---

10 See again *R. Wagner*, in: FS Kropholler (2008) 715, 722.

11 Based on a ROME II study on compensation of cross-border victims in the EU conducted by Demolin Brulard Barthelemy (a law firm) for the Commission and published on 29 January 2009 (available at http://ec.europa.eu/internal_market/insurance/docs/motor/20090129report_en.pdf), the Commission launched a Consultation Paper on the Compensation of Victims of Cross-Border Traffic Accidents in the European Union on 26 March 2009 (available at http://ec.europa.eu/internal_market/consultations/docs/2009/cross-border-accidents/rome2study_en.pdf) followed by a Feedback Statement of 7 October 2009 (available at (available at http://ec.europa.eu/internal_market/consultations/docs/2009/cross-border-accidents/feedback.pdf) in both of which it developed and discussed 8 policy options on compensation awards and 9 policy options on limitation periods.

12 See Art. 5 of the European Parliament's legislative resolution after the first reading (P6-TA(2005)0284 of 6 July 2005).

rule (proposals were ranging from the law of the seat of the media company to the law of the habitual residence of the injured party).[13] Eventually, the issue was excluded from the material scope of the Regulation. At the same time, the Commission was put under an obligation to submit a study on the law applicable in the field of privacy and personality rights by 31 December 2008.[14] In contrast to the treatment of foreign law the Commission shall not only be prepared, but *will* take appropriate measures if necessary (see the first Commission Statement).

Article 31
Application in time

This Regulation shall apply to events giving rise to damage which occur after its entry into force.

Article 32
Date of application

This Regulation shall apply from 11 January 2009, except for Article 29, which shall apply from 11 July 2008.
This Regulation shall be binding in its entirety and directly applicable in the Member States in accordance with the Treaty establishing the European Community.

---

13 See *R. Wagner*, in: FS Kropholler (2008) 715, 722.

14 In February 2009 the Commission published a Comparative Study on the Situation in the 27 Member States as regards the Law Applicable to Non-Contractual Obligations Arising out of Violations of Privacy and Rights Relating to Personality (JLS/ 2007/C4/028. Final Report; available at http://ec.europa.eu/justice_home/doc_centre/civil/studies/doc/study_privacy_en.pdf), and the Committee on Legal Affairs of the European Parliament (rapporteur *Diana Wallis*) has produced a Working Paper on 23 June 2010 (available at http://conflictoflaws.net/2010/rome-ii-and-defamation-diana-wallis-and-the-working-paper).

A. The Rule

1 The rules on the temporal scope of the Rome II Regulation in Art. 31 and 32 are unfortunately rather ambiguous and unclear. This has given rise to a variety of interpretations.

I. Literal Interpretation

2 The starting point must be the **wording of Art. 31 and 32**.

3 Art. 31 looks to the event giving rise to the damage. The Regulation shall apply to any such event that occurs after the Regulation's entry into force. The entry into force is, however, not specified in the Regulation. This has lead to a considerable amount of debate and eventually to a reference to the ECJ.

4 Drawing from the general provision of Art. 254(1)2 EC Treaty (which was applicable at the time), a Regulation is deemed to enter into force on the 20th day from its publication in the Official Journal. Since the Rome II Regulation was published on 31 July 2007,[1] it entered into force on 20 August 2007.[2] This means that the Regulation applies to events giving rise to damage that occurred on or after 20 August 2007.

---

1 OJ of 31 July 2007, L 199/40.

2 *Kadner Graziano*, 73 RabelsZ (2009) 1, 3; *Dicey, Morris & Collins*, para. S 35-168; *Hartley*, 57 ICLQ (2008) 899; *Rushworth/Scott*, LMCLQ 2008, 274, all state 19 August 2007 as the relevant date, but starting to count on the day following publication in the Official Journal as the predominant opinion does, 20 August 2007 appears to be the correct date.

Art. 32 concerns the date of application of the Regulation which it sets to 11 January 2009, thus 18 months after its adoption (apart from the obligation of the Commission to publish the list of conventions under Art. 29 applying from 11 July 2008). This means that the Regulation will be applied by the Member States as of 11 January 2009. 5

The combined effect of a literal interpretation of Art. 31 and 32 would therefore amount to the following rule on the Regulation's temporal scope: The Member States would have to apply the Regulation as of 11 January 2009 to events giving rise to damage that occurred on or after 20 August 2007.[3] 6

The **systematic interpretation** supports this view to some extent. The report on the application of the Regulation under Art. 30(1) is due no later than 20 August 2011, a date that is referred to in the corresponding Commission Statement on the treatment of foreign law[4] as "four years after the entry into force of the 'Rome II' Regulation". This supports 20 August 2007 as the date of entry into force. Furthermore, the studies on violations of privacy and personality rights as well as traffic accidents are due by the end of 2008. This presupposes an entry into force before that date.[5] 7

---

[3] Such interpretation is favoured by *Dickinson*, para. 3.319; *Dicey, Morris & Collins*, para. S 35-168; *Hartley*, 57 ICLQ (2008) 899; *Wilderspin*, NIPR 2008, 408, 412; *Légier*, La Semaine Juridique. Edition générale 2007 I 207, 13 seq.; *Glöckner*, IPRax 2009, 121; *Staudinger*, in: FS Kropholler (2008) 691, 692; *Handig*, GRUR Int. 2007, 24, 25; in that direction also *Rushworth/Scott*, LMCLQ 2008, 274 (application to proceedings commenced after 11 January 2009); not convincing is the view taken by *Cheshire, North & Fawcett*, p. 775 (entry into force on 11 July 2007 based on an alleged intention stemming from earlier versions of the Regulation).

[4] OJ 2007 L 199/49.

[5] *von Hein*, ZEuP 2009, 1, 11 (who eventually takes a different view though).

II. The Majority View to the Contrary

8 The result of such literal and systematic interpretation has been described as very unsatisfactory and highly undesirable even by its proponents.[6] It creates the odd situation that a Regulation applied to acts as of 20 August 2007 while the courts were not allowed to apply the Regulation for nearly 17 months (from 20 August 2007 to 10 January 2009).[7] If an action was brought before 11 January 2009 in relation to an event that occurred on or after 20 August 2007, the court would have had to apply its national conflict rules until 10 January 2009 to then switch to the conflict rules of the Rome II Regulation. This would have led to great uncertainty as well as procedural inefficiency and it would have opened the door to abusive tactics by either expediting or delaying the proceedings.[8]

9 Consequently, many authors favour an interpretation according to which the application in time and the date of application coincide: the regulation applies as of 11 January 2009 to events giving rise to damage that occurred on or after 11 January 2009.[9] The

---

6 See *e.g. Dickinson*, para. 3.319 ("extremely unsatisfactory"); *Wilderspin*, NIPR 2008, 408, 412 ("alarming").

7 *Junker*, in: Münchener Kommentar BGB, Arts. 31, 32 para. 4 regards this as so far out of place that it is not even worth considering ("so abwegig, dass man darüber nicht ernsthaft diskutieren kann").

8 *Dickinson*, para. 3.322; *von Hein*, ZEuP 2009, 1, 11; *Bücken*, IPRax 2009, 125, 127.

9 *Bücken*, IPRax 2009, 125; *von Hein*, ZEuP 2008, 1, 11; G. *Wagner*, IPRax 2008, 1, 17; *R. Wagner*, IPRax 2008, 314, 316; *Kramer*, NIPR 2008, 414, 417; *Thorn*, in: Palandt, Art. 30 para. 1; *Junker*, in: Münchener Kommentar BGB, Arts. 30, 31 para. 4; *Spickhoff*, in: Bamberger/Roth, Anh. zu Art. 42 EGBGB para. 150; *Mankowski*, RIW 2008, 177; *Leible/Lehmann*, RIW 2007, 721, 724; *Heiss/Loacker*, JBl. 2007, 613, 618; *Hohloch*, 9 YbPIL (2007) 1; *Ofner*, ZfRV 2008, 13, 15; *De Lima Pinheiro*, Riv. dir. int. priv. proc. 2008, 5, 12; *Garcimartín Alferéz*, EuLF 2007, I-77, 81.

main, **pragmatic argument** is to **avoid uncertainty and a change of conflict rules while the proceedings are pending** which is regarded as unacceptable. Several proponents of this interpretation suggest reading the reference to the Regulation's entry into force in Art. 31 Rome II not as a reference to Art. 254(1)2 EC Treaty (now Art. 297(1)2 TFEU) but rather as a reference to the Regulation's date of application in Art. 32 Rome II.[10] Alternatively, it is suggested to apply Art. 32 Rome II by way of analogy to the Regulation's entry into force in Art. 31.[11]

The **legislative history** of the respective provisions on the Regulation's temporal scope is of some guidance. Both proposals by the Commission contained no provision on the date of application, but merely a specific date of the Regulation's entry into force to which the application in time was linked.[12] This constituted a straight-forward and unequivocal rule. While the link to the entry into force was kept, the sentence providing for a specific date got lost during the legislative process without any explanation or even mention in the legislative materials.[13] Instead, a specific date of application was introduced. This indicates that with regard to the application in time the date of application effectively replaced the date of entry into force while it was inadvertently 10

10 See *e.g. von Hein*, ZEuP 2008, 1, 11; *Garcimartín Alferéz*, EuLF 2007, I-77, 88.

11 *Bücken*, IPRax 2009, 125, 127; to overcome Art. 254(1)2 EC Treaty (now Art. 297(1)2 TFEU), *Bücken* argues that the missing specification of the entry into force was an unintended omission so that the gap may be filled by an analogy within the scheme of the Regulation itself.

12 Art. 27 of the initial proposal reads: "This Regulation shall enter into force on 1 January 2005. It shall apply to non-contractual obligations arising out of acts occurring after its entry into force." (the amended proposal merely left the date open but to be filled in later).

13 See *Bücken*, IPRax 2009, 125, 126 and *Glöckner*, IPRax 2009, 121, 122 f. for further details.

omitted to link the application in time to the date of application instead of the entry into force.[14] The former was introduced when the latter was abandoned.[15] Application in time and the date of application were not intended to differ.

11 A **systematic comparison** with the respective provisions of the Rome I Regulation (Art. 28, 29) does not lead to a clear result. The provisions on temporal scope were initially modelled after those of the Rome II Regulation.[16] They were amended during the legislative process when the problems concerning Art. 31, 32 Rome II became apparent so as to avoid the ambiguities and uncertainty of those provisions. As a result, Art. 28 Rome I contains a specific date as regards the Regulation's application in time irrespective of the Regulation's entry into force. The entry into force as stated in Art. 29(1) Rome I merely reproduces Art. 254(1)2 EC Treaty. The date of application in Art. 29(2) Rome I concurs with the application in time pursuant to Art. 28 Rome I. The implications for the Rome II Regulation depend on the point of view. One may either point at the differences in order to argue in favour of a split regime (application as of 11 January 2009 to events after 20 August 2007) or vice versa regard the Rome I Regulation's scheme as expressing what the European legislator really intended in relation to the Rome II Regulation already.[17] It is submitted that the latter view is more convincing. First, it accords with the indication of the legislative history as explained above. Secondly, it accords with the intention of the European legislator as expressed in the Rome I Regulation to align application in time and the date of application even if an earlier entry into force is provided for.[18] And finally, the consequences of a

14 *Bücken*, IPRax 2009, 125, 126.

15 This appears to be the justification for interpreting the reference to the Regulation's entry into force in Art. 31 Rome II as referring to the Regulation's date of application in Art. 32 Rome II.

16 See Council Document 11150/07 of 25 July 2007 (Art. 25 and 26).

17 To that end *Bücken*, IPRax 2009, 125, 126 seq.

split regime during the intermediate period from 20 August 2007 until 11 January 2009 appear to be unacceptable from a practical point of view. Thus, for reasons of consistency a concurrent regime of application in time and date of application should be pursued before and after 11 January 2009.

12 In the author's opinion, therefore, the majority view is the more convincing one: the Regulation applies as of 11 January 2009 in relation to events giving rise to damage which occurs as of 11 January 2009. While the troubling issue of a change of conflict rules during the proceedings has become irrelevant as of 11 January, the discourse over the Regulation's temporal scope is still relevant for the question whether to apply the Rome II Regulation to events that occurred after 20 August 2007 or only to those that occurred after 11 January 2009.

III. Case Law

13 **National courts** applying the Rome II Regulation currently **take different views** in relation to the Regulation's temporal scope. While the German courts follow the majority view,[19] English

---

18 For that reason a comparison with other European Regulations differentiating between entry into force and date of application (*e.g.* Art. 33 Uncontested Claims Regulation (Regulation 805/2004) and Art. 24 Evidence Regulation (Regulation 1206/2001)) is not convincing; regularly the date of application and the time of application concur regardless of the date of entry into force.

19 Bundesgerichtshof, 20 May 2010 – Xa ZR 68/09 at para. 16, not yet published; Bundesgerichtshof (Germany), 11 February 2010 – I ZR 85/08 at para. 19, not yet published; Bundesgerichtshof, 29 April 2010 – Xa ZR 5/09, NJW 2010, 1958 at para. 12; Bundesgerichtshof, 22 April 2010 – I ZR 89/08, WRP 2010, 896 at para. 60; Bundesgerichtshof, 9 July 2009 – Xa ZR 19/08, NJW 2009, 3371 (para. 17); Hanseatisches Oberlandesgericht Hamburg, 19 February 2009 – 3 U 225/06, APR 2009, 32 at para. 63.

courts are split.[20] The matter will soon be clarified by the ECJ since the English High Court referred the matter to the ECJ.[21]

B. Application of the Rule

14 Art. 31 attaches the application in time to the event giving rise to the damage occurring on or after 11 January 2009. Drawing from the distinction in Art. 4 and 7 this refers to the act or omission giving rise to the damage. By contrast, the date when the direct damage occurs and the date of indirect consequences are irrelevant.[22] In case of a choice of law it is likewise the date of the event giving rise to the damage and not the date of the choice of law that is determining the temporal application of the Rome II Regulation.[23]

15 In case of **torts/delicts stretching over a longer period** one has to distinguish. If the event is of a singular nature taking place before

---

20 See *Maher v Groupama Grand Est* [2009] EWHC 38 at para. 16 (Blair J in favour of an application as of 11 January 2009 to events which occur after 20 August 2007); *Robert Bacon v Nacional Suiza* [2010] EWHC 2017 at paras. 37 et seq. (Tomlinson J equally in favour of an application as of 11 January 2009 to events which occur after 20 August 2007, regarding any other result as "simply unsustainable" [para. 55]); *Homawoo v GMF Assurance*, 27 July 2010 [2010] EWHC 1941 at paras. 41 et seq. (Slade J, taking only a preliminary view, in contrast in favour of an application as of 11 January 2009 to events which occur after that date, particularly stressing the need for legal certainty even if no court proceedings are initiated, *i.e.* in case of settlement negotiations or mediation).

21 *Homawoo v GMF Assurance* [2010] EWHC 1941 at paras. 50 et seq. (the case is listed in the ECJ register under C-412/10).

22 Concurring *von Hein*, ZEuP 2008, 1, 11; *Garcimartín Alferéz*, ELF 2007 I-77, 81; *Thorn*, in: Palandt, Art. 31 para. 1; *Junker*, in: Münchener Kommentar BGB, Arts. 31, 32 para. 6.

23 *Junker*, in: Münchener Kommentar BGB, Arts. 31, 32 para. 5; *Spickhoff*, in: Bamberger/Roth, Anh. zu Art. 42 EGBGB para. 150.

11 January 2009 with the damage materializing on or after 11 January 2009, the Rome II Regulation does not apply.[24] Examples for this type of tort/delict are the marketing of a product on 4 November 2008 with injury to the purchaser resulting from a defect in the product on 13 March 2009 or a leak in a cooling system of a factory on the river banks of the Oder river in Poland detected on 28 December 2008 but fixed on 30 December 2008, resulting in a pollution of the German river banks upstream occurring after 11 January 2009. If, in contrast, the event is of a continuous nature commencing before 11 January 2009 but continuing until after that date, a change of the governing conflict rules takes place: national conflict law with regard to the events taking place before, the Rome II Regulation's conflict regime with regard to the events taking place on or after 11 January 2009.[25] In such a case the parties may well consider to agree on one applicable law to all events as far as the choice of law provisions of the respective conflict regimes allow them to do so.

In cases of **strict liability** the event giving rise to the damage is not the creation of the generally dangerous situation to which the strict liability regime attaches (*e.g.* registering a car, manufacturing a product, keeping a dog), but the concrete event giving rise to the damage (*e.g.* the dangerous turn with the car resulting in the accident, the marketing of the product by selling it, the attack of the dog left unattended).[26] 16

In case of **events giving rise to damage that are likely to occur** (Art. 2(2) and (3)(a) Rome II),[27] Art. 31 refers to the likelihood of the event. If the event was likely to occur already before 11 Jan- 17

---

24 *Junker*, in: Münchener Kommentar BGB, Arts. 31, 32 para. 6; too undifferentiated in that respect: *Thorn*, in: Palandt, Arts. 31, 32 para. 1.

25 *Spickhoff*, in: Bamberger/Roth, Anh. zu Art. 42 EGBGB para. 151; *Junker*, in: Münchener Kommentar BGB, Arts. 31, 32 para. 10; *Leible/Lehmann*, RIW 2007, 721, 724.

26 *Von Hein*, ZEuP 2008, 1, 11; *Thorn*, in: Palandt, Arts. 31, 32 para. 2.

27 For details and examples see Art. 2 paras. 6 seq.

uary 2009, the Rome II Regulation is not applicable even if such likelihood has not changed on 11 January 2009 and an action for injunctive relief was only brought after 11 January 2009.[28] If, however, the event became likely to occur only after 11 January 2009, the Rome II Regulation applies.

18 If the time of the event giving rise to the damage is contested between the parties, the ordinary rules on burden of proof of the *lex fori* apply (Art. 1(3) Rome II subject to the exception in Art. 22 Rome II). Hence, the burden of proof does not automatically lie with the party relying on the Rome II Regulation as the new law. Rather, the burden of proof in relation to a specific date of the event giving rise to the damage will usually lie with the party that wants to rely on that date since it results in the application of the conflict regime (national regime of the forum or Rome II Regulation) that is more favourable to him.[29] This will regularly be the injured party. He has to establish the specific date as a prerequisite for the application of the respective conflict regime leading to the applicable law under which the claim is brought. If the allegedly liable party contests such date, the injured party must prove it.

---

28 *von Hein*, ZEuP 2009, 1, 11 f.; *Heiss/Loacker* JBl. 2007, 613, 618; *Junker*, in: Münchener Kommentar BGB, Arts. 31, 32 para. 12.

29 *Spickhoff*, in: Bamberger/Roth, Anh. zu Art. 42 EGBGB para. 151; *Junker*, in: Münchener Kommentar BGB, Arts. 31, 32 para. 13; *Thorn*, in: Palandt, Arts. 31, 32 para. 3.

Index